# Firewall Policies and VPN Configurations

Anne Henmi   Technical Editor

Mark Lucas

Abhishek Singh

Chris Cantrell

| KEY | SERIAL NUMBER |
| --- | --- |
| 001 | HJIRTCV764 |
| 002 | PO9873D5FG |
| 003 | 829KM8NJH2 |
| 004 | 78GHTYPM99 |
| 005 | CVPLQ6WQ23 |
| 006 | VBP965T5T5 |
| 007 | HJJJ863WD3E |
| 008 | 2987GVTWMK |
| 009 | 629MP5SDJT |
| 010 | IMWQ295T6T |

PUBLISHED BY
Syngress Publishing, Inc.
800 Hingham Street
Rockland, MA 02370

Firewall Policies and VPN Configurations

Printed in Canada
1 2 3 4 5 6 7 8 9 0
ISBN: 1-59749-088-1

Publisher: Andrew Williams
Acquisitions Editor: Erin Heffernan
Technical Editor: Anne Henmi
Cover Designer: Michael Kavish

Page Layout and Art: Patricia Lupien
Copy Editor: Judy Eby, Beth Roberts
Indexer: Nara Wood

Distributed by O'Reilly Media, Inc. in the United States and Canada.
For information on rights, translations, and bulk sales, contact Matt Pedersen, Director of Sales and Rights, at Syngress Publishing; email matt@syngress.com or fax to 781-681-3585.

# VISIT US AT

## www.syngress.com

Syngress is committed to publishing high-quality books for IT Professionals and delivering those books in media and formats that fit the demands of our customers. We are also committed to extending the utility of the book you purchase via additional materials available from our Web site.

## SOLUTIONS WEB SITE

To register your book, visit www.syngress.com/solutions. Once registered, you can access our solutions@syngress.com Web pages. There you will find an assortment of value-added features such as free e-booklets related to the topic of this book, URLs of related Web sites, FAQs from the book, corrections, and any updates from the author(s).

## ULTIMATE CDs

Our Ultimate CD product line offers our readers budget-conscious compilations of some of our best-selling backlist titles in Adobe PDF form. These CDs are the perfect way to extend your reference library on key topics pertaining to your area of expertise, including Cisco Engineering, Microsoft Windows System Administration, CyberCrime Investigation, Open Source Security, and Firewall Configuration, to name a few.

## DOWNLOADABLE EBOOKS

For readers who can't wait for hard copy, we offer most of our titles in downloadable Adobe PDF form. These e-books are often available weeks before hard copies, and are priced affordably.

## SYNGRESS OUTLET

Our outlet store at syngress.com features overstocked, out-of-print, or slightly hurt books at significant savings.

## SITE LICENSING

Syngress has a well-established program for site licensing our e-books onto servers in corporations, educational institutions, and large organizations. Contact us at sales@syngress.com for more information.

## CUSTOM PUBLISHING

Many organizations welcome the ability to combine parts of multiple Syngress books, as well as their own content, into a single volume for their own internal use. Contact us at sales@syngress.com for more information.

SYNGRESS®

# Acknowledgments

Syngress would like to acknowledge the following people for their kindness and support in making this book possible.

Syngress books are now distributed in the United States and Canada by O'Reilly Media, Inc. The enthusiasm and work ethic at O'Reilly are incredible, and we would like to thank everyone there for their time and efforts to bring Syngress books to market: Tim O'Reilly, Laura Baldwin, Mark Brokering, Mike Leonard, Donna Selenko, Bonnie Sheehan, Cindy Davis, Grant Kikkert, Opol Matsutaro, Steve Hazelwood, Mark Wilson, Rick Brown, Tim Hinton, Kyle Hart, Sara Winge, Peter Pardo, Leslie Crandell, Regina Aggio Wilkinson, Pascal Honscher, Preston Paull, Susan Thompson, Bruce Stewart, Laura Schmier, Sue Willing, Mark Jacobsen, Betsy Waliszewski, Kathryn Barrett, John Chodacki, Rob Bullington, Kerry Beck, Karen Montgomery, and Patrick Dirden.

The incredibly hardworking team at Elsevier Science, including Jonathan Bunkell, Ian Seager, Duncan Enright, David Burton, Rosanna Ramacciotti, Robert Fairbrother, Miguel Sanchez, Klaus Beran, Emma Wyatt, Krista Leppiko, Marcel Koppes, Judy Chappell, Radek Janousek, Rosie Moss, David Lockley, Nicola Haden, Bill Kennedy, Martina Morris, Kai Wuerfl-Davidek, Christiane Leipersberger, Yvonne Grueneklee, Nadia Balavoine, and Chris Reinders for making certain that our vision remains worldwide in scope.

David Buckland, Marie Chieng, Lucy Chong, Leslie Lim, Audrey Gan, Pang Ai Hua, Joseph Chan, June Lim, and Siti Zuraidah Ahmad of Pansing Distributors for the enthusiasm with which they receive our books.

David Scott, Tricia Wilden, Marilla Burgess, Annette Scott, Andrew Swaffer, Stephen O'Donoghue, Bec Lowe, Mark Langley, and Anyo Geddes of Woodslane for distributing our books throughout Australia, New Zealand, Papua New Guinea, Fiji, Tonga, Solomon Islands, and the Cook Islands.

# Technical Editor

**Anne Henmi** is an Information Security Engineer at Securify, Inc. She works with development to contribute to the improvement of the security posture of Securify's products and services.

Her specialties include Linux, Secure Shell, public key technologies, penetration testing, and network security architectures. Anne's background includes positions as a Course Developer at Juniper Networks, System Administrator at California Institute of Technology, Principal Security Consultant at SSH Communications Security, and as an Information Security Analyst at VeriSign, Inc.

# Contributing Authors

**Mark J. Lucas** (MCSE and GIAC Certified Windows Security Administrator) is a Senior System Administrator at the California Institute of Technology. Mark is responsible for the design, implementation, and security of high availability systems such as Microsoft Exchange servers, VMWare ESX hosted servers, and various licensing servers. He is also responsible for the firewalls protecting these systems. Mark has been in the IT industry for 10 years. This is Mark's first contribution to a Syngress publication. Mark lives in Tujunga, California with his wife Beth, and the furry, four-legged children, Aldo, Cali, Chuey, and Emma.

**Chris Cantrell** is a Presales System Engineer for Riverbed Technology, the leading pioneer in the wide-area data services (WDS) market. Before joining Riverbed, Chris spent 8 years focusing on network security and intrusion prevention. He has held various management and engineering positions with companies such as Network Associates, OneSecure, NetScreen, and Juniper

Networks. Chris was a contributing author for *Configuring Netscreen Firewalls* (ISBN: 1-93226-639-9), published by Syngress Publishing in 2004.

Chris lives in Denver, Colorado with his loving and supportive wife, Maria, and their two children, Dylan and Nikki.

**Laura E. Hunter** (CISSP, MCSE: Security, MCDBA, Microsoft MVP) is an IT Project Leader and Systems Manager at the University of Pennsylvania, where she provides network planning, implementation, and troubleshooting services for various business units and schools within the university. Her specialties include Windows 2000 and 2003 Active Directory design and implementation, troubleshooting, and security topics. Laura has more than a decade of experience with Windows computers; her previous experience includes a position as the Director of Computer Services for the Salvation Army and as the LAN administrator for a medical supply firm. She is a contributor to the TechTarget family of Web sites, and to *Redmond Magazine* (formerly *Microsoft Certified Professional Magazine*).

Laura has previously contributed to the Syngress Windows Server 2003 MCSE/MCSA DVD Guide & Training System series as a DVD presenter, author, and technical reviewer, and is the author of the *Active Directory Consultant's Field Guide* (ISBN: 1-59059-492-4) from APress. Laura is a three-time recipient of the prestigious Microsoft MVP award in the area of Windows Server— Networking. Laura graduated with honors from the University of Pennsylvania and also works as a freelance writer, trainer, speaker, and consultant.

**Abhishek Singh** works as a security researcher for Third Brigade, a Canadian-based information security company. His responsibilities include analysis, deep packet inspection, reverse engineering, writing signatures for various protocols (DNS, DHCP, SMTP, POP, HTTP, and VOIP), Zero day attacks, Microsoft Tuesday critical, and vulnerabilities.

In Information security, Abhishek likes to research intrusion detection/prevention systems, firewalls, two factor authentication, wireless security, cryptography, and virtual private networks. He has an invention disclosure in firewalls and holds one patent in two factor authentication. The patent involves secure authentication of a user to a system and secure operation thereafter. In cryptography, he has proposed an algorithm in learning theory which uses Context Free Grammar for the generation of one-time authentication identity. One-time authentication identity generates one-time passwords, disposable SSNs, and disposable credit card numbers. To prevent high-bandwidth and malicious covert channels, he has proposed enforcing semantic consistency in the unused header fields of TCP/IP, UDP, and ICMP packets. Abhishek's research findings in the field of compiler, computer networks, mobile agents, and artificial neural networks have been published in primer conferences and journals.

He holds a B. Tech. in Electrical Engineering from IIT-BHU, a Master of Science in Computer Science and in Information Security from the College of Computing Georgia Tech. While pursuing his education, he was employed with Symantec Corporation as a Senior Software Engineer and has worked on a consulting project for Cypress Communication, which won third prize at the 2004 Turn Around Management Competition. He was also employed with VPN Dynamics and with Infovation Inc.

Presently he lives in Banglore with his lovely wife, Swati.


**James McLoughlin** (CISSP, CCSP, CCSE) is a security engineer for Lan Communications, an Irish integrator/reseller. He is currently working towards achieving his CCIE in Security, and has over a decade of experience in the security field.

James lives in Dublin, Ireland

**Susan Snedaker** (MBA, BA, MCSE, MCT, CPM) is Principal Consultant and founder of VirtualTeam Consulting, LLC (www.virtualteam.com), a consulting firm specializing in business and technology consulting. The company works with companies of all sizes to develop and implement strategic plans, operational improvements and technology platforms that drive profitability and growth. Prior to founding VirtualTeam in 2000, Susan held various executive and technical positions with companies including Microsoft, Honeywell, Keane, and Apta Software. As Director of Service Delivery for Keane, she managed 1200+ technical support staff delivering phone and email support for various Microsoft products including Windows Server operating systems. She is author of *How to Cheat at IT Project Management* (Syngress Publishing, ISBN: 1-597490-37-7) *The Best Damn Windows Server 2003 Book Period* (Syngress Publishing, ISBN: 1-931836-12-4) and *How to Cheat at Managing Windows Small Business Server 2003* (Syngress, ISBN: 1-932266-80-1). She has also written numerous technical chapters for a variety of Syngress Publishing books on Microsoft Windows and security technologies and has written and edited technical content for various publications. Susan has developed and delivered technical content from security to telephony, TCP/IP to WiFi, CIW to IT project management and just about everything in between (she admits a particular fondness for anything related to TCP/IP).

Susan holds a master's degree in business administration and a bachelor's degree in management from the University of Phoenix. She also holds a certificate in advanced project management from Stanford University. She holds Microsoft Certified Systems Engineer (MSCE) and Microsoft Certified Trainer (MCT) certifications. Susan is a member of the Information Technology Association of Southern Arizona (ITASA) and the Project Management Institute (PMI).

**Jennifer Davis** is a senior system administrator with Decru, a Network Appliance company. Decru develops storage security solutions that help system administrators protect data. Jennifer specializes in scripting, systems automation, integration and troubleshooting, and security administration.

Jennifer is a member of USENIX, SAGE, LoPSA, and BayLISA. She is based in Silicon Valley, California.

# Contents

# Part I
# Security Policy

# Chapter 1

# Network Security Policy

## Topics in this chapter:

- Defining Your Organization
- Trusted Networks
- Untrusted Networks

☑ Summary

☑ Solutions Fast Track

☑ Frequently Asked Questions

# Introduction

Deploying a network security policy is a significant and serious undertaking. Making good decisions in this matter will save a great deal of money and prevent many future security issues on your network, while making incorrect or hasty decisions will lay the foundation for an insecure network infrastructure. Creating a network security policy will affect your organization in a number of ways, including (but not limited to):

- **Financial** A new network security policy may require you to purchase new equipment and software, such as firewalls, IPS (intrusion protection/prevention system), anti-virus software, new routers, and more. You'll likely also incur additional salary costs for security personnel trained to manage the new hardware and software.

- **Network availability** You may have to install new hardware and software on your network to comply with a new network security policy, which may impact your overall network availability as you install and configure this infrastructure. Therefore, the process needs to be well planned to reduce risks, costs, and downtime for your clients and internal users.

- **Usability** In almost every case, the security of a computer system is inversely related to its usability. As a result of your network security policy, you may reach a state where the usability of the network is drastically reduced. Your network security policy needs to balance security against usability, so that your security policy does not become so rigid that your users cannot perform their job functions.

- **Legal** Depending on your country and the activity of your business, you may be required to comply with legislative measures such as HIPPAA or Graham-Leach-Bliley. You need to consider these regulations when designing your network security policy.

Before you can begin to implement a new network security policy, you need to perform extensive planning and preparation before writing documents and configuring new hardware or software. It is important to know your network, to understand the reasons for every network device, to know the vulnerabilities of every technology in use, the strength of each device, and the way devices are connected to each other.

It's also crucial to understand how your network is going to be used, to know the requirements of your business, how many and what kind of users will have access to the network. You should also understand why the network was installed (or is going to be installed) and whether you have sufficiently trained staff and budget to manage the network. In any case, every network has its own requirements and objectives. Every network is different, and not many countermeasures applied in one network to reduce the risks to it will be directly applicable to another network.

It is easy to find the differences between a campus network in a large university and the network of a small office, the network of a big enterprise or that of a small home network. They are all networks, and they will perform the same basic operations; however, the security requirements may vary greatly.

As with most matters relating to Information Technology, the budget available to you to enforce network security is a real issue when designing and implementing your policies and procedures. Your requirements need to be sufficiently affordable for your company or client. Sometimes, it is better to generate a procedure that every user will need to know and follow, rather than try to implement a complex and expensive technical control.

Many organizations now realize the need to have an articulated information security policy, to be more effective in their preventative, detective, and responsive security measures. Moreover, because of government regulations, organizations in certain vertical industries are required to have formally documented information security policies.

In addition, an information security policy is also extremely beneficial to the security manager because it provides, at an executive level, a mandated framework for ensuring the confidentiality, integrity, and availability of an organization's information assets. What this means is that the security manager has some weight in his or her corner for budget requests when he or she has an approved information security policy.

Finally, for the security administrator, having a written and approved policy can ensure that you are able to deploy different technologies in a way that minimizes disruption to business. Think of the written policy as a recipe to ensure you configure everything correctly. Moreover, a policy is the best way to ensure you will keep your job, should something happen.

---

**NOTE**

Whatever type of network you are deploying, you need to keep your feet on the ground; a company's network needs to allow the company to produce more earnings than costs. In other words, you shouldn't spend more money protecting an asset than the asset is actually worth.

---

When tackling this issue, it's also critical to keep in mind the differences between a security *policy* and a security *procedure*. Your network security policy needs to be a high-level and fairly stable document that can withstand a certain amount of change to the operating systems your clients and servers are running, so you are not issuing changes to the policy every time Microsoft releases a new service pack. You can implement network security *procedures* to support the security policy; these procedures will discuss specific operational or procedural details that will allow you to comply with the high-level security policy. "All Internet-connected computers must be secured against malicious intrusion" is an example of an edict you might find in a network security policy, whereas "all Windows XP computers must have Service Pack 2 installed and the Windows Firewall enabled" is an example of a specific procedure you might put in place.

# Defining Your Organization

You just received the task to define a network security policy for your network. As mentioned in the introduction of this chapter, you need to think about several topics before defining your new network security policy.

A good way to start is to think about your organization. How well do you know your organization's business processes, both as an individual company and the needs and requirements of its industry as a whole? Sometimes, when an information security engineer or a consultant is asked to design a network security policy, he or she realizes that it is imperative to develop a better understanding of the organization before beginning.

To be able to design a useful network security policy, you need to know what the network is designed for. You need to design and deploy a network security policy that secures a company's resources, while still allowing people to do their jobs. Therefore, think about the department, the business, what the company produces or sells, whether the business is seasonal or cyclical, or if its activity remains roughly the same year round. Does the company have any business with foreign customers, vendors, or business partners? Are any governments involved in the operations of the business, and does the business require any kind of government security accreditation or clearance?

For example, imagine an organization that uses a remote access server that's based on passwords. Does the network security policy reference the proper procedures in case of a forgotten password, or do users know whether they should call their boss, the IT department, or even the Information Security office for a new password?

In an organization with a well-defined network security policy, users will have a procedure to follow to get a new password. That procedure needs to be secure enough to guarantee the password is being given to the right person and not to an intruder!

> **NOTE**
>
> A password recovery procedure needs to be secure, but sufficiently flexible to allow your users to recover a password and continue working even if they are away from the office or working remotely. Consider using telephone security checks or other offline methods for password resets.

It is nearly impossible to define a "typical" organization, as all are different. As such, you need to develop a way to define your own organization. You can choose several criteria, such as the size of the company, its geographical location, the different activities it performs, and so forth. Regardless of any idiosyncrasies that make your organization different from one down the street or across the country, you should always develop your network security policy as a means to protect your company's assets while allowing it to perform its needed tasks—not simply focus on closing ports, denying Internet access, and the like. Before you can begin to create a network security policy, you should perform a *security assessment* of your organization and its assets. There are two distinct parts to this process: audit and assessment. An *assessment* is intended to look for issues and vulnerabilities that can be mitigated, remediated, or eliminated prior to a security breach. An *audit* is normally conducted after an assessment with the goal of measuring compliance with policies and procedures. Typically, someone is held accountable for audit results. Some people don't like the term *auditing;* perhaps it's too reminiscent of ol' Uncle Sam scouring through your tax return from three years ago when you claimed that one vacation as a business trip because you talked to your boss on your cell phone while waiting for the shuttle to your beachfront hotel. Although the terms *assessment* and *audit* are often used interchangeably, in this chapter we focus on assessments.

Throughout the audit and assessment phase, remember that there are three primary components of IT security: *people, process,* and *technology.* A balanced approach addresses all three areas; focusing on one area to the exclusion of others creates security holes. People, including senior management, must buy into the importance of security, and must understand and participate in maintaining it. The process includes all the practices and procedures that occur and reoccur to keep the network secure. Technology obviously includes all hardware and software that comprises the network infrastructure. Part of the technology assessment required to assess and harden infrastructure security includes deploying the right technological solutions for your firm and not the "one size fits all" or the "it was all we could afford" solution. In IT, we often focus a disproportionate amount of time and energy on securing the technology and overlook the importance of people and process to the overall security environment.

To secure your infrastructure, you need to understand its building blocks. These include:

- Network perimeter protection
- Internal network protection
- Intrusion monitoring and prevention
- Host and server configuration
- Protection against malicious code
- Incident response capabilities
- Security policies and procedures
- Employee awareness and training
- Physical security and monitoring

Security assessments should begin by looking at the overall environment in which security must be implemented. Looking at the relative importance of your company's information is a good starting point, because you need to find the right balance between security and information criticality. As part of that analysis, you also need to look at the impact of a network infrastructure intrusion and what it would cost to defend and repair. You need to define the various systems you have in place and look at how information flows through your organization to understand the infrastructure you're trying to protect. Finally, you need to create an initial assessment of scope to define what *is* and *is not* included in your project.

# Information Criticality

It's important to begin by looking at information criticality. You'll find that this is a common theme throughout most security texts, because there's no point in securing something no one wants. Information criticality is an assessment of what your network holds and how important that is in the overall scheme of things. Not all data is created equal, and if your company manufactures steel troughs for horse feed, there's a good chance your network data is not nearly as interesting to a potential attacker as the data in an online stock brokerage firm or a bank or credit card processing house network. Therefore, you need to look at the criticality of your information and decide how much you're willing to spend to secure that information. No one wants a security breach, but it would not make good business sense to spend $15 million to secure a network for a company that pulls in $5 million annually and doesn't store sensitive personal data such as credit card numbers or medical records. That said, just because your company makes $5 million annually doesn't mean that you *shouldn't* look seriously at the criticality of your data, to be sure you don't have excessive exposure. If you are storing credit card numbers or medical records, you'd better be sure your security solutions are up to standards, because your legal liability could significantly outstrip that $5 million annually in a big hurry.

## Impact Analysis

You'll notice as you read the chapters for the individual security area plans that some of the information overlaps. It's hard to perform an impact analysis on an infrastructure breach without also seeing how it would affect your wireless network components, your Web site, or your policies and procedures. However, in looking at the impact to your infrastructure, you'll need to understand how a breach could affect the very foundation of your organization. The impact analysis should include:

- **Cost of network infrastructure—failure (downtime)** Server down, database server down, routers down, etc.

- **Cost of network infrastructure—unavailable (slow or unresponsive)** Denial-of-service (DoS) attacks, packet flooding, etc.

- **Cost of network infrastructure breach—data confidentiality, integrity, availability** Man-in-the-middle, spoofing, phishing, etc.

- **Cost to company reputation** Lost sales, lost customers, loss of long-term business relationships.

- **Cost to company** Cost of remediation, cost of litigation.

You should combine information criticality with the findings of your impact analysis to form a clear picture of what you're trying to protect and why. When you understand the impact, you can see where the important areas are in your organization, and can use this information, in part, to prioritize your approach to securing the network.

# System Definitions

Infrastructure systems clearly include the "backbone" services, including DHCP servers, DNS servers, Directory Services servers, e-mail servers, database servers, firewalls, DMZs, routers/switches, operating systems, Web servers, and security applications (antivirus, antispyware, IDS/IPS, etc.). If it's helpful, you can also look at your systems from the OSI model perspective—from the physical layer up through the application layer, whatever makes the most sense to you and your team.

Creating (or updating) network diagrams can also be included in the system definitions overview, since the way everything fits together is part of understanding the whole.

# Information Flow

One area that is sometimes overlooked in the assessment phase is the flow of information through the infrastructure. This area can be used in conjunction with your systems definitions to help map your network and to discover the key areas that need to be protected and how an attacker would get to those assets.

It sometimes helps to look at information flow from different perspectives. For example, how does information from a user computer flow? How does DNS or DHCP traffic flow through the network? How is external traffic coming into the network managed, and where and how does it enter? How is traffic leaving the network for the public network (Internet) managed? Creating a map of your network infrastructure and information flow will help you visualize your network and identify potential weak spots.

# Scope

You might want to limit the scope of your infrastructure security project for a variety of reasons. "Scoping" is often done when you're engaging an external security consultant. However, if you're doing this work internally, you may limit your scope here, or you may choose to do a full assessment and then limit the scope after you see what's what.

# People and Process

Clearly, people and processes will also impact network security in a big way. Most security breaches occur from the inside, not the outside, despite the media's sensationalized focus on external security breaches. The people in your organization can be your defenders or your downfall, depending on how they approach security. Savvy, well-informed users can augment the technical security measures by avoiding becoming victims of social engineering, reporting suspicious activity, avoiding phishing e-mail, or not leaving their computer logged in and unattended. All the security in the world can't prevent problems if users are not pulling their weight. There are many ways to inform and involve users, and unfortunately, many IT departments don't leverage these opportunities very successfully, because they often fall victim to a "user as pain in the hind quarters" mentality. Let's look at how users and organizational processes should be reviewed during an infrastructure assessment.

## User Profiles

What kinds of users do you have? Where and how do they work? If you begin by looking at your user population, you will see segments that have higher and lower risk profiles. The clerk in the mailroom might only have access to e-mail and the mailroom application, but does he or she also have Internet access and the ability to download and install programs? What about the marketing staff who travel world-wide? What kinds of information do they keep on their laptops (usernames, passwords, domain names, sensitive documents, contacts, and the like), and how does this affect your network security?

Users can be categorized in whatever ways work for you in your organization, but here's a list of potential risks by employee type, to get you thinking:

- **Executive** High-profile targets, often not "tech savvy," potentially easy to get information about (from press releases, public filings, legal filings, and so on).

- **Director** High-profile targets, may travel extensively with sensitive information, may need to connect to the network in a variety of insecure locations.

- **Finance**, **marketing**, **HR, legal** Access to extremely sensitive data, may be high-profile targets due to their access to sensitive data, may travel extensively and be desirable targets of social engineering.

- **IT staff** Access to network resources, ability to grant/deny access, potentially desirable targets of social engineering (especially via help desk), highly desirable targets (IT usernames and passwords with administrative privileges are the Holy Grail for hackers).

- **Users** Access to sensitive company information, often targets of social engineering.

In addition to these categories, you may have user groups defined in your network security management system (which manages access control) you want to use.

Microsoft defines users as administrators, power users, and the like, which might work for you. Again, the point is to use a categorization method that's meaningful to the way your company and your existing network infrastructure are organized, so you can understand the risks users bring into the organization and the strategies for keeping the network secure in light of the way various users work.

## Policies and Procedures

Infrastructure policies and procedures touch on the day-to-day operations of the IT staff, including the way security is monitored (auditing functions, log files, password policies, alerts) and how it is maintained (backups, updates, upgrades). Policies regarding user behavior are also crucial to ensuring that the network infrastructure remains safe. Finally, corporate policies regarding the use of data, computer and electronic equipment, and building access, to name just three, are areas that should be reviewed and revised to support and enhance security across the enterprise.

## Organizational Needs

The internal environment is shaped by the organization's business profile, including the type of business, the nature of sales and marketing functions, the types of customers, the kinds of employees, and the flow of work through the company. What does your company require from the network services you provide, and how can these needs be secured? If you believe your organization's network, data, and computer needs are being met, delineate what they are, and check with a few users to see if you're on the mark. Make sure you understand how the network fits into the organization, not the other way around, and then design your security solution accordingly.

## Regulatory/Compliance

Any infrastructure assessment and security plan must incorporate regulatory and compliance requirements. These vary greatly from state to state and country to country, and keeping up with them can be more than a full-time job. Many companies are hiring compliance officers whose primary job is to manage corporate compliance. If your company has a compliance officer, make sure he or she is a member of your IT project team, at least during the definition phase, when you're developing your functional and technical requirements, since these are often the method by which compliance occurs. We've included a short list here with a few Web site links, but it's not exhaustive; you should seek legal advice regarding regulatory and compliance requirements for your firm if you don't have a knowledgeable and experienced compliance officer in place.

## Business Intelligence...

# Common Compliance Standards

There are numerous compliance issues facing organizations today. Following are just a few of the compliance standards you should be aware of and should evaluate whether your firm is subject to these regulations.

**British Standard 7799** (BS7799)  Eventually evolved into ISO17799.

**Child Online Protection Act** (COPA)  www.copacommission.org.

**Health Insurance Portability and Accountability Act** (HIPAA)
www.cms.hhs.gov/hipaa/hipaa1/content/more.asp.

**Family Educational Rights and Privacy Act** (FERPA)
www.ed.gov/policy/gen/guid/fpco/ferpa/index.html.

**Federal Information Security Mgmt Act** (FISMA)  csrc.nist.gov/seccert/.

**Gramm-Leach Bliley Act** (GLBA)  www.ftc.gov/privacy/glbact/.

**Homeland Security Presidential Directive 7** (HSPD-7)  www.white-house.gov/news/release/2003/12/20031217-5.html.

**ISO 17799**  www.iso.org (International Organization for Standardization's INFOSEC recommendations).

**National Strategy to Secure Cyberspace**  www.whitehouse.gov/pcipb/.

**Sarbanes-Oxley Act** (SOX)  www.aicpa.org/sarbanes/index.asp.

# Establishing Baselines

The point of performing these assessments is not to prove that your network is secure or insecure, but to find out exactly what level of security you actually have and to establish baselines. When you know the starting point, you can improve security incrementally and document it as you go. Baselines are created by establishing a known starting point, in this case your current settings.

It might be tempting to correct problems as you perform this assessment, but it's not the best way to proceed. As you know, making a configuration change at Point A can cause a ripple effect through your network and show up at Point C in a strange and unexpected way. As you develop your project plan, be clear with your project team that they need to document existing configurations, settings, versions, and so on, without making changes. If a team member finds a serious security hole, it should be brought to your attention immediately for action. The problem should be quickly assessed and addressed in a calm, rational, thoughtful manner, and possibly incorporated into your project plan. Does that mean that you wait until your project planning is complete to address a serious security hole? Absolutely not. You should, however, use a well thought-out strategy for addressing it outside the project planning cycle, and then document the changes and incorporate them into your project plan. What you want to avoid is having every person looking at the network making small tweaks here and there to "tighten up security" as they go, because you'll end up with a mess at the end of your evaluation period. Serious problems should be brought to your immediate attention, and minor issues should be well documented.

# Addressing Risks to the Corporate Network

Once you have created a prioritized list of risks to your network and their associated costs, your next step is to determine a course of action in handling each risk. When deciding how to address risks to your network, you typically have one of four options:

- **Avoidance**  You can avoid a risk by changing the scope of the project so the risk in question no longer applies, or change the features of the software to do the same. In most cases, this is not a viable option, since eliminating a network service such as e-mail to avoid risks from viruses is not an appropriate measure. (Network services exist for a reason; your job as a security professional is to make those services as secure as possible.) One example of how avoidance would be a useful risk management tactic is if a company has a single server that acts as both a Web server and a database server housing confidential personnel records, when there is no interaction whatsoever between the Web site and personnel information. In this scenario, purchasing a second server to house the employee database, removing the personnel database from the Web server entirely, and placing the employee database server on a private network segment with no contact to the Internet would be a way to avoid Web-based attacks on personnel records, since this plan of action "removes" a feature of the Web server (the personnel files) entirely.

- **Transference**  You can transfer a risk by moving the responsibility to a third party. The most well-known example of this solution is purchasing some type of insurance—let's say flood insurance—for the contents of your server room. Although the purchase of this insurance does not diminish the likelihood that a flood will occur in your server room, it does ensure that the monetary cost of the damage will be borne by the insurance company in return for your policy premiums. It's important to note that transference is not a 100-percent solution—in the flood example, your company will likely still incur some financial loss or decreased productivity in the time it takes you to restore your server room to working order. As with most risk management tactics, bringing the risk exposure down to zero is usually an unattainable goal.

- **Mitigation** Mitigation is what most IT professionals think of when implementing a risk management solution. It involves taking some positive action to reduce the likelihood that an attack will occur or to reduce the potential damage that would be caused by an attack, without removing the resource entirely, as is the case with avoidance. Patching servers, disabling unneeded services, and installing a firewall are some solutions that fall under the heading of risk mitigation.

- **Acceptance** After you have delineated all the risks to your infrastructure that can be avoided, transferred, or mitigated, you are still left with a certain amount of risk that you won't be able to reduce any further without seriously impacting your business (taking an e-mail server offline as a means to combat viruses, for example). Your final option is one of acceptance, where you decide that the residual risks to your network have reached an acceptable level, and you choose to monitor the network for any signs of new or increased risks that might require more action later.

There is no one right way to address all risks to your infrastructure; you'll most likely take a blended approach to security. There are some risks you absolutely need to avoid, other risks you can reasonably transfer or mitigate, and still others that you simply accept because the cost of avoiding them is just not worth it.

# Drafting the Network Security Policy

Now that you know what is necessary, you can begin to write your network security policy. Writing a security policy is a logical progression of steps. Briefly, the structure of the policy should include the following:

- **Introduction** In this section, you should state the purpose of this policy. What is the objective of the policy? Why it is important to the organization?

- **Guidelines**  In this section, you should detail guidelines for choosing controls to meet the objectives of the policy. These are the basic requirements. Typically, you will see the word *should* in these statements.

- **Standards**  In this section, you should detail the standards for implementing and deploying the selected controls. For example, this section will state the initial configuration or firewall architecture. This section tends to detail the requirements given in the meeting with the interested departments and business units. This section is written with the words such as, "It is the policy that... ."

## NOTE

Remember that any type of traffic that takes place on your network should be defined somewhere within your network policy.

- **Procedures**  In this section, you should detail the procedures for maintaining the security solution, such as how often the logs should be reviewed and who is authorized to make changes.

- **Deployment**  The purpose of the deployment section is to assign responsibilities and specific steps for implementation of the policy. Think of it as a mini project plan. In a perimeter network security policy, this section translates the standards and guidelines into language the security administrator can enforce on the firewall.

- **Enforcement**  Although many policies lack this component, all policies require a method for enforcement. A popular and effective method for enforcement is auditing. In this section, you could state that the firewall rule base would be subject to an external audit yearly. In addition, this section should detail the enforcement and consequences if someone was to circumvent the firewall or its rules.

- **Modification or exceptions**  No policy is perfect, and the policy may require modifications or exceptions. In this section, you should detail the methods for obtaining modifications to the policy or exceptions.

The following series of headings could be considered a sample of a perimeter network security policy.

# Introduction

Due to Company X's required connection and access to the public Internet, it is essential that a strong perimeter firewall exist that sufficiently separates the internal private LAN of CompanyX and the public Internet. The firewall should provide preventative and detective technical controls for access between the two networks.

# Guidelines

The implementation of any firewall technology should follow these basic rules:

- The firewall should allow for filtering of communication protocols based on complex rule sets.
- The firewall should provide extensive logging of traffic passed and blocked.
- The firewall should be the only entry and exit point to the public Internet from the CompanyX LAN.
- The firewall operating system should be sufficiently hardened to resist both internal and external attacks.
- The firewall should fail closed.
- The firewall should not disclose the internal nature, names, or addressing of the CompanyX LAN.
- The firewall should only provide firewall services. No other service or application should be running on the firewall.

# Standards

The implementation of any firewall must follow these basic rules:

- It is the policy that only the identified firewall administrator is allowed to make changes to the configuration of the firewall.
- It is the policy that all firewalls must follow the default rule: That which is not expressly permitted is denied.

In addition, the following standards for perimeter networks are as follows:

- The deployment of public services and resources shall be positioned behind the firewall in a protected service net.
- The firewall shall be configured to disallow traffic that originates in the service net to the general LAN.

- Any application or network resource residing outside the firewall and accessible by unauthorized users requires a banner similar to the following:

A T T E N T I O N! PLEASE READ CAREFULLY.

This system is the property of CompanyX. It is for authorized use only. Users (authorized or unauthorized) have no explicit or implicit expectation of privacy. Any or all uses of this system and all files on this system will be intercepted, monitored, recorded, copied, audited, inspected, and disclosed to CompanyX management, and law enforcement personnel, as well as authorized officials of other agencies, both domestic and foreign. By using this system, the user consents to such interception, monitoring, recording, copying, auditing, inspection, and disclosure at the discretion of CompanyX. Unauthorized or improper use of this system may result in adminis-trative disciplinary action and civil and criminal penalties. By contin-uing to use this system, you indicate your awareness of and consent to these terms and conditions of use. LOG OFF IMMEDI-ATELY if you do not agree to the conditions stated in this warning.

# Procedures

Firewall will be configured to allow traffic as defined here:

- TCP/IP suite of protocols allowed through the firewall from the inside LAN to the public Internet is as follows:
  - HTTP to anywhere
  - HTTPS to anywhere
- TCP/IP suite of protocols allowed through the firewall from the inside LAN to the Service Net is as follows:
  - HTTP to Web server
  - SMTP to Mail server
  - POP3 to Mail server
  - DNS to DNS server
- TCP/IP suite of protocols allowed through the firewall from the Service Net to the public Internet is as follows:

- DNS from DNS server to anywhere

- TCP/IP suite of protocols allowed through the firewall from the public Internet to the LAN is as follows:

  - None

- TCP/IP suite of protocols allowed through the firewall from the public Internet with specific source, destination, and protocols is as follows:

  - SMTP to Mail server

  - HTTP to Web server

  - FTP to Web server

## Deployment

The security administrator will define the rule base and configure the firewall as defined above, in addition to other industry standard properties as appropriate.

## Enforcement

Traffic patterns will be enforced by the firewall's technical controls as defined by the firewall administrator. Periodically, an external vulnerability assessment will be performed to assure the proper configuration of the firewall. Additionally, an independent third party will annually audit the configured firewall.

## Modifications or Exceptions

Request for modification to the firewall configuration must be submitted via e-mail to the security manager and firewall administrator, accompanied by justification and the duration of the requested change.

# Different Access for Different Organizations

Before developing your security policy, determine whether you will need to have different policies for different locations or if you will have only one. If you have a single security policy, you can enforce the same policy on all firewalls and other security devices, usually from a single management station. Otherwise, you will have to maintain a different policy for different locations. Although for business reasons this might be necessary, it can add a level of complexity to your environment that could decrease your overall effective security. If it is necessary, make sure it is thoroughly documented. Some different types of organizations that may have differing access requirements include:

- **SOHO** The Small-Office-Home-Office network is often more concerned with accessibility than security, since these organizations often do not have dedicated IT professionals on hand, or may have an "IT person" who is doing double-duty while performing accounting or other administrative duties. In most cases, SOHO offices aren't terribly concerned with accessing resources hosted by remote networks; most SOHO access rules will pertain to a self-contained environment. (One major exception to this is that many small businesses will outsource services such as e-mail rather than run their own local servers.) Despite this focus on accessibility and ease of use, it's just as critical to maintain the security of desktops and servers within a SOHO environment as in the largest of enterprise networks.

- **Small/medium enterprise** When networks become larger than the typical SOHO configuration, you'll begin to see networks that run more infrastructure services in-house, including DHCP, DNS, e-mail, and VPN services. Here you'll also see the beginnings of access requirements that cross the boundaries of trusted networks, where you may need to configure a trust relationship or a federated access for a B2B arrangement between vendors or suppliers. Small- to medium-sized enterprise networks will typically have one or more dedicated IT staff available of varying skill levels who can implement network security policies and procedures.

- **Large enterprise** The largest organizations will typically have an extensive IT infrastructure to match. This typically means multiple layers of firewalls in place, both perimeter firewalls and internal firewalls to protect high-security areas on an internal LAN such as Human Resources or Research & Development. Enterprise networks will also usually have IT personnel of several levels of expertise, ranging from desktop or help desk support representatives to specialized network, firewall, or e-mail server administrators.

## Trusted Networks

It is not easy to define what a trusted network consists of, or what comprises a trusted network even within a single corporation or entity, since the concept of "trust" doesn't apply equally even within a single company—you'll still want to control access to sensitive information such as payroll or HR information. The old concept of firewalls and networking dictated that we have an Internet connection coming into a firewall from a single point, and this firewall would protect our inside networks from all attackers. Today, the idea of the network *perimeter* is expanding and shifting; many technologies make this previous definition outdated. Today we are remotely accessing our network via mobile phones, VPN clients from a personal DSL connection in our homes; we are also providing access to our network for our employees, and often for our suppliers and customers. The idea of perimeter security is disappearing because of the prevalence of wireless and home-based high-speed Internet connections in such a way that old concepts are no longer valid. Attackers are not always coming from outside your network; insiders may become the most dangerous attackers, as they have access to the intranet and may get proprietary information. Therefore, it should be mandatory to restrict the accesses and privileges in a "Need to Know" or "Need to Access" policy, giving access and privileges just when necessary and not by default to all your users. You have to update your mental schemas to protect your networks from today's threats.

## NOTE

One of the challenges of defining a trusted network is: Would you trust a network that can be remotely accessed by someone you don't know?

As always, identify the data that is going through each network segment to be able to apply the appropriate security measures. This is a crucial step because, in a typical environment, an Engineering department's requirements would differ from Human Resources', and the network running the fileservers would be different from the network supporting the Web server. And what about your financial departments, or the differences between the procurement and the sales departments? Each group of users needs different accesses and privileges, and you will have to provide them all in a way that is easy and productive.

# Defining Different Types of Network Access

Not every network segment is used by the same users or applications; moreover, usually the user defines which applications need to be run in a network segment. Each application has its own requirement regarding bandwidth and security, and the network security policy has to be defined with all those requirements in mind.

Let us imagine a hypothetical network that has been designed to support a large financial company. In our example, we have a company with:

- **The Board of Directors and high-level executives** These are either nontechnical users or ones whose computer knowledge is not very current (they may have left a technical position some years ago). The challenge here is that they usually want access to everything and want to be able to do what they want, no matters what it is; it's incredibly common to find organizations with firewall and proxy server rule-sets that have exceptions called something to the effect of "Allow VPs All Access." You need to gain buy-in from these high-level executives for your network security policy to succeed, even when it means their own access needs to be curtailed.

- **Engineering** These may be users with a high computer and networking knowledge, and possibly know more than you do! On the other hand, you may be dealing with people with a great deal of knowledge in their own specific field, but with no knowledge about computer networks or security.

- **Sales, Procurement, Financial** These users usually do not have a strong technical and security knowledge, but may be managing valuable data such us provider information, future projects, products prices, confidential commercial operations, etc. These users usually require a fairly free level of Internet access to interact with and research customer and suppliers networks.

- **Human Resources department** It is critical to secure this area, not because of any Internet access requirements, but because this department manages personal data. Depending on the country you are doing business in, there are numerous laws and regulations to protect employee and customer personal data. You will need to fulfill all the requirements of such laws while allowing your HR staff enough privileges to perform their jobs.

- **Marketing, Public Relations, and similar departments** These users may have specific requirements of network access. Talk with them, analyze their answers, and define a policy that suits their needs and allows them to do their work without compromising the business security.

**NOTE**

Involving the directors in security managing will greatly improve the success of your security policy—not an easy task, but essential. They may need to be informed, for example, that having full and unfiltered Internet access poses a risk to the security of their business.

# Untrusted Networks

The federation of networks that became the Internet consisted of a relatively small community of users by the 1980s, primarily in the research and academic communities. Because it was rather difficult to get access to these systems and the user communities were rather closely knit, security was not much of a concern. The main objective of connecting these various networks together was to share information, not keep it locked away. Technologies such as the UNIX operating system and the TCP/IP networking protocols that were designed for this environment reflected this lack of security concern; security was simply viewed as unnecessary.

By the early 1990s, however, commercial interest in the Internet grew. These commercial interests had very different perspectives on security, often in opposition to those of academia. Commercial information had value, and access to it had to be limited to specifically authorized people. UNIX, TCP/IP, and connections to the Internet became avenues of attack and did not have much capability to implement and enforce confidentiality, integrity, and availability. As the Internet grew in commercial importance, with numerous companies connecting to it and even building entire business models around it, the need for increased security became acute. Connected organizations now faced threats they never had to consider before.

When the corporate computing environment was a closed and limited-access system, threats mostly came from inside the organizations. These *internal threats* came from disgruntled employees with privileged access who could cause a lot of damage. Attacks from the outside were not much of an issue since there were typically only a few, if any, private connections to trusted entities. Potential attackers were few in number, since the combination of necessary skills and malicious intent were not widespread.

With the growth of the Internet, *external threats* grew as well. There are now millions of hosts on the Internet as potential attack targets, which entice the now large numbers of attackers. This group has grown in size and skill over the years as its members share information on how to break into systems for both fun and profit. Geography no longer serves as an obstacle, either. You can be attacked from another continent thousands of miles away just as easily as from your own town.

Threats can be classified as structured or unstructured. *Unstructured threats* are from people with low skill and perseverance. These usually come from people called *script kiddies*—attackers who have little to no programming skill and very little system knowledge. Script kiddies tend to conduct attacks just for bragging rights among their groups, which are often linked only by an Internet Relay Chat (IRC) channel. They obtain attack tools that have been built by others with more skill, and use them, often indiscriminately, to attempt to exploit vulnerability in their target. If their attack fails, they will likely go elsewhere and keep trying. Additional risk comes from the fact that they often use these tools with little to no knowledge of the target environment, so attacks can wind up causing unintended results. Unstructured threats can cause significant damage or disruption, despite the attacker's lack of sophistication. These attacks are usually detectable with current security tools.

*Structured attacks* are more worrisome because they are conducted by hackers with significant skill. If the existing tools do not work for them, they are likely to modify them or write their own. They are able to discover new vulnerabilities in systems by executing complex actions the system designers did not protect against. Structured attackers often use so-called *zero-day exploits*, which target vulnerabilities the system vendor has not yet issued a patch for or does not know about. Structured attacks often have stronger motivations behind them than simple mischief. These can include theft of source code, theft of credit card numbers for resale or fraud, retribution, or destruction or disruption of a competitor. A structured attack might not be blocked by traditional methods such as firewall rules or detected by an IDS. It could even use noncomputer methods such as social engineering.

## NOTE

*Social engineering,* also known as *people hacking*, is a means of obtaining security information from people by tricking them. The classic example is calling up a user and pretending to be a system administrator. The hacker asks the user for his or her password to ostensibly perform some important maintenance task. To avoid being hacked via social engineering, educate your user community that they should always confirm the identity of any person calling them and that passwords should never be given to *anyone* via e-mail, instant messaging, or the phone. To guard against social engineering and similar security hazards, user education should be an integral part of any network security policy.

Another key task in securing your systems is closing vulnerabilities by turning off unneeded services and bringing them up to date on patches. Services that have no defined business need present an additional possible avenue of attack and are just another component that needs patch attention. Keeping patches current is one of the most important activities you can perform to protect yourself, yet one that many organizations neglect.

The Code Red and Nimda worms of 2001 were successful primarily because so many systems had not been patched for the vulnerabilities they exploited, including multiple Microsoft Internet Information Server (IIS) and Microsoft Outlook vulner-abilities. Patching, especially when you have hundreds or even thousands of systems, can be a monumental task. However, by defining and documenting processes, using tools to assist in configuration management, subscribing to multiple vulnerability alert mailing lists, and prioritizing patches according to criticality, you can get a better handle on the job.

One useful document to assist in this process has been published by the U.S. National Institute of Standards and Technology (NIST), which can be found at http://csrc.nist.gov/publications/nistpubs/800-40/sp800-40.pdf (800-40 is the document number).

Also important is having a complete understanding of your network topology and some of the key information flows within it, and in and out of it. This under-standing helps you define different zones of trust and highlights where re-archi-tecting the network in places might improve security—for example, by deploying additional firewalls internally or on your network perimeter.

# Identifying Potential Threats

As you prepare your overall security plan and de-militarized zone (DMZ), it is important to identify and evaluate the potential risks and threats to your network, systems, and data. You must evaluate your risks thoroughly during the identification process to assign some sort of value to the risks to determine priorities for protec-tion and likelihood of loss resulting from those risks and threats if they materialize. You should be looking at and establishing a risk evaluation for anything that could potentially disrupt, slow, or damage your systems, data, or credibility. In this area, it is important to assign these values to potential threats such as:

- Outside hacker attacks
- Trojans, worms, and virus attacks
- DoS or Distributed Denial of Service (DDoS) attacks
- Compromise or loss of internal confidential information
- Network monitoring and data interception
- Internal attacks by employees
- Hardware failures
- Loss of critical systems

This identification process creates the basis for your security plan, policies, and implementation of your security environment. You should realize that this is an ongoing evaluation that is subject to change as conditions within your company and partners, and employee need for access, change and morph over time. Security is a process and is never truly "finished." However, a good basic evaluation goes a long way toward creating the most secure system we can achieve.

# Using VPNs in Today's Enterprise

Ensuring that your data arrives safe and sound when it passes through a network is something everyone wants to have. In an ideal world, your data's integrity and confidentiality would be guaranteed. If this sounds like a fantasy, you are wrong. These types of guarantees can be made when you use IPSec VPN technologies. When you use an IPSec connection between two networks or a client and a network, you can ensure that no one looked at the data and no one modified it. Almost every company today uses VPN technologies to secure its data as it passes through various networks. In fact, many regulations specify that a VPN connection must be used to pass specific types of data.

IPSec provides integrity checking to ensure your data was not modified. It also provides encryption, ensuring no one has looked at the data. When two sides create a VPN connection, each side is authenticated to verify that each party is who they say they are. Combined with integrity checking and encryption, you have an almost unbeatable combination.

# The Battle for the Secure Enterprise

This book covers the NetScreen firewall product line and focuses on that specific product and technology. A firewall is the core of securing your network, but other products should also be implemented in your network. These additional devices help ensure a network that has security covered from all angles. The following technologies are usually the minimum that companies should implement to provide security in the organization.

A *firewall* can contain many different types of technology to increase its importance in your network. Many firewall products today can integrate several different technologies, and almost all provide VPN services. This allows secure streams of data to terminate to your firewall. This is usually over the Internet, but also over other unprotected networks. When the traffic gets to your secured network it no longer requires encryption. You can also force users to authenticate before accessing resources through the firewall. This commonly used practice denies access to systems until the user authenticates. When doing this, clients cannot see the resource *until authentication has occurred.*

*URL filtering* is another requirement in many organizations, and provides a way to accept or reject access to specific Web sites. This allows companies to reduce liability by users accessing inappropriate Web content. Many firewalls can integrate with this type of scanning when used with another product.

*Anti-virus* is a requirement for any organization today. With more viruses being written, the last thing you want in your network is a virus outbreak. The Windows operating system is built to provide so many different functions that there are many ways it can be exploited. In recent months, Microsoft has done a great job of coming out with security patches when or before an exploit is discovered. Typically, though, when vulnerability is discovered an anti-virus company has a way to stop it much faster than Microsoft. An outbreak on your network can mean disaster, data loss, or loss of your job. Data is a company's most valuable asset today, and loss of that data or access to it can cost companies millions of dollars or more per day. Firewalls can be used to perform virus scanning. These devices are usually deployed in a central area on the network. A tiered anti-virus solution is a requirement for any organization.

You should have anti-virus scanning on all your desktops and servers to stop infections at the source. This will help prevent most virus outbreaks. In addition, you should have anti-virus scanning on your Simple Mail Transfer Protocol (SMTP) mail forwarder and should be resident directly on your mail server. Your chances for a virus outbreak should be small as long as you keep all of those devices up to date with the appropriate virus definitions. New technologies such as inline virus scanning in firewalls and other network appliances can provide extra protection from viruses.

Patch management has become a Herculean effort with all of the software an organization needs to run today. Patching operating systems and applications as soon as a vulnerability occurs is a must. With limited staff and increased software deployed, this task is almost impossible to accomplish. However, by providing an anti-virus system, you can provide a first level of defense against the spreading of malicious software or malware.

No matter what device or security you provide, everything usually comes down to some type of access token, usually a username and password. Using static usernames and passwords is not enough anymore. Even 15 to 30 days may be too long to keep the same password. Two-factor authentication, digital certificates, and personal entropy are leading the march to provide a stronger nonstatic type of authentication that is hard to break.

Your network has millions of packets traversing it every day. Do you know what they are all doing? This is where an intrusion detection or intrusion detection and prevention device comes into play. These devices detect application- and network-based attacks. Intrusion detection devices sit on your network and watch traffic. They provide alerts for unusual traffic, and TCP resets to close TCP sessions. The newer technology of intrusion detection and prevention provides the ability to stop malicious traffic altogether and alert on it. However, heavy tuning of the products is required to make them effective.

Access into your network should be encrypted whenever possible. This ensures that parties not authorized to see your data do not get access to it by any means. IPSec VPN clients are one of the most popular ways to do this. This type of client provides strong encryption of your data and access to your internal resources without having them publicly accessible. A new trend in VPN solutions is the Secure Sockets Layer (SSL) VPN. These products allow you to put more behind them and do not require predeployment of a VPN client.

## External Communications (also see "Remote Access")

- **Modems are not disconnected** The problem with unsecured modems is that they can be attacked by wardialers who simply look for modems connected to corporate networks. These can create significant security holes and are often overlooked in our quest to lock down the wired network.

- **An ISP connection exists without written approval** In most companies, this might be a difficult trick to achieve, but it certainly warrants examination to ensure the ISP connection(s) is managed by the IT department and not some errant user who managed to get the local ISP provider to run a cable into the office on a Saturday morning.

- **Communications devices are not password protected** This seems like a giant "Duh!" but you'd probably be surprised how often communication devices such as modems, routers, switches, and other "smart" devices are left unprotected by even a simple password, or use the default password that came with the device out of the box.

- **No warning banner** Failure to display the required login banner prior to logon attempts will limit the site's capability to prosecute unauthorized access. It also presents the potential for criminal and civil liability for systems administrators and information systems managers. Not displaying the proper banner will also hamper the site's capability to monitor device usage. Displaying a banner warning users of the consequences of unauthorized access helps ward off the bad guys and draws a line in the legal sand that you might need later.

# DMZ Concepts

The use of a DMZ and its overall design and implementation can be relatively simple or extremely complex, depending on the needs of the particular business or network system. The DMZ concept came into use as the need for separation of networks became more acute when we began to provide more access to services for individuals or partners outside the LAN infrastructure. One of the primary reasons why the DMZ has come into favor is the realization that a single type of protection is subject to failure. This failure can arise from configuration errors, planning errors, equipment failure, or deliberate action on the part of an internal employee or external attack force. The DMZ has proven more secure and offers multiple layers of protection for the security of the protected networks and machines. It is also very flexible, scalable, and relatively robust in its capability to provide the protection we need. DMZ design now includes the ability to use multiple products (both hardware- and software-based) on multiple platforms to achieve the level of protection necessary, and are often designed to provide failover capabilities as well.

When we are working with a DMZ, we must have a common ground from which to work. To facilitate understanding, we examine a number of conceptual paths for traffic flow in the following section. Before doing so, however, let's make sure we understand the basic configurations that can be used for firewall and DMZ location and how each can be visualized. In the following figures, we'll see and discuss these configurations. Please note that each of these configurations is useful on internal networks needing protection, and protecting your resources from networks such as the Internet. Our first configuration is shown in Figure 1.1.

## Designing & Planning...

### Know What You Want to Secure First

As you begin your DMZ design process, you must first be clear about what your design is intended for. A design that is only intended to superficially limit internal users' access to the Internet, for instance, requires much less planning and design work than a system protecting resources from multiple access points or providing multiple services to the public network or users from remote locations. An appropriate path to follow for your predesign path might look like this:

- Perform baseline security analysis of existing infrastructure, including OS and application analysis

Continued

- Perform baseline network mapping and performance monitoring
- Identify risk to resources and appropriate mitigation processes
- Identify potential security threats, both external and internal
- Identify needed access points from external sources
- Public networks
- VPN access
- Extranets
- Remote access services
- Identify critical services
- Plan your DMZ

**Figure 1.1** A Basic Network with a Single Firewall

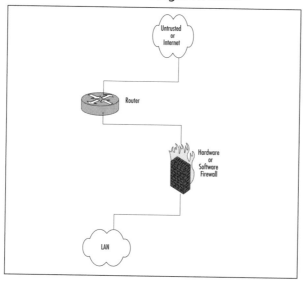

Figure 1.1 shows the basic configuration that would be used in a simple network situation in which there was no need to provide external services. This configuration would typically be used to begin to protect a small business or home network. It could also be used within an internal network to protect an inner network that had to be divided and isolated from the main network. This situation could include Payroll, Finance, or Development divisions that need to protect their information and keep it away from general network use and view.

Figure 1.2 details a protection design that would allow for the implementation and provision of services outside the protected network. In this design, it would be imperative that rules be enacted to not allow the untrusted host to access the internal network. Security of the bastion host machine would be accomplished on the machine itself, and only minimal and necessary services would be enabled or installed on that machine. In this design, we might be providing a Web presence that did not involve e-commerce or the necessity to dynamically update content. This design would not be used for provision of virtual private network (VPN) connections, FTP services, or other services that required other content updates to be performed regularly.

**Figure 1.2** Basic Network, Single Firewall and Bastion Host (Untrusted Host)

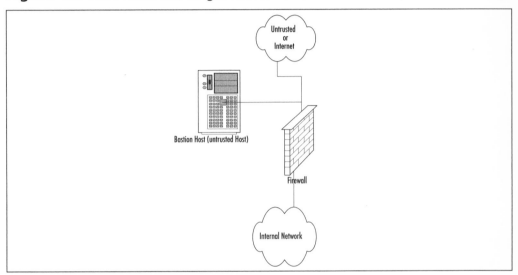

Figure 1.3 shows a basic DMZ structure. In this design, the bastion host is partially protected by the firewall. Rather than the full exposure that would result to the bastion host in Figure 1.2, this setup would allow us to specify that the bastion host in Figure 1.2 could be allowed full outbound connection, but the firewall could be configured to allow only port 80 traffic inbound to the bastion host (assuming it was a Web server) or others as necessary for connection from outside. This design would allow connection from the internal network to the bastion host if necessary, and potentially allow updating of Web server content from the internal network if allowed by firewall rule, which could allow traffic to and from the bastion host on specific ports as designated.

**Figure 1.3** A Basic Firewall with a DMZ

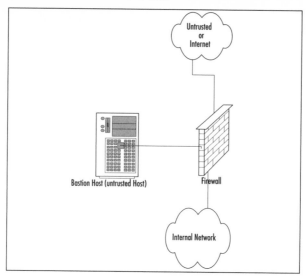

Figure 1.4 shows a generic dual-firewall DMZ configuration. In this arrangement, the bastion host can be protected from the outside and allowed to connect to or from the internal network. In this arrangement, like the conditions in Figure 1.3, flow can be controlled to and from both of the networks away from the DMZ. This configuration and method is more likely to be used if more than one bastion host is needed for the operations or services being provided.

**Figure 1.4** A Dual Firewall with a DMZ

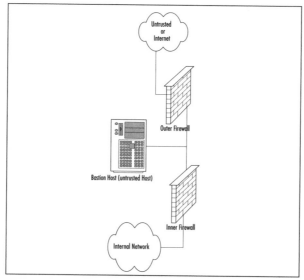

# Traffic Flow Concepts

Now that we've had a quick tour of some generic designs, let's look at the way network communications traffic typically flows through them. Be sure to note the differences between the levels and the flow of traffic and protections offered in each.

Figure 1.5 illustrates the flow pattern for information through a basic single-firewall setup. This type of traffic control can be achieved through hardware or software and is the basis for familiar products such as Internet Connection Sharing (ICS) and the NAT functionality provided by digital subscriber line (DSL) and cable modems used for connection to the Internet. Note that flow is unrestricted outbound, but the basic configuration will drop all inbound connections that did not originate from the internal network.

**Figure 1.5** Basic Single-Firewall Flow

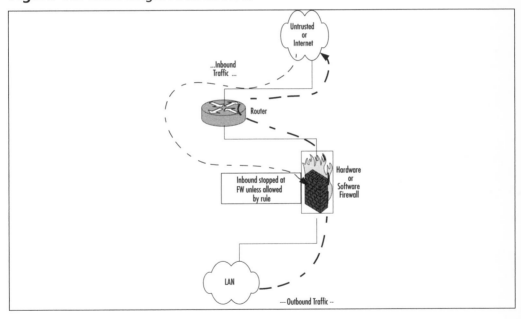

Figure 1.6 reviews the traffic flow in a network containing a bastion host and a single firewall. This network configuration does not produce a DMZ; the protection of the bastion host is configured individually on the host and requires extreme care in setup. Inbound traffic from the untrusted network or the bastion host is dropped at the firewall, providing protection to the internal network. Outbound traffic from the internal network is allowed.

**Figure 1.6** A Basic Firewall with Bastion Host Flow

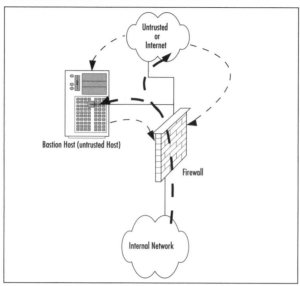

Figure 1.7 shows the patterns of traffic as we implement a DMZ design. In this form, inbound traffic flows through to the bastion host if allowed through the firewall and is dropped if destined for the internal network. Two-way traffic is permitted as specified between the internal network and the bastion host, and outbound traffic from the internal network flows through the firewall and out, generally without restriction.

**Figure 1.7** A Basic Single Firewall with DMZ Flow

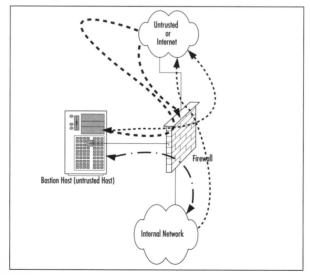

Figure 1.8 contains a more complex path of flow for information, but provides the most capability in these basic designs to allow for configuration and provision of services to the outside. In this case, we have truly established a DMZ, separated and protected from both the internal and external networks. This type of configuration is used quite often when there is a need to provide more than one type of service to the public or outside world, such as e-mail, Web servers, DNS, and so forth. Traffic to the bastion host can be allowed or denied as necessary from both the external and internal networks, and incoming traffic to the internal network can be dropped at the external firewall. Outbound traffic from the internal network can be allowed or restricted to the bastion host (DMZ network) or the external network.

**Figure 1.8** A Dual Firewall with DMZ Flow

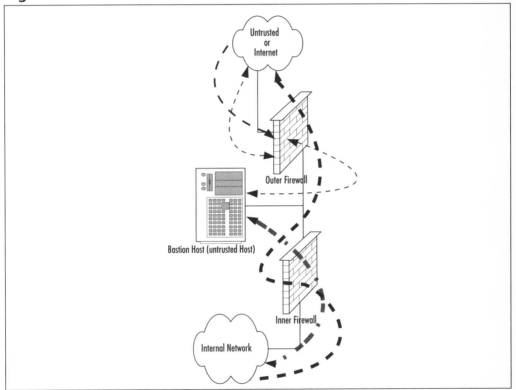

As you can see, there is a great amount of flexibility in the design and function of your protection mechanisms. In the sections that follow, we expand further on conditions for the use of different configurations and on the planning to implement them.

# Networks with and without DMZs

As we pursue our discussions about the creation of DMZ structures, it is appropriate to also look at the reasoning behind the various structures of the DMZ, and when and where we'd want to implement a DMZ or perhaps use some other alternative.

During our preview of the concepts of DMZs, we saw in Figures 1.5 to 1.8 some examples of potential design for network protection and access. Your design may incorporate any or all of these types of configuration, depending on your organization's needs. For instance, Figure 1.5 shows a configuration that may occur in the case of a home network installation or perhaps with a small business environment that is isolated from the Internet and does not share information or need to provide services or information to outside customers or partners. This design would be suitable under these conditions, provided configuration is correct and monitored for change.

Figure 1.6 illustrates a network design with a bastion host located outside the firewall. In this design, the bastion host must be stripped of all unnecessary functionality and services and protected locally with appropriate file permissions and access control mechanisms. This design would be used when an organization needs to provide minimal services to an external network, such as a Web server. Access to the internal network from the bastion host is generally not allowed, because this host is subject to compromise.

Figure 1.7 details the first of the actual DMZ designs and incorporates a screened subnet. In this type of design, the firewall controls the flow of information from network to network and provides more protection to the bastion host from external flows. This design might be used when it is necessary to regularly update the content of a Web server, or provide a front end for mail services or other services that need contact from both the internal and external networks. Although better for security purposes than Figure 1.6, this design still produces an untrusted relationship in the bastion host in relation to the internal network.

Finally, Figure 1.8 provides a design that allows for the placement of many types of service in the DMZ. Traffic can be very finely controlled through access at the two firewalls, and services can be provided at multiple levels to both internal and external networks.

In the next section, we profile some of the advantages and disadvantages of the common approaches to DMZ architecture and provide a checklist of sorts to help you to make a decision about the appropriate use (or not) of the DMZ for protection.

# Pros and Cons of DMZ Basic Designs

Table 1.6 details the advantages and disadvantages of the various types of basic design discussed in the preceding section.

**Table 1.6** Pros and Cons of Basic DMZ Designs

| Basic Design | Advantages | Disadvantages | Appropriate Use |
|---|---|---|---|
| Single firewall | Inexpensive, fairly easy configuration, low maintenance | Much lower security capabilities, no growth or expansion potential | Home, small office/home office (SOHO), small business without need to provide services to others |
| Single firewall with bastion host | Lower cost than more robust alternatives | Bastion host extremely vulnerable to compromise, inconvenient to update content, loss of functionality other than for required services; not scalable | Small business without resources for more robust implementation or static content being provided that doesn't require frequent updates |
| Single firewall with screened subnet and bastion host | Firewall provides protection to both internal network and bastion host, limiting some of the potential breach possibilities of an unprotected bastion host | Single point of failure; some products limit network addressing to DMZ in this configuration to public addresses, which might not be economic or possible in your network | Networks requiring access to the bastion host for updating information |

**Continued**

**Table 1.6 continued** Pros and Cons of Basic DMZ Designs

| Basic Design | Advantages | Disadvantages | Appropriate Use |
|---|---|---|---|
| Dual firewall with DMZ | Allows for establishment of multiple service-providing hosts in the DMZ; protects bastion hosts in DMZ from both networks, allows much more granular control of resources and access; removes single point of failure and attack | Requires more hardware and software for implementation of this design; more configuration work and monitoring required | Larger operations that require the capability to offer multiple types of Web access and services to both the internal and external networks involved |

## Configuring & Implementing...

### Bastion Hosts

Bastion hosts must be individually secured and hardened because they are always in a position that could be attacked or probed. This means that before placement, a bastion host must be stripped of unnecessary services, fully updated with the latest service packs, hot fixes, and updates, and isolated from other trusted machines and networks to eliminate the possibility that its compromise would allow connection to (and potential compromise of) the protected networks and resources. This also means that a machine being used for this purpose should have no user accounts relative to the protected network or directory services structure, which could lead to enumeration of your internal network.

# DMZ Design Fundamentals

DMZ design, like security design, is always a work in progress. As in security planning and analysis, we find DMZ design carries great flexibility and change potential to keep the protection levels we put in place in an effective state. The ongoing work is required so that the system's security is always as high as we can make it within the constraints of time and budget, while still allowing appropriate users and visitors to access the information and services we provide for their use. You will find that the time and funds spent in the design process and preparation for the implementation are very good investments if the process is focused and effective; this will lead to a high level of success and a good level of protection for the network you are protecting. In this section of the chapter, we explore the fundamentals of the design process. We incorporate the information we discussed in relation to security and traffic flow to make decisions about how our initial design should look. Additionally, we'll build on that information and review some other areas of concern that could affect the way we design our DMZ structure.

**NOTE**

In this section, we look at design of a DMZ from a logical point of view. Physical design and configuration are covered in following chapters, based on the vendor-based solution you are interested in deploying.

## Why Design Is So Important

Design of the DMZ is critically important to the overall protection of your internal network—and the success of your firewall and DMZ deployment. The DMZ design can incorporate sections that isolate incoming VPN traffic, Web traffic, partner connections, employee connections, and public access to information provided by your organization. Design of the DMZ structure throughout the organization can protect internal resources from internal attack. As discussed in the security section, much of the risk of data loss, corruption, and breach exists *inside* the network perimeter. Our tendency is to protect assets from external harm but to disregard the dangers that come from our own internal equipment, policies, and employees.

These attacks or disruptions do not arise solely from disgruntled employees. Many of the most damaging conditions occur because of inadvertent mistakes made by well-intentioned employees. Each and all of these entry points is a potential source of loss for your organization and ultimately can provide an attack point to defeat your other defenses. Additionally, the design of your DMZ will allow you to implement a multilayered approach to securing your resources that does not leave a single point of failure in your plan. This minimizes the problems and loss of protection that can occur because of misconfiguration of rule sets or access control lists (ACLs), and reduces the problems that can occur due to hardware configuration errors. In the last chapters of this book, we look at how to mitigate risk through testing of your network infrastructure to make sure your firewalls, routers, switches, and hosts are thoroughly hardened so that when you do deploy your DMZ segment, it is secure from both internal and external threats.

# Designing End-to-End Security for Data Transmission between Hosts on the Network

Proper DMZ design, in conjunction with the security policy and plan developed previously, allows for end-to-end protection of the information being transmitted on the network. The importance of this capability is explored more fully later in the chapter, when we review some of the security problems inherent in the current implementation of TCP/IPv4 and the transmission of data. The use of one or more of the many firewall products or appliances currently available will most often afford the opportunity to block or filter specific protocols and protect the data as it is being transmitted. This protection may take the form of encryption and can use the available transports to protect data as well. Additionally, proper use of the technologies available within this design can provide for the necessary functions previously detailed in the concepts of AAA and CIA, using the multilayer approach to protection we discussed in earlier sections. This need to provide end-to-end security requires that we are conversant with and remember basic network traffic patterns and protocols. The next few sections further illustrate the need to design the DMZ with this capability in mind.

# Traffic Flow and Protocol Fundamentals

Another of the benefits of using a DMZ design that includes one or more firewalls is the opportunity to control traffic flow into and out of the DMZ much more cohesively and with much more granularity and flexibility. When the firewall product in use (either hardware or software) is a product designed above the home-use level, the capability usually exists to control traffic flowing in and out of the network or DMZ through packet filtering based on port numbers, and allow or deny the use of entire protocols. For instance, the rule set might include a statement that blocks communication via ICMP, which would block protocol 1. A statement that allowed IPSec traffic where it was desired to allow traffic using ESP or AH would be written allowing protocol 50 for ESP or 51 for Authentication Header (AH). (For a listing of the protocol IDs, visit www.iana.org/assignments/protocol-numbers.) Remember that like the rule of security that follows the principle of least privilege, we must include in our design the capability to allow only necessary traffic into and out of the various portions of the DMZ structure.

# Making Your Security Come Together

In today's security battlefield, it almost seems impossible to win. You must identify the best products and procedures for your organization. If you have all of the suggested security solutions, but not enough staff to manage them, the solutions may not be effective enough. Simply having the appropriate products is not going to resolve all of your problems; you must effectively understand how to use and configure the products. There is no easy solution regarding the best way to go about securing your organization. This is why companies all over the world spend hundreds of millions of dollars on consulting companies to come in and make security decisions for them.

# Summary

We've covered a lot of ground in this chapter because your network infrastructure is literally and figuratively the backbone of your network. Creating a network security policy touches every aspect of your network, and a thorough assessment will take time and careful effort to complete so your network is as secure as it can reasonably be, given the organizational constraints and considerations you'll have to deal with. It's often helpful to break the network infrastructure down into its systems or areas to help ensure that you cover all the areas, including devices and media, topology, intrusion detection and prevention, system hardening, and all the network components such as routers, switches, and modems. Once you've identified all the areas, you need to take a top-to-bottom look at how security is currently implemented and what threats exist. By looking at issues such as information criticality and performing an impact analysis, you can decide what should be included in your project and what can reasonably be left out or delayed for a later phase if needed. Understanding the threat environment and your network's vulnerabilities is also important during your planning phase.

Requirements need to be thoroughly developed because they form the foundation of your project's scope. Functional requirements should be developed first, followed by technical, legal, and policy requirements. Be sure to build these into your task details when you create your WBS so that all required elements will be present and accounted for in your project plan.

In an infrastructure security project, you'll need a wide variety of skills that span the depth and breadth of networking knowledge. Be sure you define those skills so you can assess your team and your organization to identify skills gaps. These will have to be addressed before your project can proceed, and often requires hiring outside contractors or providing training for internal staff members. Either way, this can affect both your budget and your schedule, so be sure you do a gap analysis between needed and available skills prior to proceeding with your project.

The WBS defines the scope of your project, so once you've identified all the work through delineating the tasks, be sure to do a scope check. If the defined scope is smaller than the scope outlined in your WBS, you need to reconcile the differences. Also, be sure to discuss any scope changes with your project sponsor so you start with the same expectations about project results.

Scheduling an infrastructure security project can be challenging due to all the moving parts involved. You'll run into scheduling conflicts, resource usage conflicts, timing issues, and more. These should be resolved to the greatest degree possible before starting the project, because things will only get more complicated and difficult to resolve once project work is underway. One important scheduling note is that with all areas of your network being poked and prodded, you'll need to make sure subproject teams are not working at cross-purposes and undoing work just done or inadvertently injecting false indicators into the process through their own task work.

When it's all said and done, you should be able to define, implement, and manage a very useful network security policy if you follow a consistent methodology and make teamwork and quality topmost priorities. This is the foundation of all other security projects; it touches on everything in your organization, so success here will create the framework for a very secure network that will help you sleep at night, knowing you've done everything possible to keep your organization's assets secure.

# Solutions Fast Track

## Defining Your Organization

- You need to understand your organization's business and business processes before you can craft a network security policy.

- Consider the IT needs and characteristics of different areas within your company; e.g., your application developers may have differing security requirements than members of your Human Resources area.

- Be aware of any legal or regulatory requirements that your company needs to comply with, such as compliance measures like SOX or HIPPAA.

## Trusted Networks

- As much as possible, you should define the difference between trusted and untrusted networks in your environment; i.e., those networks that can safely transmit sensitive data versus those that are at risk by internal or external attackers.

- The increased availability of home-based high-speed Internet access and wireless hotspots has made it much more difficult to create a line of demarcation between trusted and untrusted networks.

- Even on trusted networks, your network security policy should dictate the protection measures that should be put in place to protect your data as it traverses the network.

## Untrusted Networks

- Any time your data traverses a network where it is at risk of being intercepted or manipulated by a malicious user, you need to outline the steps that will minimize the risk of this occurring.

- Whenever possible, business data should not be transmitted over an untrusted network in a clear-text or other easily readable format.

- Technologies such as Network Quarantine and Federation Services will make an increasingly large impact on your ability to secure your network as the line between trusted and untrusted networks continues to blur.

# Frequently Asked Questions

The following Frequently Asked Questions, answered by the authors of this book, are designed to both measure your understanding of the concepts presented in this chapter and to assist you with real-life implementation of these concepts. To have your questions about this chapter answered by the author, browse to **www.syngress.com/solutions** and click on the **"Ask the Author"** form.

**Q.** I've already configured a perimeter firewall and numerous other resources for my company, aren't we already secure?

**A.** The only way to make a computer or network *completely* secure is to never ever connect it to a network or plug in a floppy or USB drive. (Dropping it overboard in the middle of the ocean helps as well.) In the modern computing environment, the phrase that pays is "defense in depth"—configuring multiple layers of security (within the limits of budgets and reason) so that if one layer fails, another layer will be present to secure your resources.

**Q.** How can I determine which resources on my network should receive priority when crafting our security policy?

**A.** In a perfect world, you would have an unlimited budget to deploy perfect security for all aspects of your network. In reality, you only have so much money to spend—and it's usually not worth spending more on securing an asset than that asset is worth. In many ways, this decision is not a technical one, but must be made in conjunction with data owners and decision-makers in your organization to determine which resources need to be given priority in a finite budget.

**Q.** What is the difference between a policy and a procedure?

**A.** Your network security policy should be a high-level document that can withstand changes in technology without needing constant revision. In addition to your security policy, you can specify a number of procedures that detail how to secure specific technologies or products; these procedures are much more technical in nature and can be updated as the technology they refer to changes. In other words, your network security policy should specify the "What," "When," "Where," and "Who," while your procedures can focus more on the specifics of "How."

**Q.** How do I respond to the CEO or other VP who insists that he or she should be exempt from all security restrictions?

**A.** This is a delicate political needle to thread, but you are doing a disservice to your organization if you do not at least make the attempt. For example, you might point out that a network virus will do the same amount of damage regardless of whether it originated from a secretary's computer or the CEO's laptop. It's the "weakest link" adage in action—if a certain segment of your network is left unsecured, it can potentially reduce the security of the entire network.

# Chapter 2

# Using Your Policies to Create Firewall and VPN Configurations

## Topics in this chapter:

- **Logical Security Configurations**

- **Profiling Network Assets**

- **Users and User Groups**

- **Security Areas**

- **Security Area Risk Ratings**

- **Writing Firewall and VPN Logical Security Configurations**

☑ **Summary**

☑ **Solutions Fast Track**

☑ **Frequently Asked Questions**

# Introduction

As we learned in the previous chapter, securing your network starts with creating various security policies that articulate the rules, requirements, standards, and recommendations specific to your environment. As our businesses depend more and more on networks and the resources they provide, it is increasingly important that we protect these resources from unauthorized access, attacks, and exploits against vulnerabilities. As security professionals, our success is not dependant on fixing these inherent and ongoing problems, but relies on our abilities to select, implement, and configure solutions that protect our resources. The threats, attacks, and abuse will always be present as long as we have networks and provide services on those networks. It all starts with written security polices, which are our roadmaps—and the single most important documents you can have. Whether it is an Acceptable Use Policy, Remote User VPN Policy, or the Perimeter Access Policy, each will have a long-term impact on the security of your network.

Unfortunately, security policies are afterthoughts in many companies. It is not uncommon to find companies that have selected a security product, vendor, or even a complete security solution without ever writing a security policy. As a result, the security posture of these networks is ineffective in many respects. Their configurations and rules probably do not reflect the requirements or desires of the organization. In other situations in which security policies are not an afterthought, it is common to find that those policies are outdated and probably had little or no impact on the product selection or configurations of their security solutions. The most successful organizations with respect to strong security have a commonality between them—security policies. They review, update, and leverage best practice security principals when selecting and configuring their security solutions.

Another area commonly overlooked is security policy sponsorship. As important as developing the policies themselves, it is equally as important to get sponsorship for their content and implementation. This helps drive and support the entire process you will go through when creating, maintaining, and implementing your security solutions. Many organizations spend the time, resources, and money to create security policies, and fail to support them after their initial creation. Their failures are usually not a result of their efforts or even part of the original plan. Many recommendations and policies never get implemented or enforced long term because of two key missing elements: sponsorship and acceptance.

Sponsorship is key because it provides the support by someone who has authoritative power in the organization to oversee your success. This entire process is largely a team effort and without a sponsor, it will become challenging and often difficult to complete all the steps necessary to develop and implement the organizational policies.

Equally important is the acceptance and understanding from the entire team on the project goals and charter. While it might be impossible to always get 100 percent from everyone on the team, everyone must agree to support the team decisions and help enforce the policies. This is an area in which facilitation skills have a major impact. Helping lead others to understand the positive impact the policies will have on them personally will aid in their long-term support. If an individual or group of people does not general accept or believe in the goals, why would they support them? Finally, keep in mind that everyone on the team should have input and understand his or her participation is critical to the success of the project.

This chapter discusses how to take your written security policies and convert them into logical security configurations. Logical security configurations are used by technical administrators to guide them through the implementation and configuration of your firewall and VPN devices. You might be thinking that we have yet to discuss a specific firewall or VPN appliance. Well, you are right! In fact, this is a mistake commonly made by security professionals when they go through this step. By abstracting vendor-specific technology or features, you are able to think about the goals of the policies versus writing policy around a vendor's product. This step might seem somewhat insignificant; however, it is a vital step that should not be overlooked or skipped. The primary goal of this chapter is to create concise and clear objectives that are specific to actual configurations of the firewall and VPN devices.

### NOTE

It is important to understand these processes are not the end-all, be-all of security policy development. They are guidelines and should be interpreted as such. In addition, it is easy to stray from the goals of this step, which is to develop effective and clear running configurations for your devices.

# What Is a Logical Security Configuration?

Once you have developed and received approval for your written security policies, the next major step is to convert them into logical security configuration documents. You might ask, what is a logical security configuration and how is it different from an actual configuration you will create for your firewall or VPN device? This is a great question, and one that is might or might not be easily answered. Logical security configurations are documents that interpret written security policy requirements and define configuration requirements for a specific type of enforcement device, like a firewall or VPN products. Based on standard capabilities of these various devices, these documents will be used to build device-specific configurations that ultimately enforce your policy requirements.

For example, a firewall device provides access control between different networks to which it connects. At a basic level, they will provide these controls from Layer 3 and layer headers, which include source IP, destination IP, source port, and destination port. Even though you might select two different firewall devices for your network, this information will be important as the administrator configures the device. Keep in mind that we are not discussing or using actual features found in a specific vendor's product or solution offerings. Instead, we are creating a logical configuration that will map our written security policy to the common capabilities of these devices.

While there is not a definitive correlation of logical configurations to written policies or logical configurations to specific devices, it is important that you create documents that can be easy to maintain and have focus. As a result, we recommend creating logical configurations for each group or type of devices you will be using in your environment. For our example, Example Corporation, we have created the following five categories and will create a logical configuration for each of these groups.

- Firewalls
- VPN
- Workstations
- Servers
- Routers

Once our logical configurations are complete, we should have a series of documents that accurately represent the rules, policies, configurations, and procedures that will be configured on the specific firewall and VPN devices in your organization.

# Planning Your Logical Security Configuration

Now we are ready to start the planning phase of our logical configuration process. It is recommended you complete the following four steps before starting the actual writing of your logical security configuration documents.

1. Identifying network assets.

2. Profiling your network assets.

3. Creating security areas.

4. Assigning network assets to security areas.

Keep in mind, once you capture some of this information, it can be leveraged in each of the logical configuration documents we identified in the previous step.

# Identifying Network Assets

One of the first steps is to identify the network assets we are trying to protect and provide secure access to or from. It is important to understand what devices and services are on the networks you are protecting. The more information you capture about your assets, the more informed you will be when you have to make decisions. This information will be useful when you create your logical security policies and for ongoing management and auditing of your systems and configurations.

Since you will be collecting a lot of information, we highly recommend you take some time before starting this process to determine what method or system you can use to help organize this information. While outside the context of this book, it is common for customers to use a network inventory system and other network scanning tools to locate and profile each device. Open source projects like Open Computer and Software Inventory Next Generation (OCSng— http://ocsinventory.sourceforge.net/) and NMap (http://insecure.org/nmap/) are two places to start. Even though we recommend long-term using network inventory solutions like these, it is not required to continue. A simple spreadsheet like the following (see Table 2.1) can also be used.

**Table 2.1** Example Corporation

| Device | Location | POC | Notes |
| --- | --- | --- | --- |
| Web server | Corporate HQ | Joe Smith | Public Web server |
| Mail server | Corporate HQ | Joe Smith | Public Mail server |
| Exchange server | Corporate HQ | Joe Smith | Internal Exchange server |
| Web server | Corporate HQ | Joe Smith | Internal Web server |
| File server | Corporate HQ | Joe Smith | Internal File/CIFS server |

**Continued**

**Table 2.1 continued** Example Corporation

| Device | Location | POC | Notes |
| --- | --- | --- | --- |
| Domain server | Corporate HQ | Joe Smith | Domain controller, DHCP, P-DNS |
| Domain server | Corporate HQ | Joe Smith | BDC, S-DNS |
| User network | Corporate HQ | Bob Green | All corporate workstations |
| IT network | Corporate HQ | Bob Green | All IT workstations |
| Conference | Corporate HQ | Bob Green | All conference rooms network |
| Internet router | Corporate HQ | Bob Green | Internet router |

**N**OTE

Remember, at this point you are identifying assets and not their complete configurations or services. In the next step, Profiling Your Network Assets, you will capture the configurations of each of these devices. In addition, we are not covering the switching and routing infrastructure devices and their security aspects. A common best practice is to limit their remote access and centralize their authentication and logging.

# Profiling Your Network Assets

In this step, you will profile each of the network assets you identified in the identification step in the previous section. The network asset profile is a report on the various attributes that are important to you and your organization.

First, we need to determine what information we are going to collect about our network assets. It is recommended you identify as much information as possible and clearly mark which attributes are required and which are optional. For our example, we are going to use the following attributes for Example Corporation (see Table 2.2 and Table 2.3):

**Table 2.2** Attributes for Example Corporation

| |
|---|
| Device Name: |
| Device Type: |
| IP Address: |
| DNS Name: |
| Physical Location: |
| Services: |
| Access Requirements: |

**Table 2.3** Defined Attributes for Example Corporation

| | |
|---|---|
| Device Name: | Web server |
| Device Type: | Server, Red Hat Enterprise Server 3.0 |
| IP Address: | 10.1.1.10 |
| DNS Name: | webserver1.example.com |
| Physical Location: | Server farm |
| Services: | Apache, SSH, mySQL |
| Access Requirements: | Internet hosts, internal employees |

For each of your network assets, you should collect similar information and record it in your asset management system or in a spreadsheet similar to the preceding template. While the device administrator might be able to provide it for you, it is recommended you verify the information yourself and use various security tools to verify which services are available.

**NOTE**

Profiling your assets is an important process and one that is often done with the aid of tools and management systems.

As you plan and implement your written security policies, understanding and using a concept of "security areas" will be very beneficial. They will have impact from the beginning network architecture and design phases through the ongoing, daily management and maintenance of your security systems. In this section, we discuss what security areas are and how they will be used as you design your logical security configurations of your firewall and VPN solutions.

# What Are Security Areas?

Security areas are logical and sometimes physical groupings of network assets and resources that share a common set of security attributes. At first you might ask, what is the difference between security areas and VLANs? Don't VLANs create a separate logical and physical separation between systems? The quick answer is yes and yes.

While different in many ways, VLANs and security areas are commonly used with one another but don't have to be per se. Based on the requirements of a given security area, a network administrator might create a VLAN that will be used by the systems that are assigned to a security area or not. The main difference is, security areas are created by analyzing and grouping devices together based on the security attributes and not just on the physical separation. For example, what if your written security policy states that all hosts that belong to a "special group" are allowed to talk to one another but are required to pass through a firewall access policy first? Just defining a VLAN will not allow us to enforce our policy when these hosts communicate with one another. Using the concept of security area provides an abstraction that will help ensure our written policy can be enforced and ultimately help us in our actual design and configurations.

# Implied Security Areas

If you are like many security professionals today, early in our careers we were introduced to implied security areas when we were asked to help protect our networks from the Internet. The Internet connections were assigned to an implied interface known as "untrusted," while our networks connected to an interface known as "trusted." These are two examples of implied security areas. Another example is the now famous "DMZ." As pictured in Figure 2.1, an interface called the DMZ interface of the firewall connects to a network that provides DNS, mail and Web services for our example company. Based on the fact that these devices provide public services and are likely to be targets for attacks, we separate them from other hosts based on best security practices.

**Figure 2.1** Legacy and common DMZ architecture

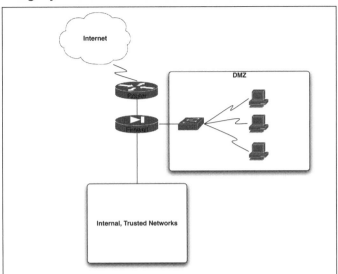

While much focus is put on protecting our "perimeters" from the Internet, it is not the only area that needs to be protected. It is now common security practice to view internal, traditional "trusted" networks and resources as important as protecting our perimeters.

The real question behind the implied groups like "trusted" and "untrusted" is what defines and constitutes these groupings? In our opinion, this is a great question and one that could be the basis for a very long discussion. In fact, as you probably know, many firewall vendors hard-code these implied areas and assign them to default physical interfaces. Since firewalls originally were designed to protect our company resources from the Internet, it was easier to have these defaults versus introducing a more complex concept like security areas. While it is still very common to see and use these implied security areas, it is not as simple as just assigning your resources to one of these groups.

The real reason to create security areas is not because of physical groupings. It is because it allows us to understand the inter- and intra-relationships between the devices that are part of a security area. For example, it is very common to have a written security policy that requires traffic traversing between security areas be inspected for violation of a specific access policy. Based on this requirement, we must implement some access control and logging for all traffic between these two areas. This point of inspection is known as an enforcement point (see Figure 2.2).

**Figure 2.2** Logical Enforcement Point Diagram

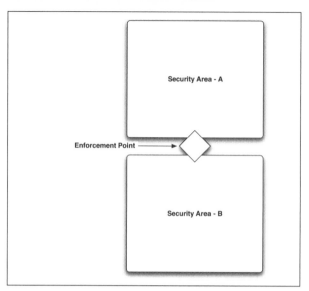

# Enforcement Points

Now that we have created an abstraction between security areas and enforcement points, it is easy to convert written security policies to logical security configurations that are not limited by feature or functionality of a device. In fact, this process becomes invaluable later as we use this information to help us select the right type of device to implement between our security areas. In our previous example, our enforcement point is the intersection between our two security areas. An important point is that an enforcement point does not just imply using a firewall to apply a policy to the traffic. It allows us to understand the security requirements at a specific point in our network, which might mean using a product, products, and or features of a product to enforce our written security requirements.

# Creating Security Areas

In this step, we will create security areas that are specific to your network. Before we start, however, we need to define the attributes we will use.

## *Security Area Attributes*

Before creating your security areas, we recommend you write down and agree to a set of attributes that are important to your organization. While there is not a clearly defined group of attributes to use, some common ones include:

- Access rights
- Services offered
- Risk profile

For our discussion, we are going to use three attributes: access rights, services, and risk.

**NOTE**

While we are going to use these attributes, you can use your own, based on your specific environment. For example, the Federal Government has developed strict guidelines that are used to classify systems, their services, and their users.

Access rights define who and what needs access to use a resource or series of resources on an end device, such as a server. It is common for a single server to host multiple services.

In our network example, we have three servers that provide Internet-based services to the world. These services include mail, Web, and name services. Each of our servers is dedicated to one of these functions. Since all of these servers provide public services, they all require access to and from the Internet. For security purposes, we have decided to separate these servers onto a dedicated network and assign them to the DMZ–Server1 security area.

## Assigning Network Assets to Security Areas

Now that we have created our security areas, we will need to assign our network assets to one of these areas. This step is pretty simple and straightforward. For each of our network assets, assign them to one of your security areas. Here is our example for Example Corporation (see Table 2.4):

**Table 2.4** Assignment of Network Assets to Security Areas

| Network Asset | Security Area |
| --- | --- |
| Web server | DMZ-1 |
| Mail server | DMZ-1 |
| DNS server | DMZ-1 |

**Continued**

**Table 2.4 continued** Assignment of Network Assets to Security Areas

| Network Asset | Security Area |
| --- | --- |
| Exchange server | Internal-IT |
| Web server | Internal-IT |
| File server | Internal-IT |
| Domain server | Internal-IT |
| Domain server | Internal-IT |
| User network | User-Network |
| IT network | IT-Network |
| Conference network | Conference-Network |
| Internet | Untrusted |

# Security Area Risk Rating

An optional set we like to use and recommend is to assign a risk rating to each of your security areas. While not necessary, risk ratings are a subjective numerical rating that you assign to each particular security area. The main reason to assign this rating is to help understand the risk level between areas, and how access rights between those areas might apply. Risk ratings typically correlate to attributes like:

- Access and availability
    - Public
    - Private
- Data sensitivity
    - Critical, high sensitivity
    - Sensitive
    - Low, informational
- Security and encryption
    - Encrypted
    - Clear

An example to discuss is the DMZ security area, where many companies place their Internet services and servers. The DMZ is a common location for those companies that host their own Web, mail, and DNS services. Access to these services is general not authenticated or encrypted, and the trust of the client systems is very low. Taking these attributes in consideration, most companies will not allow access to more secure areas, such as their intranet, from this security zone.

While there are not specific rules for assigning risk ratings, it is common to find customers using a 1 through 10 scale. In our example, 1 represents high risk and 10 represents low risk. This might sound counterintuitive at first; however, it allows an easy understanding for assigning access rights based on security areas. For example, a risk rating has access rights to any security area with a risk rating equal to or below its own.

Table 2.5 is an example chart illustrating security risk ratings.

**Table 2.5** Example Chart Illustrating Security Risk Ratings

| Security Area Name | Risk Rating | Notes |
| --- | --- | --- |
| DMZ-1 | 2 | Internet services |
| VPN Network | 4 | VPN segment |
| User-Network | 5 | User workstations |
| IT-Network | 4 | File servers, network services |
| Conference-Network | 1 | Untrusted hosts, guest access |
| Untrusted | 1 | Internet router, firewall |

# Users and User Groups

Your firewall and VPN devices both might use users and user groups in their configurations and policies. While most firewalls use location, such as source IP and or destination IP for their access control, VPN solutions typically grant access based on the user or user group to which an individual is assigned. In both cases, however, it is important to understand who your users are, where they access resources from, and when they will be accessing these resources.

We could dedicate a whole chapter, if not a whole book, on secure and effective user management. Since we can't, we will have to assume our firewalls and VPNs will leverage an existing user management infrastructure. Examples include Microsoft Windows Active Directory, Kerberos, and Radius. While each has strengths and weaknesses from a technical standpoint, they all are designed to provide a centralized user management system to various client systems. We recommend leveraging one of these solutions versus using a built-in authentication service you will find in the various firewall and VPN products. When building our logical security configurations for our firewall and VPN solutions, we will need to reference and use information about our user community.

Examples of user groups include:

- Corporate employees
- Remote corporate employees
- Corporate temporary employees
- Remote temporary employees
- Human resources
- Executive staff
- Executive administration
- IT management
- IT engineering
- IT help desk

# Writing Logical Security Configurations

Are you ready to start writing your logical security configurations? If you are like most security professionals, this is what we like to do. While we all understand planning is a critical process for success, it is the actual configurations and implementations we like to spend our time working on. Since firewall and VPN solutions provide different capabilities, we have divided this section into two parts. The first part covers Firewall logical security configurations, and the second part covers VPN logical security configuration. Both parts will use a lot of information we gathered in previous sections, such as security areas.

## Logical Security Configuration: Firewall

As discussed in the introduction, the Firewall Logical Security Configuration is a document that correlates security policy information into common security feature and functionality. Again, it is important to reiterate this process is not trying to write a device-specific configuration file. While there are many methodologies and process you could follow during this phase, we are going to take a simple, yet effective approach to building your first configurations. We will further divide this section into two components: general security and access policies.

# General Security for Firewall Configurations

Anything that relates to the secure deployment of your firewall devices should be documented in this section. We recommend using a spreadsheet similar to the example following. It will allow you to convert your policies requirements into logical configurations in an easy way. While this might seem obvious, converting your security policies into these specific details will help in deployment and auditing of your devices. For our example, we have broken the spreadsheet into four columns.

- **AREA and ITEM**   General and specific categories used to help organize and sort the spreadsheet.

- **DESCRIPTION**   Statements found in our security policies that need to be configured or supported.

- **REQUIREMENT**   Specific information that will be used to configure the devices during implementation.

While the description and requirement might both be defined in your security policy, it is important to break them out in your logical security configurations. In some cases, the requirements are loosely defined in security policies, and this exercise (see Table 2.6). will help articulate a specific requirement for a given area and item.

**Table 2.6** General Security: Articulation of a Specific Requirement for a Given Area and Item

| Area | Item | Description | Requirement |
|------|------|-------------|-------------|
| Management | Access Control | All remote management must be limited to side-band, dedicated management interfaces. | Each firewall will be required to support a dedicated network interface on the 10.10.10.0/24 network. |
| Management | Protocol Support | All remote management must be secure and encrypted. | Secure shell access will be limited to SSHv2, and secure Web access will be limited to SSL. |

**Continued**

**Table 2.6** General Security: Articulation of a Specific Requirement for a Given Area and Item

| Area | Item | Description | Requirement |
|------|------|-------------|-------------|
| Behavior | Default Access Policy | If a rule or policy does not grant or restrict access, the default access policy should be deny. In addition, only IP traffic is allowed to traverse between segments. | Implied access policy will be to drop all connection attempts and log. |
| Logging | Default Level Logging | All connection attempts originating from the Internet must be logged. | Internet to Trusted Security Areas— Logging = True |
| Access | From Internet Zone | All connections originating from untrusted sources, such as the Internet, should be dropped and logged. | Source=Internet Destination=Any Access=Drop Logging=True |
| Access | To DMZ Security Area | All connections from an untrusted security zone, such as the Internet, with a destination to the DMZ will be limited to HTTP, HTTPS, and SMTP. | Source=Internet Destination=DMZ Access=HTTP/HTTPS/ SMTP Logging=True |
| Policy | Access | All connections originating from a security area with a risk greater than the destination must be dropped and logged. | Source=DMZ Destination=Internal Access=Drop Logging=True |

# Access Policies for Firewall Configurations

Access policies are more specific and include a lot of information we developed earlier in the chapter. This includes things such as security areas and security area risk ratings (see Table 2.7).

**Table 2.7** Security Areas and Security Area Risk Ratings

| Source | Destination | Access | Protocols | Logging | Notes |
|---|---|---|---|---|---|
| User-Network, VPN-Network | DMZ-1 | Allowed | HTTP, HTTPS | Enabled | Internal user access to DMZ servers |
| Internet | DMZ-1 | Allowed | HTTP, HTTPS, SMTP | Enabled | Internet access to DMZ servers |
| User-Network Conference-Network, VPN-Network | Internet | Allowed | HTTP, HTTPS | Disabled | Internet access |
| User-Network | IT-Network | Allowed | CIFS, HTTP, HTTPS, DNS | Disabled | Internal server access |
| VPN-Network | IT-Network | Allowed-Authenticated | CIFS, HTTP, HTTPS, DNS | Disabled | Internal server access |
| IT-Network | Internet | Allowed-Authenticated | HTTP, HTTPS, DNS | Disabled | Internal server Internet access |
| DMZ-1 | Internet | Allowed | DNS | Disabled | |
| DMZ-1 | Internet | Allowed-Authenticated | HTTP, HTTPS | Enabled | Allows Internet access after authentication |

# Logical Security Configuration: VPN

Virtual private networks, commonly referred to as VPNs, are deployed in most companies today. While there are many types and uses for VPNs, many are deployed to provide secure, remote access to the companies' network resources to remote employees. In today's distributed environments, field sales teams, home-office based employees, and consultants are all great examples and users of VPN solutions. As VPNs provide the necessary communication links between these users and resources, they also bring new challenges to security professionals. They are common targets for attackers and are considered one of the weakest points in the overall security posture of an organization.

VPNs are also used when an organization wants to connect remote sites together or with a central site. These deployments might use one of many types, but often are found using the Internet as their transport. Using the Internet as a transport has many advantages. They often are more cost effective, easily deployed, and use standardized protocols such as IPSec. The more common VPN solutions include:

- Gateway-to-gateway IPSec
- Gateway-to-gateway PPTP
- Gateway-to-gateway L2TP
- Gateway-to-gateway IPSec
- Gateway-to-gateway SSL

# Best Security Practices for VPN Configurations

Your first goal is to ensure your VPN solution can be configured to enforce the requirements defined in your security policies. However, there are many common, best security practices we recommend for all VPN deployments. These include:

- Deploy VPN termination devices on dedicated network segments.
- Require secure access control for all VPN traffic.
- Use dedicated devices for VPN termination.
- Limit management access to side-band/out-of-band interfaces.
- Require additional or complementary authentication to standard username and passwords.
- Enable auditing, providing detailed audit trail for access, authentication, and use.

- Limit rules or configurations to specific users and, instead, design around groups.

- Use recent software versions.

- Audit logs and authentication records on a daily basis.

It is imperative to evaluate and integrate best security practices when deploying your VPNs. VPNs are one of the weakest areas of your network and can lead to breaches in your network security. An old cliché in security is, "security is only as strong as the weakest link." Keep in mind, no system or device is 100-percent protected and secure from attacks or vulnerabilities. If someone wants access, he or she will gain it. Many times, your configurations and security policies only need to be as strong as the information they are protecting. As security professionals, you have learned security is a trade-off of risk versus reward. Keeping this in mind is useful when creating your VPN logical security configurations.

Once a host authenticates, it is common to authorize the specific user. While host authentication is recommended, it does not ensure the person using that host is who you believe him to be. A common best practice is to deploy a strong, two-factor user authentication system such as RSA SecurID tokens and Aladdin Knowledge Systems' eToken solutions. Other solutions include biometric systems, smart cards, USB tokens, and random one-time-password token systems. When deploying VPN access for remote users, it is recommended one of these systems be used versus a standard username- and password-based system.

# Who Needs Remote Access?

Determining who needs to use your VPNs is not an easy task that can be done in just minutes. It is not uncommon for almost every employee to need some form of VPN access at one point or another. This introduces many challenges from user management to the auditing of your systems and individual access logs. This is an area in which your user groups and centralized user management systems will play an important role. It will help ensure your access rights are secure and granted to only those individuals or groups that need access. As you implement a remote access VPN solution, keep your access controls simple and easy to audit. Long term, this will help you maintain a strong security posture with your remote access solutions.

Many organizations deploy their remote access solutions granting their users unrestricted access to all internal network resources. This is probably one of the most critical mistakes you can make as a security professional. Access controls should be specific and related to the requirements defined by your written security policies. Some additional best practice recommendations for remote VPN users include:

- Grant access to user groups and not individual users.

- Implement access control, granting access only to those resources that are required.

- Require a strong authentication system, based on a user and not a device.

- Enable strong audit capabilities.

- Require password changes twice as often as policy requirements or internal systems for remote VPN users.

# Access Policies for VPN Configurations

VPN access policies are more specific and include a lot of information we developed earlier in the chapter. This includes things such as security areas and security area risk ratings. Table 2.8 is an example remote access VPN logical configuration policy for our example company.

**Table 2.8** Remote Access VPN Logical Configuration Policy

| Source | Destination | Access | Protocols | Logging | Notes |
|---|---|---|---|---|---|
| VPN-Remote Employees VPN-Contractors | DMZ-1 | Allowed-Authenticated | HTTP, HTTPS | Enabled | Remote user access to DMZ servers |
| VPN-Users-ALL | Internet | Allowed | HTTP, HTTPS with URL Filtering | Disabled access | Internet |
| VPN-Remote-Employees | IT-Network | Allowed-Authenticated | CIFS, HTTP, HTTPS, DNS | Disabled | Internal server access |
| VPN-Contractors | IT-Network | Allowed-Authenticated | CIFS, HTTP, HTTPS, DNS | Enabled | Internal server access |

The most important concept to remember is you should only grant access to remote users based on their requirements. Granting unrestricted access might be easier to manage, but creates a security risk that will likely lead to an attack or security incident.

# Summary

Creating logical security configurations for firewalls and VPN devices is not a trivial task. It takes time and patience to create a strong security posture for any organization. Since these devices are common targets for attack and exploitation, they are the areas that require a lot of attention. With practice and over time, the process to effectively convert your written policies into logical security configurations will become easier. As discussed early in the chapter, our primary goal is to create a roadmap that is abstracted from specific vendors' devices or product feature set. This very important step will help create an overall more secure environment. This process helps security administrators implement secure configurations that reflect the business goals of the organization. While it is not important to rank each step as it relates to another, it is easy to understand how focusing time and effort to each can help achieve success during implementation, and to maintain it through the entire management lifecycle.

# Solutions Fast Track

## Logical Security Configurations

☑ Logical security configurations are documents that interpret written security policy requirements and define configuration requirements for a specific type of enforcement device, like a firewall or VPN product.

☑ Unlike a device configuration for a specific vendor's product or version, logical security configurations are written to common feature sets found in the target enforcement devices.

☑ Logical security configurations are developed for a type or group of enforcement devices versus one for each device in your environment.

☑ A specific written policy requirement or item is commonly used by many logical security configuration documents across the enterprise.

## Planning Logical Security Configurations

☑ Identification of network assets is a critical requirement in the overall security posture of an organization.

☑ Networks evolve and constantly change and as a result, a method to capture, organize, edit, and audit this information is recommended.

☑ Network asset profiling is an exercise to capture and validate information specific to each device. A combination of automated tools and interviews is commonly used by security professionals.

☑ *Security area* is a term used to group together network assets based on common attributes of those devices.

☑ Security area risk rating is a numerical value assigned to each area that helps a security professional understand the relationship between those two areas. As traffic passes from one area to another area, this rating helps understand the policy that should be enforced for that traffic.

☑ Users and user groups are a key element in security policy development. Most access is granted to user groups versus individual users.

# Writing Logical Security Configurations

☑ Logical security configurations are written for each type of device that will be used to enforce an organization's written security policies.

☑ VPN remote access to your company's resources is considered high risk, and as a result, additional user authentication and access restrictions are recommended to reduce the chance of a security breach.

☑ Logical security configurations, once written, should be audited and reviewed against actual configurations on a regular basis.

☑ It is a best practice to separate the responsibilities for writing security policies, logical configurations, and implementation guides.

# Frequently Asked Questions

The following Frequently Asked Questions, answered by the authors of this book, are designed to both measure your understanding of the concepts presented in this chapter and to assist you with real-life implementation of these concepts. To have your questions about this chapter answered by the author, browse to **www.syngress.com/solutions** and click on the **"Ask the Author"** form.

**Q.** Since we have already standardized on a specific vendor's firewall and VPN solution, should we still create a logical security policy?

**A.** It is recommended you go through the process to develop your logical security policies even if you have already bought a vendor's product or solution. Doing so will help you understand your security policy in more detail and ensure you have the right product and features to enforce your organization's requirements. In many cases, this exercise will help discover other features in your products that might not enabled or could be configured that result in an overall, better security posture for your organization.

**Q.** I don't understand the concept of a security area risk rating and how it relates to the logical security configuration.

**A.** A security area risk rating is numerical value you assign to each security area, and as a result, allows you to understand the relationship of risk between those two areas. This will be helpful when evaluating traffic that traverses between two security areas and applying a specific enforcement policy to the traffic.

**Q.** Why is it recommended to implement VPN termination devices on a dedicated, separate network?

**A.** Terminating remote access on a dedicated segment provides many security benefits, including auditing, management, and security policy enforcement. This is a best-practice design and not a requirement.

**Q.** With new remote access solutions such as SSL clientless VPNs, how do they compare from a security perspective to traditional IPSec VPN solutions?

**A.** The main difference between using an SSL and an IPSec-based solution has more to do with the management of remote clients than with the security of the system. The overall security effectiveness is in the strength and implementation of the encryption algorithms.

**Q.** In our DMZ, we allow access to internal resources for the system administrators and developers. Reading this chapter, you recommend not allowing access to internal systems. Why?

**A.** DMZs are traditional security areas that host servers and services that are more subjective to external attacks. As a result, compromised systems on your DMZ will have a high likelihood of becoming a launch system. By limiting access to other internal security areas, a system compromised could be contained and limit the attacker's ability to gain additional access to other areas of your network.

**Q.** Our authentication for remote access users currently uses the built-in features. Is our solution secure?

**A.** While this is not insecure per se, it is not a strong solution. You should make it a priority to implement a strong authentication system to replace the built-in controls you are using today. In addition, it is recommended you audit your access logs often and educate your users about ensuring they maintain strong passwords that are not easily guessed.

**Q.** Our network design limits our ability to control specific access for our remote users, and as a result, we grant unrestricted access. Are we secure?

**A.** Again, while not insecure, this is an area that would be considered high risk and likely to lead to a security incident. A network design in which security has been an afterthought is challenging and difficult to secure. In these cases, it is recommended you gain executive support to create a project that will address all the security concerns of your organization. Remember the old saying, "security is only as strong as the weakest link in the system."

# Part II
# Firewall Concepts

# Chapter 3

# Defining a Firewall

## Solutions in this chapter:

- **Threats and Attacks**
- **TCP/IP Protocol**
- **Application Proxy/Gateway**
- **Packet Inspection**
- **Stateful Inspection**

☑ **Summary**

☑ **Solutions Fast Track**

☑ **Frequently Asked Questions**

# Introduction

When most people think about Internet security, the first thing that comes to mind is a firewall, which is a necessity for connecting online. In its simplest form, a firewall is a chokepoint from one network (usually an internal network) to another (usually the Internet). However, firewalls are also being used to create chokepoints between other networks in an enterprise environment. There are several different types of firewalls.

# Why Have Different Types of Firewalls?

Before we delve into what types of firewalls there are, we must understand the present threats. While there are many types of threats, we only discuss a few of them in this chapter, paying the most attention to those that can be mitigated by firewalls.

Ensuring a physically secure network environment is the first step in controlling access to your network's data and system files; however, it is only part of a good security plan. This is truer today than in the past, because there are more ways into a network than there used to be. A medium- or large-sized network can have multiple Internet Service Providers (ISP's), virtual private network (VPN) servers, and various remote access avenues for mobile employees including Remote Desktop, browser-based file sharing and e-mail access, mobile phones, and Personal Digital Assistants (PDAs).

# Physical Security

One of the most important and overlooked aspects of a comprehensive network security plan is physical access control. This matter is usually left up to facilities managers and plant security departments, or outsourced to security guard companies. Some network administrators concern themselves with sophisticated software and hardware solutions to prevent intruders from accessing internal computers remotely, while at the same time not protecting the servers, routers, cable, and other physical components from direct access. To many "security-conscious" organization's computers are locked all day, only to be left open at night for the janitorial staff. It is not uncommon for computer espionage experts to pose as members of cleaning crews to gain physical access to machines that hold sensitive data. This is a favorite ploy for several reasons:

- Cleaning services are often contracted out and their workers are often transient, so your company's employees might not know who is a legitimate member of the cleaning company staff.

- Cleaning is usually done late at night when all or most company employees are gone, making it easier to surreptitiously steal data.

- The cleaning crew members are paid little attention by company employees, who take their presence for granted and think nothing of them being in areas where the presence of others would normally be questioned.

Physically breaking into a server room and stealing a hard disk where sensitive data resides is a crude method of breaching security; nonetheless, it happens. In some organizations, it may be the easiest way to gain unauthorized access, especially for an intruder who has help "on the inside."

It is beyond the scope of this book to go into detail about how to physically secure your network, but it is important for you to make physical access control the outer perimeter of your security plan, which means:

- Controlling physical access to the servers

- Controlling physical access to networked workstations

- Controlling physical access to network devices

- Controlling physical access to the cable

- Being aware of security considerations with wireless media

- Being aware of security considerations related to portable computers

- Recognizing the security risk of allowing data to be printed

- Recognizing the security risks involving floppy disks, CDs, tapes, and other removable media

There are also different types of external intruders who will physically break into your facility to gain access to your network. Although not a true "insider," because he or she is not authorized to be there and do not have a valid account on the network, this person still has many of the advantages (refer to the "Internal Security Breaches" section.) Your security policy should take into account the threats posed by these "hybrid" intruders. Remember, someone with physical access to your servers has complete control over your data. Someone with physical access to your authentication servers owns everything.

# Network Security

Virtual intruders can access your network from across the street or from halfway around the world. They can do as much damage as a thief that breaks into your company headquarters to steal or destroy data, and are much harder to catch. The following sections examine specific network security risks and ways to prevent them.

For a number of years, firewalls were used to divide an organization's internal network from the Internet. There was usually a demilitarized zone (DMZ), which contained less valuable resources that had to be exposed to the Internet (e.g., Web servers, VPN gateways, and so forth), and a private network that contained all of the organization's resources (e.g., user computers, servers, printers, and so forth). Perimeter defense is still vitally important, given the ever-increasing threat level from outside the network. However, it is no longer adequate by itself.

With the growth of the Internet, many organizations focused their security efforts on defending against outside attackers (i.e., those originating from an external network) who are not authorized to access the systems. Firewalls were the primary focus of these efforts. Money was spent building a strong perimeter defense, resulting in what Bill Cheswick from Bell Labs famously described years ago as, "A crunchy shell around a soft, chewy center." Any attacker who succeeded in getting through (or around) the perimeter defenses, would have a relatively easy time compromising internal systems. This situation is analogous to the enemy parachuting into the castle keep instead of breaking through the walls. Perimeter defense is still vitally important, given the increased threat level from outside the network; however, it is simply no longer adequate by itself.

Various information security studies and surveys have found that the majority of attacks come from inside an organization. Given how lucrative the sale of information can be, people inside organizations can be a greater threat than people outside the organization. These internal threats can include authorized users attempting to exceed their permissions, or unauthorized users trying to go where they should not be. Therefore, an insider is more dangerous than an outsider, because he or she has a level of access to facilities and systems that the outsider does not. Many organizations lack the internal preventive controls and other countermeasures to adequately defend against this threat. Wide open networks and servers sitting in unsecured areas provide easy access to the internal hacker.

The greatest threat, however, arises when an insider colludes with a structured outside attacker. With few resources exposed to the outside world, it is easier for the bad guys to enlist internal people to do their dirty work. The outsider's skills combined with the insider's access could result in substantial damage or loss to the organization.

# Attacks

Attacks can be divided into three main categories:

- **Reconnaissance Attacks**  Hackers attempt to discover systems and gather information. In most cases, these attacks are used to gather information to set up an access or a Denial of Service (DoS) attack. A typical reconnaissance attack might consist of a hacker pinging Internet Protocol (IP) addresses to discover what is alive on a network. The hacker might then perform a port scan on the system to see which applications are running, and to try to determine the operating system (OS) and version on a target machine.

- **Access Attacks**  An access attack is one in which an intruder attempts to gain unauthorized access to a system to retrieve information. Sometimes the attacker has to gain access to a system by cracking passwords or using an exploit. At other times, the attacker already has access to the system, but needs to escalate his or her privileges.

- **DoS Attacks**  Hackers use DoS attacks to disable or corrupt access to networks, systems, or services. The intent is to deny authorized or valid users access to these resources. DoS attacks typically involve running a script or a tool, and the attacker does not require access to the target system, only the means to reach it. In a Distributed DoS (DDoS) attack, the source consists of many computers that are usually spread across a large geographic boundary.

# Recognizing Network Security Threats

In order to effectively protect your network, you must consider the following question: From who or what are you protecting it? In this section, we approach the answer to that question from three perspectives:

- Who are the people that break into networks?

- Why do they do what they do?

- What are the types of network attacks and how do they work?

First we look at intruder motivations and classify the various types of people who have the skill and desire to hack into others' computers and networks.

## *Understanding Intruder Motivations*

There are probably as many different specific motives as there are hackers, but the most common intruder motivations can be broken down into a few broad categories:

- **Recreation** Those who hack into networks "just for fun" or to prove their technical prowess; often young people or "antiestablishment" types.

- **Remuneration** People who invade the network for personal gain, such as those who attempt to transfer funds to their own bank accounts or erase records of their debts, and "hackers for hire" who are paid by others to break into the network. Corporate espionage is also included in this category.

- **Revenge** Dissatisfied customers, disgruntled former employees, angry competitors, or people who have a personal grudge against someone in the organization.

The scope of damage and the extent of the intrusion are often tied to the intruder's motivation.

# Recreational Hackers

Teen hackers who hack primarily for the thrill of accomplishment, often do little or no permanent damage, perhaps only leaving "I was here" messages to "stake their claims" and prove to their peers that they were able to penetrate your network's security.

There are also more malevolent versions of the fun-seeking hacker. These cyber-vandals get their kicks out of destroying as much of your data as possible or causing your systems to crash.

**NOTE**

The following is one example of a recreational hacker:

October 17, 2005 (Computerworld) — Using a self-propagating worm that exploits a scripting vulnerability common to most dynamic Web sites, a Los Angeles teenager made himself the most popular member of community Web site *MySpace.com* earlier this month. While the attack caused little damage, the technique could be used to destroy Web site data or steal private information, even from enterprise users behind protected networks.

The unknown 19-year-old, who used the name 'Samy,' put a small bit of code in his user profile on MySpace, a 32-million-member site, most of whom are under age 30. Whenever Samy's profile was viewed, the code was executed in the background, adding Samy to the viewer's list of friends and writing at the bottom of their profile, "Samy is my hero."

# Profit-motivated Hackers

Hackers who break into your network for remuneration of some kind—either directly or indirectly—are more dangerous. Because money is at stake, they are more motivated than other hackers to accomplish their objective. Unfortunately, the number of these hackers is increasing dramatically, especially with the profitability of identity theft. Furthermore, because many of them are "professionals", their hacking techniques could be more sophisticated than those of the average teenage recreational hacker.

Monetary motivations include:

- Personal financial gain

- Corporate espionage

- Third-party payment for the information obtained

Those motivated by the last goal are almost always the most sophisticated, and the most dangerous. Money is often involved in the theft of identity information. Identity thieves can be employees who have been approached by any number of malicious organizations and offered money or merchandise or even threatened with blackmail or physical harm.

In some instances, hackers go "undercover" and seek a job with a company in order to steal data that they can give to their own organizations. To add insult to injury, these "stealth spies" are then paid by your company at the same time they're working against you.

There are also "professional" freelance corporate spies that can be contracted to obtain company secrets, or they might do it on their own and auction the data off to competitors.

These corporate espionage agents are often highly skilled. They are technically savvy and intelligent enough to avoid being caught or detected. Fields that are especially vulnerable to the threat of corporate espionage include:

- Oil and energy

- Engineering

- Computer technology

- Research medicine

- Law

Any company on the verge of a breakthrough that could result in large monetary rewards or worldwide recognition, should be aware of the possibility of espionage and take steps to guard against it.

*Phishing,* the new information gathering technique, is spreading and becoming more sophisticated. Phishing e-mails either ask the victim to fill out a form or direct them to a Web page designed to look like a legitimate banking site. The victim is asked for personal information such as credit card numbers, social security number, or other data that can then be used for identity theft. There has been at least one insidious phishing scheme that uses a Secure Sockets Layer (SSL) certificate so that the data you give to the hacker is safely encrypted on the network.

## Notes from the Underground…

### "Cybercrime on the rise, survey finds. Criminal attacks online are on the upswing and they are getting stealthier," according to Symantec.

By Amanda Cantrell, *CNNMoney.com* staff writer

March 7, 2006: 11:51 AM EST

NEW YORK (*CNNMoney.com*) - Cybercrime is on the rise, and today's attacks are often silent, hard to detect and highly targeted, according to a new survey.

Danger in the ether

Symantec (down $0.57 to $15.96, Research), which makes anti-virus software for businesses and consumers, found a notable increase in "cybercrime" threats to computer users, according to the latest installment of its semiannual Internet Security Threat Report. Cybercrime consists of criminal acts performed using a computer or the Internet. Symantec also found a rise in the use of "crimeware," or software used to conduct cybercrime.

Cybercriminals are also getting more sophisticated. Attacks designed to destroy data have now given way to attacks designed to steal data outright, often for financial gain, according to the survey, which covers the six-month

**Continued**

period from July 1, 2005 to December 31, 2005. Eighty percent of all threats are designed to steal personal information from consumers, intellectual property from corporations, or to control the end user's machine, according to Symantec.

Moreover, today's attackers are abandoning large-scale attacks on corporate firewalls in favor of targets such as individual desktop computers, using Web applications that can capture personal, financial, and confidential information that can then be used for financial gain. That continues a trend Symantec found in its survey covering the first half of 2005."

# Vengeful Hackers

Hackers motivated by the desire for revenge are also dangerous. Vengeance seeking is usually based on strong emotions, which means that these hackers could go all-out in their efforts to sabotage your network.

Examples of hackers or security saboteurs acting out of revenge include:

- Former employees who are bitter about being fired or laid off, or who quit their jobs under unpleasant circumstances.

- Current employees who feel mistreated by the company, especially those who are planning to leave soon.

- Current employees who aim to sabotage the work of other employees due to internal political battles, rivalry over promotions, and the like.

- Outsiders who have grudges against the company, such as dissatisfied customers or employees of competing companies who want to harm or embarrass the company

- Outsiders who have personal grudges against someone who works for the company, such as employees' former girlfriends or boyfriends, spouses going through a divorce, and other relationship-related problems

Luckily, the intruders in this category are generally less technically talented than those in the other two groups, and their emotional involvement could cause them to be careless and take outrageous chances, which makes them easier to catch.

## Notes from the Underground...

### New Directions in Malware

Kaspersky Labs reports on extortion scams using malware:

"We've reported more than once on cases where remote malicious users have moved away from the stealth use of infected computers (stealing data from them, using them as part of zombie networks, and so forth) to direct blackmail, demanding payment from victims. At the moment, this method is used in two main ways: encrypting user data and corrupting system information.

Users quickly understand that something has happened to their data. They are then told that they should send a specific sum to an e-payment account maintained by the remote malicious user, whether it be EGold, Webmoney or some other e-payment account. The ransom demanded varies significantly depending on the amount of money available to the victim. We know of cases where the malicious users have demanded $50, and of cases where they have demanded more than $2,000. The first such blackmail case was in 1989, and now this method is again gaining in popularity.

In 2005, the most striking examples of this type of cybercrime were carried out using the Trojans GpCode and Krotten. The first of these encrypts user data; the second restricts itself to making a number of modifications to the victim machine's system registry, causing it to cease functioning.

Among other worms, the article discusses the *GpCode.ac* worm, which encrypts data using 56-bit Rivest, Shamir, & Adleman (RSA). The whole article is interesting reading.

Posted on April 26, 2006 at 01:07 PM on *www.schneier.com*."

## Hybrid Hackers

The three categories of hacker can overlap in some cases. A recreational hacker who perceives himself as having been mistreated by an employer or in a personal relationship, could use his otherwise benign hacking skills to impose "justice," or a vengeful ex-employee or ex-spouse might pay someone else to do the hacking.

It is beneficial to understand the common motivations of network intruders because, although we might not be able to predict which type of hacker will decide to attack our networks, we can recognize how each operates and take steps to protect our networks from all of them.

Even more important than the type of hacker in planning our security strategy, is the type of attack. In the next section, we examine specific types of network attacks and ways in which you can protect against them.

---

**NOTE**

Social engineering, also known as people hacking, is a means for obtaining security information from people by tricking them. The classic example is calling up a user and pretending to be a system adminis-trator. The hacker asks the user for his or her password to perform some important maintenance task. To avoid being hacked via social engi-neering, educate your user community that they should always confirm the identity of any person calling them, and that passwords should never be given to anyone over e-mail, instant messaging, or the tele-phone.

It is beyond the scope of this book to address social engineering and ways to educate employees against it. However, SysAdmin, Audit, Network, Security (SANS) Institute (*http://www.sans.org*) has both full courses and step-by-step guides to help with this process.

---

# Back to Basics—Transmission Control Protocol/Internet Protocol

Transmission Control Protocol/Internet Protocol (TCP/IP) is the network protocol that pushes data around the Internet. (Other protocols you may have heard of are Windows NETBeui, Mac Appletalk, and Novell IPX/XPS, however none of these concern us.) You don't need to understand the intricacies of TCP/IP; however, a basic understanding will make your firewall deployment much easier.

TCP/IP is based on the idea that data is sent in packets, similar to putting a letter in an envelope. Each packet contains a header that contains routing informa-tion concerning where the packet came from and where it is going (similar to the address and return address on an envelope), and the data itself (the letter contained in the envelope). Figure 3.1 illustrates a typical TCP/IP packet

**Figure 3.1** Layout of a Typical TCP/IP Packet

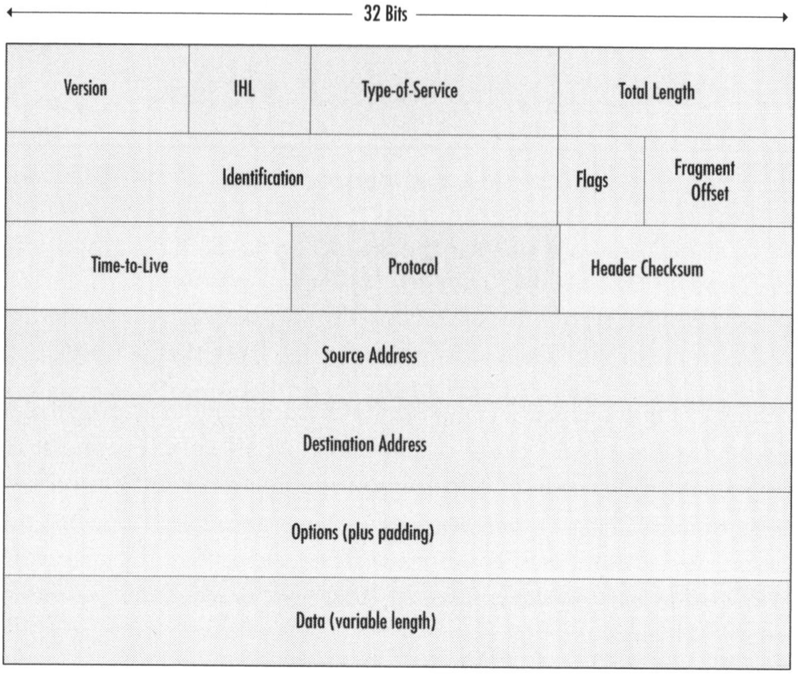

- **Version**  Indicates the version of IP currently used.

- **IP Header Length (IHL)**  Indicates the datagram header length in 32-bit words.

- **Type of Service**  Specifies how an upper-layer protocol wants a current datagram to be handled, and assigns various levels of importance to datagrams.

- **Total Length**  Specifies the length, in bytes, of the entire IP packet, including the data and header.

- **Identification**  Contains an integer that identifies the current datagram. This field is used to help piece together datagram fragments.

- **Flags**  Consists of a 3-bit field of which the two low-order (least significant) bits control fragmentation. The low-order bit specifies whether the packet can be fragmented. The middle-order bit specifies whether the packet is the last fragment in a series of fragmented packets. The third or high-order bit is not used.

- **Fragment Offset**  Indicates the position of the fragment's data relative to the beginning of the data in the original datagram, which allows the destination IP process to properly reconstruct the original datagram.

- **Time-to-live**  Maintains a counter that gradually decrements down to zero, at which point the datagram is discarded. This keeps packets from looping endlessly.

- **Protocol**  Indicates which upper-layer protocol receives incoming packets after IP processing is complete.

- **Header Checksum**  Helps ensure IP header integrity.

- **Source Address**  Specifies the sending node.

- **Destination Address**  Specifies the receiving node.

- **Options**  Allows IP to support various options, such as security.

- **Data**  Upper-layer information.

# TCP/IP Header

The "envelope" or header of a packet contains a great deal of information, only some of which is of interest to firewall administrators, who are primarily interested in source and destination addresses and port numbers. Only application proxies deal with the data section.

## IP Addresses

Source and destination addresses reference the exact machine a packet came from and the corresponding machine receiving the packet. These addresses are in the standard form of four sets of three-digit numbers separated by periods (i.e., the IP version 4 standard). Table 3.1 shows the various classes of IP addresses.

**Table 3.1** IP Address Classes

| Class | Start Address | Comment |
| --- | --- | --- |
| A | 0.0.0.0 | Standard internet addresses available to all users, except private 10.0.0.0 subnet |
| B | 128.0.0.0 | Standard internet addresses available to all users, except private 172.16.0.0 – 172.31.255.255 range |

**Continued**

## Table 3.1 continued IP Address Classes

| Class | Start Address | Comment |
|-------|---------------|---------|
| C | 192.0.0.0 | Standard internet addresses available to all users, except private 192.168.0.0 subnet |
| D | 224.0.0.0 | Multicast address class |
| E | 240.0.0.0 | Research and limited broadcast class |

As noted in the table, there are three sets of addresses known as *private addresses* and there are three subnets designated as private: 10.0.0.0 to 10.255.255.255, 172.16.0.0 to 172.31.255.255, and 192.168.0.0 to 192.168.255.255. By definition, these subnets, cannot be routed on the Internet.

There is also a group of IP addresses known as *self-assigned addresses*, which range from 169.254.0.0 to 169.254.255.255. These addresses are used by the OS when no other address is available, making it possible to connect to a computer on a network that doesn't automatically assign addresses (Dynamic Host Configuration Protocol [DHCP]), and there are no valid *static IP addresses* that can be typed into the network configuration. All routers, switches, firewalls, and other appliances are designed to stop these addresses.

One address is reserved as the *loopback address.* Address 127.0.0.1 refers to the machine itself, and is generally used to confirm that the TCP/IP protocol is correctly installed and functioning on the machine.

Networks 224.0.0.0 to 254.255.255.255 are reserved for special testing and applications. While Internet-routable, the standard organization or individual does not generally use them. The Class D network provides *multicast* capabilities. A multicast is when a group of IP addresses is defined in such a way as to permit individual packets to have a destination address of all the machines, rather than a single machine. Class E is for research by particular organizations and has *limited broadcast* capabilities. A *broadcast* is when a single device sends out a packet that has no particular recipient. Instead, it goes to every machine on the subnet. On standard (non-Class E) networks, this is defined by address 255.255.255.255. The Class E network is different and is not accessible to devices on the other classes of networks.

While there are legitimate uses for broadcasts (e.g., obtaining a DHCP address), we want to keep them to a minimum. To this end, all routers and firewalls block broadcasts by default. Too many broadcasts will slow network performance to a crawl.

Every device on the Internet must have a unique IP address. If a device has a valid IP address (i.e., not a private, non-routable address or self-assigned address) and is not behind a firewall, it is available for connection to any other device on the Internet. A computer in Berlin can print to a printer in London. A mail server in Chicago can deliver e-mail directly to a machine in Singapore.

This ubiquitous communication and ability to transfer data directly from one machine to another is what makes the Internet so powerful. It is also what makes it so dangerous. It is impossible to stress strongly enough that no machine on the public Internet is hidden. No machine is safe from detection. Firewalls are the only method of safely hiding a device on a private network, while still providing access to the Internet as a whole.

Firewalls are able to hide a device by doing *address translation*. Address translation is when firewalls convert a valid Internet address to a private address on a private subnet. Almost all firewalls do this type of address translation, which has several advantages:

- **An Additional Layer of Security** Without the firewall in place to do the translations, Internet addresses can't communicate with the private network and vice versa.

- **Expansion of Available IP Addresses** Not every device in your organization needs to be accessible from the Internet. User workstations require access to the Internet, but do not need to have incoming traffic originating on the Internet. They only require responses to inquiries sent out. Most firewalls handle this by converting every internal address to a single, Internet-routable address. This address is usually the address of the firewall itself, but does not necessarily have to be.

- **Ability to Completely Hide a Device from the Internet** Is it necessary to have your printers available to the Internet? Does that Web server that is only available to employees at their desks, need to have an Internet address? The answer to both questions is probably "no." With a firewall capable of address translation, both of these examples can be assigned a private address with no translation to the outside. The device is hidden from anyone on the public Internet and is completely inaccessible.

## IP Half-scan Attack

*Half scans*, also called *half-open scans* or *Finish Packet (FIN) scans*, attempt to avoid detection by sending only initial or final packets rather than establishing a connection. Every IP connection starts with a Synchronous (SYN) packet from the connecting computer. The responding computers respond with a SYN/Acknowledgement (ACK) packet, which acknowledges the original packet and establishes the communication parameters. SYN/ACK continues until the end of the communication when a *FIN packet* is sent and the connection is broken. A half scan starts the SYN/ACK process with a targeted computer but does not complete it. Software that conducts half scans, such as Jakal, is called a *stealth scanner*. Many port-scanning detectors are unable to detect half scans.

## IP Spoofing

*IP spoofing* involves changing the packet headers of a message to indicate that it came from an IP address other than the true source. The spoofed address is normally a trusted port that allows a hacker to get a message through a firewall or router that would otherwise be filtered out. Modern firewalls protect against IP spoofing.

Hackers use spoofing whenever it is beneficial for one machine to impersonate another. It is often used in combination with another type of attack (e.g., a spoofed address is used in the SYN flood attack to create a "half-open" connection. The client never responds to the SYN/ACK message, because the spoofed address is that of a computer that is down or doesn't exist. Spoofing is also used to hide the true IP address of the attacker in ping of death, teardrop, and other attacks. IP spoofing can be prevented using source address verification on your firewall.

## Denial of Service Attacks

In February 2000, massive DoS attacks brought down several of the biggest Web sites, including *Yahoo.com* and *Buy.com*. DoS attacks are a popular choice for Internet hackers who want to disrupt a network's operations. The objective of DoS attackers is to bring down the network, thereby denying service to its legitimate users. DoS attacks are easy to initiate, because software is readily available from hacker Web sites and warez newsgroups that allow anyone to launch a DoS attack with little or no technical expertise.

> **NOTE**
>
> *Warez* is a term used by hackers and crackers to describe bootlegged software that has been "cracked" to remove copy protections and made available by software pirates on the Internet, or in its broader definition, to describe any illegally distributed software.

The purpose of a DoS attack is to render a network inaccessible by generating a type or amount of network traffic that will crash the servers, overwhelm the routers, or otherwise prevent the network's devices from functioning properly. DoS can be accomplished by tying up the server's resources (e.g., by overwhelming the central processing unit (CPU) and memory resources. In other cases, a particular user or machine can be the target of DoS attacks that hang up the client machine and require it to be rebooted.

## NOTE

DoS attacks are sometimes referred to in the security community as *nuke attacks*.

Distributed DoS (DDoS) attacks use intermediary computers (called *agents*) on which programs (called *zombies*) have previously been surreptitiously installed, usually by a virus or Trojan (see below). The hacker activates these zombie programs remotely, causing the intermediary computers (which can number in the hundreds or even thousands) to simultaneously launch the actual attack. Because the attack comes from the computers running the zombie programs—which could potentially be on networks anywhere in the world—the hacker is able to conceal the true origin of the attack.

It is important to note that DDoS attacks pose a two-layer threat. Not only could your network be the target of a DoS attack that crashes your servers and prevents incoming and outgoing traffic, but your computers could be used as the "innocent middlemen" to launch a DoS attack against another network or site.

The Domain Name Server (DNS) DoS attack exploits the difference in size between a DNS query and a DNS response, in which all of the network's bandwidth is tied up by bogus DNS queries. The attacker uses the DNS servers as "amplifiers" to multiply the DNS traffic.

The attacker begins by sending small DNS queries to each DNS server, which contain the spoofed IP address of the intended victim (see "IP Spoofing" in this chapter). The responses returned to the small queries are much larger in size, so if there are a large number of responses returned at the same time, the link will become congested and DoS will take place.

One solution to this problem is for administrators to configure DNS servers to answer with a "refused" response (which is much smaller than a name resolution response) when they receive DNS queries from suspicious or unexpected sources.

**NOTE**

Detailed information on configuring DNS servers to prevent this problem is contained in the U.S. Department of Energy's Computer Incident Advisory Capability information bulletin J-063, available at *www.ciac.org/ciac/bulletins/j-063.shtml.*

## Notes from the Underground...

### IP Version 6

You may have heard of IPv6, the new standard for Internet communications. This standard was devised to address several problems with IPv4, primarily the limited number of possible addresses available. IPv4 supports $4.3 \times 10^9$ (4.3 billion) addresses, while IPv6 supports $3.4 \times 10^{38}$ addresses. The roll out of IPv6 is occurring slowly, as more computers and network appliances become IPv6-compatible. For the foreseeable future, IPv4 will be the de facto standard. What you learn in this book will still largely apply to IPv6. Firewall concepts, filtering theories, and deployment strategies will change little, if at all.

IPv6 does not use the same classes of addresses as IPv4. Instead, there are three classes: unicast, multicast, and anycast. Broadcasts are not supported; however, multicast accomplishes nearly the same end.

Also, IPv6 has only two reserved addresses, one for internal protocol implementation and a loopback address. All other addresses are free for use on the public Internet.

The question which should come to mind is, "If my firewall supports IVv6, and I really don't use it, do I need to worry about configuring it?" The short answer is "yes." There are already exploits that take advantage of IPv6. If firewalls supporting IPv6 are configured incorrectly, they will pass unimpeded through your firewall. Remember, IPv6 is designed to travel over the same network as IPv4. All it needs are routers, switches, and firewalls that support IPv6. Most new network appliances support IPv6.

## Source-routing Attack

TCP/IP supports *source routing,* which is a means to permit the sender of network data to route the packets through a specific point on the network. There are two types of source routing:

- **Strict Source Routing** The sender of the data can specify the exact route (rarely used).

- **Loose Source Record Route (LSRR)** The sender can specify certain routers (hops) through which the packet must pass.

The source route is an option in the IP header that allows the sender to override routing decisions normally made by the routers between the source and destination machines. Network administrators use source routing to map the network or to troubleshoot routing and communications problems. It can also be used to force traffic through a route that will provide the best performance. Unfortunately, hackers can also exploit source routing.

If the system allows source routing, an intruder can use it to reach private internal addresses on the Local Area Network (LAN) (normally not reachable from the Internet), by routing the traffic through another machine that is reachable from both the Internet and the internal machine. Source routing should be, and is disabled on most routers to prevent this type of attack. If it is not disabled on your router, disable it now.

# TCP/UDP Ports

A port number is a virtual "mail slot" on each of these machines. Applications running on computers listen to the Internet for incoming information on these ports. Certain applications listen on certain ports. The Internet Assigned Numbers Authority (IANA [*www.iana.org*]) defines these ports (e.g., Web servers listen on ports 80 and 443 and File Transfer Protocol (FTP) servers listen on port 21. Hyper-text Transfer Protocol (HTTP), Hyper-Text Transfer Protocol Secure sockets (HTTPS), and FTP are examples of Internet Protocols. You will never find a legitimate FTP server listening on port 80. Ports 1 to 1023 are considered well-known ports, and have clearly defined IP's. Ports 1024 through 49151 are *registered ports.* Specific software vendors have registered these ports for use by their specific applications. Ports 49152 to 65535 are *dynamic ports.* These have no specific registration and can be used by any application at any time. Using either or both application and gateway firewalls mitigates the misuse of ports.

Ports can use either the TCP protocol or the User Datagram Packet (UDP) protocol. TCP requires a connection started with a SYN packet that receives an ACK packet in response. SYN-ACK continues until the end of the data transmission. Each ACK packet confirms the correct receipt of the SYN packet containing data. On the other hand, UDP protocols send data with no requirement for a response. UDP protocols are generally faster than TCP protocols, but there is no assurance that the data has arrived at its destination intact.

RFC 1700 documents, the official well-known port assignments, are available on the Web at *www.freesoft.org/CIE/RFC/1700/index.htm*. The IANA makes the port assignments. In general, a service uses the same port number with UDP as with TCP, although there are some exceptions. The assigned ports were originally numbered from 0 to 255, but were later expanded to 0 to 1023.

Some of the most well-known ports used are:

TCP/UDP port 20: FTP (data)

TCP/UDP port 21: FTP (control)

TCP/UDP port 22: SSH

TCP/UDP port 23: Telnet

TCP/UDP port 25: SMTP

TCP/UDP port 53: DNS

TCP/UDP port 67: BOOTP server

TCP/UDP port 68: BOOTP client

TCP/UDP port 69: TFTP

TCP/UDP port 80: HTTP

TCP/UDP port 88: Kerberos

TCP/UDP port 110: POP3

TCP/UDP port 119: NNTP

TCP/UDP port 137: NetBIOS name service

TCP/UDP port 138: NetBIOS datagram service

TCP/UDP port 139: NetBIOS session service

TCP/UDP port 220: IMAPv3

TCP/UDP port 389: LDAP

TCP/UDP port 443: HTTPS

TCP/UDP port 1433: Microsoft SQL

TCP/UDP ports 6660-6669 and 7000: IRC (Internet Relay Chat [IRC])

## Port Scanning

A total of 65,535 TCP ports and 65,535 UDP ports are used for various services and applications. If a port is open, it responds when another computer attempts to contact it over the network. Port-scanning programs such as *Nmap* are used to determine which ports are open on a particular machine. The program sends packets for a wide variety of protocols and, by examining which messages receive responses and which don't, creates a map of the computer's listening ports.

It is not possible to turn off all listening ports. If you did, you would render the computer invisible on the network and other devices would be unable to communicate with the computer. This may be exactly what you want with a workstation, but with servers, this is impossible.

Port scanning generally does no harm to your network or system, but it does provide hackers with information they can use to penetrate a network. Potential attackers use port scans in much the same way that a car thief checks the doors of parked vehicles to determine which ones are unlocked. Although this activity in itself does not constitute a serious offense and is generally not considered illegal; what the person conducting the scan does with the information can present a big problem. Intensive port scanning can cause a DoS and in some cases crash the machine being scanned. Should these situations occur, the activity is illegal.

**NOTE**

The intrusion and attack reporting center at *www.doshelp.com/PC/trojanports.htm* is an excellent resource for information on ports that should be closed, filtered, or monitored, because they are commonly used for Trojan and intrusion programs.

Firewall logs are an excellent resource to analyze and to see if you are being port-scanned. Port scans generally appear as pings to various ports on one IP address after another. Port scanners are now automated so the hacker can set it to run and come back later to a report of IP addresses with listening ports.

The logs also provide evidence should legal action be taken against the scanner. Thus, logs need to be maintained and backed up in a secure manner.

## Other Protocol Exploits

The attacks discussed so far involve exploiting some feature or weakness of the TCP/IP protocols. Hackers can also exploit vulnerabilities of other common protocols, such as HTTP, DNS, Common Gateway Interface (CGI), and other common protocols.

Active-X controls, JavaScript, and VBScript can be used to add animations or applets to Web sites, or to Hyper Text Markup Language (HTML) e-mail messages, but hackers can exploit these to write controls or scripts that allow them to remotely plant viruses, access data, or change or delete files on the hard disks of unaware users. Both Web browsers and e-mail client programs that support HTML mail are vulnerable.

# Data Packet

The data portion of the packet itself can be analyzed. Gateway firewalls generally do not perform this type of analysis, or they do it in a "rudimentary" or "simplistic" manner. Application proxies are much more thorough and examine each packet that is passed through the application proxy.

Since data packets vary greatly from application to application, it is impossible within the scope of this book to describe how packets are structured and the process for examining each type. Let's take a brief look at some ways to manipulate the data packet for nefarious purposes.

## System and Software Exploits

*System and software exploits* allow hackers to take advantage of weaknesses of particular OSs and applications (often called *bugs*). Like protocol exploits, they are used by intruders to gain unauthorized access to computers or networks, or to crash or clog up the systems to deny service to others.

Common bugs can be categorized as follows:

- **Buffer Overflows** Many common security holes are based on buffer overflow problems. Buffer overflows occur when the number of bytes or characters input exceeds the maximum number allowed by the programmer writing the program.

- **Unexpected Input** Programmers may not take steps to define what happens if invalid input (input that doesn't match program specifications) is entered. Such input could cause the program to crash or open up a way into the system.

- **System Configuration Bugs** These are not really bugs per se, but rather they are ways of configuring the OS or software that leaves it vulnerable to penetration.

Popular software such as Microsoft's Internet Information Server (IIS), Microsoft's Internet Explorer (MSIE), Linux Apache Web Server, UNIX Sendmail, and Mac Quicktime, are popular targets of hackers looking for software security holes that can be exploited.

Major OS and software vendors regularly release security patches to fix exploitable bugs. It is very important for network administrators to stay up-to-date in applying these fixes and/or service packs to ensure that their systems are as secure as possible.

## Trojans, Viruses, and Worms, Oh My!

Intruders who access your systems without authorization or inside attackers with malicious motives, could plant various types of programs to cause damage to your network. There are three broad categories of *malicious code*: Trojans, viruses, and worms.

- **Trojans** The name, short for *Trojan horse*, refers to a software program that appears to perform a useful function, but in fact performs actions that the program user is not aware of or did not intend. Hackers often write Trojans to circumvent the security of a system. Once the Trojan is installed, the hacker can exploit the security holes it creates to gain unauthorized access, or the Trojan program can perform some action such as:

  - Deleting or modifying files

  - Transmitting files across the network to the intruder

  - Installing other programs or viruses

    Basically, the Trojan can perform any action that the user has privileges and permissions to perform on the system. This means that a Trojan is especially dangerous if the unsuspecting user who installs it is an administrator and has access to the system files.

    Trojans can be cleverly disguised as innocuous programs, utilities, screensavers, or the like. A Trojan can also be installed by an executable script (JavaScript, a Java applet, Active-X control, and so forth) on a Web site. Accessing the site can initiate the installation of the program, if the Web browser is configured to allow scripts to run automatically.

- **Viruses** Includes any programs that are usually installed without the user's awareness and performs undesired actions. Viruses can also replicate themselves, infecting other systems by writing themselves to any disk used in the computer or sending themselves across the network. Viruses often distribute as attachments to e-mail or as macros in word processing documents. Some viruses activate immediately on installation; others lie dormant until a specific date or time, or when a particular system event triggers them.

  Viruses come in thousands of varieties. They can do anything from popping up a message that says "Hi!" to erasing a computer's entire hard disk. The proliferation of computer viruses has also led to the phenomenon of the *virus hoax*, which is a warning (generally circulated via e-mail or Web sites) about a virus that does not exist or does not do what the warning claims it will do. Real viruses, however, present a real threat to your network. Companies such as Symantec and McAfee make anti-virus software that is aimed at detecting and removing virus programs. Because new viruses are created daily, it is important to download new virus *definition files*, which contain the information required to detect each virus type on a regular basis, to ensure that your virus protection stays up-to-date. The most dangerous virus is a new, fast replicating virus for which no definition has been created. Fortunately, anti-virus companies now respond within hours of a new outbreak. Since nearly all anti-virus software has auto-update features, the new definitions are usually quickly put in place and effectively shut down the proliferation. This does not mean you are immune from infection if you have anti-virus software, it just means you are generally safe from older viruses.

  Both viruses and Trojans may carry a *logic bomb* (i.e., a bit of malicious code designed to "explode" under certain circumstances such as performing, or failing to perform an action). The bomb can do anything from delete files to wipe a computer. The "fun" part of a logic bomb for a hacker is letting the victim believe nothing is wrong and then at a much later time damage the computer, making it more difficult to determine where and when the infection occurred.

- A **worm** is a program that can travel across the network from one computer to another. Sometimes different parts of a worm run on different computers. Worms make multiple copies of themselves and spread throughout a network. The distinction between viruses and worms has become blurred. Originally the term *worm* was used to describe code that attacked multi-user systems (networks) and *virus* was used to describe programs that replicated on individual computers.

The primary purpose of a worm is to replicate. Worm programs were initially used for legitimate purposes in performing network management duties, but their ability to multiply quickly has been exploited by hackers, who create malicious worms that replicate wildly and might also exploit OS weaknesses and perform other harmful actions.

Unfortunately, nearly all these now contain a *root-kit*. This is a series of tools that take control of your machine and create a zombie that will do the bidding of the malicious writer. Once a root-kit is installed on your machine, your only choice is to flatten the machine and rebuild from scratch. Root-kits notoriously have subprograms that hide their presence from the OS. While there are tools such as Root-kit Revealer by SysInternals (www.sysinternals.com), there is no sure way to confirm that all pieces of the root-kit have been removed. Any remaining bits have the potential to reinstall the entire root-kit and begin transmitting information to the owner.

## Buffer Overflow

In general, most data packets can be manipulated in an attempt to create a *buffer overflow*, which is a specific condition in an application where more data is written to an area of memory than has been allocated. The extra data then flows into the next area of memory, where it should not be. If the application design doesn't consider this possibility, it may be possible to leverage this situation to execute the code in the second memory area. This situation can yield many unwanted results including: application hang or crash, server hang or crash, or even worst, compromise of the machine where control is given to the sender of the packet.

*White hat hackers*, people who attempt to find vulnerabilities in software and then report them to the manufacturer for correction, are constantly working to find buffer overflow errors in software and OSs. Because humans write all software and humans are prone to error, it is highly unlikely that there will ever be "perfect software" with no vulnerability. Therefore, it is in the best interest of network administrators to protect the most valuable assets with firewalls as best we can.

## Notes from the Underground…

### Do Firewalls Have Buffer Overflows?

Short answer, "Yes." However, there are far fewer than most other software, because firewalls are stripped down to the bare essentials. Firewall software is also scrutinized more closely due to the task the firewall is attempting to perform. Most firewall vulnerabilities result in DoS's rather than access violations or compromise. Firewalls are designed to *fail closed* so that the firewall cuts off network access rather than permitting unauthorized access.

Also realize that some firewalls are designed to be installed on existing OSs. If the underlying OS has vulnerabilities, your firewall will only be as good as the OS its running on.

In addition, a poorly configured firewall can leave gaping holes that a malicious person could walk through with ease. This book is a good start to configure your firewall securely; however, don't stop here. Read the manufacturer's documentation, white papers provided by the manufacture, and blogs, newsgroups, and discussion groups related to your model of firewall. Learn from other's mistakes and don't make them yourself. Most of these resources are freely available on the Web; a few searches should turn up starting points that will lead you to more resources.

To a determined hacker, discovering a firewall is tantamount to throwing down a gauntlet and posing the challenge of how to exploit the permitted access. The good news here is that such determined hackers are fewer than the *script kiddies* (less experienced hackers who rely on pre-written scripts and tools to compromise machines) who look for easy targets with well-known vulnerabilities. Therefore, be certain that the script kiddies will walk away after knocking on the door and getting no answer. Then delve into the literature mentioned above and make your network unwelcoming to even determined hackers.

# Firewall Types

There are two basic types of firewalls: Application Proxy and Gateway. Gateways are divided into packet filters and stateful inspection firewalls. These differ in function and design and have different uses in network architecture. Never try to have one type of firewall do the duty of another type. It is better to have a well-run and securely configured firewall doing its intended job, than to have something doing a job for which it wasn't designed. This is an invitation for disaster. Let's look at these firewalls and how they should be used.

# Application Proxy

An application proxy firewall takes apart each packet that comes in, examines it to see if it meets the criteria set, rewrites it, and sends it on its way. The proxy terminates the connection from the outside source and starts a new connection from the proxy to the destination. This offers great protection to the servers, because there is no direct interaction between the source and the destination. In addition, the proxy is greatly hardened against attacks and has a very small attack surface. It is very difficult for a hacker to take control of an application proxy firewall.

These firewalls are very specific and a proxy must be written for each supported application. The advantage to this is that you will have the exact needs of your particular application addressed; however, you are at the mercy of the vendor should there be an update to your application that the firewall doesn't support. Delays may occur in upgrading your application until the firewall vendor catches up.

Application proxies are usually "invisible" on the network. Often, they have no IP address themselves, or, if they do, they sometimes masquerade as the destination server. Thus, application proxies may not do address translation.

Application proxies work at the application level of the OSI Model (see Figure 3.2).

**Figure 3.2** The OSI Model

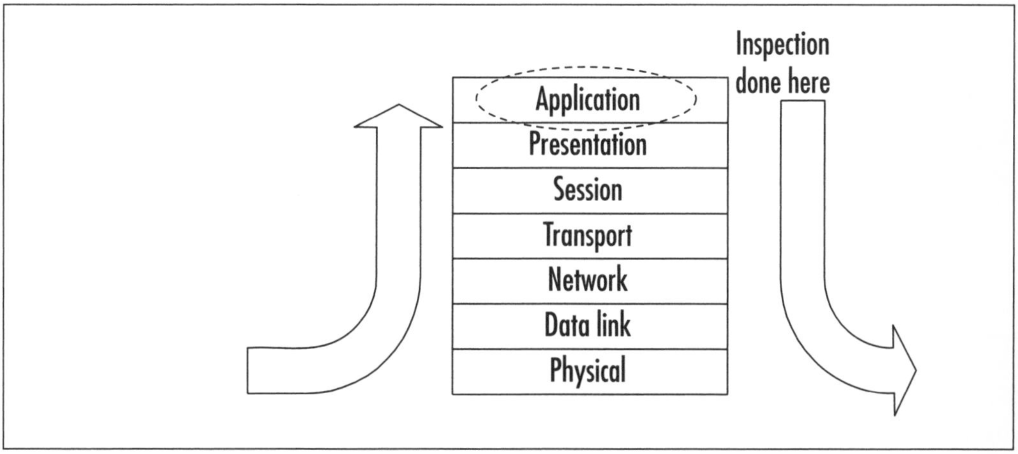

As the name implies, application proxy firewalls act as intermediaries in network sessions. The user's connection terminates at the proxy, and a corresponding separate connection is initiated from the proxy to the destination host. Connections are analyzed all the way up to the application layer to determine if they are allowed. It is this characteristic that gives proxies a higher level of security than packet filters, stateful, or otherwise. However, as you might imagine, this additional processing extracts a toll on performance. Figure 3.3 shows how packet processing is handled at the application layer before it is passed on or blocked.

**Figure 3.3** Application Proxy Data Flow

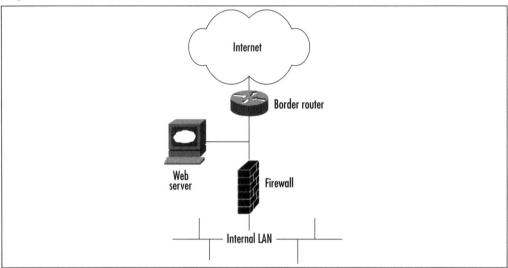

Depending on how the application proxy is written, it is possible to permit only those packets that are specific for the target application, and reject all others. Typically, these firewalls check against such factors as buffer overflows, hidden malicious code, correct source and destination IP addresses, and correct port usage using algorithms and international Internet standards. Any packet that doesn't pass the tests is rejected. This makes for very clean packets arriving at the server; however, it also requires a great deal of processing power.

# Pros

For a high level of security, an application proxy is the appliance of choice. The detail of control permitted is unmatched by any other device.

# High Security

An application proxy is generally far more secure than a gateway. By breaking down each packet to its basic parts and rewriting it, the firewall discovers and drops hidden malicious code. These firewalls can, and have, prevented zero-day attacks.

# Refined Control

Application proxies also provide the opportunity to fine tune exactly what you will let into your protected network, and, depending on the design of the firewall, what you will allow out. A *reverse proxy* handles controlling the outgoing of information. Reverse proxies can play a very important role in high security environments by examining the contents of outgoing packets for sensitive information.

# Cons

While providing high security, application proxies cannot and should not be used in every situation. There are severe drawbacks to using these devices.

# Slower Network Performance

Due to the work an application proxy must perform to dissect each packet and then rewrite it properly to pass on, they tend to be slower than a gateway. Depending on the volume of traffic across the firewall and the complexity of the data, you may see a significant performance hit with an application proxy.

# Update Schedule Governed by Vendors

Since vendors specifically write the OS of these appliances, it may take time for them to catch up to the latest release of a particular application. Until your proxy is up-to-date with the application it is protecting, you cannot update the application itself.

# Limited Control, Depending on Vendor

While some application proxies can be tweaked, others cannot. In most cases, if you are using standard protocols and the application proxy at your border to the Internet, it will not matter if you can finely control what does and doesn't enter your protected network. However, using an application proxy to protect an entire server room from the rest of the organization can prove to be disastrous if not tested. Note that neither of these scenarios are typical uses for an application proxy. Most often, an application proxy will be placed in front of a specific type of server, not at a border or subnet (see Figure 3.4).

**Figure 3.4** Example Positioning of an Application Proxy Firewall

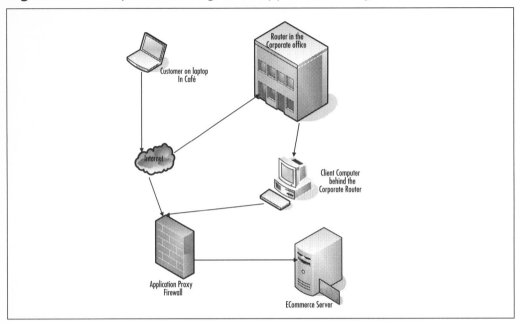

In this example, the corporate offices have a direct connection to the Internet, and there are mobile users directly on the Internet. Due to the sensitivity of the e-mail communications, all e-mail passes through Microsoft Internet Security and Acceleration (ISA [*www.microsoft.com/isaserver/default.mspx*]) server. ISA server is Microsoft's application proxy. Built for various applications including Exchange, Structured Query Language (SQL), and Terminal Server, it analyzes the data for appropriateness to the backend application, terminates the connection from the client, and establishes a new connection from ISA server to the backend Exchange. The reverse is done as the Exchange server answers the client's query.

## Tools & Traps …

### Evaluate, Test, Evaluate, and Test Again

I was offered the opportunity to evaluate a new application proxy firewall. The marketers promised this would be the "golden bullet" that would solve all our problems and prevent zero-day attacks. They also promised that their algorithms

**Continued**

were perfectly safe and compatible with the servers we had deployed. We already had a well-configured gateway firewall in front of our servers, protecting them from the Internet and the rest of the organization. If we didn't have the option of putting this application proxy device at the border, we would place it in-line with the gateway in front of the servers.

To start, we weren't certain that there were significant risks to our servers from zero-day attacks. We patched early and often and the number of ports open to the local network was small, even with a smaller subset open to the Internet. All of these ports were well-known and well-established protocols.

I used my own workstation as a guinea pig. I could afford to be offline; our production servers could not. Within 5 minutes, Outlook stopped talking to the Exchange server; my e-mail was offline. In my mind, I could hear the mail users screaming and the phones ringing off the hook if we had listened to the marketers and placed this inline with the gateway, as they suggested. The application proxy had "decided" that the packets between Outlook and Exchange didn't match what it considered a legitimate protocol.

I examined both the Web interface to the application proxy device and the logs, to determine if I could figure out why it thought this was unacceptable traffic and if I could fix or reconfigure the logic to mark these packets as acceptable. Alas, neither was possible.

Beware of placing such black boxes in your environment. Not knowing how they work or why they mark traffic as unacceptable can be almost as destructive as an attack. Having to explain why the device you put on the network performed a DoS against the network it was meant to protect, is no fun. Faced with a choice between two devices, one that logged everything it did and why, and one that did its thing with little or no feedback to you, I'd always go with the first.

# Gateway

By far, the most commonly deployed firewall is the gateway. This firewall examines the source and destination addresses and ports, and determines if the packet meets the designated rules to pass through the firewall to the servers. There are various levels of gateways. Some are extremely simplistic and only filter packets by port, others can filter by IP address and port, and still others perform various checks on the legitimacy of some or all IPs. Gateways come in two flavors: packet filters and stateful inspection gateways. Let's examine each in turn.

# Packet Filters

These are basic firewalls with very little flexibility or functionality. Often, these are built into OSs, such as Mac OS X, to provide rudimentary protection for the individual workstation. Windows and Linux have more advanced firewalls built in.

Windows firewall has some features of stateful inspection, while Linux has IPChains, which can be used as a full-function firewall (explored in the next chapter.) Packet filters also have their place in the network architecture. Network routers will function as packet filters.

# Technical Description

In its most basic form, a *packet filter* makes decisions about whether to forward a packet based only on information found at the IP or TCP/UDP layers (transport and network layers, respectively, in the Open Systems Interconnection (OSI) model. See Figure 3.1). In effect, a packet filter is a router with some intelligence. However, a packet filter only handles individual packets; it does not keep track of TCP sessions. Thus, it is poorly equipped to detect spoofed packets that come in through an outside interface. These specifically crafted packets will pretend to be part of an existing session by setting the ACK flag in the TCP header. Packet filters are configured to allow or block traffic according to source and destination IP addresses, source and destination ports, and type of protocol (TCP, UDP, (Internet Control Message Protocol [ICMP], and so on).

While rudimentary, packet filters can provide an effective barrier that reduces your *attack surface*. An attack surface, in network speak, refers to the number of ports you have available for someone to try to exploit. A Web server, which is only serving unencrypted pages, only requires port 80 open to the Internet. Using a packet filter, you can block all incoming traffic except that destined for port 80. You have just reduced your attack surface from 65535 ports to 1. While any hacker worth their salt will find your single open port, you have greatly reduced their toolset for breaking into your machine. In addition, if there is vulnerability, even a zero-day vulnerability, on one of the other ports, it will be impossible to reach *from the outside*.

Another example of packet filter use involves limiting the IP addresses permitted to contact a server. Let's assume you have a business that has a specific subnet, 192.168.50.x. Your financial application server should only provide services to this subnet. Simply block all other traffic. Now, the only way someone can get to your application server is to be on your specific subnet. Packet filters usually have their own address and address translation. Some of the specific techniques addressed in the following chapters can be applied to packet filters, just be aware of their limitations and potential vulnerabilities.

The ultimate example of a simplistic port-only packet filter is the old Microsoft Windows TCP/IP filter available in advanced network properties. This is so simplistic, it is only worthwhile to use in a few cases.

Figure 3.5 shows an example using a router as a packet filter. This situation is often found in academia where open communication is considered more important than security. In this case, the router selectively blocks certain protocols that are determined to be dangerous, and all other traffic is permitted. In this case, the blocked protocols are insecure because they transmit usernames and passwords in clear text, or, they can be used by hackers to gain control over machines. Simple Network Management Protocol (SNMP) can transfer various commands to devices. These commands range from information gathering to actual control of the devices. IRC is a common protocol used by hackers to communicate with zombies. Blocking this at the border, both incoming and outgoing, removes a control channel for hackers should a machine inside become compromised. Telnet and FTP are protocols that transmit both data and authentication credentials in clear text. Telnet is a remote command-line protocol and FTP is used to transfer files to and from servers. Better choices are Secure Shell (SSH) and Secure File Transfer Protocol (SFTP) both of which encrypt data and authentication. Simple Message Block (SMB) file sharing, while not insecure in and of itself, has been found to have numerous vulnerabilities in the implementation in Windows and older Linux system. These vulnerabilities can be used to compromise machines, and therefore should be blocked at the border router. Also note the Peer-to-Peer (P2P) file sharing, which is not uncommon in academic settings and should be taken into consideration when designing network security.

**Figure 3.5** Using a Router as a Packet Filter

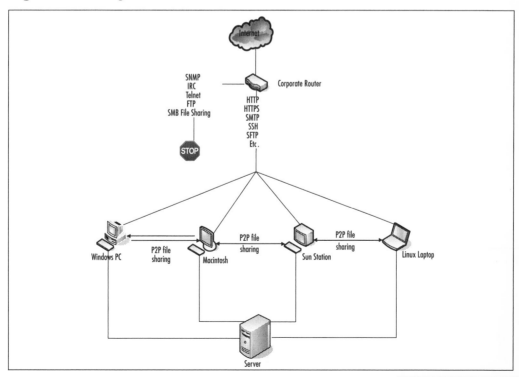

# Pros

Packet filters are extremely useful in certain situations. Primarily they should be deployed at the perimeter of your organization where coarse filtering is the best option.

## Speed

Packet filters are extremely fast. Since they only examine the destination port and/or the source/destination IP address, they have very little work to do. Simple packet filters are an excellent choice if you have an extremely high traffic resource that must process packets in and out very quickly. A high-traffic Web site is an ideal application for a packet filter. You can also throw a packet filter at your corporate border. Perhaps you only need ports such as SSH (22) or Remote Desktop Protocol (RDP) (3365) open for remote administration and VPN for remote access by users. Perfect. None of the cons below applies to these protocols and you don't need anything fancy to get the job done.

## Rapid Implementation

Quick deployment is also a major plus to packet filters. As long as you know the necessary ports and/or subnets, you can have a packet filter set up in literally minutes. There are no complicated rule sets and no extra protocols to deal with. What ports do you need open and where can the traffic come from? Answer those two questions and you are on your way.

# Cons

While packet filters have the advantages of speed and simplicity, they suffer from problems of security and other limitations that more complicated firewalls do not.

## Less Secure

Because packet filters are basic and do simple packet inspection, they are less secure than an application proxy. They pass through anything arriving from a permitted subnet to a permitted port, no questions asked.

## Port Limitations

Packet filters do not track where an incoming packet came from, or insure that the return packet goes to the same location (see "Stateful Inspection"). This also means that the conversation cannot be moved from lower static ports to higher dynamic ports. Remember the high dynamic ports we discussed earlier? Many applications use these after making the initial handshake and the two machines agree how to communicate. The application will request a move to higher ports to free up the lower static ports for other initial handshakes. With a packet filter, this requires opening most, if not all, of the dynamic ports, which, of course, makes the firewall useless.

The Windows mail application, Outlook, and its corresponding server, Exchange, demonstrate this very well. Initial communications are started on TCP port 135. Once the connection is established and authenticated, Exchange requests that the communication be moved up to ports around 5000. By default, this could include any number of possible ports that would require too many holes in the packet filter.

FTP, a "standard" protocol, can behave strangely with a packet filter. Since communication happens on port 21 but data transfer is switched to port 20, many packet filters fail to correctly pass FTP packets; therefore, the file transfer is interrupted.

# Stateful Inspection

The Stateful Inspection gateway is the standard type of firewall deployed to protect servers and other network resources. There are many companies that provide this type of firewall with varying degrees of features (explored in Chapter 4). For now, let's look at how these firewalls work in general.

## Technical Description

Stateful inspection is important to security because it provides a deeper level of filtering than Access Control Lists (ACL's) found in routers, which may only filter based on header information. Firewalls that perform stateful inspection analyze individual data packets as they traverse the firewall. In addition to the packet header, stateful inspection also assesses the packet's payload and looks at the application protocol. It can filter based on the source, destination, and service requested by the packet. The term "stateful inspection" refers to the firewall's ability to remember the status of a connection and thereby build a context for each data stream in its memory. With this information available, the firewall is able to make more informed policy decisions.

Stateful inspection is several steps below an application proxy and much better than a packet filter. In this case, the firewall keeps track of the TCP SYN/ACK packets that initiate and continue the conversation between two machines in a *connection table*. UDP protocols are monitored in a similar fashion, but the table is far less complete, because there is no detailed information. Stateful inspection firewalls also handle protocols such as Generic Route Encapsulation (GRE) and Protocol 47 used in VPN communications, and ICMP.

All of these types of firewalls have the concept of "inside" versus "outside." While there may be several insides that have various levels of security (private, users, DMZ, and so forth), there is only one outside and it is completely untrusted. By default, nothing is permitted to cross the firewall from the outside. Conversely, devices on a higher security interface, such as users, are permitted access to a lower security interface such as DMZ or outside. All of these parameters are configurable; however, before we begin discussing the configuration, let's get a better understanding of how a firewall decides what can and cannot pass through.

## The Inspection Process

The inspection of TCP/IP packets is a multi-step procedure. What follows is a summary of the steps, not necessarily in order (see Figure 3.6):

1. A packet arrives at the outside interface. It is checked for *permitted* or *denied* ports and IP addresses. Note that stateful inspection firewalls require both a port and an IP address. IP addresses can be in the form of a single machine, group of IP addresses, or "any," meaning any valid IP address on the specified network.

2. The firewall checks the source IP address for validity. This feature prevents spoofed packets from being transmitted, by allowing only packets whose source addresses match the subnet of the firewall's incoming interface or routing table. Therefore, if the packet has inconsistent information concerning its origins, it is unlikely that it is legitimate and is dropped.

3. The firewall compares the ports and addresses to the ACL, and either clears the packet for further processing or drops the packet.

4. The packet's *from* and *to* addresses, as well as other tracking information, is recorded in a table for reference when a return packet is sent. Stateful inspection firewalls keep track of who is talking to whom. This is extremely important for the correct use and protection of the dynamic ports. Should the packet be part of an ongoing connection, there is an entry in the connection table and the packet information is compared to the table for consistency.

5. If the packet is a well-known protocol such as SMTP (Internet mail), HTTP (Web), or FTP (file transfer), the packet may be checked against the IANA standards or a vendors private standards for compliance. This insures that packets containing malformed data are dropped and do not reach the servers where they may cause harm. This is not, however, equivalent to the application proxy's inspection of packet data. Application proxies inspect

data contained in the packet to conform to a specific application's require-ments and rewrite the packet. Stateful inspection firewalls simply look for standards compliance and only address translation. They do not wholesale rewrite the packet. They are not application-specific nor do all stateful inspection firewalls perform this type of check.

6. Finally, the firewall rewrites the destination IP address from the valid Internet address to the private address, and sends it on its way.

**Figure 3.6** Stateful Packet Inspection Example

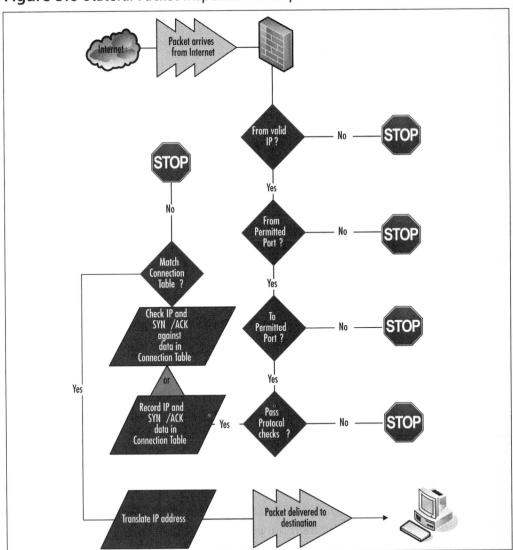

Packets sent from the inside to the outside follow a similar process:

1.  The firewall checks for a valid IP address and permitted IP address destina-
    tions. By default, most firewalls assume that a higher security interface is
    permitted to access any location outside the firewall. However, this can be
    overridden and best practices suggest doing this (see Chapter 4).

2.  A comparison is done between the outgoing packet parameters and the
    entries in the connection table. The firewall confirms that the entries match
    and that the packet is headed to the appropriate destination.

3.  The firewall may confirm the outgoing protocols, although in most cases,
    firewalls assume that trusted networks use valid protocols.

4.  Addresses are translated and the packet is sent on its way to the destination.

## Stateful Inspection Gateway Features

Let's take a look at some of the features that make the Stateful Inspection Firewall so
popular. While not every model of firewall will contain all, or even most of these
features, some will be in nearly every one:

- **Purpose-built OS**  Eliminates the weaknesses found in most general OSs.
  Because the firewall's OS has a single purpose—filter TCP/IP traffic from
  one interface to another—it does not have extras that could be leveraged as
  a point of entry for compromise. It also means that the OS that does the
  filtering can be separated completely from a Graphical User Interface
  (GUI) interface for configuration and maintenance.

- **Connection Table**  The method the firewall uses to provide stateful packet
  filtering, which analyzes each packet to ensure that only legitimate traffic
  traverses the interface. This is the module that maintains the connection
  table and validates destination and source addresses.

- **Universal Resource Locator (URL) Filtering**  Can limit URLs
  accessed by the user's base on a policy defined by the network administrator or a security policy. This feature can be considered a reverse proxy.
  Users inside the firewall can be prevented from accessing certain Web sites
  based on the address of the Web site.

- **Content Filtering**  Can block ActiveX or Java applets. This is a simplistic
  application filter that is beginning to blur the line between application
  proxies and gateways. The firewall can block either specific ActiveX and/or
  Java applets, or all such applets.

- **Network Address Translation (NAT) and Port Address Translation (PAT)**  Hides internal addressing from the Internet and makes more efficient use of private address space. As stated above, this is the standard for gateways. As both a security measure and a way to extend a limited Internet address space, NAT turns valid Internet addresses into private addresses. PAT can be used to redirect a standard port (e.g., HTTP Port 80) to a non-standard port (Port 8080). This is often used for security or to mask the service from other internal machines.

- **Cut-through Proxy**  Authenticates users accessing resources through the firewall. With a single authentication event, the firewall permits users to access file and print services that would otherwise be inaccessible outside the firewall.

- **VPN**  Capable of handling mobile user access and site-to-site VPNs utilizing Data Encryption Standard (DES), 3DES, and Advanced Encryption Standard (AES) methods. Thus, a mobile user creates an encrypted "tunnel" from his computer to the firewall, permitting secure access to the resources behind the firewall, as if the computer was physically behind the firewall.

- **Intrusion Detection**  Enables the firewall to protect against various forms of malicious attacks, as well as the ability to identify attacks via attack "signatures." Yet another feature that makes the stateful inspection firewall appear a bit like an application proxy. Remember, these are general validations of the protocols and are not specific for a given application. Application proxy firewalls are written for specific applications and do much more precise checks on each data packet.

- **DHCP**  Can act as a DHCP client and/or server. While not so much a security feature, it provides the opportunity to automatically assign IP addresses to machines inside the firewall, which eliminates the need for a second device. There are some arguments against using this feature, because if an intruder gains access to your private network and is able to automatically obtain a valid IP address, it makes it much easier to begin the malicious work. (If an intruder has access to your private network, you have much larger concerns.)

- **Routing Functionality**  Can support static routes, Routing Information Protocol (RIP), and Open Shortest Path First (OSPF). Not strictly a security feature, but an elimination of other network appliances that must be maintained.

- **Support for Remote Authentication Dial-in User Server/Service (RADIUS) or Terminal Access Controller Access Control System Plus (TACACS+)** Authenticating, authorizing, and accounting for users passing through the firewall, or to enable authentication for those connecting to the management interfaces. RADIUS and TACACS+ are basic, cross-platform authentication services that eliminate the need to maintain multiple sets of usernames and passwords that increase security.

- **Failover** Provides a resilient, high-availability solution in case of failure. A network is only useful if it is available. Providing failover not only protects against hardware failure, but also against failure due to a DoS attack or other non-destructive interruption of service.

# Pros

Stateful inspection firewalls are the best balance between the performance of a packet filter and the security of an application proxy. There's a wide selection of these firewalls available and they have few, if any drawbacks.

## Networking Standard

A stateful inspection firewall is the de facto standard for network protection at this time. Installing less is not a wise move without good reason (e.g., a requirement for the fastest possible data transfer while maintaining some protection for the internal network).

## Performance and Protection

The balance of performance versus protection between a packet filter and an application proxy is excellent. Since stateful inspection is the current standard, most vendors support this type of firewall and offer it in many levels of data transfer rates and cost.

# Cons

There are very few reasons not to use a stateful inspection firewall; however, there are a few possible considerations.

## Lower Data Transfer Rates Than a Packet Filter

As stated above, there is performance degradation over a packet filter. Tables are maintained and logic is used to parse the access lists, costing memory and processor power.

## Lack of Fine Control

Fine control of application proxies is lost in favor of better performance. Stateful inspection firewall software is written to be generic (i.e., usable in nearly any environment), whereas application proxies are specific and therefore provide fine control for the specific applications.

# Summary

The number and variety of threats on the Internet increase every day. With increased connection speeds and the wide availability of fast connections, hackers have more access to more potential targets than ever before. Weaknesses in the TCP/IP protocol combined with weaknesses in the OSs provide "hooks" for malicious persons to gain control of valuable resources for fun and profit.

Data is pushed around the Internet using the TCP/IP protocol. The protocol uses headers as envelopes for the data, and firewalls use the information in these headers to control what data is permitted through to the protected servers and what data is dropped.

Two types of transmission protocols create the headers. TCP protocol uses SYN and ACK packets to confirm the successful receipt of data. UDP protocol sends the data off with no regard whether the information reaches its intended target or not. Packet filter firewalls disregard much of the packet information and permit/block based solely on the port number and/or destination/source IP address. Both application proxies and stateful inspection firewalls create tables of source and destination addresses and ports, and monitor communications based on these tables.

Application proxy firewalls are written to the specifications of particular applications, and the selection of a particular application proxy is mostly determined by the type of application server being protected. Fine control of information is favored over performance.

Packet filters favor speed over control. They are basic and only monitor if a particular source or destination address or port is permitted through. A particular port can be used for any type of information, not just the information for which the port was defined. Packet filters are favored when performance outweighs all other considerations.

Stateful inspection gateways are the best balance of application proxy fine control and packet filter performance. They are the standard for most network infrastructures. While they are generic and can be used in any environment, they often provide good basic inspection of various IPs to maintain network integrity.

# Solutions Fast Track

## Threats and Attacks

- ☑ Physical access
- ☑ Network access
- ☑ Reconnaissance, Access, DoS attacks
- ☑ Hacking for fun and profit/Identity theft
- ☑ Trojans, viruses, and worms

## TCP/IP Protocol

- ☑ Packet structure
- ☑ IP addresses
- ☑ TCP/UDP ports, their uses, and vulnerabilities
- ☑ Data packet vulnerabilities

## Application Proxy/Gateway

- ☑ Fine control of data
- ☑ Written for specific applications
- ☑ Performance sacrificed for data integrity
- ☑ At mercy of vendor for updates supporting application updates

## Packet Inspection

- ☑ High performance, high data transfer rates
- ☑ Block/permit based solely on Internet address and/or port number
- ☑ Least secure of the technologies
- ☑ Extremely quick to implement

## Stateful Inspection

- ☑ Excellent balance between Application Proxy and Packet Inspection
- ☑ Provides good generic data integrity
- ☑ Widely supported
- ☑ Monitors data destinations and ports
- ☑ Provides support for transmissions changing from low-static ports to high-dynamic ports without loss of connection

# Frequently Asked Questions

The following Frequently Asked Questions, answered by the authors of this book, are designed to both measure your understanding of the concepts presented in this chapter and to assist you with real-life implementation of these concepts. To have your questions about this chapter answered by the author, browse to **www.syngress.com/solutions** and click on the **"Ask the Author"** form.

**Q:** Can I deploy a firewall in my environment?

**A:** Almost undoubtedly. No matter what your environment, deploying a firewall to protect your infrastructure from the hostile Internet is a wise move. With proper planning, a firewall will improve your security and reduce your attack surface without degrading your data transfer performance or causing unwanted communication problems.

You may begin by using your existing router to block unneeded or vulnerable services. Check, check, and recheck to ensure whatever ports you block will not turn off vital business services. There is nothing worse than making a change in the name of security and then having the CEO who is on an important business trip, call angry and in a panic because he or she cannot obtain the data needed.

**Q:** What type of firewall should I deploy?

**A:** Ultimately, only you can answer this question. Consider what you are trying to protect, where in your network infrastructure you are planning to place the firewall, and how much control you want to exert over the data transmission.

**Q:** Can I deploy more than one type of firewall?

**A:** Absolutely. Defense in depth is standard practice, like putting a lock on your motorcycle so that the wheels cannot roll, putting a second lock on the steering column so it cannot be turned, chaining the motorcycle to an immovable object, and activating an alarm that will sound if moved. The more hoops a malicious person must jump through to obtain access to your valuable resources, the less likely that person will bother. Figure 3.7 shows a highly protected network where the most valuable resources are completely isolated, not only from the Internet, but also from the users.

In the figure, untrusted servers may be servers run by a consultant or other third party. The public access Web application servers could be e-commerce servers housing customer private information such as credit card numbers. User access servers could be mail servers or file servers for use inside the organization. Protected private application servers could house organizational financial information or employee records. Note that in this particular setup, it would likely be necessary to have VPN access between the users and the Web application servers so that authorized users could access the credit card data.

By dividing the network in this way, it is unlikely that the compromise of one portion of the network will result in the compromise of the entire network. With this type of strict division of networks, most users would not be able to access sensitive information. It also limits the damage that an internal user can do, even with sophisticated hacking tools.

**Q:** Where should I put the various firewalls?

**A:** Packet filters are best deployed at the border of your organization, between your final router and your Internet Service Provider (ISP). This is where all of the traffic in and out of your organization occurs. Performance is essential here, and fine control is nearly impossible due to the variety of protocols and information types passing through. The packet filters will most likely be set to accept most connections and only deny some potentially dangerous ones such as Telnet. Outbound, you may wish to block the IRC ports. Hackers often use IRC to communicate with the malicious software (*bots*) that they install on compromised machines.

**Figure 3.7** Defense In-depth Example

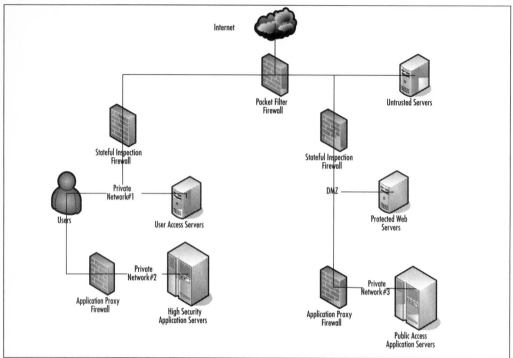

Stateful inspection gateways can be used internally to further protect subnets and filter the information coming in from the Internet. Stateful inspection gateways are often used to protect a more secure area (e.g., financials) from the rest of the organization.

Finally, application proxies are used to protect your most valuable applications from attack. An e-mail application proxy is a good example of this type of deployment. The proxy can be configured to not only accept e-mail from certain locations, but also to filter for unwanted data and protect internal data from either accidental or purposeful transmission outside the organization. There are even e-mail proxies which scan every e-mail for keywords or attachment types that could contain valuable private data. The proxies stop this data cold.

**Q:** If I deploy all three types of firewalls exactly to the best practices, will I be 100 percent safe?

**A:** Nothing short of using wire cutters to cut the cables connecting you to the Internet, will keep any network 100 percent safe from outside threats. Even if you took this step, you still have people inside that could compromise your data. You cannot ignore patching your internal computers nor can you ignore patching your firewall. You must maintain vigilance and check your firewall logs for problems. DoS attacks can still render your communications to the Internet impossible. However, you will be better protected with a firewall than without.

**Q:** What if a hacker manages to take control of a machine inside my firewall?

**A:** This is every network and system administrator's greatest nightmare. Several steps can be taken to mitigate the damage such a situation would cause.

1.  Use host-based firewalls such as IPChains or Windows Firewall to limit the access one machine has to other machines. This limits the available ports available for a hacker to exploit from the compromised machine.

2.  Monitor your network with intrusion detection systems (IDS) such as Snort (*www.snort.org*), which will alert you to malicious behavior before it spreads.

3.  Monitor your important systems for unauthorized changes with system auditing and third-party products such as Tripwire (*www.tripwire.com*).

**NOTE**

To fully explore IDSs is far beyond the scope of this book and has filled several volumes by itself. Two places to start learning more about intrusion detection are SANS (*www.sans.org/resources/idfaq/*) and WindowSecurity (*www.windowsecurity.com/whitepaper/info/misc/network-intrusion-detection.html*)

5.  Divide your network following the example above to minimize the possibility of a single compromise permitting access to every system.

6.  Employ *bastion hosts* to access the most valuable systems. Bastion hosts are machines who's sole function is to provide an access portal to other, more vulnerable systems. These machines must be individually secured and hardened, because they are always in a position of being attacked or probed. This means that before placement, a bastion host must be stripped of unnecessary services, fully updated with the latest service

packs, hot fixes, and updates, and isolated from other trusted machines and networks to eliminate the possibility that its compromise would allow for connection to (and potential compromise of) the protected networks and resources. This also means that a machine being used for this purpose should have no user accounts relative to the protected network or directory services structure, which could lead to enumeration of your internal network. See Figure 3.8 for placement and use.

**Figure 3.8** Bastion Host Placement and Use

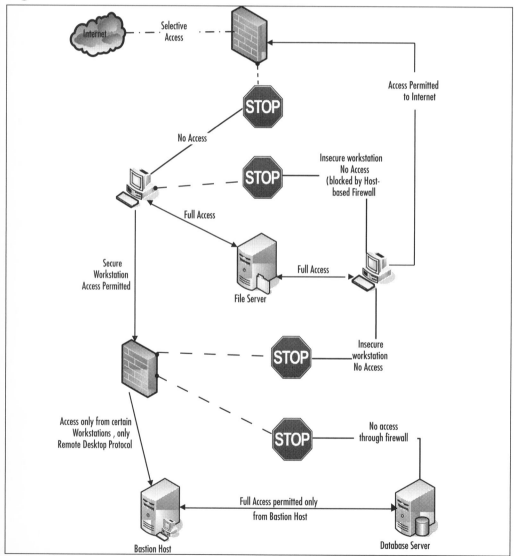

**Q:** It would be easier for me to administer my firewall via HTTP or Telnet. Why are clear text protocols so dangerous?

**A:** There are numerous versions of a type of tool called a *packet sniffer* available. A packet sniffer captures the TCP/IP packets passing between devices and records the data. These devices can be used to "steal" data as it travels across the network. The sniffer captures individual data packets and allows hackers to view and analyze the message contents and packet headers. Should you use a plain text protocol, not only will all the commands be passed for a potential intruder to see, but so will your username and password. It would then be trivial for an intruder to access your firewall and change the configuration to suit his needs.

---

**NOTE**

Packet sniffers are also called *protocol analyzers* or *network analyzers*. Sniffer and Sniffer Pro are two packet-sniffer products marketed by Network Associates.

---

Below is a plain text capture of a packet from a Web site captured on TCP Port 80:

```
HTTP/1.1 200 OK
Accept-Ranges: bytes
Date: Sun, 11 Jun 2006 02:49:58 GMT
Content-Length: 450
Content-Type: text/plain
Server: Apache/1.3.33 (Darwin)
Last-Modified: Thu, 04 May 2006 16:02:47 GMT
ETag: "eb1be3-1c2-445a25a7"
Via: 1.1 netcache03 (NetCache NetApp/5.5R6)
{
configURL =
"http://configuration.apple.com/configurations/internetservices/dotmackit/1/
clientConfiguration.plist";
    accountInfoURL =
"https://www.mac.com/WebObjects/Info.woa/wa/XMLRPC/accountInfo";
    signUpURL = {
            en = "http://www.mac.com";
```

```
        ja =
"http://www.mac.com/WebObjects/Welcome.woa/wa/default?lang=ja&cty=JP";
    };
    referralLookupURL =
"http://homepage.mac.com/dotmackitsupport/Referrals";
    otherParameters = {};
}
```

As you can see, this is completely legible. If there was a username and password in this conversation, it would be available. (*www.mac.com*).

Below is an encrypted session captured on TCP Port 443. This was captured by accessing *https://www.mac.com*, my personal page:

```
n_9¡R⌐h□Ébà,ö∞ôÿ#πç}(″∂qÏ□,ö4п□"µî™È′at⍀rãiaɒ»gt‰□Ë ˋv□,TÂ⌐Ê⌐Ûv„fiòÙ*Cçk[ê‹œÍú
□Èß•0€và÷Ô□i□S&wi□ßûÚ_Ïq[□{(„U⊛□ˋúéu~ ˊ;M¿áqÁ□‡,Èî⁻Å¨2˜í∑ç□ù2¶á.~Û‰0LÏF□□v¬Ç>
□Åû□ùî†°ñˇé□_2[‡„YÁ«ÿì‹≥¶K` ˋïßXô£§□Yèоà,ÕYiænɸ ª è î≥¨öeKò≥rÑ3iûçk□¥□8}k¨n_\◊'K
Àni″;"ɾIæóⱽ4¸Ì□L6Ôоèₚ()□èª˜ØµcV$Èa]‰°fiÎPÏ∞òexªŸ7ð⍺⊛°ÊÜé/I˜ª□‹ó»¸Õˆ/å□Z"[wE⁻≥
óÖ≥□Z]Ön•□[3w‰+Lô□$‡□1G≠⁻,{pÎZnà80‡Å»»‰Üî»∞‹e□□B¬óR>£Ê™«`?Å^∑□⁻⌐□æ[Ó\Düœ‰⁻˜k
.µ{iFÀµ°æ*ÃF'V˜î¥w∅□Î±k{ˋô°ÊÎ⊛Q‹ ˋŸ4∑□xZ˜hjtÛH□□X□□^‰L/1□√=wq□ëªUfg•п:ù□«!ò°
a˜Ã˜ˇøÑ5Gð™ô,ÿÇífi□qÅ˜°œ.a□Íë]§=ò¡Xù¸ð§ˋs‹ •ß⊛fl°!,∂[9ÜⱭÅãrüÀz⍀T◊□□dGÔX□,a~w~
‹û□ÿ⊛]]zü›¬jy‹□ù□?tæˇrK2◊éGL⊛|ûÂ⊛C°\±ö⍀[üé□ÕⱭⱲx◊□p_d!ôíPg,□h¶
```

As you can see, this is completely illegible. This was transmitted with 128-bit encryption, which is nearly unbreakable. This is typical of any encrypted protocol, HTTPS, SSH, SFTP, and so forth. While it is not necessarily easy to sniff network traffic, it can be done. Particularly vulnerable are unencrypted wireless connections, Internet Café's, and networks connected via hubs rather than switches. Therefore, never, under any circumstances, enable clear text protocols on a network connection to important data or the devices protecting that data.

# Chapter 4

# Deciding on a Firewall

## Solutions in this chapter:

- **Appliance/Hardware Solution**
- **Software Solutions**

☑ **Summary**

☑ **Solutions Fast Track**

☑ **Frequently Asked Questions**

# Introduction

Choosing a firewall solution involves many factors, some that can be controlled (e.g., features and cost) and others that cannot be controlled (e.g., overall network structure, history, and politics). This chapter presents the benefits and the drawbacks of various firewalls. The final decision of what will work best in your environment rests on your shoulders and on those who control the budget.

# Appliance/Hardware Solution

## Basic Description

Considered the most secure approach, a *network appliance* is a highly specialized device that is placed on the network between a hostile environment and a safe environment. A "hostile" environment could mean the Internet with access open to anyone; the network containing the user base vs. the network containing servers, which should have limited access; or dividing the network into segments of varying security or access, where some areas have less access due to the sensitive data stored there.

Compliance with various laws is particularly important for government and private agencies when choosing between firewall types. Such laws include the Federal Information Processing Standards (FIPS) (www.itl.nist.gov/fipspubs) and the Health Insurance Portability and Accountability Act (HIPAA) (www.hhs.gov/ocr/hipaa) in the US, and the Canadian Security of Information Act (SOIA) (www.tbs-sct.gc.ca/pubs_pol/gospubs/tbm_12a/sia-lpi1_e.asp#effe). These laws require that certain standards be met, including hardware firewall standards. If you fall under one of these laws, you may not have the option of a software firewall.

## Hardware

With a hardware-based solution, you have a network appliance whose sole purpose is to provide a firewall that will pass packets in and out quickly, while inspecting them based on a defined security policy. A network device's hardware provides the single function of packet filtration and/or inspection.

In its simplest form, a network router configured as a packet filter is a hardware-based firewall. In its most complex form, it is an application proxy on specialized hardware protecting a specific application package.

## Damage & Defense ...

### Packet Filter Warning!

Do *not* depend on packet-filtering routers for your firewall needs; these attacks can go straight through a packet filter (e.g., the Microsoft Structured Query Language (SQL) server has an exploit that can be compromised using the well known SQL port 1433). Blocking all other ports to the SQL server so that users can query the database decreases the attack surface, and won't protect you against an attack to that port. Using an application proxy allows you to analyze the packets and reduce the possibility that a malicious packet will traverse the firewall and compromise your server.

The operating system (OS) and inspection software are sometimes modified for a particular hardware. It is rare for network hardware to be sold without an integrated OS; however, that OS may not be unique to the hardware. Linux, UNIX, and Windows are often the base OS. Even with this, the OS is usually hardened against network attacks and/or stripped down to provide a specific set of functions.

It is difficult to add third-party products or change the basic functionality of a hardware-based firewall. Consider the security implications of changing the functionality of a well-designed and hardened OS. Teams of dedicated people have worked to design hardware and software to use together for the greatest functionality and security. You don't have to worry about how the OS functions; just plug it in, define the rule sets, and go. Your sole responsibility concerning the OS and filtering software is maintaining up-to-date patches.

## Hardware-based Firewalls

The following section looks at some of the hardware-based firewalls and the advantages they offer, including Cisco Private Internet Exchange (PIX), Juniper NetScreen, SonicWall, and Nokia Security Platform (NSP) firewalls. It then touches on other hardware-based firewalls (e.g., using routers as packet filters). Some manufacturers offer additional appliances that work with firewalls to protect data in transit (e.g., virtual private network [VPN] appliances, content filtering (anti-phishing, anti-spam, and antivirus), and content blocking (e.g., Universal Resource Locator [URL] filtering/reverse proxy). This section focuses solely on the firewalls offered by these companies.

# PIX

Cisco PIX firewalls offer world–class security and high levels of performance and reliability, and have been a part of enterprise and service provider networks since 1995. Cisco PIX firewalls fit into a wide range of environments, from small office/home office (SOHO) environments to large enterprises and service providers. With support for complex protocols, the latest VPN technologies, and intrusion detection features, PIX firewalls are leaders in the market and have the widest deployment of any firewall.

## *Introduction*

Cisco firewalls utilize a proprietary OS and command language. Version 7.0 of the PIX OS introduced some new features into the Cisco product line (e.g., switches and routers). One new feature is security zones within a single interface. In previous versions, security zones were limited to the number of physical network interfaces a device had. Now, a single interface can be split into several security zones. Active/active device failover is also an option; previously, only active/passive was offered.

Version 7.0 also introduced the Adaptive Security Device Manager (ASDM), which is a useful graphical tool used for managing the PIX. The actual physical device runs on flash memory so that the only moving parts are the fans. This improves the reliability of the PIX, because there are no hard drives to fail. Models 515 and higher are generally upgradeable, both in interface number and memory size.

## Tools & Traps...

### Command Line Interface (CLI) vs. Graphical User Interface (GUI)

While the GUI is attractive to many Windows and Mac administrators (and even some Linux administrators), ease of use is limited. The CLI provides the ability to enter a number of commands into a text file, confirm the order and configuration, copy and paste it into a command window, and execute all of them correctly the first time. In addition, reading the CLI flat file configuration is much easier than searching through various windows, and it is searchable. Where did I use this particular Internet Protocol (IP) address? Which object-group did I use in this access list? These answers are much easier to find in a text file.

**Continued**

A GUI can be very useful for moving access-list lines, or adding a single Internet Protocol (IP) or port to an object-group. The PIX GUI has an excellent interface for checking firewall statistics, complete with colored graphs indicating the device's health.

Both interfaces have their strong points. Don't disregard one for the other; learn them both. This applies to all firewalls with both interfaces, not just the PIX.

## Embedded OS

Many firewalls are based on general-purpose OSs, which means maintenance is required to ensure that the correct configuration is used and that the base OS is patched and secured. This requirement offers a higher long-term cost and the potential for security weaknesses.

An embedded OS is one where the OS is self-contained in the device and resident in Read-Only Memory (ROM). This involves reduced maintenance costs, and because no customizations or OS configurations are required, a single image is downloaded and stored to flash. There is little that can go wrong with the OS itself; you cannot accidentally leave an unnecessary service running, because the firewall's services are tuned to only those features appropriate for a security device.

Unlike appliances based on a general-purpose kernel such as Linux or Windows CE, the PIX is based on a hardened, specialized OS specific to security services. This OS allows for kernel simplification, which supports explicit certification and validation. The PIX OS has been tested for vendor certifications such as International Computer Security Association (ICSA) Labs' Firewall Product Certification Criteria and the very difficult-to-obtain International Standards Organization (ISO) Common Criteria EAL4 certification. This testing allows for maximum assurance in deployment from Cisco's positive security engineering based on good commercial development practices.

Kernel simplification has advantages in throughput as well; the PIX 535 will support up to 256,000 simultaneous connections, far exceeding the capabilities of a UNIX- or Windows-based OS on equivalent hardware.

One key advantage to PIX firewall software is its command-line structure similarity to Cisco Internetwork Operating System (IOS). This means that firewall administrators have the ability to rapidly master management of the PIX, thereby reducing deployment costs and supporting management using Network Operations Center (NOC) personnel.

## Notes from the Underground…

### Cisco OS Upgrade/Update Warning

In addition to learning the new commands, it is vital to examine each release closely and determine if it is *necessary* to update. Read the release notes carefully and check to see if any of the fixes apply to your environment. Will new functionality be useful? Are security fixes needed to protect either your firewall or your internal network? Most importantly, search the Internet discussion groups for any potential problems with an update/upgrade.

I discovered through painful personal experience that PIX version 7.1(2) had a bug that dropped all network connectivity through the firewall on a regular basis, and then restored it over a period of about 5 minutes. Version 7.1(2)4 solved the problem, but it wasn't until after consultation with other PIX administrators and a call to Cisco's support team, that I found the updated version. Cisco's support team said I should have stayed with 7.0(2).

Cisco's first question regarding any support call concerning an update is, "Why did you update?" If there isn't a security problem, the PIX is functioning, and you don't need the new functionality, don't apply an update.

## *The Adaptive Security Algorithm*

The heart of the PIX is the Adaptive Security Algorithm (ASA). The ASA is a mechanism used to determine if packets should be passed through the firewall if they are consistent with the information flow control policy implemented in the access control list (ACL) table. The PIX evaluates packet information against a developed state and decides whether to pass the packet. ASA allows traffic to flow from a higher security level to a lower security level, unless modified by access-list commands. More formally, the manual notes:

- No packets can traverse the PIX firewall without a connection and state.

- Outbound connections or states are allowed, except those specifically denied by ACLs. An outbound connection is one where the originator or client is on a higher security interface than the receiver or server.

- Inbound connections or states, except those specifically allowed, are denied access. An inbound connection or state is one where the originator or client is on a lower security interface or network than the receiver or server. Multiple exceptions can be applied to a single translation (xlate), which lets you permit access from an arbitrary machine, network, or any host on the Internet to the host defined by the xlate.

■ All Internet Control Message Protocol (ICMP) packets are denied unless specifically permitted.

■ All attempts to circumvent the previous rules are dropped. A message is generated and sent to a management device (e.g., local buffer, Simple Network Management Protocol (SNMP) trap, syslog, console), depending on the severity of the attempt and the local configuration. (Normal traffic may also trigger logging, again depending on configuration. At the highest debugging mode, every packet generates an alert.

## Damage & Defense …

### ICMP & the PIX

By default, the PIX will respond to a ping request sent directly to the outside interface. Best practices recommend turning this off with command:

```
Icmp deny any outside
```

Turning off the ICMP response denies access to a potential hacker. However, any decent hacker will figure out that your network has a firewall; what they will not know is the location or the IP address of the firewall.

## Advanced Protocol Handling

The PIX combines *stateful* packet filtering with advanced protocol handling with proxies via application inspection. Application inspection provides a tighter security model for that given protocol. Don't confuse an application inspection with an application proxy. Application inspection doesn't inspect packets for a specific application, but rather for compliance to the Internet Assigned Numbers Authority (IANA) standards for a particular protocol.

For example, if we configured an access list for SMTP, we could filter on port, source IP, and destination IP. When the SMTP inspection engine is used in conjunction with an access list, only the seven basic SMTP commands are allowed and restricted by the ACL. The inspection command also allows you to change the port assignment of the protocol. Using the above SMTP example, we would use port 8080 along with the default inspect SMTP (port 25). In pre-7.0 code, we used the **fixup** command; however, now we need to use two commands. The **class-map** command is used to name the mapping (i.e., SMTP-INSPECTION-8080) and the **match** command is used to specify the port, protocol, and port number:

```
PIX1(config)# class-map SMTP-INSPECTION-8080
PIX1(config-cmap)# match port tcp eq 8080
PIX1(config-cmap)# exit
PIX1(config)#
```

The final result in the configuration looks like this:

```
!
class-map SMTP-INSPECTION
match port tcp eq smtp 8080
class-map inspection_default
match default-inspection-traffic
!
```

Cisco PIX is now listening for SMTP traffic on port 8080 and port 25. You can also inspect a range of ports:

```
class-map RANGEOPORTS
match port tcp range 1024 1055
```

The class-map of RANGEOPORTS now matches from 1024 to 1055. Providing support for complex protocols is a distinguishing characteristic of the PIX. The default class-map includes File Transfer Protocol (FTP), Hypertext Transfer Protocol (HTTP), H.323, Remote Shell (RSH), Real Time Streaming Protocol (RTSP), Simple Mail Transfer Protocol (SMTP), Extended Simple Mail Transfer Protocol (ESMTP), Serial Interface Protocol (SIP), skinny, SNMP, Media Gateway Control Protocol (MGCP), ICMP, Network Basic Input/Output System (NetBIOS), Domain Name Server (DNS), and Structured Query Language Network (SQLNET).

Application support of this type is the real power of the PIX firewall. The PIX is more than just a gatekeeper passing or blocking packets; it understands the underlying protocol and actively rewrites the communications (e.g., enforcing RFCs, eliminating dangerous commands, and preventing the leakage of information) to provide the highest level of security available, consistent with application functionality. The following example uses the FTP inspection engine that is enabled by default, and tightens things up by restricting which FTP commands can be used through the PIX. This FTP inspection engine was configured the same as the previous one, but with a twist.

```
PIX1(config)# ftp-map FTP-INSPECTION
PIX1(config-ftp-map)# request-command deny ?
ftp-map mode commands/options:
appe Append to a file
cdup Change to parent of current directory
dele Delete a file at server site
get FTP client command for the retr command - retrieve a file
help Help information from server
mkd Create a directory
put FTP client command for the stor command - store a file
rmd Remove a directory
rnfr Rename from
rnto Rename to
site Specify server specific command
stou Store a file with a unique name
PIX1(config-ftp-map)# request-command deny dele
```

In this example, the delete function of FTP is blocked using the **request-command deny dele** command. You can also see the range of FTP commands options that can be blocked.

## VPN Support

An important aspect of network security is the confidentiality of information. Packets flowing along a network are much like postcards sent through the mail; if you don't want the world reading your messages, you have to take additional steps.

To achieve the kind of confidentiality offered on a private network, several approaches can be used. One uses encryption to conceal (encrypt) the information. An early standard, supported by Microsoft, is the Point-to-Point Tunneling Protocol (PPTP). Much like putting a letter inside a sealed envelope, this standard allows for encapsulating (and concealing) network traffic inside a transport header. A similar but more comprehensive approach is to use the layer 2 Tunneling Protocol (L2TP). This protocol is native to many Microsoft deployments; therefore, PIX support for PPTP and L2TP is an important element of the feature set.

In the fall of 1998, the Secure Internet Protocol (IPSec) was published in RFC 2401. Cisco took the lead in IPSec implementation by coauthoring many of the IPSec RFCs and providing solutions for some of the stickier IPSec issues. Trying to use NAT with L2TP/IPSec is one of the biggest issues with VPNs. NAT rewrites the IP header, thereby defeating the purpose of L2TP/IPSec, which ensures the authenticity of the IP header. RFC 3193 details how NAT Traversal is used to allow User Datagram Protocol (UDP) encapsulation of the authenticated IP packet using port 4500.

The PIX is an excellent IPSec tunnel termination point. It has a wide range of interoperable standards and is used to configure preshared keys and Certificate Authority's (CA). Many companies use PIX as an integrated firewall/VPN termi-nator (particularly in SOHO environments), and as a stand-alone VPN terminator in conjunction with another (dedicated) firewall. By using PIX, remote offices can con-nect securely to a central point or to each other. Instead of incurring high costs, a VPN can be configured between two PIX firewalls with all information traversing the VPN encrypted and authenticated, making it nearly impossible for someone to sniff the wire and steal the data.

One of the PIX's best features is VPN performance. The simplicity of the PIX firewall appliance makes it a sound choice for VPN termination in many enterprise and carrier-class environments.

## URL Filtering

URLs identify user-friendly addresses on the World Wide Web (WWW). The PIX firewall supports URL filtering by intercepting a request and validating its permissi-bility against a database located on a N2H2 or Websense server. The N2H2 server can run Linux (*www.n2h2.com/products/bess.php?os=lnx&device=pix*) or Microsoft Windows (*www.n2h2.com/products/bess.php?os=win&device=pix*); the Websense server can use these platforms or be installed on a Solaris server (*www.websense.com/prod-ucts/integrations/ciscoPIX.cfm*).

URL filtering provides the means to apply and enforce an acceptable use policy for Internet browsing, as well as to capture and analyze how personnel use the Internet. The servers provide reporting capabilities so that you can determine if the policy is being followed.

## NAT

NAT is a key feature of the Cisco PIX. Interestingly, the PIX was originally created by a company called Network Translations Inc., and its first role was performing address translation

PIX Version 7 also supports transparent mode, which is a special mode where the PIX doesn't address translation, but still separates the network into secure and insecure areas. The IP address space is flat and there is no private network.

A single interface can be subdivided into several logical areas known as *security contexts*, each with a different security level. This is known as multiple context mode, and makes it possible to have more security areas than interfaces. Transparent mode and multiple context mode are generally used together. For a complete discussion on security contexts and how to configure them, go to *www.cisco.com/en/US/products/ps6120/products_configuration_guide_chapter09186a0080450b90.html.*

## High Availability

The three fundamental concepts of information security are confidentiality, integrity, and availability. The PIX addresses the availability by providing a robust, fault-tolerant environment: if an error or failure occurs, alerts are triggered, thereby allowing corrective actions to be taken.

The term High Availability (HA) usually refers to hardware fault tolerance. Obviously, a firewall is a critical piece of equipment: to effectively perform its function, it is placed in the middle of multiple data streams. Cisco hardware is very high quality, and the PIX has no moving parts (except the cooling fans). Nonetheless, problems will occur; even the best-made equipment fails. HA is a device configuration that is used to ensure that isolated failure of the hardware does not bring down your network.

To achieve high availability requires multiples of hardware. In this case, two identical PIX firewalls are configured exactly the same and maintain communications between themselves. Loss of these special communications equates to a failure, allowing corrective actions to occur automatically. If one firewall in the pair fails, the other transparently picks up the traffic, and alarm messages are sent to the network management console.

HA can be configured in several ways. The simplest and least expensive way is through a serial cable, which is provided with the purchase of a failover license. Alternately, a LAN interface can be dedicated to the failover process. With the failover cable, hello packets containing the number of bytes seen by the interfaces are transmitted between the two boxes; if the values differ, failover occurs. With the LAN interface, full state information is transmitted so that in the event of a failover, the Transmission Control Protocol (TCP) sessions can keep running without reinitialization. PIX 7.0 also allows firewalls to run in active/active mode, enabling the ability to balance some of the traffic across a pair of firewalls.

## PIX Hardware

The PIX has many different configuration models to ensure that a product is suitable to different environments. The requirements of a SOHO user are different from a service provider. Cisco provides various classes with different price points to ensure optimum product placement.

Five models are currently supported: the 501, the 506E, the 515E, the 525, and the 535. However, there are three models that you may see deployed in enterprise environments: the 515, the 525, and the 535. As it turns out, these are the three models that the new 7.0 code runs on. Table 4.1 shows the vital characteristics of each model.

**NOTE**

At the time of this writing, version 7.0 code does not run on the SOHO models i.e., the 501 and 506E models: nor are there plans to support version 7.0 OS on these two models.

- **PIX 501** The PIX 501 is the basic entry model for the PIX line, with a fixed hardware configuration. It has a four-port 10/100Mbps switch for inside connectivity, and a single 10/100Mbps interface for connecting to the Internet upstream device (such as cable modem or Digital Subscriber Line [DSL] router). It provides 3 megabits per second (Mbps), throughput on a Data Encryption Standard (DES) IPSec connection, which satisfies most SOHO requirements. The base license is a 10-user license with 3Data Encryption Standard (3DES)

- **DES IPSec** There is an optional 50-user upgrade and/or 3DES VPN support. There is also an unlimited user count version available. The 501 is based on a 133 MHz AMD SC520 processor with 16 MB of RAM and 8 MB of flash. There is a console port, a full-/half-duplex RJ45 10BaseT port for the outside, and an integrated, auto-sensing, auto-MDIX 4 port RJ45 10/100 switch for the inside.

**Table 4.1** PIX Model Characteristics

| Model | Processor Type | Interfaces | Maximum Support | Failover Throughput | Clear-Text Available Throughput | VAC RAM Memory | 3DES |
|---|---|---|---|---|---|---|---|
| 501 | 133MHz AMD SC520 | 2 | No | 8Mbps | No | 3 Mbps | 16 Mb |
| 506E | 300MHz Intel Celeron | 2 | No | 20Mbps | No | 16 Mbps | 32 MB |
| 515E | 443MHz Intel Celeron | 6** | Yes | 188Mbps | Yes | 63 Mbps* | 64 MB** |
| 525 | 600MHz Intel PIII | 8 | Yes | 360Mbps | Yes | 70 Mbps* | 25 6MB** |
| 535 | 1GHz Intel PIII | 10 | Yes | 1Gbps | Yes | 100 Mbps* | 1 GB** |
| FWSM | No | 25600 VLANS | | | Yes | 5.5Gps | NA    1 Gb |

\* Maximum 3DES throughput is achieved with the VPN Accelerator.

\*\* Maximum requires the unrestricted license.

- **PIX 506E** The 506E product is an enhanced version of the 506. The chassis' are similar, but the 506E has a beefier central processing unit (CPU), a quieter fan, and a new power supply. The CPU is a 300 MHz Intel Celeron, and the random-access memory (RAM) and flash are of the same capacity as the original 506. Clear-text throughput has been increased to 100Mbps (wire speed), and 3DES throughput has been increased to 16 Mbps. Licensing on the 506E (and 506) is provided in single, unlimited-user mode. The only extra license you may need is the 3DES license. The 506E has one console port and two RJ45 10BaseT ports, one for the outside and one for the inside.

- **PIX 515E** The 515E replaced the 515 in May 2002. It has a higher-performing 433MHz Intel Celeron and an increasing base firewall performance, and is intended for the enterprise core of small-to medium-sized businesses. The 515E can offload the arithmetic load of DES computation from the OS to a dedicated VPN accelerator card (VAC+), delivering up to 135Mbps 3DES throughput and 2,000 VPN tunnels. The licensing is similar: a restricted license limits you to three interfaces and no failover, whereas an unrestricted license has the memory upgrade, the VAC+, and up to six interfaces.

  The chassis is a 1 Unit (1U) pizza-box, which is intended for rack mounting. The most important difference between the 506E and the 515E is that the 515E chassis is hardware-configurable. It provides a slot for an additional single-port or four-port Fast Ethernet (FE) interface, allowing for an inside port, an outside port, and up to four additional service networks. The licensing is flexible, allowing enterprises to purchase only what they need. The restricted license limits the number of interfaces to three and does not support HA. The unrestricted license allows for an increase in RAM (from 32MB to 128MB) and up to six interfaces, together with failover capability.

- **PIX 525** The PIX 525 is designed for large enterprise- or small-service provider environments. The 525 supports three single- or four-port 10/100 FE cards, or three single-port fiber channel gigabit Ethernet cards. Performance tells the story: The 525 with its 600MHz Intel Pentium III boasts 330Mbps clear-text throughput and, with the VPN+ accelerator card, 145Mbps of 3DES IPSec tunnel traffic.

  As with the other models, licensing is based on interface counts and failover. The restricted license limits the PIX 525 to 128MB of RAM and six interfaces. The unrestricted license bumps RAM to 512MB, allows up to eight interfaces, and supports failover. As before, 3DES licensing is separate, if desired.

- **PIX 535** The PIX 535 is the top-of-the-line model, suitable for service provider environments. Performance is the key: up to 1.7Gbps clear-text throughput, half a million simultaneous connections, and 7000 connection initialization/teardowns per second. With the VAC+, you can get 425Mbps 3DES throughput, with up to 2,000 simultaneous security associations (VPN tunnels).

  In terms of hardware, the PIX 535 is based on a 1GHz Intel Pentium III, with up to 1GB of RAM. It has a 16MB flash and 256K cache running at 1GHz, as well as a dual 64-bit 66MHz PCI system bus. In terms of interfaces, the 535 supports the installation of additional network interfaces via four 66 Mhz/64-bit and five 33 MHz/32-bit Peripheral Component Interconnect (PCI) expansion slots. The slots support expansion cards including single-port FE, four-port FE and single-port Gigabit Ethernet cards. The 535 is also the only model to support redundant power supplies.

- **Cisco ASA 5500 Series Firewall Edition** Recently, Cisco introduced a new line of firewall appliances called the ASA Series. These new firewall appliances build on the PIX technology and add a new features including enterprise-wide management and monitoring tools, and a modular design that permits easy integration with new sister products. The other products in the ASA line are VPN Edition Security Service Modules (SSMs), which are designed for secure communications between remote locations. The IPS Edition is designed for application-level packet inspection and intrusion detection, and the Anti-X Edition is designed for virus protection. The series is comprised of four models (using 64MB flash memory) for the OS, configuration storage, support application layer filtering, and layer 2 transparent mode.

  The following are used throughout:

  - **Security Services Card (SSC)** A lower-end implementation of a Security Services Module (SSM).

  - **SSM** (see above).

  - **Advanced Inspection and Prevention Security Services Module (AIP-SSM)** An intrusion prevention service designed to stop malicious traffic, including worms and network viruses.

- **Content Security and Control Security Services Module (CSC-SSM)** A threat protection and content control product designed to be placed at the Internet edge, providing antivirus, anti-spyware, file blocking, anti-spam, anti-phishing, URL blocking and filtering, and content filtering.

- **4 Gigabit Ethernet Security Services Module (4GE-SSM)**

- **Power over Ethernet (PoE)** The ability for the LAN-switching infrastructure to provide power over a copper Ethernet cable to an endpoint such as an IP telephone.

- **ASA 5505** Designed for the SOHO/Enterprise Teleworker, the 5505 provides a maximum throughput of 150Mbps with 100 Mbps during 3DES VPN connectivity. 256MB of RAM supports the series standard 64MB flash memory. There are eight 10/100 ports that support three VLANs. There is an SSC slot, which will be supported in the future. No SSMs are supported. While active/passive failover is supported, it is stateless; therefore, any existing connections will be lost.

- **ASA 5510** This model is targeted to small businesses and enterprises. 300Mbps standard throughput and 170Mbps VPN throughput raise this above the 5505. More significantly, this model supports up to 50 10/100 ports with one dedicated out-of-band management port. It also supports up to 25 VLANs. This and all subsequent models share support for active/active stateful failover and the CSC-SSM, AIP-SSM, and 4GE-SSM modules.

- **ASA 5520** Targeted to small enterprises, this model provides up to 45Mbps standard throughput and 225Mbps VPN throughput. This is the first in the series to support four gigabit ports and up to 100 VLANs, and memory is increased to 512MB. This and all subsequent models support VPN clustering and load balancing.

- **ASA 5540** Medium-sized enterprises would benefit from this model, boasting 650Mbps standard throughput and 325Mbps VPN. Memory is up to 1024MB and 200 VLANs are supported in this and the next model.

- **ASA 5550** This model is strictly for large enterprises. While it has a maximum throughput of 1200Mbps and a VPN throughput of 425Mbps, it does not support any plug-in modules. Instead, separate appliances must be purchased to enhance the filtering capabilities. It also supports up to eight gigabit interfaces and the memory is 4096MB.

## Software Licensing and Upgrades

The PIX uses software licensing to enable or disable features within the PIX OS. Although the hardware is common to all platforms (except certain licenses that can ship with additional memory or hardware accelerators) and the software is common, features differ depending on the activation key.

The activation key allows you to upgrade features without acquiring new software, although the process is similar. The activation key is computed by Cisco, depending on what you have ordered and your serial number, which is different for each piece of PIX hardware. The serial number is based on the flash; thus, if you replace the flash, you have to replace the activation key.

The activation key enables feature-specific information such as interfaces, HA, and type of encryption.

For more information about the activation key, use the **show version** command, which provides code version information, hardware information, and activation key information. Alternately, the **show activation-key** command provides this printout:

```
PIX1# show activation-key
Serial Number: 809411563
Running Activation Key: 0xf9202218 0x4c4b6b1f 0x253532cd 0x8c5e626b
Licensed features for this platform:
Maximum Physical Interfaces : 10
Maximum VLANs : 100
Inside Hosts : Unlimited
Failover : Active/Active
VPN-DES : Enabled
VPN-3DES-AES : Enabled
Cut-through Proxy : Enabled
Guards : Enabled
URL Filtering : Enabled
Security Contexts : 2
GTP/GPRS : Disabled
VPN Peers : Unlimited
This platform has an Unrestricted (UR) license.
The flash activation key is the SAME as the running key.
PIX1#
```

Updating the activation key in version 7.0 of the PIX OS couldn't be simpler. The command **activation-key** sets the key to the new value. Note that activation *tuples* are in hexadecimal, are case insensitive, and don't require you to start the numbers with 0x. Thus, the previously mentioned machine could be set with:

```
PIX1(config)# activation-key 75fe7c49 c08b4082 08979930 e4b4c4b0 004b4ccd
```

## Licensing

Generally, Cisco PIX licensing falls into one of four types: restricted, unrestricted, failover, and failover active/active. Restricted and unrestricted licenses apply to all Cisco PIX firewalls except the 501 and the 506, and the failover applies to only the 515, the 525, and the 535. The 501 and 506 do not have the required interfaces for the failover. With the release of the PIX 7.0 code, the failover method has added an active/active feature to its active and standby model.

Various pieces make up the licensing or feature set for the Cisco PIX. In Table 4.2 there are several key features of each license type and how they differ between the licenses.

**Table 4.2** PIX 500 Series Licensing

| PIX 515/515E | Restricted | UR (Unrestricted) | FO (Failover) | FO-AA (Failover Active/Active) |
|---|---|---|---|---|
| Security contexts | No support | 2 Default up to 5 | 2 Default | 2 default up to 5 |
| Failover | No support | Active/Standby Active/Active | Active/Standby Active/Active | Active/Standby |
| Standby | | | | |
| Max VLANs | 10 | 25 | 25 | 25 |
| Concurrent connections | 49K | 130K | 130K | 130K |
| Max. physical interfaces | 3 | 6 | 6 | 6 |
| Encryption | None default Base DES or 3DES/AES | None default Base DES or 3DES/AES | None default Base DES or 3DES/AES | None default Base DES or 3DES/AES |

**Continued**

**Table 4.2 continued** PIX 500 Series Licensing

| PIX 515/515E | Restricted | UR (Unrestricted) | FO (Failover) | FO-AA (Failover Active/Active) |
|---|---|---|---|---|
| Min RAM | 64MB | 128 MB | | 128 MB |

| PIX 525 | Restricted | UR (Unrestricted) | FO (Failover) | FO AA (Failover Active/Active) |
|---|---|---|---|---|
| Security contexts | No support | 2 or 5,10,20,50 | 2 or 5,10,20,50 | 2 or 5,10,20,50 |
| Failover | No support | Active Standby Active/Active | Active Standby | Active Active/Active |
| Max VLANS | 25 | 100 | 100 | 100 |
| Concurrent connections | 110K | 280K | 280K | 280K |
| Max. physical interfaces | 6 None Base DES 3DES/AES | 10 None Base DES 3DES/AES | 10 None Base DES 3DES/AES | 10 None Base DES 3DES/AES |
| Min RAM | 128 MB | 512 MB | 512 MB | 512 MB |

| PIX 535 | Restricted | UR (Unrestricted) | FO-AA (Failover) | FO-AA (Failover Active/Active) |
|---|---|---|---|---|
| Security contexts | No support | 2,5,10,20, 50,100 | 2,5,10,20, 50,100 | 2,5,10,20,50,100 |
| Failover | | No support Active/Active | Active Standby | Active Standby Active/Active |
| Max VLANs | 50 | 200 | 200 | 200 |
| Concurrent connections | 250K | 500K | 500K | 500K |
| Max physical interfaces | 8 | 14 | 14 | 14 |
| Encryptions | None Base DES 3DES/AES | None Base DES 3DES/AES | None Base DES 3DES/AES | None Base DES 3DES/AES |
| Min RAM | 512 MB | 1024 MB | 1024 MB | 1024 MB |

Note that new appliances 5505, 5510, 5540, and 5550 have very similar licensing to the previous 515, 525, and 535 series. The primary difference is that "bundles" are now offered, comprising different licensing features and different interface configurations. In all cases, a single model can be upgraded to a higher bundle by purchasing a new license and additional interfaces.

## Management Access

Management access is used to access the Cisco PIX for configuration and management. The Cisco PIX is very flexible. You can connect through a console port and a simple eight-wire cable, or through Telnet, Secure Shell (SSH), or Hypertext Transfer Protocol Secure (HTTPS) using a browser. This provides a lot of options for configuring the Cisco PIX management access in a secure manner based on your own situation.

- **Console Port** The default mechanism for talking to a PIX is via the console port. This is the connection you use to configure the PIX the first time, or if you cannot access the PIX via a network port. Some devices have old DB9 connectors (i.e., nine-pin D-subminiature connectors similar to those found on the back of many PCs). The newer devices use the Cisco standard RJ45 connector, similar to those used with most Cisco routers and switches. In each case, an appropriate cable is provided with your equipment and generally connects to the DB9 serial port on your PC. Any terminal program such as TeraTerm or Windows HyperTerminal can be used to connect to the PIX.

- **Telnet** Telnet is the antiquated way to access a network device. Even though the Cisco PIX supports Telnet access it should never be used. Disable Telnet entirely by removing any existing Telnet command using:

```
no telnet [ip address] [interface]
```

Then set the Telnet timeout to one second:

```
telnet timeout 1
```

Telnet is strongly discouraged in favor of using SSH, which is encrypted.

- **SSH** The preferred method of connecting over a network to the Cisco PIX firewall. SSH is a suite of encrypted applications that replaces Telnet, copy, and FTP with SSH, SCP, and SCP. SSH uses port 22 and is not enabled by default. To enable SSH, a public/private DES or 3DES key must be generated and the interfaces must be configured to permit SSH. For full details on using and enabling SSH on the Cisco PIX firewall, please see Cisco documentation.

All three of the above interfaces use the CLI. In the case of the Cisco PIX firewall, the command line is a flexible way to configure the Cisco PIX. With the new 7.0 code, it is easier if you already know the Internetwork Operating System (IOS) command structure, because many old PIX commands were updated to reflect the IOS command line structure. In rare cases, the command line is the only way to configure certain features that the ASDM does not yet support.

The PIX firewall builds help functionality into the CLI. At any point, typing **?** will help you complete your commands. In addition, "man page" or "manual page" functionality is built in (e.g., if you want to ping something and forgot the syntax, type **ping ?**. If you don't remember what the ping command does, type **help ping**. This provides usage, description, and syntax for the command).

■ **Web** The Cisco PIX can be managed by a Web interface called the ASDM, which replaces the PIX Device Manager (PDM). The new ASDM can be accessed using HTTPS or using a Windows application installed on the management console. The Web-based interface is Java-based, so any Java-enabled Web browser can be used to manage the PIX, including Firefox, Internet Explorer, Mozilla, Opera, and Safari. The installed application is downloaded directly from the PIX. The option to use Java or the downloaded application (if running a Windows-based browser) is presented when you connect to *https://[firewall IP address]*. Figure 4.1 shows the home page of the ASDM using Java and FireFox.

# Juniper NetScreen Firewalls

Juniper Networks delivers an integrated firewall and VPN solution called the NetScreen firewall. This firewall product line has several tiers of appliances and systems, which allow you to choose the right hardware for your network.

**Figure 4.1** Running ASDM in the FireFox Web Browser

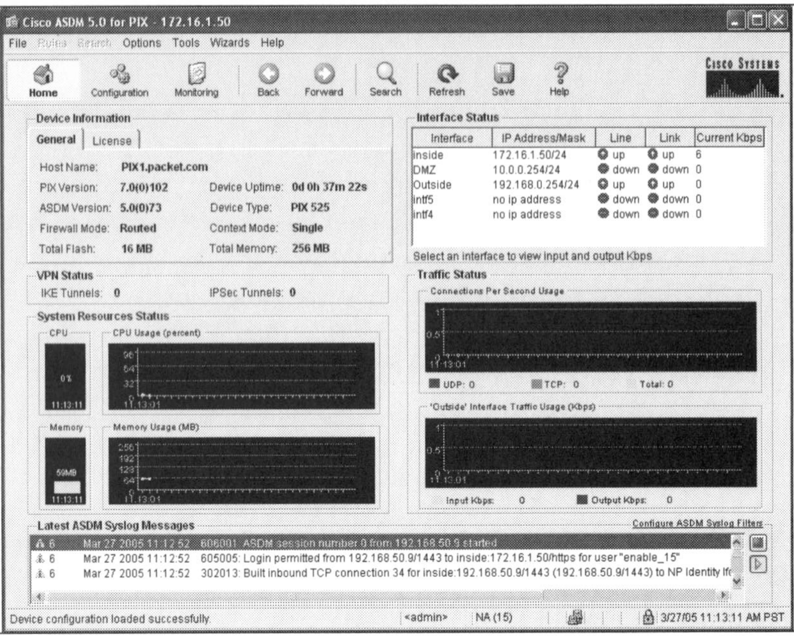

## Introduction

NetScreen is the fastest growing firewall product line on the market today, and has clinched the number two spot among the worldwide security appliance market. The NetScreen product line is robust and competitive, and is now part of Juniper Networks. As of April 16, 2004, Juniper Networks completed its purchase of NetScreen for four billion dollars, which it chose to purchase in order to enter the enterprise market. Previously, Juniper Networks focused on the carrier class market for high-end routers; however, now it is attempting to compete directly with Cisco for the number one firewall appliance vendor and the number one router vendor in the world.

The NetScreen firewall appliance is Juniper Network's firewall/VPN solution. Throughout this section, the firewall is referred to as a NetScreen firewall. This product line provides integrated firewall and IPSec VPN solutions in a single appliance.

## Core Technologies

- **Ground-up Design** The NetScreen hardware architecture was developed to be a purpose-built device. Developed from the ground up to provide exceptional throughput, the firewall devices provide an amazing device that leads the pack in firewall design. Juniper Network's NetScreen firewall product line is a layered architecture, designed to provide optimal performance for critical security applications. The top layer of the NetScreen firewall architecture is the integrated security application, which integrated with the OS to provide a hardened security solution. The integrated security application provides all of the VPN, firewalling, Denial of Service (DoS), and traffic management.

- **Dedicated OS** The second layer in the NetScreen firewall platform is the OS. The OS for the NetScreen firewall product is called ScreenOS, which is designed as a Real-time Operating System (RTOS). An RTOS is defined as an OS that can respond to external world events in a time frame defined by the external world. Because only one task can run at a time for each CPU, the idea is to minimize the time it takes to set up and begin executing a task. A large challenge for RTOS is memory allocation. Allocating memory takes time, which can slow down the OS from executing a task. ScreenOS reallocates memory to ensure that it has enough memory to provide a sustained rate of service. Some people argue that ScreenOS is more secure than open source OSs, because the general public cannot review the source code for vulnerabilities. The OS on a NetScreen firewall provides services such as dynamic routing, HA, management, and the ability to virtualize a single device into multiple virtual devices.

- **High-speed Hardware** The third layer in the NetScreen architecture is the hardware components. The NetScreen firewalls are based on a custom-built architecture consisting of Application-Specific Integrated Circuit (ASIC) technology. ASIC is designed to perform a specific task at a higher performance level than a general-purpose processor. ASIC connects over a high-speed bus interface to the core processor of the firewall unit; a reduced instruction set computer (RISC) CPU. The firewall connects all of its components together with a high-speed multi-bus configuration. The bus connects each ASIC with a RISC processor, Synchronous Dynamic Random Access Memory (SDRAM), and the network interfaces. An ASIC is a chip designed for a single purpose, which allows that single purpose to be performed much faster than if you were using a general-purpose microprocessor.

- **Stateful Inspection** The NetScreen firewall core is based on the stateful inspection technology. Stateful inspection provides a connection-oriented security model by verifying the validity of every connection while providing a high-performance architecture.

- **Deep Inspection** The firewall platform also contains additional technologies to increase your network's security. First, the products support deep inspection. This technology allows you to inspect traffic at the application level to look for attacks. This can help prevent the next worm from attacking your Web servers, or someone from trying to send illegal commands to your SMTP server. The inspection technology includes a regularly updated database as well as the ability to create your own regular expression-based signatures.

Deep inspection technology is the next step in the evolution of firewalls. It allows you to inspect traffic at the application layer, relying on regular expressions (Regex) to determine what content in a packet is malicious (e.g., if a worm on the Internet attempts to exploit your Internet Information Server (IIS) Web server vulnerabilities by sending a specific string of characters to your Web server, a custom signature can be written to identify that attack string. By applying the custom signature to a policy, the traffic in that policy would be inspected for that specific string).

A smaller network may not have the same management needs and financial means to gainfully install an Intrusion and Detection and Protection (IDP) device. The integration of application-level inspection may be a better fit. Application-level scanning in an integrated device can also be used to provide a second level of protection to your network by blocking specific attacks.

## Damage & Defense ...

### Application Level Inspection

Firewalls have conventionally focused on layer 3 and layer 4 filtering, which means that the connection is only filtered based on IP addresses and TCP and UDP ports and the options set at those layers. This can prevent systems from accessing your servers. What do you do when an attacker uses your firewall configuration against you?

The attacker passes right through your allowed port and manipulates your Web application without your detection. Now, even though your Web server is on a separate demilitarized zone (DMZ) than your database server, the attacker uses your Web application to access the secured database and take your customers' credit card information and identities. This type of attack goes on every day; however, many organizations are not aware of this kind of threat. Talented individuals that understand Web applications and their designs can easily snake through your applications and extract data from your database.

**Continued**

Does this mean that you have to disable access to your Web server and dismantle your e-commerce efforts? Of course not. You must, however, use security products that provide application-level inspection to attempt to identify these attacks. The best method is to have a penetration test done on your application to determine what type of vulnerabilities your applications may have. Next, begin implementing products that can determine what are attacks and what is normal traffic. The deep inspection software integrated into the NetScreen firewall can help protect against many of the unstructured attacks that can be damaging to your Web server. However, structured attacks need a stronger tool such as the IDP to mitigate the risks of these attacks.

To make IDPs and the deep inspection technology work effectively, you need to tune them for your network. It can take a great deal of effort and time to ensure that your network is using these devices effectively. Sometimes, simple programming techniques can greatly enhance the security of your applications.

All of the appliances include the ability to create IPSec VPNs to secure your traffic. The integrated VPN technology has received both the Common Criteria certificate and the ICSA (*www.icsalabs.com*) Firewall certificate, which means that the IPSec VPN technologies have good cross-compatibility and standards compliance. Juniper Networks also offers two client VPN solutions to pair with the NetScreen firewall. The NetScreen-Remote provides the ability to create an IPSec connection to any NetScreen firewall or any IPSec-compliant device. The NetScreen-Security client creates IPSec tunnels and also includes a personal firewall to secure the end user's system.

The NetScreen firewall product line leverages the technologies of Trend Micro's industry-leading antivirus software, which allows you to scan traffic as it passes directly through the firewall, thus mitigating the risks of viruses.

## Zones

Zones are the core of the NetScreen architecture and one of the unique features of the Netscreen firewall series. A zone is defined as a *logical* area, and several types of zones can exist on a NetScreen firewall. The most commonly used zone is the *security* zone, which is the segment of the network space where security measures are applied. These measures are used to determine the different network locations assigned to a NetScreen firewall. The two most commonly used security zones are *trust* and *untrust*. The *trust* zone is assigned to the internal local area network [LAN] and the *untrust* zone is assigned to the Internet. The name of the zone is arbitrary, but is used to help the administrator determine what the zone is used for. Security zones are a key component in policy configuration. A security zone can encompass any number of physical or virtual interfaces, including VPN tunnels, which permit an administrator to join the Finance or Marketing departments in various subnets and locations under a single protection policy. The Finance department in the main office, the Cashier's office, and the Finance department located in a remote city connected via VPN, can all be in the same zone with the same rule set. If you add a second remote office connected by a second VPN to the zone, and the rule set is automatically applied—no further configuration is necessary. Juniper Networks is the only company that provides this type of functionality, which is what sets the NetScreen apart from other firewalls and provides a unique functionality that makes administration much easier.

Another zone type is the *tunnel* zone, which is used in conjunction with tunnel interfaces. Tunnel zones are defined as a logical segment where the VPN tunnel interface is bound.

The last type of zone is a *function* zone, which specifies that an interface is used only for management traffic and will not allow traffic to be routed over it. A function zone is defined as a physical or logical entity that performs a specific function. The use of zones allows you to clearly define the separation between two or more areas.

## *Virtual Routers*

A firewall is nothing more than a glorified router. It essentially sends traffic from one location to another, determining the best path based on its routing table. What makes a firewall different from a standard router is its ability to allow or deny traffic. The NetScreen firewall provides simple routing services and more. A normal device that uses IP has a single routing table, which contains all of the known or learned routes. A NetScreen device uses a virtual router (VR), which are most important in the high-end firewalls such as the NetScreen 200 series and above.

A VR is a logical construct within a NetScreen device that provides multiple routing tables on the same device. The VR has many uses. VRs are bound to zones and the zones are bound to interfaces. The NetScreen router functions much like a standard firewall device with one routing table. However, using two separate routing tables gives you the ability to separate your routing domain (e.g., if you ran Open Shortest Path First (OSPF) internally and Border Gateway Protocol (BGP) externally, you would have two separate routing domains, which would allow you to securely separate your internally trusted routes with your externally untrusted routes. For an in-depth discussion of Netscreen VRs, see the Juniper documentation at *www.juniper.net/techpubs/software/erx/junose72/swconfig-system-basics/html/virtual-router-config2.html#58658*.

# VPN

Juniper's NetScreen firewall supports all of the standard elements you expect on a VPN device, including:

- Internet key exchange (IKE)
- Authentication header (AH)
- Encapsulating security payload (ESP)
- Tunnel mode
- Transport mode
- Aggressive mode
- Quick mode
- Main mode
- Message Digest Algorithm 5 (MD5)
- Secure Hash Algorithm 1 (SHA-1)
- DES
- 3DES
- AES-128
- Perfect forward secrecy

Juniper provides several options when configuring a firewall on a NetScreen appliance. There are two different methodologies that can be used: a *route-based* VPN or a *policy-based* VPN.

A policy-based VPN allows for the creation of a VPN through a policy or rule, which gives you a simplified method to create VPNs.

A route-based VPN uses a special type of virtual interface, called a *tunnel* interface, to connect via a VPN. This virtual interface allows you to provide special types of services (e.g., run routing protocols between two virtual interfaces; run OSPF, which requires two devices be directly connected). This would not normally be possible over the Internet, but if you create a route-based VPN between two NetScreen firewalls, the OSPF limitation is removed because of the special virtual interface.

# Interface Modes

By default, a NetScreen firewall operates initially as a router. It allows each physical interface to use an IP address, thereby allowing traffic to be forwarded between each interface. A NetScreen firewall, however, is not limited to this traditional type of firewall configuration.

A NetScreen firewall allows its physical interfaces to run in a special mode called *transparent* mode. Transparent mode allows you to put the NetScreen firewall into layer 2 mode, which operates at the network layer, allowing a NetScreen firewall to act as a switch while still providing normal firewall filtering. This serves many purposes. (e.g., if you have a flat network with one subnet and no routing, but still want to separate your network and provide security for a few critical devices, you can install a NetScreen firewall in transparent mode).

## Policies

A *policy* is a statement that allows or denies traffic based on a defined set of specifications. Every brand of firewall has a version of policies; however, the base specifications include the source IP address, destination IP address, source zone, destination zone, and service or port. There are three types of policies: *intrazone, interzone*, and *global*. By default, there is an invisible global policy that denies any traffic from passing through the NetScreen. Therefore, if the traffic is not implicitly allowed by another policy, it is denied. Creating policies allows you to perform one of three actions on the traffic: *allow, deny*, or *tunnel*.

You *allow* traffic when you let it pass through the firewall. You *deny* traffic if you want to prevent it from passing through the firewall. Finally, you *tunnel* traffic when you want to permit traffic and put the traffic into a VPN tunnel. Each NetScreen device has a limited number of policies, which is a license restriction and a capacity restriction. You cannot create new policies once you reach the maximum amount of policies per device. Juniper Networks does this to ensure that the performance numbers are specified for the specification sheets. Other firewalls do not impose this limit; it is up to you to configure your policies to optimize performance. It would not make sense to allow a low-end 5-GT appliance to run 40,000 policies, only to have the performance be at 1Mbps. These restrictions are not modifiable and are on each platform. There are many different elements involved in configuring an advanced policy, including traffic shaping, user authentication, NAT, alarms, URL filtering, and scheduling.

Administering policies can be done from the Web User Interface (WebUI), the CLI, or the NetScreen Security Manager (NSM). Each method creates the same end result; however, performing each task is slightly different. On some competitive firewall products, using access lists can be frustrating because of the hassle of reordering, viewing, and managing them. When the NetScreen platform was designed, it was calculated with those hassles in mind. The WebUI of the Netscreen is often touted as the easiest to use in the industry.

## Management

The NetScreen firewall platform provides three management options:

- **CLI**  Provides the most granular control over the platform through straightforward interaction with the operation system (ScreenOS).

- **WebUI**  A streamlined Web-based application with a user-friendly interface that allows you to easily manage the NetScreen appliance. Both WebUI and CLI are consistent among all of the NetScreen firewall products (i.e., once you learn one firewall model, you can easily apply your knowledge to the other models in the NetScreen firewall product line.

- **NSM**  This is a centralized enterprise class solution that allows you to manage your entire NetScreen firewall infrastructure. The NSM not only provides a central console to manage your firewalls, it also provides consolidated logging and reporting. This great option allows you to see all of your network's activity from a central location.

## The NetScreen Firewall Product Line

The NetScreen firewall product line has several tiers of products that span over its entire product line. One of the great things about the NetScreen firewall product line is that the configuration of each device remains similar, which allows you to configure each device the same. Every device supports the same three management options; the WebUI, CLI, and NSM configuration of each device is relatively similar. However, the higher up the firewall product line, the more ports and options are available.

Every firewall device is configured using the same methods, no matter what tier the device is in. Some vendors offer inconsistent configurations among their devices, but the NetScreen remains unvarying. The architecture on all of the platforms remains very similar, leveraging the power of a RISC processor and ASICs to provide a high-performance OS. Many familiar systems  (e.g., Intel-based Pentium systems) use the less efficient complex instruction set computer (CISC) processor. All of the devices use flash memory for the long-term storage option. None of the firewalls rely on hard disks.

The NetScreen-Security manager provides lasting storage for the firewall devices, eliminating the need for long-term storage on the devices for logs. You can also stream logs to a syslog server for storage.

In Table 4.3, you can see the layout of the product line from the low end to the high end. We concentrate on the hardware and feature differences between the many models. For more information, visit the Juniper Web site *(www.juniper.net/products/glance/)* for the latest numbers.

**Table 4.3** The NetScreen Device Architecture

| Integrated Security Application |
| :--- |
| VPN |
| Firewall |
| Denial of Service protection |
| Traffic Management |

| Security Specific Real Time OS |
| :--- |
| Dynamic Routing |
| High Availability |
| Virtualization |
| Centralized Management |

| RISC CPU | Memory | ASIC | Interfaces |
| :--- | :--- | :--- | :--- |

| Purpose-Built Hardware Platform |
| :--- |

## Tools & Traps...

## Choosing the Right Tool for the Job

If you plan to purchase a NetScreen device, make sure you examine your specific needs; most of the devices cannot be upgraded. When purchasing a Juniper Networks device, realistically you should look at the life of the product over the next three to five years, which will provide the right amount of growth for your network. Many companies never need more than the NetScreen-208 product. Providing eight total interfaces and up to seven hundred megabits per second throughput, it can suffice for most networks.

In many lower-end networks where there is just an internal LAN and an Internet connection, four interfaces and a lower amount of throughput are required. Even the lowest end NetScreen firewall device can easily handle a hefty DS3 circuit to the Internet providing 45 Mbps.

**Continued**

This said, choosing a firewall can be hard work. Because of the low upgrade ability and large selection, many people looking at a NetScreen might think twice. However, with careful planning, the proper selection of a device can be easily accomplished.

- **NetScreen-Remote Client**—NetScreen-Remote VPN Client and NetScreen-Remote Security ClientRemote access to company resources is a requirement for most organizations. Company resources have to be accessible away from the office in a secure manner. For remote access security, Juniper Networks offers NetScreen-Remote VPN Client and NetScreen-Remote Security Client, which provide an easy-to-use interface to configure and connect to IPSec gateway endpoints. You are not limited to client access of the NetScreen-based VPN firewalls; it is capable of connecting to any IPSec gateway. NetScreen-RemoteVPN Client also supports the Extended Authentication (XAuth) protocol. XAuth supports distribution of IP address and DNS settings to a virtual interface on the client. The remote VPN client is capable of supporting up to 100 concurrent IPSec VPN tunnels. The NetScreen-Remote VPN and Security clients provide easy, secure access to your mobile workforce. The NetScreen-Remote Security client has an integrated client firewall to protect remote user systems, and allows end users to connect securely to the enterprise network over IPSec. The client interface allows user's to quickly configure a VPN connection. It also provides administrator's with the ability to create, export, and deploy a VPN policy to all remote users. Another feature of the security client is the integrated firewall. While not available natively on most OSs (Linux, Mac, and Windows), this firewall allows you to protect the end user's system using centrally configured policies. This is especially handy for stand-alone machines that are not part of a managed domain such as Windows Active Directory (AD).

- **SOHO—NetScreen-Hardware Security Client and NetScreen 5GT** For remote locations or remote users that need a dedicated security appliance, the SOHO line of NetScreen firewall appliances provide enterprise-class security at a low-cost entry point. This product line has a small footprint, which is ideal for offices where space is at a premium.

  The *NetScreen-Hardware Security Client* is currently at the low end of NetScreen's firewall product line, and was designed as a hardware-based version of the remote software client. The Hardware Security Client can easily support the fastest residence-installed broadband connection.

Protecting home users from viruses is easy with this device, because it includes Trend Micro's scan engine embedded directly into the device. This allows you to scan Post Office Protocol 3 (POP3), SMTP, and HTTP Web mail in real time to protect users from viruses. This is a great way to reduce infections on home machines and prevent infected home users from spreading viruses to the company's network. Deep inspection is supported to help protect against application-level attacks and vulnerabilities. The NetScreen-Hardware Security Client must be managed from a NetScreen Security Manager.

The NetScreen 5-GT is the answer to your needs if you want a low-end remote appliance. The only things low-end about this device are the price and the model number. Anti-phishing and anti-spyware are supported on the Juniper-Kaspersky Antivirus engine and standard antivirus filtering comes embedded. This device has five 10/100 Ethernet ports and comes in an Ethernet-only model, an Asymmetric Digital Subscriber Line (ADSL) model, and a wireless model, which allow two Internet-connected interfaces to provide redundant connectivity in case one Internet Service Provider (ISP) experiences a failure. HA Lite is an option where you can have two 5-GT's with configuration synchronization and maintain a connection if one of the devices fail. However, it doesn't allow you to fail all of your active sessions. All active sessions are lost when one device fails over to the backup device when using an HA Lite configuration.

- **Mid-Range—NetScreen–25 and NetScreen–50** The NetScreen-25 and NetScreen-50 are the next step up the NetScreen ladder. These devices are a perfect fit for branch and remote offices, or for medium- and small-size companies. The only difference between these two devices is the performance they provide. Both devices are physically identical. These devices and all higher level devices also provide deep inspection scanning. (In some cases, this is only an option with advanced licensing and not included in the baseline license.)

  The NetScreen-25 is the weaker of the two devices in the mid-range category. It has slower performance, but like the NetScreen-50, it has a total of four 10/100 Ethernet ports, a console port, and a modem port. The console port provides access for console CLI management. The modem port allows you to connect a modem for out-of-band management capabilities. The NetScreen-25 (and all devices upward) allows you to configure the network ports to your liking. This gives you total control over the network, providing for multiple configuration options. You can have four separate security zones for these interfaces. The NetScreen-25 device only allows for

HA Lite mode. In both models, an external Trend Micro antivirus server does the antivirus scanning.

The NetScreen-50 is the performer of the two devices in the mid-range category. With faster throughput, the NetScreen-50 device also allows for HA in active/passive mode. This mode provides for failover in case of a hardware failure; however, it would also failover all of your sessions for a seamless failover.

- **High-Range—NetScreen-204 and NetScreen-208** The NetScreen 200 series is the first model of high-end NetScreen features, which is the first series of devices designed that support an active/active HA configuration. This allows both of the NetScreen appliances in an HA cluster to be active at the same time, allowing for higher throughput and maximum capacity. This class of firewall is typically required for one of three reasons: it requires four or more interfaces; a higher throughput is needed on these devices; and, to take advantage of the advanced features available for the NetScreen-200 series.

  The NetScreen-204 provides double the performance of the NetScreen-50. Much like the other devices of the same form factor, this device provides four 10/100Base-T ports, as well as the console and modem ports for out-of-band management. This is the first platform that allows a function in active/passive mode or active/active mode. An external Trend Micro antivirus server does the antivirus scanning on both models.

  The NetScreen-208 comes with a similar one-rack unit form factor, but it is the first device to have over four physical interfaces. The NetScreen-208 has the capability to easily support an e-commerce type of deployment. This device provides eight 10/100Base-T ports. An additional feature of the 208 is the ability to use a Personal Computer Memory Card International Association (PCMCIA) CompactFlash card to back up your configuration. This model adds the active/active full mesh configuration to the active/passive and active/active configurations.

- **Enterprise Class —SSG-520 and SSG-550** If you are looking for high performance and HA, the Enterprise class of NetScreen products is where you should browse. Both systems are the first devices in the NetScreen firewall line to provide redundant power supplies. This is a great option when uptime is crucial. Both devices also have interchangeable interface modules, which allow you to have up to eight 10/100 base-T ports or four gigabit fiber ports. Presently, there is only support for fiber connections; copper gigabit ports are unsupported at this time.

The SSG-500 series are Enterprise class devices capable of providing a highly available firewall scenario. Redundant power supplies combined with redundant support components (e.g., fans) are essential when managing a network that requires 99 percent or better uptime. As far as HA modes go, the SSG-550 supports all three modes: active/passive, active/active, and active/active full mesh, while the SSG 520 only supports active/passive. When using a NetScreen device in HA mode, you must have ports dedicated to enable both a heartbeat and the passing of session synchronization information. The SSG-500 series provides these two dedicated ports.

The SSG-550 ships with a feature called Virtual Systems (VSYS0), which allows you to segment a device into several virtual systems. These virtual systems allow you to have a completely separate management domain provide virtual firewalls within the single physical device.

Finally, the 500 series is expected to have embedded antivirus, including anti-phishing and anti-spyware, in the second half of 2006, which will eliminate the need for an additional server to house the antivirus software.

- **Next Generation Enterprise Class—NetScreen-ISG 1000 and ISG 2000** The NetScreen Integrated Security Gateway 2000 or NetScreen ISG-2000 is Juniper Network's next generation firewall. This device is built on fourth-generation ASICs, and the chips are specialized for performing specific tasks. Its architecture is designed for more then just firewall security purposes, and it has four expansion ports that permit adding more interfaces. In the future, it will allow users to add products such as the NetScreen IDP to allow for application-level scanning of all traffic. The IDP module will be ASIC-based, and will provide excellent performance while scanning at the application layer.

  These devices have two important features that put them at the top of their class: enormous throughput and port density. The throughput of the Integrated Security Gateway (ISG) series is one of the highest in the industry. The NetScreen-ISG 2000's four expansion slots allow you to combine any of the following: four-port 10/100 Ethernet module, eight-port 10/100 Ethernet module, or a dual-port mini-Gigabit Interface Converter (GBIC) module to provide the exact interface configuration you require.

  In the advanced license model, the NetScreen-ISG 2000 supports the active/passive, active/active, and active/active full mesh HA configurations.

It can also support up to 50 virtual systems, 512,000 concurrent sessions, and 10,000 concurrent VPN tunnels.

■ **Carrier Class—NetScreen-5200 and NetScreen-5400** Welcome to the top of the NetScreen firewall product line. While impressive, these devices are only suitable for the most demanding environments. Both devices are nearly identical except for two things: port density and throughput. The NetScreen-5200 series appliance can have a maximum of eight mini-GBIC ports or two mini-GBIC ports and 24 10/100BaseT Ethernet ports. It has a maximum throughput of 4 gigabits per second firewall inspection.

The NetScreen-5400 has even more impressive performance and port density. This device can have either a maximum of 24 mini-GBIC ports, or six mini-GBIC ports and 72 10/100BaseT Ethernet ports.

For the most part, these two appliances have identical performance statistics. The NetScreen-5000 product line can support up to one million concurrent sessions. In addition, they can support up to 25,000 VPN tunnels, a total of 500 virtual systems, and up to 4,000 VLANs. Both devices can support all three modes of HA active/passive, active/active and active/active full mesh. Both devices come equipped with HA ports to provide both heartbeat and session synchronization.

# Sonicwall

SonicWALL offers a variety of firewall products designed to meet the needs of anyone from the home office to the enterprise. Since coming to the market in 1991, SonicWALL has become one of the top players in the industry. Today, with over a half-million units in the field, they continue to be touted as one of the best firewall appliances on the market.

## Introduction

SonicWALL's firewall product line provides integrated firewall and IPSec VPN solutions in a single appliance. Antivirus and content filtering are also built into the SonicWALL firewalls. The core of the SonicWALL firewall is based on stateful inspection technology, which provides a connection-oriented security model by verifying the validity of every connection while still providing a high-performance architecture. The SonicWALL firewalls, like the NetScreens, are based on a custom-built architecture consisting of ASIC technology with a main processor.

SonicWALL uses two distinct hardware architectures. In home office and small business appliances such as the TZ 170, SonicWALL utilizes a SonicWALL security processor to handle the workload. Throughout the higher-end appliances, such as the SonicWALL PRO 3060, SonicWALL utilizes an Intel or x86-based main processor, along with a Cavium Nitrox cryptographic accelerator. The combination of the cryptographic accelerator and the x86 architecture has proven to be an effective hardware design, as shown in the SonicWALL product line's overall stability and high throughput in processing VPN and firewall traffic.

The firewall platform also contains additional technologies to increase your network's security. The products support deep inspection like the NetScreens; all of the appliances include the ability to create IPSec VPNs to secure traffic; and the integrated VPN technology has received the ICSA (*www.icsalabs.com*) Firewall Certifications. This means that the IPSec VPN technologies have good cross-compatibility and standards compliance.

SonicWALL also offers three client VPN solutions to pair with the SonicWALL firewall. The SonicWALL VPN client provides the ability to create an IPSec connection to any SonicWALL firewall or any IPSec compliant device. The SonicWALL Global VPN Client is custom-engineered software designed to easily create tunnels with the SonicWALL firewall. It is designed for enhanced security as well as ease of management. The SonicWALL Global Security Client work similarly to the Global VPN client, adding a software firewall to its functionality.

The SonicWALL firewall product line also leverages a subscription-based antivirus software. This allows you to scan traffic as it passes directly through the firewall, thus mitigating the risks of viruses spreading throughout your network.

The SonicWALL firewall platform provides three management options:

- **CLI** Available only on certain SonicWALL models, and only by using a serial cable. Although SonicWALL has support for the CLI, it is not full-featured; you cannot set up access rules using the CLI.

- **WebUI** The WebUI is a streamlined Web-based application with a user-friendly interface that allows you to easily manage the SonicWALL appliance. This is the preferred method for configuring the SonicWALL appliance.

- **SonicWALL Global Management System (GMS)** A centralized enterprise-class solution that allows you to manage your entire SonicWALL firewall infrastructure. The GMS not only provides a central console to manage your firewalls, it also provides consolidated logging and reporting. This is a great option that allows you to see all of your network's activity from a central location.

# The SonicWALL Firewall Core Technologies

Sitting at the core of every SonicWALL appliance is SonicOS, which is the firmware developed by SonicWALL engineers that give the appliance its features and functionality. All SonicWALL appliances are built on and rely on SonicOS to do its job policing network traffic.

There are two modern versions of SonicOS: *SonicOS Standard* and *SonicOS Enhanced*. Often you will see the enhanced version listed with a trailing "e" signifying "enhanced." The differences between SonicOS Standard and SonicOS Enhanced include SonicOS Enhanced's ability to provide ISP failover, wide area network (WAN) load balancing, and zone-based management. Tables 4.4 and 4.5 list detailed feature comparisons of SonicOS Standard and SonicOS Enhanced on two of the available SonicWALL models.

**Table 4.4** Comparison of SonicOS Standard vs. SonicOS Enhanced—SonicWALL TZ170

| Feature | SonicOS Standard | SonicOS Enhanced |
| --- | --- | --- |
| Zones | No zone support | 20 maximum |
| Policy-based firewall access rules | N/A | Yes |
| Address objects/groups | N/A | 100 objects/20 groups |
| User objects/groups | N/A | 150 objects/32 groups |
| Schedule objects/groups | N/A | 50 objects/10 groups |
| Service objects/groups | N/A | 100 objects/20 groups |
| VPN zone support and rules per Security Association | N/A | Yes |
| Bandwidth management on all interfaces and VPN tunnels | N/A | Yes |
| WAN/WAN ISP failover and load balancing | N/A | Yes |
| User-definable IKE entries | N/A | Yes |
| Redundant peer gateway/ secondary IPSec gateway | Yes | Yes |
| Site-to-site VPN tunnels | Max. 10 with unlimited node license | Max. 10 with unlimited node license |

**Continued**

**Table 4.4 continued** Comparison of SonicOS Standard vs. SonicOS Enhanced—SonicWALL TZ170

| Feature | SonicOS Standard | SonicOS Enhanced |
|---|---|---|
| DHCP scopes/address leases | 2/255 | 2/255 |
| Hardware failover | N/A | N/A |

**Table 4.5** Comparison of SonicOS Standard vs. SonicOS Enhanced - SonicWALL Pro3060

| Feature | SonicOS Standard | SonicOS Enhanced |
|---|---|---|
| Zones | No zone support | 20 maximum |
| Policy-based firewall access rules | N/A | Yes |
| Address objects/groups | N/A | 256 objects/64 groups |
| User objects/groups | N/A | 500 objects/64 groups |
| Schedule objects/groups | N/A | 50 objects/10 groups |
| Service objects/groups | N/A | 100 objects/20 groups |
| VPN zone support and rules per Security Association | N/A | Yes |
| Bandwidth management on all interfaces and VPN tunnels | N/A | Yes |
| WAN/WAN ISP failover and load balancing | N/A | Yes |
| User-definable IKE entries | N/A | Yes |
| Redundant peer gateway/ secondary IPSec gateway | Yes | Yes |
| Site-to-site VPN tunnels | 500 | 1,000 |
| DHCP scopes/address Leases | 2/1024 | 255/4096 |
| Hardware failover | N/A | Yes |

If you purchase a SonicWALL appliance with the standard OS and decide later that you want the more feature-rich enhancements provided by SonicOS Enhanced, don't worry. SonicWall has made the process of upgrading an appliance to the enhanced OS relatively easy. Simply purchase the upgrade license to SonicOS Enhanced, download the new firmware, and follow the included instructions to upgrade your appliance. This is a good point to recall that to enable advanced features on the Cisco PIX, you simply enter a new license code. No installation is necessary, thus, there is no downtime.

## Notes from the Underground…

### SonicOS Standard vs. SonicOS Enhanced?

With today's network security needs and architectures, is there a reason to purchase a SonicWALL appliance with SonicOS Standard rather than start off with the more functional SonicOS Enhanced? To me the answer is clearly "no." Other than SonicWALL, no reputable security vendor still has a product with pre-zone-based management architecture. The convention of zones makes firewall management an easier task and provides more flexibility in how to divide up your network. Object-based management also makes access rules and traffic flow easier to follow and manage. When these features are combined with the other features provided in SonicOS Enhanced, there is no reason anyone should purchase an appliance with SonicOS Standard.

## Zones

Originally, SonicWALL's security model was going to allow administrators to create rules based on traffic flowing in one physical interface and out another. With the release of SonicOS 2.0 enhanced firmware came the introduction of security zones in the SonicWALL firmware. A security zone is a logical method of grouping one or more interfaces or subinterfaces and applying security rules to traffic as it passes between zones. To protect departments and more restricted resources from internal malicious intent, an administrator can enable zones, place different departments into different zones, and create rules to police the traffic between the zones. As discussed, zones are not unique to SonicWALL appliances; they are used industry-wide in the firewall and networking world.

## Interface Modes

When you first power up a SonicWALL and begin to deploy it, the default configuration is for the SonicWALL to utilize NAT and act as a router. In this instance, devices inside the firewall are assigned private IP addresses that are not routable on the Internet. As traffic traverses the SonicWALL, the firewall creates a session and provides translation to ensure traffic is properly delivered.

However, there may be instances where you need to assign public IP addresses to servers or systems, but still want to provide firewall filtering to the traffic. To do this, SonicWALL provides the ability to operate in transparent mode. When operating in transparent mode, the SonicWALL acts as a bridge between the WAN interface and one or more of the internal interfaces, assigning both interfaces the same address as is assigned to the WAN interface. Public addresses can then be assigned to devices behind the internal interface. When traffic is transmitted, no translation of addresses is performed.

## Access Rules

An access rule is a statement that allows or denies traffic based on a defined set of specifications. The base specifications are the source IP address, destination IP address, source zone, destination zone, and service or port.

SonicWALL appliances have a couple of default access rules built into the SonicOS. By default, there is a global access rule that denies traffic from passing through the SonicWALL from the public network to the private network. Therefore, if traffic is not implicitly allowed by another policy, it is denied. There is also a default access rule that allows traffic to pass from the private interface to the public interface.

Each SonicWALL device has a limited number of policies, including a license restriction and a capacity restriction. As with NetScreen firewalls, you cannot create new policies once you reach the maximum number of policies per device. This is set to ensure that the performance numbers are specified in the specification sheets. It doesn't make sense to allow a low-end TZ 150 appliance to run 40,000 policies, only to have the performance at 1Mbps. These restrictions are on each platform and are not modifiable.

There are many different elements involved in configuring an advanced policy, including traffic shaping, user authentication, NAT, alarms, URL filtering, and scheduling. These elements provide a great deal of configuration options.

Administering policies can be done from the WebUI or by using the SonicWALL GMS. Each method creates the same end result, but performing each task is slightly different.

## VPN

SonicWALL firewalls also provide VPN functionality and support. They can terminate most VPN tunnels (e.g., site-to-site tunnels, dial-up VPNs, and so forth).
SonicWALL firewalls support all of the standard elements you expect a VPN device
to including:

- IKE
- AH
- ESP
- Tunnel mode
- Transport mode
- Aggressive mode
- Quick mode
- Main mode
- MD5
- SHA-1
- DES
- 3DES
- AES-128
- Perfect forward secrecy

SonicWALL's appliance VPN capabilities are interoperable with most other VPN
appliances on the market.

## Deep Inspection

Deep inspection allows you to inspect traffic at the application layer, relying on signatures to determine what content in a packet is malicious. SonicWALL incorporates this technology in its Intrusion Prevention System (ISP) or IPS. The
SonicWALL IPS uses a database of signatures similar to those that antivirus software
uses to scan files, except that it scans the packets as they traverse the firewall for possible matches to its signature database. When a match is detected, the SonicWALL
can either log or reset the session and drop the packet; whichever is configured.
SonicWall dynamically and automatically updates the signature database.

## Tools & Traps…

### Automatic Updates on Your Firewall?

A firewall is a major network component; if it goes down for any reason or incorrectly passes or doesn't pass traffic, many services and users are affected. The worst scenario is a firewall that suddenly starts passing undesirable traffic. Do you want your firewall automatically updated without knowing exactly what is being put on it? What if the update is corrupt and stops all scanning?

In many cases, a firewall is the defense for a network. Can you afford to not use every available technology to block hostile attacks on our infrastructure? As system administrators, do you have the time to spend manually examining every definition update and then manually installing them? Would you know a corrupt update if you saw it? Your data is extremely valuable; even a minor breach could wreck havoc. You must use every available measure to protect it.

You must evaluate your environment, the risks of exposure, the cost of a security breach, and the cost of a firewall failure (both failing open and closed). Automatic updates are always a double-edged sword. When they work, they provide the most comprehensive detection of hostile traffic available. When they fail, they can leave you more vulnerable than if you didn't scan in the first place. Most companies are well aware of their responsibility to provide accurate and completely automatic updates; therefore, the worst case scenario rarely happens.

## Device Architecture

The SonicWall firewall connects all of its components together using a high-speed bus configuration. The product line also utilizes a cryptographic accelerator to perform services such as encrypting and decrypting VPN traffic, thus reducing the load across the system and increasing throughput. The hardware contained within the appliances cannot be upgraded.

## The SonicWALL Product Line

The SonicWALL product line is very diverse, with products designed for everything from home office use to enterprise-class networks. All SonicWALL appliances support the WebUI and the SonicWALL GMS. Additionally, some models include support for a CLI. Models that include limited management with CLI are the SonicWALL TZ 170, SonicWALL Pro 2040, and the SonicWALL Pro 4060, all running the enhanced firmware. All of the devices use flash memory as the long-term storage option. Like all of the previous brands, none of the firewalls rely on a hard disk to run. For the full and current throughput numbers on all appliances, go to *www.sonicwall.com/products/vpnapp.html*.

**Table 4.6** Overview of the SonicWALL Product Line

| Model | Product Class | Maximum Interfaces | Firewall Throughput | Estimated Price Range |
|---|---|---|---|---|
| TZ 150 | SOHO | 5 (includes 4-port switch) | 30 Mbps | $330–400 |
| TZ 150 Wireless | SOHO | 5 (includes 4-port switch) | 30 Mbps | $430–500 |
| TZ 170 | Remote/branch office | 7 (includes 5-port switch) | 90 Mbps | $370–1300 |
| TZ 170 SP | Remote/branch office | 7 (includes 5-port switch) Analog modem | 90 Mbps | $600–750 |
| TZ 170 Wireless | Remote/branch office | 7 (includes 5-port switch) | 90 Mbps | $500–1100 |
| TZ 170 SP Wireless | Remote/branch office | 7 (includes 5-port switch) Analog modem | 90 Mbps | $825–1100 |
| PRO 1260 | Mid range | 26 (includes 24-port switch) | 90 Mbps | $825–1600 |
| PRO 2040 | Mid range | 3 (4 with Enhanced OS) | 200 Mbps | $1,675–2,700 |
| PRO 3060 | High range/ enterprise | 3 (6 with Enhanced OS | 300 Mbps | $2,325–2,800 |
| PRO 4060 | High range/ enterprise | 6 | 300 Mbps | $4,500–5,000 |
| PRO 4100 | High range/ enterprise | 10 (Gigabit) | 800 Mbps | N/A |
| PRO 5060c/ PRO 5060f | High range/ enterprise | 6 Copper (5060c) 4 Copper; 2 Fiber (5060f) | 2.4 Gbps | $11,000–13,000 |

**Continued**

**Table 4.6 continued** Overview of the SonicWALL Product Line

| Model | Product Class | Maximum Interfaces | Firewall Throughput | Estimated Price Range |
|---|---|---|---|---|
| Content Security Manager 2100 CF | Content filter | N/A | N/A | $2,000–1,0000 |
| SSL-VPN 200 | SSL VPN appliance | N/A | N/A | $575–700 |
| SSL-VPN 2000 | SSL VPN appliance | N/A | N/A | $1,950–2,500 |
| Global VPN Client | VPN Client | N/A | N/A | $50– |
| Global Security Client | VPN Client/ Security software | N/A | N/A | $250– |
| GMS | SonicWALL Appliance Management Software | N/A | N/A | $2000– |

- **SOHO** Designed for remote locations or remote users that need a dedicated security appliance, the SOHO line of SonicWALL firewall appliances provides enterprise-class security at a low-cost entry point. These appliances terminate a site-to-site VPN from a corporate office to a remote site for a small number of users. They have a small footprint and can easily be stacked on a table or desk. When using IPS or Gateway Antivirus for the SOHO line, the appliance does not have the ability to support a DS3 circuit's full speed.

  The *SonicWALL TZ 150* is designed for small office and home office users. The TZ 150 has an integrated four-port Auto-MDIX 10/100 switch, and supports up to 2000 concurrent sessions from a maximum of 10 nodes. Firewall throughput is around 30 Mbps, with VPN throughput around 10 Mbps. The SonicWALL TZ 150 supports two site-to-site VPN policies, and a maximum of two client VPN licenses. Like the midrange and higher-end models, the TZ 150's firewall utilizes deep packet inspection.

  The *SonicWALL TZ 150 Wireless* contains many of the same features as the TZ 150, but also provides support for 802.11b/g wireless networks. The TZ 150 Wireless has a built-in access point, and provides wireless guest services and wireless IDP.

Both the SonicWALL TZ 150 and the TZ 150 Wireless ship with SonicOS Standard. It is important to note that neither of the TZ 150 series can be upgraded to SonicOS Enhanced. The inability to upgrade the OS is a good reason to step up one level and deploy the TZ 170.

The *SonicWALL TZ 170* is an ideal solution for any small office or home office user. The base model is very versatile. The TZ 170 can be purchased with the ability to support ten, twenty-five, or an unlimited number of nodes. This model provides seven 10/100 interfaces, including a five-port switch. At 90 Mbps, the TZ 170 can easily support a DS3 circuit. The TZ 170 can also support up to 30 Mbps throughput for VPN traffic. The TZ 170 supports up to ten site-to-site VPN policies, and a maximum of 50 client VPN tunnels.

If running SonicOS Enhanced, the SonicWALL TZ 170 is the lowest-end model in the SonicWALL product line that can support features such as WAN failover and load balancing. The TZ 170 also provides an optional (OPT) port, which is used to provide these services. It can also be used to provide a DMZ.

The *SonicWALL TZ 170 SP* is the TZ 170 with an additional piece of hardware. The TZ 170 SP ensures continuous uptime for VPN connectivity by automatically failing over to either a second WAN connection or an integrated analog modem. Once the broadband connection has been re-established, the TZ 170 SP detects the restored connection and automatically fails back, ensuring the best possible connectivity.

- **Midrange** The SonicWALL PRO 1260 and SonicWALL PRO 2040 fall into the midrange category. These appliances are designed for use in branch and remote offices and small- or medium-sized businesses. They provide a solid gateway and firewall solution, and provide secure VPN access. Both appliances can be rack-mounted.

The *SonicWALL PRO 1260* was designed to be the core of a small business or branch office network integrated into a single appliance. The PRO 1260 provides deep inspection firewall and VPN capabilities, and a 24-port 10/100 Ethernet switch. The integrated switch also includes Auto-Medium Dependent Interface, Crossover (MDIX) support (negating the need for cross-over cables) with an unlimited number of nodes.

The SonicWALL PRO 1260 has a unique feature called PortShield architecture, which provides the ability to configure each port as an individual security zone. Not only is traffic from the WAN inspected and filtered, but it can effectively filter traffic from other ports on the firewall, including the other LAN ports. It's as if each port has a firewall running on it.

The *SonicWALL PRO 2040* is designed to be a midrange workhorse rather than an out-of-the-box core network solution. It provides three available 10/100 interfaces, and supports an additional fourth 10/100 interface when utilizing SonicOS Enhanced. There is no built-in switch on the PRO 2040; however, it supports an unlimited number of nodes. Like the SonicWALL PRO 1260, the PRO 2040 provides a small- or medium-sized business network with a deep inspection firewall as well as a VPN gateway. Unlike the SonicWALL PRO 1260, the PRO 2040 supports hardware failover when SonicOS Enhanced is installed.

Both the SonicWALL PRO 1260 and the PRO 2040 support several advanced features, including WAN/WAN failover, ISP failover, and load balancing. Both appliances come bundled with a 30-day subscription of services, including gateway antivirus, anti-spyware, IPS, and the SonicWALL Premium content filter service.

- **Enterprise Class** These appliances are designed for use in large, complex networks, where higher throughput and additional segmentation of the network is needed. They are designed to provide a solid gateway and firewall solution, and to provide secure VPN access. All appliances in this class are rack-mountable.

    Although at the lower end of the large business and enterprise-class appliances, the SonicWALL PRO 3060 is well-suited for any complex environment. It comes standard with SonicOS Standard and includes six customizable 10/100 network interfaces. With support for up to 128,000 concurrent connections, the PRO 3060 is designed to handle a large amount of traffic without losing efficiency.

    The *SonicWALL PRO 4060* steps up the performance from the SonicWALL PRO 3060. It ships from SonicWALL with SonicOS Enhanced preinstalled, providing for object-based management out-of-the-box. Like the SonicWALL PRO 3060, the PRO 4060 provides six 10/100 user-configurable network interfaces. What separates the PRO 4060 from the SonicWALL PRO 3060 is the emphasis placed on acting as a VPN concentrator. The VPN throughput is more than double that of the PRO 3060 and has a larger connection table, supporting up to a half million concurrent connections. Distributed wireless LAN capabilities allow easy integration of advanced WLAN services within existing network and security architectures utilizing SonicWALL SonicPoints.

    The *SonicWALL PRO 4100* is designed for higher traffic environments with many network segments. Providing 10GB network interfaces, the

PRO 4100 builds on the high-end VPN performance of the SonicWALL PRO 4060 and introduces the SonicWALL Clean VPN feature. This ensures that mobile user connections and branch office traffic are decontaminated to prevent vulnerabilities form being introduced via remote connections. SonicOS Enhanced is standard.

The SonicWALL PRO 5060c and 5060f round out the SonicWALL firewall appliance offerings. Both the PRO 5060c and the PRO 5060f have similar specifications, the major difference being the available interfaces. The PRO 5060c offers six copper interfaces, while the PRO 5060f offers four copper interfaces along with two fiber interfaces. These two appliances offer the utmost in network throughput and comes standard with SonicOS Enhanced.

## Management

SonicWALL offers the easy-to-use WebUI integrated into SonicOS to manage SonicWALL appliances. The WebUI is an ideal solution to manage a small number of appliances (e.g., four to five remote sites or a few telecommuters). However, what if your organization consists of ten or more branch offices? What if you are a managing many SonicWALL appliances for clients? Managing each individual firewall is a huge chore. Furthermore, how do you consolidate the logs of these devices? Is it practical to use a simple syslog server to manage all of those devices? The solution is the SonicWALL GMS, which can manage many SonicWALL appliances from one easy-to-use interface.

The SonicWALL GMS provides administrators with the following benefits:

- Unified management interface
- Lower administrative costs
- Centralized logging
- Simplified VPN deployment

Each individual device is imported into the GSM where individual aspects of the firewall can be managed. You can add and delete security zones, create new access rules, and tweak existing access rules. If you have dozens of locations that need the same policy, you can easily deploy that policy to all of those devices. If you need to make a change to that policy, instead of accessing each device individually, you can make the change to the policy and then update all of the policies at once. This simplifies large-scale deployments and allows you to gain more control over the enterprise's security as a whole. The GMS also brings logging to one central location to be stored for historical purposes and monitors it in real time. This takes the guess-work out of determining what is happening to your secured infrastructure.

# Nokia Hardened Appliances

The NSP offers enterprise-class security with Check Point software running on Nokia IPSO, a hardened OS on purpose-built, high-performance hardware.

## *Technologies*

Nokia IPSO is a UNIX-based, appliance-optimized, security-hardened, cluster-able OS capable of supporting a wide range of Nokia and partner security applications. Built-in IP routing functionality, including IPV6 standards compliance, makes it capable of internetworking with customer IP networks. Nokia's Web-based administrative interface, the *Voyager*, can be used for just about anything, including point-and-click OS and firewall software upgrades (see Figure 4.2).

**Figure 4.2** Interface Configuration Through the Voyager Web

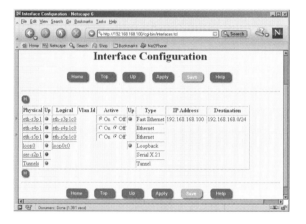

If you only have a console connection to your Nokia device or prefer a com-mand prompt interface, you can use Voyager over a console connection from the IPSO shell (see Figure 4.3).

A command-line tool called *iclid* can be used to show and monitor various con-figuration settings. It has a syntax similar to Cisco's IOS command shell, and offers the tabbed command completion and the command display present in most modern UNIX shells (see Figure 4.4).

**Figure 4.3** Package Management Through the Lynx Interface

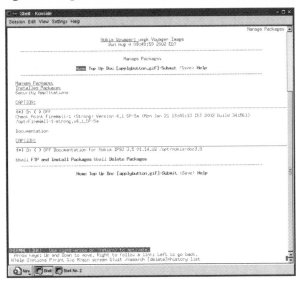

**Figure 4.4** Output of Common Shell Commands

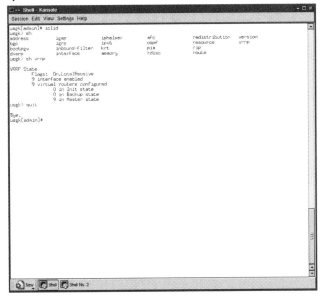

IPSO is based on UNIX and boots into a standard C-shell (csh) (see Figure 4.5). Configuration files do not normally persist across system reboots or across changes made with Voyager. However, there are ways to use the standard tools to make permanent changes.

**Figure 4.5** Output of Common Shell Commands

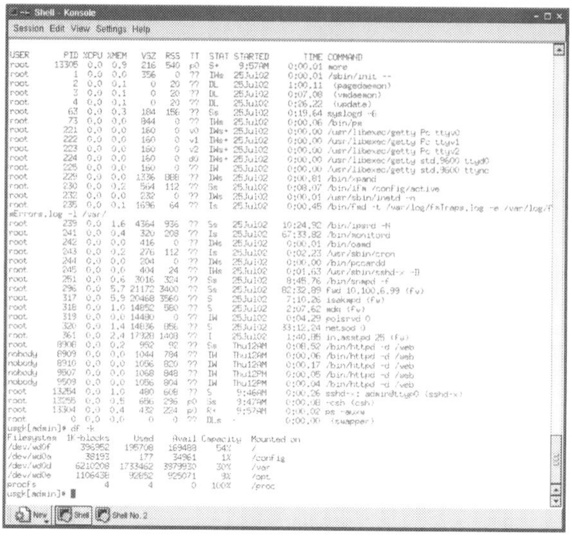

Most models offer Virtual Router Redundancy Protocol (VRRP), which enables implementation of hot-standby firewall appliances in a way that is transparent to host systems. Hosts can utilize a hot-standby firewall appliance if the primary appliance fails without any direct host involvement. Combining VRRP with Check Point Firewall Sync (i.e., a technology that replicates the configuration parameters between devices), Nokia firewall appliances can be deployed in configurations that support integrated, redundant, hot-standby routing and firewall services.

The Nokia Horizon Manager reduces the time spent manually installing and upgrading software and applications, by managing multiple IP network security appliances and their IPSO OS settings. It allows you to stage new appliance rollouts according to enterprise standards with consistent configuration changes across the network.

Network managers can access Nokia Horizon Manager, with its remote secure GUI client, to implement configuration changes across multiple Nokia IP security platforms. In addition, management tools such as configuration templates can be edited and stored to form a set of common, standardized configurations. A task scheduler feature also increases operational efficiency by implementing best-practice security management such as system backups, upgrades, and password changes.

The Appliance Manager is a software-based management solution that enables centralized scalable monitoring, fault management, and reporting for multiple Nokia Security appliances and applications. The real-time and historical monitoring and reporting on inventory, network traffic, faults, and security events provides key information for security appliance maintenance, capacity planning, and audit and device lifecycle management.

## Nokia Models

All of the models are standardized on the common Web interface called Voyager, through which you can remotely administer and configure almost any aspect of the OS or firewall, as well as a CLI. Serial console access is standard. The NSP consists of 12 different hardware models, all part of the IP series. All models offer various additional software packages to add such features as VPN, intrusion detection, and virus scanning. As the model numbers increase, the performance and throughput increase. For full and current specifications on these appliances reference *www.nokiausa.com/ business/security/product/1,8193,pid:fw_vpn_app%7Ctab:0,00.html*. Given the number of models and similarities between models, it would be wise to use Nokia's Platform Recommendation Tool available at *www.nokia-platformtool.com/scripts/main.html.* Below are some examples of the myriad of models available:

- **Nokia IP45**  The Nokia IP45 firewall appliance is the optimal remote connectivity and perimeter security solution for enterprise remote office branch office (ROBO), work extenders, and small- and medium-size business that need robust VPN connectivity. This appliance combines Check Point firewall software with a purpose-built, Nokia-designed hardware platform. The desktop-sized firewall appliance offers high reliability with no moving parts, out-of-the-box deployment (pre-licensed and pre-configured), multiple connection types, and ease-of-maintenance (including automatic upgrading of firewall/VPN appliances) without network downtime. Four models are available with 8, 16, 32, and unlimited nodes.

- **Nokia IP350 and IP355**  The Nokia IP350 and Nokia IP355 deliver performance for real-world mixed-traffic environments, and offer high-port density in a 1RU system. They are designed for small- to mid-sized enterprise customers or small, standalone companies.

    Key features available with Nokia IP350 and Nokia IP355 include on-board encryption, large routing tables, highly reliable flash-based storage (Nokia IP355) or disk-based storage on the IP350, maximum expansion capacity with up to ten 10/100 Ethernet ports, synched firewalls in HA environments, and the hardened Nokia IPSO OS with its Web and CLI interface. Nokia IPSO includes Nokia IP clustering, and supports a wide array of protocols, such as the remote authentication protocols Authentication Dial-In User Server (RADIUS) Client/Server and Terminal Access Controller Access Control System (TACACS+) Client. The IP350

ships with 256MB RAM and the IP355 has 1GB RAM. Both have two
Type II PCMCIA slots and an encryption accelerator.

■ **Nokia IP1220**   The Nokia IP1220 supports the traffic requirements present in large business and service provider networks with a high-speed
encryption accelerator card and up to 2GB of RAM. Its redundant hardware capabilities include hot swap interface cards, optional mirrored hot
swap capable hard disks, and an optional load-sharing power supply and
fan. VRRP and Nokia IP Clustering support additional redundancy.

With its expansion capacity in a 3 Unit (3U) form factor, the IP1220
can service a multitude of network segments for a large and growing network infrastructure with up to 20 10/100 Ethernet or four 10/100
Ethernet and eight 1000 Gigabit Ethernet (GigE) connections in a variety
of customer-selected configurations.

Like most Nokia Firewall/VPN appliances, the IP1220 offers the
option of either disk- or flash-based storage configurations. Additionally, it
can be configured with hybrid (flash and compact disk) local storage. The
hybrid configuration uses flash storage for Nokia IPSO and the Check
Point enforcement module, and local disk for management and logging.

Nokia IP1220 features Nokia IPSO™, a secure OS with Web or
CLI, as well as support from Nokia Horizon Manager, which provides
secure robust system management, version control, and backup and
restore.

■ **Nokia IP2250**   The Nokia IP2255 is the top level of the Nokia firewall
line and is designed specifically for the demanding performance and port-
density requirements of carriers, service providers, e-commerce sites, and
enterprise data center cores. It is a 3U form factor, flash-based security
appliance providing in excess of 8 Gbps of performance with up to 20 Gbs
Ethernet interfaces or up to 36 10/100 Ethernet interfaces for the Check
Point VPN-1 Power application. Harnessing the power of two network
processors and Nokia Accelerated Data Path (ADP) software acceleration
technology, the Nokia IP2255 running Check Point VPN-1 Power provides up to 8.9 Gbps of firewall throughput with 87,000 firewall connections per second 2.3 Gbps of AES256 encrypted VPN throughput.

The Check Point SMART Management framework simplifies complex
policy definition and deployment. Nokia Network Voyager and Cluster
Voyager provide complete local and remote WebUI appliance management,
and Nokia Horizon Manager and Nokia Appliance Manager provide

simple, comprehensive, centralized management of multiple appliances. All of these software enhancements are included standard.

The IP2255 includes redundant, hot-swappable power supplies and fans. In addition, it includes VRRP and IP Clustering for HA. In short, if Nokia offers the option, it is either included or available for add-on to this model.

## Others

The four examples above should provide a good overview of the features the range of possibilities available to a network administrator. While some are not Enterprise-class solutions, AlphaShield, D-Link, Hawking, Linksys, NetGear, SMC, Symantec, WatchGuard and Zyxel (among others) produce either hardware firewalls or network routers with firewall capabilities built in. In most cases, the lower-end capabilities are limited to packet filtration and rudimentary DMZ configurations. Sites such as *zdnet.com* and *pcmag.com* provide reviews of low-end, consumer firewalls. For enterprise firewalls, *networkcomputing.com* and *networkworld.com* are helpful starting points.

Even the simplest router can be used to effectively protect a small home network, and some can create a VPN to an Enterprise firewall to enable telecommuters to work efficiently and safely from home. Cost is often (but not always) an indicator of the number of features and network throughput. Always examine the specification sheets and compare one model against another. Where one model is upgradable and another is not, the cost difference must be weighed against the growth potential.

It is important to remember that despite simple firewall features, it is still imperative to correctly configure the firewall to keep out unwanted visitors. If a VPN is used, the configuration must be even more carefully scrutinized lest the tunnel be used as a mile-wide hole for a malicious person to walk through.

# Software Solutions

## Basic Description

Software firewalls are specialized applications designed to run on generic hardware and OSs. Containing most, if not all, of the features found in hardware firewalls, they can be a cost effective alternative, providing care is taken to harden the underlying OS and to choose the appropriate hardware platform to run on.

# Hardware Platform

Using a software-based firewall, you have both the option and the responsibility to choose a hardware platform. Reviewing the hardware-based firewalls above, gives you some idea of the necessary requirements needed to produce the desired performance. However, with a software-based firewall, you are relying on a non-optimized OS. Typical OSs such as Linux, UNIX, and Windows, are optimized for other uses such as file sharing and application hosting. They are not designed specifically to pass through IP packets after being scanned by a piece of software. You may require more horsepower to achieve the performance you need.

When choosing a hardware platform, you should consider purchasing accelerator cards to reduce the load on the CPU. Cards such as VPN or IPSec offload Network Interface Cards (NICs) transfer the load of encryption/decryption from the CPU to the specifically designed processor on the NIC itself.

While considering accelerator cards, you need to consider how many network interfaces you want and then plan for possible expansion. In all cases, you should purchase the fastest cards possible. Do not try to save money using 10/100MB cards when 1GB cards are available for a small increase in cost. It is likely that you will end up switching to faster cards before the life of the server is complete. The only reason to use a 10/100MB card is if you plan to have a dedicated management-only interface utilized by that card.

Some commercial firewalls come with a modem for out-of-band management. Consider this addition carefully. Will you use it? While dial-up access still exists, do you use it? When was the last time you tried to manage something over dial-up? If you feel it's valuable, include a modem card. If you think you might need one in the future, or major firewall manufactures include it, then think twice. While not an expensive addition, it is one more item that must be maintained, find drivers for, and still potentially fail. Remember, firewall hardware should be simple and stripped to the bare bones.

Finally, you need to select a hardware platform that is supported by your OS of choice. Linux and Windows run on just about any PC on the market. For optimal performance, UNIX needs to be on a Sun (*sun.com*).

# Harden the OS

As stated above, OSs are not optimized to function as hosts for firewalls. Often, there are services running that are unnecessary when used as a firewall host (e.g., file sharing and print services should be completely disabled or removed). Functions such as network browsing should also be disabled. Most OS manufacturers have hardening guides to assist administrators with this task. The Center for Internet

Security (CIS) (cisecurity.org) provides "one stop shopping" for hardening guides, as does the System Administration, Networking, and Security Institute (SANS) (sans.org).

## Hardening Examples

Below are some steps that should be taken to harden your OS in order to use it as a firewall host. These are not complete steps; check for the latest hardening recommendations before deploying your firewall in production.

RedHat Linux:

- If machine is a new install, protect it from hostile network traffic until the OS is installed and hardened.

- Set a Basic Input/Output System (BIOS)/firmware password and/or configure the device boot to prevent unauthorized booting from alternate media.

- Install OS and application services security patches.

- Configure SSH.

- Enable and test the OS and applications logging.

- Consider installing the Bastille Linux. The Bastille Hardening (*bastille-linux.org*) program "locks down" an OS, proactively configuring the system for increased security, and decreasing its susceptibility to compromise. Bastille Linux can also assess a system's current state of hardening, granularly reporting on each of the security settings that it works with.

- Disable any services, and any application and/or user accounts that are not being utilized

- Disable GUI login, if possible.

- Configure an NTP server.

- Log all administrator or root access.

- Integrity checking of system accounts, group memberships, and their associated privileges should be enabled and tested.

- Ensure that the configuration files for Pluggable Authentication Modules (PAM) are secure (*/etc/pam.d/**).

- Enable the terminal security file/restrict root logins to system console.

- Install and enable antivirus software.

- Configure to update signature daily on antivirus software.

- Enable integrity checking of critical OS files using third-party tools such as Tripwire (tripwire.com).

Windows:

- If the machine is a new install, protect it from hostile network traffic until the OS is installed and hardened.

- Set a BIOS/firmware password and/or configure the device boot order to prevent unauthorized booting from alternate media.

- Install OS and application services security patches.

- Always utilize the New Technology File System (NTFS) file system.

- Enable auditing.

- Limit user rights.

- Use registry entries to reduce the possibility of TCP/IP vulnerabilities being exploited.

- Set a secure location to retrieve secure system files such as a read-only CD, and ensure that Windows File Protection (WIP) is configured for regular scans.

   1. Utilize Tripwire for full system protection, if possible.

- Utilize restricted groups in the Group Policy to ensure that only authorized users are included in sensitive groups (e.g., administrators).

- Secure terminal services (if being used) by requiring high encryption.

- Run the Security Configuration Wizard to disable and/or remove unnecessary services.

As you can see, the basic procedure is the same. Isolate, install, patch, audit, disable. Hardening is all about reducing your host OS to the minimal configuration necessary to run the firewall software.

# Keep Up With OS Patches and Firewalls

Your OS also needs to be completely patched, not just at rollout, but updated and maintained as they are released. Although hardware firewalls with dedicated OSs must be maintained, your host OS was designed for multiple purposes and is more likely to have a vulnerability in some other component. These other components can compromise your firewall, and from there, compromise your entire protected network. No OS is immune to the need for patches. Larry Ellison, Oracle's CEO in early 2005, stated that the new version of Oracle was "unbreakable," only to require its first patch soon thereafter.

In addition to patching your OS, you must maintain up-to-date firewall software, which is also susceptible to coding errors. As errors are found, they need to be patched so that the vulnerabilities cannot be exploited.

Some manufacturers offer auto-updates of firewalls, which also extends to the OS. In the case of software firewalls running on a separate OS, it would be wise to manually install the updates so that you can schedule your downtime (e.g., Windows requires a restart for most updates, thus causing a few minutes of downtime. In some environments, this is not a problem; in others, such unscheduled downtime can be akin to a crisis.

# Examples

We explore several options of software firewalls and the advantages and disadvantages of each. Recall that one of the primary advantages of software firewalls is the cost savings on hardware firewalls. However, much more labor is required in order to provide a secure firewall.

# Checkpoint FW-1

Check Point's product line is split into three main areas. Perimeter security relates to security at the edge of your network. Internal security protects data inside your network. Web security is for locking down Web-based applications and encrypted tunnels in your network.

## *Perimeter*

Check Point's solution for enforcing perimeter security includes FireWall-1/VPN-1 Pro, VPN-1 Edge, VPN-1 VSX, Web Intelligence, and SmartCenter. VPN-1 Pro enables secure, encrypted tunnels for data to pass through. VPN-1 Edge allows remote offices to have firewall security and VPN endpoints at the edge of your network. VPN-1 VSX allows for virtual security gateways with VLAN security, and multiple policies per gateway. Web intelligence enables you to inspect Web content and look for vulnerabilities. SmartCenter enables you to tie it all together into a central management system.

The new Check Point NGX product line adds several new features. The SmartCenter NGX Management Server can now manage VPN-1, VPN-1 Edge,

Connectra, and InterSpect gateways, all from a centralized management console. SmartDefense, Application Intelligence, and Web Intelligence engines include enhanced peer-to-peer (PTP) protection, Voice Over IP (VoIP) DoS protection, and enhanced security servers. The VPN-1 Pro NGX product also includes the ability to run dynamic routing protocols on the firewall, as well as enhanced VPN routing.

## Internal

To enforce security inside your network, sometimes a bit more security is in order. Use FireWall-1 inside your network to secure internal segments. Check Point has two additional products to help secure the enterprise: InterSpect and Integrity.

InterSpect can stop the spread of worms through your network. InterSpect understands common internal protocols, such as Microsoft file sharing, and has the ability to block unwanted traffic using those protocols.

The Integrity product enables you to enforce desktop security. Integrity has plug-ins for SecureClient or can run in stand-alone mode, The stand-alone version is based on the ZoneAlarm desktop firewall.

## Web

Check Point has three products made specifically for Web traffic: Connectra, Web Intelligence, and the Secure Sockets Layer (SSL) Network Extender.

Connectra is Check Point's SSL VPN product. With Connectra, remote users can access the network through an SSL-encrypted Web browser.

Web Intelligence integrates with Check Point's FireWall-1 gateway software, and allows you to do application-level scanning at wire speed. Web content can be inspected and Web-based vulnerabilities can be stopped at the gateway. Check Point NGX adds the ability to prevent directory listings, Lightweight Directory Access Protocol (LDAP) injection, and Web-server error messages.

The SSL Network Extender is a Web-based plug-in that allows network-level access through your Web browser. Every time users' access the firewall, they get a new client. The SSL Network Extender can be used with Connectra to provide a complete SSL VPN solution. Check Point NGX adds the ability to centralize management of the SSL Network Extender into the SmartDashboard console. NGX also adds enhanced SecurID features and ClusterXL functionality.

## INSPECT Script

Check Point firewalls use the INSPECT engine to do stateful inspection. When a policy is pushed to a firewall, it is converted into INSPECT script. All of Check Point's advanced functionality is modifiable via INSPECT script, and custom

INSPECT script can be inserted automatically into policies before they are pushed to firewall gateways.

> **NOTE**
>
> Custom INSPECT code can be inserted into policies by editing files in the $FWDIR/lib directory.

Check Point has documentation available for custom INSPECT programming, but is not often needed because the SmartDashboard gives you the ability to create custom objects. The primary reason to write custom INSPECT code is to create a custom protocol for an application that Check Point does not yet support.

## FireWall-1 Decision Making

When a packet reaches the FireWall-1 several things happen. First, Check Point goes through anti-spoofing rules to make sure the packet is coming in the correct interface. Then, IP options and packet checksums are checked. If any errors are found the packets is discarded. After the initial checks, the packet hits the FireWall-1 daemon.

Figure 4.6 shows what the Check Point INSPECT engine goes through with every packet. First, the firewall looks at its rule base for a match. Rules are parsed from top to bottom, one rule at a time. Once a rule is matched, the connection is logged and the firewall makes a determination to pass, reject, or drop the packet based on the policy. A rejected packet sends a negative acknowledgment (NACK) packet to the server to close the connection. Normally you would not do this, because tells the hacker that something is rejecting packets. Reject typically is used when you want to avoid a timeout on a service your users use frequently.

## SmartPortal

SmartPortal allows you to extend read-only browser-based access to the SmartCenter server to people outside the security team, and to those on PCs without the GUI clients. It's essentially a secure Web interface into your SmartCenter server that enables you to see the security policy and the logs. The SmartPortal license is included in the SmartCenter Pro license; otherwise, it has to be purchased separately.

**Figure 4.6** The Check Point INSPECT Engine

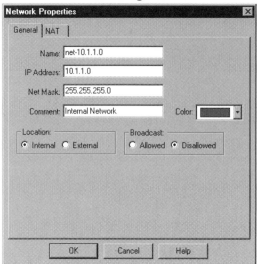

## SmartDefense/Web Intelligence

In the early days of firewalls, it was sufficient to inspect packets at the network layer (layer 3) and transport layer (layer 4) and then base filtering decisions on these simple identifiers. Within a couple of years, these battles were essentially over, with firewalls consistently winning the day. A well-configured firewall could stop just about all attacks directed at closed ports.

The problem now is that the battles are being waged through the open ports. If your firewall allows Web traffic to reach your Web server, or allows insiders to go out on most services, all sorts of new attack opportunities are available to those who would do you harm. SmartDefense/Web Intelligence is Check Point's way of providing an intelligent defense against attacks directed at open ports, as well as against other more sophisticated types of attacks.

SmartDefense and Web Intelligence have capabilities in three broad categories:

- Defenses against attacks
- Implicit defenses
- Abnormal behavior analysis

## Defenses Against Attacks

SmartDefense provides defenses against the following attacks:

- DoS

- TCP/IP

- Web and application vulnerabilities

- Network probing

- HTTP worms

- Microsoft Network-specific vulnerability

- Protocol vulnerability

- Buffer-overflow attacks

- Implicit defenses

These defenses include fingerprint spoofing and other tricks to reduce the ability of outside observers to reach conclusions about your internal network based upon information carried in packets leaving your network. The goal is to increase the difficulty your enemy will have in fingerprinting your network.

## Abnormal-Behavior Analysis

SmartDefense can report on and analyze traffic patterns, alerting you when certain criteria are met. Components include successive events detection, port scan detection, and sweep scan detection.

### Tools & Traps…

### DNS Protocol Enforcement

DNS traffic usually gets special treatment in firewalls. Because it's easy to forget that UDP DNS resolutions need to pass through the firewall in order for other services to work, administrators often create a rule allowing all DNS traffic (UDP and possibly TCP) to traverse the firewall.

This is overly permissive and a security risk, and SmartDefense has a partial answer to the problem. By configuring the settings properly, SmartDefense can look inside each DNS packet and confirm whether they're genuine and unmodified, and block packets that someone is trying to tunnel through an otherwise open Port 53.

## SmartDefense Subscription Service

Check Point offers a subscription service called SmartDefense Services. This is an annual subscription program (separate from and in addition to your software subscription and support contract) that is licensed to each individual enforcement module. The goal is to provide ongoing and real-time updates and configuration advisories for defenses and security policies.

## SmartDefense and Web Intelligence

If you're using FireWall-1/VPN-1 to protect Web servers, you'll be particularly interested in what's available to configure in Web Intelligence. The HTTP protocol has all sorts of risks, and Web Intelligence offers a robust array of countermeasures.

Web Intelligence is a separate license that must be purchased for the number of servers you want to protect. In NGX, you have the ability to configure individual filters and tests to monitor but not drop packets, which enables you to see the effect of implementation without causing unexpected network problems. If you subscribe to the SmartDefense Services, new filters and options are added dynamically to the lists through automatic updates.

## Eventia Reporter

With the passage of Sarbanes-Oxley and the increased demand for auditing, the portion of firms requiring their firewall administrators to log all traffic continues to grow. Anyone who's had much experience working with software that produces logs knows how large and unwieldy they can become, particularly in organizations with large traffic flows or multiple gateways.

Eventia Reporter is a log analysis tool that provides fairly straightforward ways to audit and monitor network traffic. You can use it to create detailed or summary reports in a variety of formats (e.g., list, vertical bar, pie chart, and so on).

## Dynamic Routing

Check Point includes a dynamic routing functionality in the Pro version of SecurePlatform (SPLAT). For some administrators, this is their long-awaited opportunity to further integrate their FireWall-1/VPN-1 gateways into their network infrastructure and provide additional redundancy. For others (primarily in smaller organizations), its additional cost, risks, and complexities argue against implementation.

It's generally considered a security risk to configure your firewall to accept any more information from external sources than is absolutely necessary. The stealthier your firewall is, the better it can resist attacks. For this reason, it's generally considered a risk to use any sort of dynamic routing protocol in your gateway.

It often comes as a surprise to students new to firewalls, that every firewall gateway is a router first and a border guard second. Except in unusual configurations, every firewall acts as a router. Static routes are best as they are hard-coded into the gateway's OS and don't rely on updates from any external source. It would be a particularly attractive attack vector if your enemy found out that by sending bogus dynamic routing updates to your gateway, he or she could redirect your traffic through one of his or her own routing nodes.

Static routes are also easier to debug, and given that routing problems are a frequent underlying cause of "firewall" problems, keeping all your routes static is a great way to start the debugging process with some of the potential confusion eliminated.

## *SPLAT*

SPLAT is Check Point's combined OS and the VPN-1 Pro software. The OS is a proprietary, hardened, enhanced version of Linux that easily installs on most PCs. The creation of SPLAT gives users several significant advantages:

- Avoidance of licensing fees associated with Microsoft Windows

- Avoidance of the costs of a third-party appliance platform

- The benefits of a pre-hardened, purpose-built OS

- The ability to take advantage of special Check Point-only enhancements, such as dynamic routing protocols

- The ability to automatically update the OS when updating VPN-1 Pro

SPLAT is now a split product line in version NGX. In addition to "regular" SPLAT, there's also a premium version called SPLAT Pro. The Pro version offers two distinct advantages:

- Dynamic routing

- RADIUS Authentication for SPLAT administrators

SPLAT Pro requires a separate, additional license. This license must be installed on the SmartCenter Server managing the SPLAT module.

## Notes from the Underground…

### Choosing SPLAT versus SPLAT Pro

Unless your network management team insists that your firewall support dynamic routing, there aren't many other reasons to pay for SPLAT Pro. The only advantage of SPLAT Pro is the ability for firewall administrators to authenticate with RADIUS, which isn't a crucial benefit, because it also adds risk by configuring the firewall to authenticate to an external source. It is more secure to have firewall administrators authenticate only to the SmartCenter Server itself, and leave the firewall password out of the hands of the other IT staff who manage passwords on the RADIUS server.

Check Point offers a line of hardware firewall appliances called VPN-1 Edge devices, which are small, don't have hard drives, boot a stripped down version of Linux, and run FireWall-1/VPN-1 version NG.

## IPtables

Over the years, the open source community has created firewall software that is suited for networks of any size. Linux natively supports the ability to route and/or filter packets, which means that the attractive price of "free" for both the OS and the firewall software is available. IPtables supports Linux kernel 2.4 and higher. IPchains and IPfilter were available in earlier versions of Linux; however, these are not considered because there is no reason to use an old version of the OS. The package supports packet masquerading and filtering functionality, found in the 2.3 kernel and later. This functionality is known as *netfilter*, which is what IPtables are based on. Therefore, in order to use IPtables, you must recompile the kernel so that netfilter is installed, and then you must install the IPtables package, which is found by clicking **Networking Options | IP: NetFilter Configuration**.

Depending on your kernel version, you can use these applications to configure your Linux system to act as a router, to ensure that packets are sent from one network to another. At this level, a Linux router does not examine or filter any traffic; it simply ensures that all traffic addressed to a remote network is sent to it.

IPtables also allow you to configure your Linux router to masquerade traffic (in other words, to rewrite IP headers so that a packet appears to originate from a certain host), or to examine and block traffic. It is also possible to configure your Linux router to do both. The practice of examining and blocking traffic is called *packet filtering*.

A packet filter works at the network layer of the Open System Interconnection/Reference Model (OSI/RM). Daemons such as Squid (*www.squid-cache.org*) also allow you to examine and block traffic. However, Squid is not a packet filter; it is a proxy server designed to operate at the application layer of the OSI/RM. The primary difference between a packet filtering router (e.g., one created by using IPtables) and a proxy server (e.g., one enabled by Squid) is that a packet-filtering router does not inspect network packets as deeply as a proxy server does. However, proxy servers require more system resources in order to process network packets. As a result, a proxy server can sometimes be slow when honoring requests, especially if the machine is not powerful enough. This is why packet filters and proxy servers are both necessary in a network: the packet filter blocks and filters the majority of network traffic, and the proxy server inspects only certain traffic types.

### NOTE

When considering an open source firewall, you need to consider the cost/benefit ratio. Acquisition costs are only a small part of the equation. You must also consider the cost of support. With a commercial firewall, the vendor is there to offer technical support and classes (for a fee). Open source has no such luxury. The administrator is left to his own resources and those of the colleagues using the same package. This may not pose a problem if the firewalls are administered by a group of experienced people, but in a small company, where an open source firewall is often considered, there is usually one person maintaining the device. If this person is out and there is a problem, the cost of diagnosing and fixing the problem without vendor support can be great.

## Choosing a Linux Firewall Machine

A firewall does not necessarily have to be the most powerful system on your network. It should, however, be a dedicated host, which means that you should not run any other services. The last thing you want to do is configure your firewall to also be a Samba server or print server. Additional services may cause a performance drain or open up vulnerabilities.

Ideally, a small network would be well served by a typical Pentium III or Pentium IV system with 128MB of RAM and a 500MHz processor. Depending on the amount of traffic the network generates, however, you could get by with a less powerful system. It is common to see a network with 25 systems accessing the Internet using a Linux router that is no more powerful than a low-end 300MHz system. A good NIC is vital for firewalls and routers.

Larger businesses (e.g., those with demands for Web surfing, e-mail retrieval, and additional protocols) may require a more powerful system. Considerations for more powerful systems might include a 1GHZ processor, at least 256MB of RAM (512MB of RAM or more may be preferable), quality network interfaces and Input/Output (I/O) cards, and Redundant Array of Inexpensive Disks (RAID 0) for faster data processing. RAID 0 does not provide data redundancy. It does, however, provide faster read/write time, which is helpful regarding firewalls. Although a firewall does not store data like a database application server does, fast I/O is important, because you want the machine to process data as quickly as possible. Fast I/O is especially important if you plan to log extensive amounts of data. Small Computer System Interface (SCSI) systems tend to be faster and longer-lasting than their Interactive Development Environment (IDE) counterparts, thus allowing for a more powerful firewall.

## Protecting the Firewall

One of the benefits of having a firewall is that it provides a single point that processes incoming and outgoing traffic. However, consider that a firewall can also provide a central point of attack or failure. A firewall informs a hacker that a series of networks exist behind it. If a hacker is able to defeat this one firewall, the entire network would be open to attack. Furthermore, if a hacker was able to somehow disable this host, the entire network would be denied all Internet services. Therefore, it is important to take measures to protect your firewall. Consider the following options:

- Limit router and firewall access to interactive login only, and physically secure the system. This way, your firewall is less susceptible to remote attack. It is still possible, however, that problems in the kernel (e.g., buffer overflows and other programming problems) may occur. Such problems can lead to compromise of the system, even if there are no other services running.

- If remote access is necessary, access the firewall only SSH, properly configured to use public keys to authenticate. Although SSH is not immune to security threats, it is one of the most popular and secure remote administration tools for Linux firewalls.

- Create a backup host. If your host crashes due to an attack or because of hard drive failure, you should have an identical system available as a backup.

If that is not possible, make sure you have a copy of the kernel configuration, the IPtables configuration, and everything in the */etc* directory.

- Monitor the host. Use an IDS application to listen in on connections made to your router. Installing an IDS application on a separate host on the network is usually best. This is called passive monitoring, because the remote host does not consume the system resources of the firewall. The IDS application can send a random ping to the firewall to test whether it is up, and can inform you if the host is down. Consider using an application such as Cheops.

- Watch for bug reports concerning IPtables, the Linux kernel, and any applications such as SSH that are installed. Keeping current about such changes can help you quickly upgrade your system in case a problem is discovered.

IP forwarding is the ability for a Linux system to act as a router. Packets enter the Linux kernel and are processed by the OS. The main thing to remember is that a Linux system with simple IP forwarding enabled can route any network address to another. If you are allotted a range of IP addresses from a local or regional Internet registry, you can use a multi-homed Linux system to route this set of addresses to another network (e.g., if you are allotted the 128.187.22.0/24 block of IP addresses, you can use a Linux router to route this network to the 221.9.3.0 network, or to any other). However, Internet routers do not forward traffic from private IP addresses (in other words, any network address of 10.0.0.0/8, 172.16.0.0/12, or 192.168.0.0/16). Figure 4.7 shows how traffic from the 10.1.2.0 network and the 192.168.1.0 network can reach all networks, including the 128.187.22.0 network. However, only traffic from the 128.187.22.0 can reach the Internet.

**Figure 4.7** Linux System Configured as a Forwarding Router

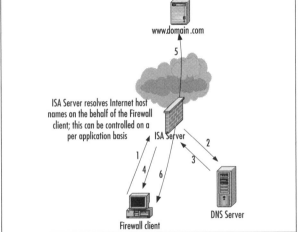

Masquerading is when your Linux system rewrites the IP headers of a network packet so that the packet appears to originate from a different host. Once the IP header has been rewritten to a nonprivate IP address, it can be rerouted over the Internet. The practice of rewriting IP packets is known as packet mangling, because it alters the contents of the packet. Masquerading is useful, because you can use it to invoke NAT, where one IP address can stand in for several.

As shown in Figure 4.8, masquerading allows the Linux-based system to translate the 10.1.2.0 network in to the Internet-addressable IP address of 66.1.5.0.

**Figure 4.8** Masquerading the 10.1.2.0 Network as the 66.1.5.1 IP Address

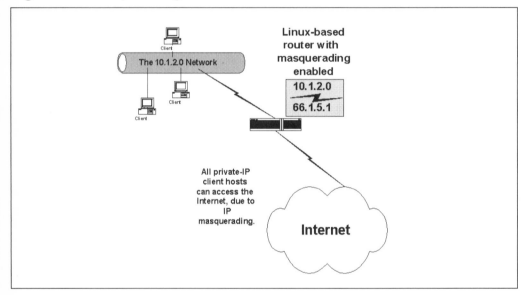

Once private network 10.1.2.0 is masqueraded as IP address of 66.1.5.1, all hosts on the network can access the Internet. Depending on the subnet mask used for the 10.1.2.0 network, hundreds, perhaps even thousands of client hosts can be masqueraded under this one IP address.

Translating the private Internet address to a routable Internet address is accomplished by the database stored on the IPtables-based Linux router. The Linux masquerading router keeps this database so that it knows how to "untranslate" the packets that have been mangled so that they can then be addressed to the local, private network. This process occurs quickly, although it is important that you have the proper amount of system power to enable the translation database to do its jobs.

Simple masquerading leaves the network "wide open," meaning that anyone who enters your firewall or router as a default gateway can have full access to all attached networks. Packet filtering is the answer to locking down access to your network.

## Customized Packet Filtering

Your firewall configuration needs will be specific to your situation. You need to consider the design of your network and the services you need to provide (e.g., if you want to allow remote clients to access certain internal hosts, such as a Web server, you can place the Web server outside the firewall, or you can allow incoming traffic to access port 80). Consider that if you place your Web server behind your firewall, you will have to ensure that this request is forwarded to a specific internal host.

## Configuring the Kernel

Most Linux OSs such as Red Hat, Slackware, SuSE, and Caldera, support IP forwarding, masquerading, and firewalling by default. However, you may have to reconfigure your kernel in order to provide full functionality. When recompiling the kernel, choose the network packet filtering option.

## Packet Accounting

Packet accounting is the ability to summarize protocol usage on an IP network, and can be used to list the amount of TCP, ICMP, and IP traffic that passes through your interfaces. Once you have recompiled the kernel and restarted your system, find out if the following file is present in the */proc virtual* file system:

```
/proc/net/ip_acct
```

If the file exists, your kernel supports IP accounting in addition to all other features.

## Automated Firewall Scripts and Graphical Firewall Utilities

The configuration of IPtables is natively done via the command line. Several attempts have been made to automate the process of creating a firewall in Linux. Similarly, developers are also busy creating GUI applications that make the job easier. Many of these utilities are quite useful, although they are mostly effective in beginning your firewall configuration. You will likely have to customize the rules these applications generate.

The more effective firewall scripts and GUI tools include the following:

- **Firestarter** A fairly sophisticated graphical tool that supports both IPtables. It can be used to create a personal firewall, but also supports multi-homed systems. Like many automated firewalls, it creates multiple rules to filter out known and expected attacks. You may need to adjust some of these automatic settings. Although Firestarter supports multiple interfaces such as most of the open-source GUI firewall applications, it is best used only as a beginning to a firewall on a multi-homed system. You can obtain Firestarter at *http://sourceforge.net/projects/firestarter*.

- **Knetfilter** A GUI firewall designed to work with the K Desktop Environment (KDE). Learn more about Knetfilter at *http://expansa.sns.it/knetfilter/*.

- **Firewall Builder** Firewall Builder is the most ambitious open-source GUI tool. It uses an object-oriented GUI and a set of compilers to create configurations for various firewall platforms. Currently there are implemented compilers for IPtables, IPfilter, OpenBSD pf, ipfw and Cisco PIX. As of this writing, there are beta packages for Mac and Windows, as well as the traditional Linux package. Learn more about Firewall Builder at *http://sourceforge.net/projects/fwbuilder*.

- **EasyChains** EasyChains has a ncurses-based GUI and supports IPtables, and can be download at *http://sourceforge.net/projects/easychains*.

## Notes from the Underground…

## Weighing the Benefits of a Graphical Firewall Utility

As you consider using any of the GUI applications covered in this section, keep the following issues in mind:

- Often, these downloads do not provide public keys or hash values for their code; therefore, before using any of the applications, make sure that you review the source code. If you cannot review the source code yourself, employ someone to check it, especially if you plan to use it in an Enterprise environment.

- Most of these applications are still in beta form; therefore, remember that they often provide limited functionality. Although some are quite impressive, limitations still persist.

- The more advanced GUI applications often require you to upgrade to either the very latest version of a particular window manager,

**Continued**

> such as KDE or Gnome, or to use an idiosyncratic version or configuration. Consequently, you may have to spend a great deal of time configuring your window manager. Generally, this time could be better spent learning how to use IPtables commands.

# Microsoft Internet Security and Acceleration (ISA) Server

ISA 2004 has many of the features that administrators expect from a firewall as opposed to previous versions of ISA Server (e.g., VPN administration, authentication, firewall rules, Outlook Web Access (OWA) publishing, FTP support, secure Web publishing, cache rules, the SMTP message screener, customization of reports, support for multiple networks, stateful filtering and inspection for VPN traffic, VPN quarantine, firewall user groups, firewall generation of forms used by OWA for forms-based authentication, link translation, and so on). Microsoft's focus is on marketing ISA 2004 first and foremost as a firewall/security product that can compete in that market, and then as a caching/acceleration server, adding value and saving money for organizations that need both functions, but don't want to buy two separate products.

ISA Server 2004 allows you to control the access and usage of any protocol, including IP level (layer 3) protocols such as the ICMP. This makes it possible for users to use applications such as ping and tracert, and also to create VPN connections using the PPTP. IPSec traffic can also be enabled through ISA Server.

At the transport layer (layer 4), ISA Server 2004 also adds new support for port redirection and better FTP support. A connection that is received on one port can be redirected to a different port and FTP servers can be published on alternate ports without requiring any special configuration on the client, by creating an FTP server publishing rule.

Streaming media and voice/video applications frequently require the firewall to manage complex protocols, which is needed to make multiple connections. With ISA Server 2004, you can easily create protocol definitions with the New Protocol Wizard. These protocol definitions can be created "on the fly" when creating an access rule, or you can create a new protocol in the Firewall Policy node of the management console.

## *Management*

Figure 4.9 shows the ISA Server 2004 console with a three–pane window that includes a tree structure in the left pane, and tabbed pages in the middle and right panes. Common management tasks are at your fingertips. Any IT administrator without extensive training can easily learn this point-and-click interface. An administrator who likes a GUI interface will love this, while a CLI administrator will quickly become frustrated.

**Figure 4.9** The ISA Server 2004 Management GUI

---

> **N**OTE
>
> You can use the management console to connect to remote ISA servers and the local ISA Server. You can also install the management console on a workstation or non-ISA server, and manage your ISA machines remotely. To select the ISA computer that you want to manage, click Connect to Local or Remote ISA Server in the right console pane on the Tasks tab. Using the "RunAs" option in Windows, you can manage ISA servers from your workstation without running as the dangerous Administrator account. (See www.microsoft.com/resources/documentation/windows/xp/all/proddocs/en-us/runas.mspx?mfr=true for more information on RunAs.)

## Monitoring

The dashboard is a "big picture" view that summarizes each of the areas represented by a tab (except logging). Like the dashboard of a car, you're able to keep an eye on what's going on with all the different areas from one interface. The dashboard is shown in Figure 4.10.

**Figure 4.10** The Dashboard

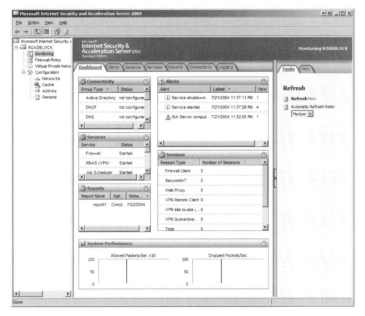

The dashboard also provides system performance information, which means that you are able to see the number of packets allowed per second (×10) and the number of packets dropped per second in graph format.

Detailed information about each monitoring area is available by clicking on the appropriate tab. You can configure what actions will trigger alerts. Figure 4.11 shows the Alert tab.

The right task pane allows you to refresh the Alerts window manually, or you can set an automatic refresh rate (none, low, medium, or high). Under "Alerts Tasks," you can reset selected alerts by clicking the alert(s) you want to reset (highlight multiple alerts by holding down CTRL while selecting them) and then clicking **Reset**. You can also choose "Acknowledge" to indicate that you are handling the alert. This will not remove it from the Alerts window; however, the alert will be removed from the dashboard view.

**Figure 4.11** The Alerts Tab

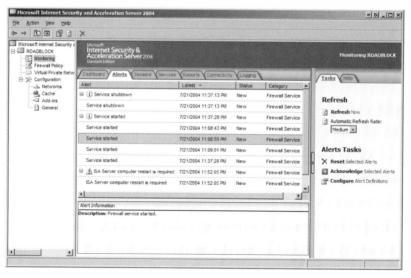

You can configure alerts by choosing from a list of predefined alert events, and you can specify the number of times an event or the number of events must occur per second in order to trigger an alert. You can also specify what should happen when an alert is triggered (e.g., send e-mail to an administrator, run a specified program, log to the Windows event log, or start or stop a specified service or services).

## Policies

If you select Firewall Policy, the middle pane displays a list of firewall policy rules, and the right pane contains tabs labeled Toolbox, Tasks, and Help, as shown in Figure 4.12.

**Figure 4.12** Firewall Policy Configure Rules

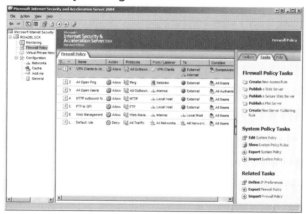

The firewall policy node is the "heart" of the ISA server interface. This is where you create access rules, Web publishing rules, mail server publishing rules, and other server publishing rules to control access to and from your network. In addition, you can edit system policy, define IP preferences, and export and import system policies and firewall policies.

Policies now work like standard firewall rules. System policy rules are processed first, then user-defined rules. The firewall rules represent an ordered list where parameters are first compared to the top-listed rule. ISA Server 2004 moves down the list of rules until it finds one that matches the connection parameters, and then it enforces the matching rule's policy. In addition, unlike previous versions, ISA Server 2004's firewall rules allow you to define the source and destination for each individual protocol that a user or group is allowed to access.

## Authentication

Users can be authenticated via the built-in Windows authentication or Remote Authentication Dial-In User Service (RADIUS) or other namespaces. You can apply rules to users or user groups in any namespace. Using the software development kit, third-party vendors have extended these built-in authentication types to provide for additional authentication mechanisms. This provides a flexible authentication environment compatible with third-party applications.

## VPN

ISA Server 2004 has VPN capabilities that allow it to create site-to-site links to other VPN servers, using IPSec in tunnel mode. This means that ISA Server 2004 can be placed at a branch office and a tunnel mode IPSec site-to-site link can connect the branch office network to the main office network, even if the main office is using a third-party edge firewall (e.g., Cisco PIX, Check Point, or any other firewall that supports IPSec VPNs).

ISA Server 2004 utilizes stateful filtering and inspection for all communications moving through a site-to-site VPN connection. This means you can control which resources specific hosts or networks can access on the opposite side of the link. User- and group-based access policies can be used to granularly control resource utilization via the link.

ISA Server 2004 leverages the Network Access Quarantine Control feature built into Windows Server 2003 to provide VPN quarantine, which allows you to quarantine VPN clients on a separate network until they meet a predefined set of security requirements. If ISA Server 2004 is installed on Windows 2000, you can still use quarantine control with some limitations.

In either case, you can specify conditions that Windows VPN clients must meet in order to be allowed on the Internal network, such as the following:

- Security updates and service packs must be installed

- Antivirus software must be installed and enabled

- Personal firewall software must be installed and enabled

VPN clients that pass the pre-defined security tests are allowed network access based on the VPN client firewall policies. VPN clients who fail security testing may be provided limited access to servers that will help them meet network security.

VPN quarantine control is an exciting feature that helps protect your Microsoft network from remote users who establish VPN connections from client computers that don't have up-to-date security patches and service packs, don't have antivirus software installed and enabled, and/or don't have personal firewalls to prevent Internet attacks. A number of other firewall vendors offer similar functionality, although usually with a different name. However, in most cases, you must use their proprietary VPN client software (at extra cost) to take advantage of this feature. With ISA Server 2004, no special client software is required; clients use the PPTP or L2TP clients built into all modern Windows OSs. However, to take full advantage of this feature, you should be running a Microsoft shop.

## New Application Layer Filtering Features

Application Layer Filtering (ALF) is one of ISA Server 2004's strong points; unlike a traditional packet filtering firewall, ISA can delve deep into application layer communications to protect your network from the many modern exploits that occur at this layer. ISA Server 2000's ALF functionality has been enhanced by the addition of the following new features:

- Per-rule HTTP filtering

- Ability to block access to all executables

- Ability to control HTTP downloads by file extension

- Application of HTTP filtering to all client connections

- Control of HTTP access based on signatures

- Control over allowed HTTP methods

- Ability to force secure Exchange Remote Procedure Call (RPC) connections

- Policy-based control over FTP
- Link translation

## OWA

OWA is a specialized function of ISA Server used in Microsoft Exchange environments. ISA server can replace both a firewall and an Exchange front end server, reducing the exposure of the Exchange database while maintaining reliable connectivity. It can also be used solely as the front-end to an Exchange server, which is often done because using ISA server to front Exchange provides the best possible protection while providing the most functionality.

The ISA Server 2004 OWA Publishing Wizard walks you through the process of setting up a firewall rule that creates an OWA SSL VPN to your Exchange server. All network elements can be created "on the fly." In addition, the OWA Publishing Wizard supports Outlook Mobile Access (OMA) and ActiveSync, which were not configurable via the wizard in ISA 2000. With ISA 2004, you can set properties individually for each Web listener, thus, you can have different parameters for OWA, OMA, and ActiveSync.

# Summary

The PIX is a dedicated firewall appliance with a special-purpose, hardened OS. The simplified kernel and reduced command structure (compared with firewalls based on general-purpose OSs) means that all other things being equal, the PIX will have higher throughput and more reduced maintenance costs than general-purpose device. The similarity to IOS provides an edge to security administrators who are familiar with the Cisco environment.

The PIX is a hybrid firewall that performs stateful packet filtering using proxies for specific protocols. The stateful packet filter is known as the ASA. ASA maintains the state of the traffic transiting the network, and dynamically allows packets through the filter. The ASA inspects packet header information (e.g., source address, destination address, and TCP and UDP socket information), and packet contents for certain protocols, to make intelligent decisions on routing the packets. As part of its inspection engine, ASA will rewrite packets where necessary, where the protocols are well known.

In addition to its native packet-filtering and access control features, the PIX provides additional common firewall services. The PIX makes an excellent VPN terminator, with the ability to pass encrypted traffic at wire speed, when an accelerator card is installed. It can provide content logging and filtering to help control Web surfing, and provides address translation to allow for either "sewing together" networks seamlessly at the perimeter or consolidating (and concealing) internal networks to present a limited number of addresses to the outside world.

Modern environments depend on firewalls; therefore, the PIX provides high resiliency through its failover mechanism. This mechanism provides for a hot spare—a second PIX with an equivalent configuration that will automatically press itself into service should the primary device fail.

As of this writing, five different models are shipping that are designed to match almost any environment. The PIX 501 is designed for the SOHO user, with a small switch built in for basic use. The PIX 506E, designed for the small or branch office, supports better performance for connecting back to the corporate hub. The PIX 515E is designed for the enterprise core of small- to medium-sized business, with a rack-mounted chassis and corresponding enterprise-class performance. The PIX 525 is designed for large enterprise or small service provider environments and has a slot-based configuration to allow for multiple interface configurations. The PIX 535 is the top-of-the-line model, designed for service provider environments, with the best possible throughput of the PIX appliances.

Licensing for the PIX features is set via an activation key. Licensing usually falls into three categories: unrestricted (all features enabled), restricted (limited features and interfaces), or failover (used for hot standby machines).

Communicating with a misconfigured PIX is easily achieved through the console cable, which is provided with each firewall kit. For standard maintenance, either SSH or using the ADSM through HTTPS is recommended.

The NetScreen firewall product line offers a core set of products to secure your network's focal points. Zones are a core part of the NetScreen firewall, because they allow you to divide networks into logical separations. This allows you to simplify the policy creation process by clearly allowing or denying access to different network segments based on their applied zones. NetScreen bends the idea of a firewall with the use of VRs, which allow you to separate all of your routing domains into separate logical entities. This allows a firewall to employ the firewall as a true router without compromising security. The NetScreen firewall can act as a transparent device in your network, while still providing full firewall features. A policy in the NetScreen firewall is the rule base, security policy, or access list of the other competitive products. It can do much more than just allow or deny traffic.

Besides being a firewall gateway, the NetScreen firewall is also a fully integrated VPN gateway, providing the ability to act as a site-to-site gateway and provide remote VPN access to mobile users. NetScreen provides an industry standard IPSec implementation. Deep inspection provides analysis of the application layer that otherwise might only be provided by a dedicated device such as the IDP product. HA is integrated into many of the NetScreen models, therefore, additional licenses are unnecessary.

The NetScreen firewall product line provides a complete selection of firewall products that can cover any company's needs. Each product has a unique feature set to provide exactly what you need. Choosing the proper model is extremely important, because most of the offerings are not upgradable.

The SonicWALL product line offers both small and large customers a good selection of products for deployment on the network. The firewall product line offers a core set of products to secure your network's focal points. To minimize your network's risk, the integrated gateway antivirus and IPS products enable you to intensely inspect your traffic. With the proper configuration, you can block malicious traffic before it affects your systems, possibly compromising them and or creating data loss. The SonicWALL firewall product strays away from the traditional look of a firewall with its ability to act as a transparent device in your network, while still providing full firewall features.

This chapter discussed the differences in SonicOS Standard and SonicOS Enhanced, their feature sets, and the options each supports. Nearly every

SonicWALL firewall appliance supports zones out-of-the-box or via a firmware upgrade, and allow you to divide networks into logical separations. This allows you to simplify the policy creation process by clearly allowing or denying access to different network segments based on their applied zones.

Besides being a firewall gateway, the SonicWALL firewall is also a fully integrated VPN gateway, providing the ability to act as a site-to-site gateway and provide remote VPN access to mobile users. The industry-standard IPSec implementation provided by SonicWALL, gives it a an enterprise-class VPN solution.

Application-level security is a must for every organization today. It provides inspection of the application layer that otherwise could only be provided by a dedicated device such as an IDP product.

The SonicWALL firewall product line provides a complete selection of firewall products that can cover any company's needs. Each product is tailored to provide exactly what you need for almost every possible solution for an enterprise's firewall needs. The GMS product manages all of your firewalls under one single solution, and provides all of the various solutions most administrators would want to centrally manage firewall products.

The Nokia Security Product Line consists of many models, from the IP45 to the IP2255. All offer a wide range of features and hardware specifications, and it is a model that fits any network architecture from the small office to the largest ISP's or Telco's. The primary feature points that distinguish one model from another include direct WAN connectivity, 16 or more network interfaces, Gb Ethernet, and hot-swappable or redundant components. All of the devices are based on the Nokia IPSO OS, and all of them can be almost entirely configured through Nokia's intuitive Voyager Web interface. These appliances' ability to function as full-fledged routers with WAN support and support for many of the most common dynamic routing protocols, means that they can function as a drop-in replacement for the commonly seen "border router-firewall" configuration. The rack-mountable appliances are becoming very popular for use in high-availability VPN deployments, where they are configured in pairs with VRRP and Check Point's gateway clustering.

Administration of the Nokia IP series devices can be accomplished in several ways: using the Voyager tool through a graphical browser, through the text-mode browser Lynx, and through command-line utilities such as iclid or even the standard UNIX shell. Nokia has hardened the IPSO OS, which is based on UNIX; as a result, these devices are ready to run out-of-the-box (after network configuration). Nokia also has a product called Horizon Manager that enables remote, centralized administration of multiple devices.

Check Point offers a complete, comprehensive security solution for network environments of every size. PIW (Perimeter/Internal/Web) allows Check Point to provide a security-rich solution. Perimeter security protects the network from the Internet. Internal security protects the internal network from internal attacks. Web security protects HTTP- and HTTPS-based connections. The INSPECT engine is programmed by INSPECT script. The Check Point SmartDashboard generates INSPECT script, which is pushed down to the firewalls. Custom INSPECT script can be written and pushed to the firewalls along with a policy. The INSPECT engine follows a process for handling network traffic. Rules are parsed from top to bottom, one at a time. Packets that do not match a rule are silently dropped. When a packet is rejected, a NACK is generated in order to properly close the connection.

Check Point SmartPortal allows administrators to extend browser-based connectivity to the SmartCenter Server. Users without the SmartConsole GUI clients and administrators at their primary workstations can connect through HTTPS. SmartDefense and Web Intelligence have a fascinating set of tools for the network security administrator to understand and configure against all sorts of higher-level attacks. Eventia Reporter provides a way to tackle those large and growing log files and provide detailed, informative reports and traffic analysis. Dynamic routing adds some risk and complexity, and is available to those larger organizations who want to fully integrate the underlying router in their Check Point firewalls into their existing dynamic routing configuration. SPLAT continues to evolve and improve. The product line is now split, with the addition of SPLAT Pro, which offers dynamic routing and support for RADIUS authentication for firewall administrators.

In this chapter, you learned about using IPtables to create firewall rules. The IPtables package supports packet masquerading and filtering functionality, as found in the v2.3 kernel and later. This functionality is known as netfilter. Therefore, in order to use IPtables, you must recompile the kernel so that netfilter is installed, and you must install the IPtables package. You were provided with practical advice concerning some of the options available with IPtables, and saw how GUI and automated applications have been created to help build firewalls.

With ISA Server 2004, Microsoft has taken another big step away from the proxy server and into the arena of serious firewall products. ISA Server now offers many features that are standard on other firewalls and the functions with the logic we expect from firewalls. The most extensive and perhaps the most welcome new feature is multi-networking support, which extends ISA Server 2004's ability to function as the firewall of choice in large, complex networking environments. New ALF features give ISA Server 2004 even more of an edge when it comes to such functions as front-line defense against spam, and VPN quarantine control gives administrators a powerful way to ensure that remote VPN clients must meet the same standards in regard to security configurations as do the clients on the Internal network.

# Solutions Fast Track

## Appliance/Hardware Solution

☑ Hardware firewalls come as a complete package, reducing the necessity to decide on hardware, OS, and firewall software separately

☑ The OS is generally hardened and optimized for network throughput and packet inspection.

☑ The PIX uses standard firewall logic: outbound is permitted by default and inbound is blocked by default. Open inbound, if necessary; close down outbound, as necessary.

☑ FixUp protocol inspection provides some inspection of protocols, mainly enforcing Internet standards.

☑ VPN functionality and URL filtering are also provided by the PIX.

☑ The PIX is primarily managed by the CLI; however, a GUI interface called the ASDM is available.

☑ Juniper NetScreen firewalls generally have the highest throughput of any firewall on the market (as of this writing) both standard throughput and when utilizing a VPN tunnel.

☑ NetScreen firewalls provide deep inspection to examine packets and prevent illegal commands from crossing the firewall.

☑ The concept of zones is used in the NetScreen, allowing you to define different levels of security to areas of the same subnet.

☑ Management of a NetScreen is accomplished via a CLI or a GUI interface, with the GUI interface being as complete and functional as the CLI. Juniper also provides the NetScreen Security Manager to configure many individual devices from one console.

☑ SonicWall provides content and antivirus filtering, which includes deep inspection, standard on all firewalls. VPN capabilities are offered on most models.

☑ Like the NetScreen, SonicWall provides CLI, GUI, and global management interfaces.

☑ SonicOU comes in "standard" and "enhanced" versions. There is rarely a reason not to purchase the enhanced version. Auto-Update is offered for the OS.

☑ Nokia appliances rely on a UNIX-based OS, which is specifically hardened and optimized for the firewalls. Check Point Firewall1 is the stateful inspection/content filtering software included.

☑ As with other firewalls, CLI, GUI, and global management applications are included with Nokia appliances.

☑ Nokia has a myriad of appliances. One helpful method for deciding on one is to use their Web-based Platform Recommendation Tool.

☑ AlphaShield, D-Link, Hawking, Linksys, NetGear, SMC, Symantec, WatchGuard, and Zyxel produce either hardware firewalls or network routers with firewall capabilities built in.

## Software Solution

☑ Software firewalls require you to choose the hardware and the OS.

☑ It is up to you to harden your OS and configure it for maximum throughput, and not for other functions such as file sharing.

☑ It is also up to you to maintain current patches and drivers on the OS, as well as patches on the firewall software. Most hardware-based firewall vendors patch both at one time.

☑ Check Point firewall software utilizes multiple technologies to inspect for the port, source, and destination rules, and also for application-level vulnerabilities. Using separate modules for the scans (e.g., Web, abnormal activity, and DoS), Firewall1 provides high throughput.

☑ Firewall1 has a convenient GUI interface for configuration.

☑ Check Point VPN works with Firewall1 to provide secure communications across geographic distances.

☑ Check Point provides for subscription updates; the software can be purchased with a specifically hardened and optimized OS.

☑ IPtables comes standard with every Linux OS and is open source, meaning that in many cases it can be obtained for free.

☑ Natively, IPtables provide a CLI for configuration. There are open-source applications that attempt to provide a more convenient GUI interface.

☑ IPtables do not have many of the advanced filtering features and application-level inspection capabilities of commercial firewalls.

☑ Microsoft ISA Server 2004 provides many advanced features found in other firewalls. It also provides features that are only available due to its integration with the rest of the Microsoft product line.

☑ ISA Server provides for the quarantine of Windows computers attempting to access protected networks, and enforces policies such as service pack level and personal firewall implementation.

☑ ISA Server provides a single tool that functions to configure and report on the function of the firewall. This tool can be used from any Windows workstation to manage one or more ISA Servers.

# Frequently Asked Questions

The following Frequently Asked Questions, answered by the authors of this book, are designed to both measure your understanding of the concepts presented in this chapter and to assist you with real-life implementation of these concepts. To have your questions about this chapter answered by the author, browse to **www.syngress.com/solutions** and click on the **"Ask the Author"** form.

**Q:** There are so many options. How do I decide?

**A:** You need to sit down and look at several factors:

1. What is your budget?
2. What throughput do you need?
3. How many subnets do you want to create behind the firewall?
4. How deeply do you need/want to inspect the packets crossing the firewall?
5. Will you be starting small and later adding more capabilities to your firewall? i.e. Is it important to be able to update the firewall in the future?
6. Evaluate the good and bad of each

Thinking of these needs will help you begin to narrow down your choices. If you must have application-level inspection, you cannot use IPtables, whereas, if you have an extremely limited budget and only a small number of machines to protect, IPtables could be the best solution. If you require maximum throughput due to excessive e-commerce traffic, you should look at the NetScreen line. If you will be updating your firewall, SonicWall or Nokia with their static hardware configurations are probably a poor choice. As unfortunate as it is, budget and institutional "tradition" often dictates the make of firewall you purchase.

**Q:** Why should I buy something when IPtables is free?

**A:** While IPtables is free and powerful, it has a steeper learning curve than most commercial products. Support is another possible problem. "The money a company may spend for technical service, support, training, customization and testing open-source applications is greater at this point [2004] than in the [Microsoft] Windows or the [Apple] Mac world, which are known entities," said Laura DiDio, senior analyst at the Yankee Group. This can, and has, changed over time and will most likely continue to do so. Currently, however, it is still a consideration.

Probably the most important reason to choose a commercial product is liability. Depending on your organization, you may have to comply with laws such as HIPPA, which have strict requirements for protecting information. Using a certified commercial product greatly reduces your liability should an incident occur. Despite their capabilities, open-source products have no such certifications.

**Q:** I have a Microsoft-only environment. Should I purchase ISA Server?

**A:** Maybe, maybe not. Will ISA server provide you the throughput you require? Are you willing to depend on a single manufacturer for both your perimeter protection and operating environment? If you diversify your environment, even a little, it is less likely that a single vulnerability will result in the compromise of your entire organization. On the other hand, if you already know Microsoft products and want to take advantage of that knowledge, it may be an appropriate answer.

**Q:** Can I mix firewalls?

**A:** Most certainly! In the previous chapter, we spoke of having a perimeter firewall and then internal firewalls to protect other more sensitive areas. You may wish to consider using a PIX, NetScreen, or IPtables to do your preliminary filtering, and then utilize Firewall1 or ISA server to protect more sensitive servers. This takes part of the load off of the more complex firewalls, because much of the chaff is dropped before it reaches them.

# Part III
# VPN Concepts

# Chapter 5

# Defining a VPN

## Solutions in this chapter:

- What IS a VPN?

- Public Key Cryptography

- IPSec

- SSL VPNs

- SSH Tunnels

- Others

☑ Summary

☑ Solutions Fast Track

☑ Frequently Asked Questions

# Introduction

In this chapter, we cover concepts of virtual private networks (VPNs), how they operate, and the different types of VPNs in use today. Before we dive into the details, you may be thinking, "What is a VPN, and why would I need to use one?" There are several good reasons to implement VPN technology in your infrastructure, starting with security. A VPN is a means of creating secure communications over a public network infrastructure. VPNs use encryption and authentication to ensure information is kept private and confidential. This means you can share data and resources among several locations without the worry of data integrity being compromised. Alone, the ability to make use of a public network to transmit data is also an advantage of VPN technology. Without using the Internet as a transport mechanism, you would have to purchase point-to-point T1s or some other form of leased line to connect multiple locations, or use frame relay service. Leased lines are traditionally expensive to operate, especially if the two points being connected are across a large geographic region. Using VPNs instead reduces the operating cost for your company.

VPNs are also cost effective for traveling users. Without VPNs, a traveling salesperson working outside the office might have to dial in to a modem bank at the office and incur long distance charges for the call. A dialup VPN is much more cost effective, allowing the salesperson to connect to a local ISP (Internet service provider) and then access the corporate network via a VPN.

Suppose your company's corporate office has a database-driven intranet site it wants your branch offices to be able to access, but does not want the rest of the world to have access to this site. Sure, you could just stick the application on an Internet-facing server and give each user a password-protected account, but the information will still be transmitted unencrypted to the user. By creating a VPN between the two sites, the branch office can access the intranet site and share resources with the corporate office, increasing productivity and maintaining a higher level of security all at the same time.

# What Is a VPN?

A traditional corporate WAN is shown in Figure 5.1. Branch office networks are connected either through a circuit-switched data path such as ISDN, providing low-end, broadband connection, or through packet-switched technologies such as frame relay or leased lines (T1, DS3, etc.). The cost of such a WAN topology increases significantly as the number of sites and interconnections between the sites increases. For a fully meshed topology with four endpoints, six frame relay or serial connections are required. In general, a full meshed network with $n$ nodes requires $(n* (n - 1)) / 2$ links. This system quickly becomes quite expensive as the number of nodes increases.

VPNs provide dramatic flexibility in network design and a reduced total cost of ownership in the WAN. A VPN can be best described as an encrypted tunnel between two computers over an insecure network such as the Internet. VPNs provide secure encrypted channel to secure communication, and cost savings in the ranges of 30 to 80 percent depending on the leased line and the destination.

There are various ways to implement VPN services, including at the enterprise-edge router, the firewall, or a dedicated VPN appliance. Additionally, MPLS can be provided by the ISP for site-to-site VPN traffic. Another possibility is the virtual private dialup network (VPDN). Primarily used for remote-access connection to an enterprise campus network, this type of VPN combines the traditional dialup network through the PSTN with either Layer 2 Forwarding (L2F) or L2TP. All of these various technologies are available in today's marketplace, but the most popular VPN technology, by far, is the IPSec VPN.

**Figure 5.1** Fully Meshed Enterprise WAN Connectivity

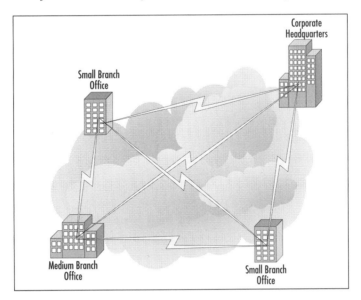

## VPN Deployment Models

One of the first decisions you must make when deploying a VPN is choosing a device to serve as the termination point for the VPN tunnel. This decision is primarily driven by the placement of the VPN tunnel endpoint, and the capabilities of the device that will serve as the tunnel endpoint. IPSec VPNs require devices capable of handling the traffic traversing outside the VPN and the VPN traffic and the encryption of the data across the VPN. Insufficient computing power results in a slow connection over the VPN and poor performance overall. Many vendors address this problem by offering VPN accelerator modules (VAMs) onboard processors designed to provide encryption services for the VPNs.

Deployment of VPNs in the enterprise DMZ is primarily done through the three models listed here and shown in Figures 5.2 through 5.4:

- VPN termination at the edge router
- VPN termination at the corporate firewall
- VPN termination at a dedicated appliance

Each of these deployment models presents its own difficulties that must be addressed for the VPN topology to be successful. One concern that must be addressed is the use of Network Address Translation (NAT). Due to its design, IPSec is not capable of traversing NAT devices. The problem comes when the NAT device changes information in the IP header of the IPSec packet. The changes will result in an incorrect IPSec checksum that is calculated over parts of the IP header. There are vendor workarounds for this problem, where the IPSec packet is encapsulated in a UDP or TCP packet and then transmitted to the other side. Currently, this solution is an Internet draft and has not reached request for comment (RFC) status. The ports to use for such communication are negotiated during tunnel setup.

# VPN Termination at the Edge Router

Termination of the VPN at the edge router has the benefit of ensuring that all VPN traffic must conform to external firewall policies to reach the internal network. This topology (shown in Figure 5.2) is best deployed for extranet connections where the business partners do not require access to the internal network but do require access to servers in the DMZ itself that might not necessarily be exposed to normal Internet traffic. As the number of business partners connecting through VPNs increases, the load on the routers due to the encryption and decryption of packets entering and exiting the VPN tunnels also increases. This situation requires the use of VAMs to offload the encryption/decryption process from the router CPU.

**Figure 5.2** VPN Termination at Edge Routers

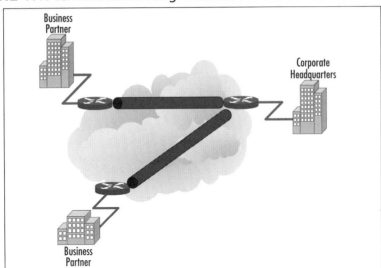

# VPN Termination at the Corporate Firewall

Termination of the VPN at the corporate firewall allows for direct access from branch networks to the internal corporate core network. Remote users can then access all internal services without having to authenticate a second time. This particular topology (shown in Figure 5.3) is best reserved for LAN-to-LAN connections such as branch-office-to-corporate-enterprise networks, but can also be used for WAN connections if there is a router in front of the firewall to direct traffic over the Internet. The drawback to this topology is that as more branch offices are connected to the corporate office, the load on the firewall increases due to the increased amount of encryption each VPN requires. When the load on the firewall reaches a point at which there is an overall impact on network connectivity, it is best to either add a VAM to the firewall or offload the VPN services to a dedicated device.

# VPN Termination at a Dedicated VPN Appliance

Dedicated VPN appliances are designed to provide VPN tunnel services for LAN-to-LAN connections. Termination of the VPN at the corporate firewall allows for direct access from branch networks to the internal corporate core network. Remote users can then access all the internal services provided without having to authenticate a second time. This particular topology (shown in Figure 5.4) is best reserved for LAN-to-LAN connections such as branch-office-to-corporate-enterprise networks. The drawback to this topology is that as more branch offices are connected to the corporate office, the load on the firewall increases due to the increased amount of encryption each VPN requires. When the load on the firewall reaches a point at which there is an overall impact to network connectivity, it is best to either add a VAM to the firewall or offload the VPN services to a dedicated device.

**Figure 5.3** VPN Termination at the Firewall

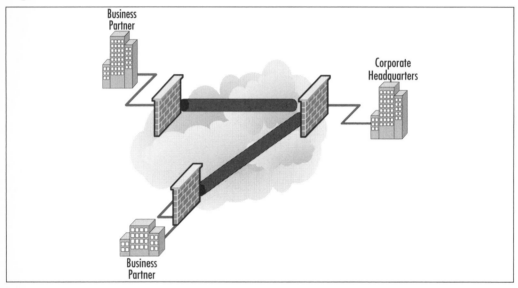

**Figure 5.4** VPN Terminations at a Dedicated VPN Appliance

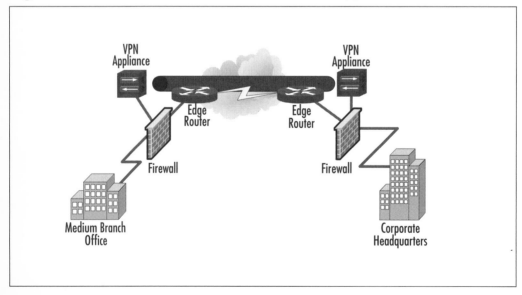

A further benefit to this deployment model is the ability to use the VPN appliances in conjunction with wireless networks.

# Topology Models

The deployment models we've discussed represent how VPNs can be implemented to provide access either to the DMZ or to the internal corporate network. This section focuses on the various topologies in which these models can be deployed. There are four general topologies to consider:

- Meshed (both fully and partially meshed)
- Star
- Hub and spoke
- Remote access

Each of these topologies is considered in greater detail in this section.

## Meshed Topology

Like their traditional WAN counterparts, meshed VPN topologies can be implemented in a fully or partially meshed configuration. Fully meshed configurations have a large number of alternate paths to any given destination. In addition, fully meshed configurations have exceptional redundancy because every VPN device provides connections to every other VPN device. This topology was illustrated in Figure 5.1. A simpler compromise is the partial-mesh topology, in which all the links are connected in a more limited fashion to other links. A partial-mesh topology is shown in Figure 5.5.

Mesh topology provides an inherent advantage that there is no single point of failure. Overall performance of the setup is independent of a single node or a single system. Sites that are geographically close can communicate with each other. Its main drawback is maintenance and key maintenance. For a fully meshed network, whenever a new node is added, all the other nodes will have to be updated. Even with the replacement of traditional WAN services such as frame relay or leased lines, fully meshed topologies can be expensive to implement due to the requirement to purchase a VPN device for every link in the mesh.

**Figure 5.5** Partial-Mesh VPN Topology

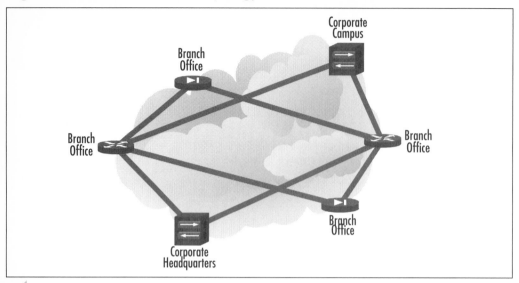

> **NOTE**
>
> Another issue you should be aware of with full versus partial-mesh topology is the number of tunnels you need to configure and manage. If you have 100 sites and add one router, think of all the connections you must make to rebuild a full mesh! In essence, the partial mesh is the way you want to go, but you might see an extra hop in the route from place to place because you will no longer have a single hop to any single destination. There is always give and take. Think about what method suits your design needs, and implement that method accordingly.

## Star Topology

In a star topology configuration, the remote branches can communicate securely with the corporate headquarters or central site. However, intercommunication between the branches is not permitted. Such a configuration could be deployed in a bank network so that compromise of one branch will not immediately lead to the compromise of a second branch without being detected. To gain access to a second branch, the attacker would have to first compromise the central network that would hopefully be able to detect such an attack. A star topology configuration is shown in

Figure 5.6. Star topologies provide an inherent advantage that a new site can be added with ease; only the central site will have to be updated.

In star topology, the central site plays an important role; if it fails, all the connections will go down. Performance of the central hub dictates the performance of the connection. For a star topology, it may happen that two nodes might be closed to each other; however, they will have to communicate via central node.

**Figure 5.6** Star VPN Deployment Topology

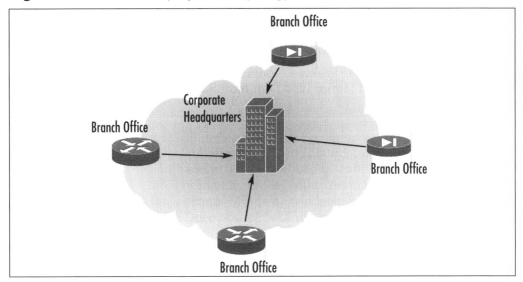

# Hub-and-Spoke Topology

A hub-and-spoke topology by design looks very similar to the star topology (Figure 5.7). However, there is one significant difference: Unlike the star topology, all branch or stub networks in a hub-and-spoke topology are able to access other branch or stub networks. The central, corporate network works as a simple transit point for all traffic from one end of the network to another. As traffic transits through the central corporate network, the data is decrypted, inspected, and re-encrypted for transmission to the final destination. This topology has more risk inherent in the design than the star topology because an attacker who is able to compromise one branch network might then be able to attack another branch network through the VPN without being required to attack the central, corporate network.

**Figure 5.7** Hub-and-Spoke VPN Topology

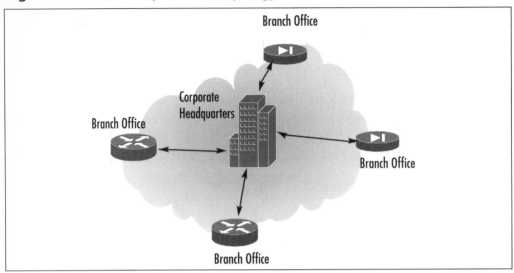

## Remote Access Topology

A final topology to consider is the remote access topology. Built on the hub-and-spoke VPN topology, this design focuses more on providing connectivity for remote users such as telecommuters, mobile workers, and other users who need access from no static IP addresses (Figure 5.8).

**Figure 5.8** Remote Access VPN Topology

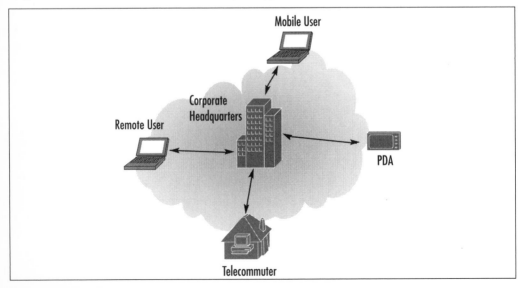

The next section presents advantages and disadvantages of VPNs.

## Pros of VPN

By using a VPN, organizations are not dependent on the expensive leased or frame relay lines. The employees are able to connect remote users to their corporate networks via a local Internet service provider (ISP) instead of via expensive 800-number or long distance calls to *resource-consuming modem banks*. This in turn will result in low cost to the companies. In addition, a VPN provides the best security using encryption and authentication protocols. By using a VPN, corporate can also use the remote access infrastructure within ISP. Corporations can add virtually unlimited amount of capacity without adding significant infrastructure. Mobile workers can access the corporate networks on their high-speed broadband connectivity. This in turn will yield flexibility and efficiency.

## Cons of VPN

Although a VPN provides security and flexibility, it does not offer quality of service. In a VPN, end-to-end throughput is not guaranteed, and there can be packet losses, delivered out of order, and fragmented. In a VPN, it is tough to achieve bandwidth reservation. Bandwidth reservation refers to the ability to reserve the bandwidth for traffic. It might be possible to reserve on out-bound traffic. For inbound traffic if you wish to have a bandwidth reservation, the VPN carrier will have to configure the VPN. For dialup users, a VPN tunnel can provide overhead in terms of additional protocol header, increase in authentication latency, and poor PPP and IP compression as compared to the direct link. This in turn will increase the latency for reconnection time. Encrypted data is not compressible, so when we use VPN to encrypt data, compression of data cannot be achieved. This in turn also means that hardware compression over the modem connection cannot be achieved.

The next section discusses public key cryptography, which will in turn help you to understand the concepts of IPSec.

# Public Key Cryptography

Public key cryptography, introduced in the 1970s, is the modern cryptographic method of communicating securely without having a previously agreed upon secret key. Public key cryptography typically uses a pair of keys to secure communications—a private key that is kept secret, and a public key that can be widely distributed. You should not be able to find one key of a pair simply by having the other. Public key cryptography is a form of asymmetric-key cryptography, since not all parties hold the same key. Some examples of public key cryptography algorithms include RSA, Diffie-Hellman, and ElGamal.

## Notes from the Underground...

### What Is Diffie-Hellman?

The Diffie-Hellman (DH) key exchange protocol, invented in 1976 by Whitfield Diffie and Martin Hellman is a protocol allowing two parties to generate shared secrets and exchange communications over an insecure medium without having any prior shared secrets. The Diffie-Hellman protocol consists of five groups of varying strength modulus. Most VPN gateways support DH Groups 1 and 2. The Diffie-Hellman protocol alone is susceptible to man-in-the-middle attacks, however. Although the risk of an attack is low, it is recommended that you enable *Perfect Forward Secrecy* (PFS discussed later in the chapter) as added security when defining VPN tunnels. For more information on the Diffie-Hellman protocol, see www.rsasecurity.com/rsalabs/node.asp?id=2248 and RFC 2631 at ftp://ftp.rfc-editor.org/in-notes/rfc2631.txt.

So, how does public key encryption work? Suppose John would like to exchange a message securely with Chris. Prior to doing so, Chris would provide John with his public key. John would then take the message he wishes to share with Chris and encrypt the message using Chris' public key. When Chris receives the message, he takes his private key and decrypts the message. Chris is then able to read the message John had intended to share with him. However, what if someone intercepts the message and has possession of Chris' public key? Absolutely nothing happens. When messages are encrypted using Chris' public key, they can only be decrypted using the private key associated with that public key.

## PKI

PKI is the meshing of encryption technologies, services, and software together to form a solution that enables businesses to secure their communications over the Internet. PKI involves the integration of digital certificates, certificate authorities (CAs), and public key cryptography. PKI offers several enhancements to the security of your enterprise.

PKI gives you the ability to easily verify and authenticate the identity of a person or organization. By using digital certificates, it is easy to verify the identity of parties involved in a transaction. The ease of verification of identity is also beneficial to access control. Digital certificates can replace passwords for access control, which are sometimes lost or easily cracked by experienced crackers.

# Certificates

Digital certificates are nothing more than a way to verify your identity through a CA using public key cryptography. There are certain steps you must take before you can use a certificate to validate your identity. First, you must generate a certificate request from within the VPN appliance. Then, the VPN appliance generates a public/private key pair. You then send a request with the public key to your CA. A response, which incorporates the public key, will be forwarded to you that will have to be loaded into the VPN appliance. This response generally includes three parts:

- The CA's certificate, which contains the CA's public key
- The local certificate identifying your VPN device
- In some cases, a certificate revocation list (CRL), which lists any certificates revoked by the CA

You can load the reply into the VPN device either through the Web UI or via TFTP (Thin File Transport Protocol) through the CLI (command line interface), whichever you prefer. Loading the certificate information into the VPN gives the following:

- Your identity can be verified using the local certificate.
- The CA's certificate can be used to verify the identity of other users.
- The CRL list can be used to identify invalid certificates.

# CRLs

A *certificate revocation list*, or CRL, is used to ensure that a digital certificate has not become invalid. VPN appliances use CRLs to check for invalid certificates before connecting VPN tunnels. When using digital certificates with VPNs, the certificate is validated during phase 1 negotiations. In the event no CRL has been loaded into the VPN, the appliance tries to retrieve a CRL via LDAP (Lightweight Directory Access Protocol) or HTTP (Hypertext Transfer Protocol), which is defined inside the CA certificate. Many VPN appliances also allow you to specify an address to refer to for the CRL. If you do not define an address, the default address within the CA's certificate is used.

# IPSec

IPSec's main design goals are to provide:

- **Data confidentiality** Encrypt data before transmission.

- **Data integrity** Each peer can determine if a received packet was changed during transit.

- **Data origin authentication** Receiver can validate the identity of a packet's sender.

- **Anti-replay** The receiver can detect and reject replayed packets, protecting it from spoofing and man-in-the-middle attacks.

## *IPSec Core Layer 3 Protocols: ESP and AH*

IPSec provides confidentiality and integrity protection for transmitted information, authentication source and destinations, and anti-replay protection. Two main network protocols, Encapsulating Security Payload (ESP) and Authentication Header (AH), are used to achieve this goal. All other parts of the IPSec standard merely implement these protocols and configure the required technical parameters. Applying AH or ESP to an IP packet may modify the data payload (not always) and may insert an AH or ESP header between the IP header and the packet contents. See Figures 5.9 and 5.10 for illustrations of how these transformations are performed.

**Figure 5.9** AH Encapsulation

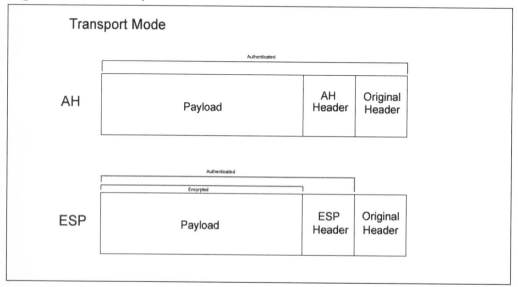

**Figure 5.10** ESP Encapsulation

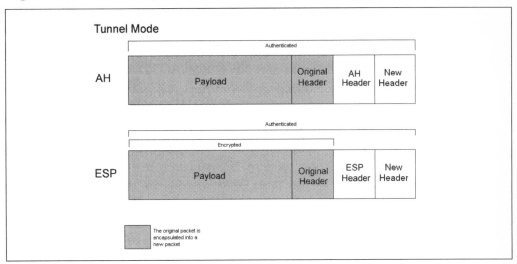

## Authentication Header

The AH, which is defined as IP protocol 51, ensures:

- **Data integrity**  Calculates a hash of the entire IP packet, including the original IP header (but not variable fields such as the TTL), data payload, and the authentication header (excluding the field that will contain the calculated hash value). This hash, an integrity check value (ICV), can be either Message Authentication Code (MAC) or a digital signature. MAC hashes are more common than digital signatures. Hashing algorithms include MD5 and SHA-1. Both are known as *keyed hashes*, meaning that they use an extra value to calculate the hash, which is known only to the participating parties. When the packet is received, its content, excluding some fields, is hashed by the receiver and the result is compared with the ICV. If they are the same, the packet is declared authentic.

- **Data origin authentication**  AH provides source IP authentication. Since the source IP is included in the data used to calculate the hash, its integrity is guaranteed.

- **Replay protection**  AH also includes an IPSec sequence number, which provides protection against replay attacks because this number is also included in authenticated data and can be checked by the receiving party.

AH provides no confidentiality because no encryption is used.

**NOTE**

Pure AH is always broken by NAT. For example, when an authenticated packet goes through an address-translation device, the IP address in its header changes and the Message Authentication Code (MAC) hash calculated by the receiver on a new packet will be incorrect, so the packet will be rejected. It is not possible for a translating gateway to recalculate the new MAC hash and insert it into the packet, because only the endpoints of a transmission know the hashing keys. This was a common problem with IPSec—trying to use AH when NAT is occurring somewhere in the path. It will simply not work.

## Encapsulating Security Payload

ESP, which is defined as IP protocol 50, provides:

- Packet padding to prevent traffic analysis, and encrypts the results using ciphers such as DES, 3DES, AES, or Blowfish.

- Optional authentication using the same algorithms as the AH protocol. IP header information is not included in the authenticated data, which allows ESP-protected packets to pass through NAT devices. When a packet is created, authentication data is calculated after encryption. This allows the receiver to check the packet's authenticity before starting the computationally intensive task of decryption.

- Optional anti-replay features.

The original ESP definition did not include authentication or anti-replay, as it was assumed the sender and receiver would use ESP and AH together to get confidentiality *and* authentication. Since ESP can also perform most of the AH functions, there is no reason to use AH. Because ESP works on encapsulation principles, it has a different format: All data is encrypted and then placed between a header and a trailer. This differentiates it from AH, where only a header is created.

## IPSec Communication Modes: Tunnel and Transport

Both AH and ESP can operate in either transport or tunnel mode. In transport mode, only the data portion of an IP packet is affected; the original IP header is not changed. Transport mode is used when both the receiver and the sender are endpoints of the communication—for example, two hosts communicating directly to each other. Tunnel mode encapsulates the entire original packet as the data portion of a new packet and creates a new external IP header. (AH and/or ESP headers are created in both modes.) Tunnel mode is more convenient for site-to-site VPNs because it allows tunneling of traffic through the channel established between two gateways.

In transport mode, the IP packet contains an AH or ESP header right after the original IP header, and before upper layer data such as a TCP header and application data. If ESP is applied to the packet, only this upper layer data is encrypted. If optional ESP authentication is used, only upper layer data, not the IP header, is authenticated. If AH is applied to the packet, both the original IP header and upper layer data are authenticated. Figure 5.11 shows what happens to the packet when IPSec is applied in transport mode.

**Figure 5.11** Packet Structure in Transport Mode

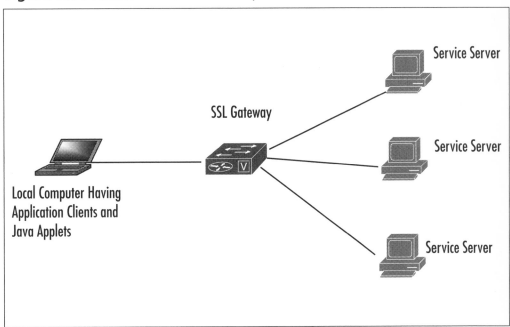

Tunnel mode is typically used to establish an encrypted and authenticated IP tunnel between two sites. The original packet is encrypted and/or authenticated and encapsulated by a sending gateway into the data part of a new IP packet, and then the new IP header is added to it with the destination address of the receiving gateway. The ESP and/or AH header is inserted between this new header and the data portion. The receiving gateway performs decryption and authentication of the packet, extracts the original IP packet (including the original source/destination IPs), and forwards it to the destination network. Figure 5.12 demonstrates the encapsulation performed in tunnel mode.

**Figure 5.12** Packet Structure in Tunnel Mode

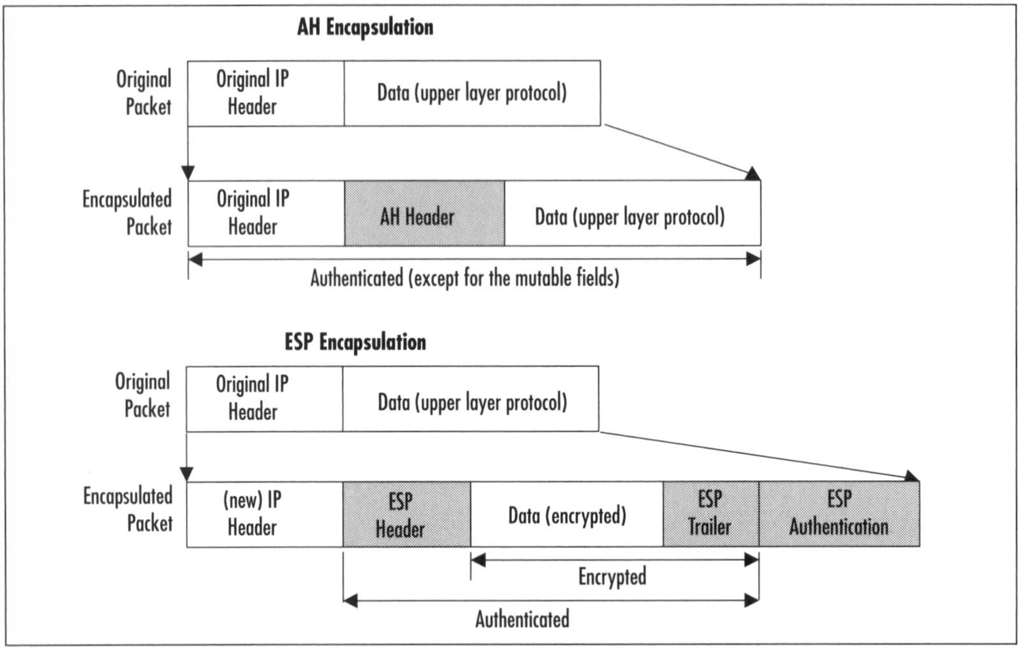

If AH is used, both the original IP header and the new IP header are protected (authenticated), but if ESP is used, even with the authentication option, only the original IP address, not the sending gateway's IP address, is protected. ESP is more than adequate since it is very difficult to spoof an IPSec packet without knowing many technical details. The exclusion of the new IP header from authenticated data also allows tunnels to pass through devices that perform NAT. When the new header is created, most of the options from the original IP header are mapped onto the new one—for example, the Type of Service (ToS) field.

# Internet Key Exchange

IPSec protocols use cryptographic algorithms to encrypt and authenticate, and requires encryption/authentication keys. It is possible to configure these keys manually, but there are disadvantages to this approach. First, it is very difficult to scale; second, it is not possible to renegotiate Security Associations (SAs) because they are fixed until manually changed. Thus, there is a strong need for tools for managing keys and SAs. Key management includes generation, distribution, storage, and deletion of the keys. The initial authentication of the systems to each other and protecting the key exchange is critical. After keys are exchanged, the channel is protected with these keys and is used to set up other parameters, including SAs.

The protocol the IETF adopted for performing these functions is Internet Security Association and Key Management Protocol (ISAKMP), defined in RFC 2408. RFC 2408 describes authenticated key exchange methods. ISAKMP has an IANA-assigned UDP port number of 500. ISAKMP is a generic protocol and is not tied to IPSec or any other key-using protocol.

ISAKMP can be implemented directly over IP or any transport layer protocol. When used with other key management protocols such as Oakley (RFC 2412) and Secure Key Exchange Mechanism (SKEME), we end up with a protocol called the Internet Key Exchange (IKE), which is defined in RFC 2409. Although not strictly correct, the abbreviations IKE and ISAKMP are often used interchangeably.

IKE has two exchange phases, and each can operate in one or two modes. IKE Phase 1 starts when two peers need to establish a secure channel—that is, they do not have IPSec SAs needed for communication over IPSec. This phase includes authentication of systems by each other, agreement on encryption and authentication algorithms used from then on to protect IKE traffic, performing a Diffie-Hellman (DH) key exchange, and finally, establishing an IKE Security Association (IKE SA). IKE SAs are bidirectional; each IKE connection between peers has only one IKE SA associated with it.

IKE Phase 2 negotiates one or more IPSec SAs, which will be used for the IPSec tunnel between these peers. It uses key material from IKE Phase 1 to derive keys for IPSec. One peer tells the other which traffic it wants to protect and which encryption/authentication algorithms are supported. The second peer then agrees on a single protection set for this traffic and establishes the keys.

While implementing different phases adds processing overhead, there are advantages to this approach:

- Trust between peers is established in the first phase and used in the second phase.

- Key material established in the first phase can be used in the second phase.

- Renegotiations of the first phase can be assisted by the second-phase data.

Phase 1 has two modes: main and aggressive. Main mode uses three exchanges between peers; each exchange consists of two messages, a request, and a reply:

- The first exchange in main mode negotiates parameters to protect the IKE connection. The initiating side sends a proposal to its counterpart, and includes parameters it supports. These parameters include one encryption algorithm (DES, 3DES, etc.) and one of three authentication algorithms: preshared secret, RSA public key encryption with Diffie-Hellman exchange group 1 and 2, or public key RSA signature (this includes use of certificates). The other peer then selects and accepts a single pair from the offered set. If there is no match or agreement, the IKE tunnel cannot be established.

- The second exchange in main mode performs DH key establishment between peers. It exchanges two values called nonces, which are hashes that only the other party can decrypt. This confirms that the message is sent by the same hosts as the previous exchange.

- The third and last exchange authenticates the peers using the agreed-on methods: public keys signatures, public key encryption, or a preshared secret. This exchange is protected by an encryption method that was selected in the first exchange.

RFC 2408 provides more details on the packet format and algorithms used. At the end of the first phase, each host has an IKE SA, which specifies all parameters for this IKE tunnel: the authentication method, the encryption and hashing algorithm, the Diffie-Hellman group used, the lifetime for this IKE SA, and the key values.

Aggressive mode exchanges only three packets instead of six, so it is faster but not as secure. Fewer packets are sent because the first two packets in this exchange include almost everything in one message; each host sends a proposed protection set, Diffie-Hellman values, and authentication values. The third packet is sent only for confirmation and after the IKE SA is already established. The weakness in aggressive mode is that everything is sent in clear text and can be captured. However, the only thing the attacker can achieve is to DoS one of the peers, because it is not possible to discover the keys that are established by the Diffie-Hellman protocol. There have been recent attacks against VPN endpoints that relied on the properties of aggressive mode.

The most important mode of Phase 2 is quick mode. It can be repeated several times using the same IKE SA established in Phase 1. Each exchange in this mode establishes two IPSec SAs by each peer. One of these SAs is used for inbound protection, and the other is used for outbound protection. During the exchange, peers agree on the IPSec SA parameters and send each other a new nonce, which is used for deriving Diffie-Hellman keys from the ones established in Phase 1. When the

IPSec SA lifetime expires, a new SA is negotiated in the same manner. Figure 5.13 summarizes the flow of the IKE protocol.

**Figure 5.13** IKE Phases and Modes

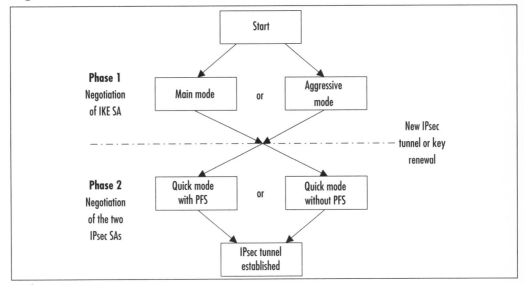

**NOTE**

Quick mode can use Perfect Forward Secrecy (PFS). PFS dictates that new encryption keys are not derived from previous ones, so even if one key is discovered, only the traffic protected by that key will be exposed. PFS is achieved by performing a new Diffie-Hellman key establishment in each quick mode.

## Security Associations

Previous sections assumed that an IPSec connection was already established and all parameters such as authentication and encryption keys were known to both parties. The data flow in each direction is associated with an entity called a *security association* (SA). Each party has at least two IPSec SAs: the sender has one for outgoing packets and another for incoming packets from the receiver, and the receiver has one SA for incoming packets from the sender and a second SA for outgoing packets to the sender.

Each SA has three parameters:

- The Security Parameter Index (SPI), which is always present in AH and ESP headers
- The destination IP address
- The IPSec protocol, AH or ESP (so if both protocols are used in communication, each has to have its own SA, resulting in a total of four SAs for two-way communication)

Each peer maintains a separate database of active SAs for each direction (inbound and outbound) on each of its interfaces. This database is known as the Security Association Database (SAD). SAs from these databases decide which encryption and authentication parameters are applied to the sent or received packet. SAs may be fixed for the time of traffic flow (called *manual IPSec* in some documents), but when a key management protocol is used, they are renegotiated many times during the connection. For each SA, the SAD entry contains the following data:

- The destination address
- The SPI
- The IPSec transform (protocol and algorithm used—for example; AH, HMAC-MD5)
- The key used in the algorithm
- The IPSec mode (tunnel or transport)
- The SA lifetime (in kilobytes or in seconds); when this lifetime expires, the SA must be terminated, and a new SA established
- The anti-reply sequence counters
- Some extra parameters such as Path MTU

The selection of encryption parameters and corresponding SAs is governed by the Security Policy Database (SPD). An SPD is maintained for each interface and is used to decide on the following:

- Selection of outgoing traffic to be protected
- Checking if incoming traffic was properly protected
- The SAs to use for protecting this traffic
- What to do if the SA for this traffic does not exist

The SPD consists of a numbered list of policies. Each policy is associated with one or more selectors, which are implemented as an access-lists. A *permit* statement means that IPSec should be applied to the matching traffic; a *deny* statement means that the packet should be forwarded without applying IPSec. The resulting map and a crypto access-list are applied to the interface, creating an SPD for this interface.

For outgoing traffic, when IPSec receives data to be sent, it consults the SPD to determine if the traffic has to be protected. If it does, the SPD uses an SA that corresponds to this traffic. If the SA exists, its characteristics are taken from the SAD and applied to the packet. If the SA does not exist yet, IKE establishes a new SA to protect the packet.

For incoming IPSec traffic, the SPI is culled from the AH or ESP header to find a corresponding SA in the SAD. If it does not exist, the packet is dropped. If an SA exists, the packet is checked/decrypted using the parameters provided by this SA. Finally, the SPD is checked to ensure this packet was correctly protected—for example, that it should have been encrypted using 3DES and authenticated with MD5 and nothing else.

## Designing & Planning...

### Cryptographic Algorithms in IPSec and Their Relative Strengths

Three types of cryptography algorithms are used in all IPSec implementations:

- Encryption
- Message authentication
- Key establishment

Encryption algorithms encipher clear-text messages, turning them into cipher text and deciphering them back to their original content via cryptographic keys. The simplest type of encryption algorithms is *symmetric encryption* where messages are encrypted and decrypted using the same key. This key must be kept a secret and well protected; otherwise, anybody can decrypt and read the message. The longer the key, the more difficult it is to "crack."

DES is an example of symmetric encryption. DES was adopted by the U.S. government as an official standard, but has now adopted the Advanced Encryption Standard (AES) for much stronger encryption. DES is obsolete and weak since messages encrypted with standard 56-bit DES can easily be cracked.

Continued

Triple DES (3DES) is a better solution, as it encrypts a message three times using DES, each time using a different 56-bit key. 3DES is still considered a strong cipher, although we see it being phased out in favor of AES.

Public-key cryptography uses complex exponential calculations and appears slow compared with symmetric-key ciphers such as 3DES or AES-128. Public-key cryptography uses two keys: one for encryption and a completely separate one for decryption. Only the decryption key (known as the *private key*) needs to be kept secret; the encryption key (known as the *public key*) can be made public. For example, if anyone wants to send Alice an encrypted message, he can use her public key to encrypt the message, but only Alice knows the key that allows her to decrypt the message. One widespread algorithm based on public keys is the Rivest, Shamir, and Adelman (RSA) algorithm.

Message authentication algorithms protect the integrity of a message. IPSec uses two types: keyed message hash algorithms and public signature algorithms. *Keyed message hashing* combines a message with a key and reduces it to a fixed-length digest. (Adding a key gives these algorithms the name *keyed*.) A *hashing algorithm* makes it almost impossible to create a spoofed message that will yield the same digest as the original message. When a receiver wants to ensure the message was not altered in transit, it performs the same calculation on the message and compares the result with the received digest. If they are the same, the message is authentic; a spoofed one would have a different digest.

IPSec uses MD5, which produces 128-bit output, and the stronger SHA-1, which produces 160-bit output. Although SHA-1 is cryptographically stronger than MD5, it requires more processing to compute the hash. IPSec uses modified versions of each, HMAC-MD5 and HMAC-SHA-1, which perform hashing twice, each time differently combining the message with the key.

Key establishment protocols securely exchange symmetric keys by both sides via an insecure medium (such as the Internet). In IPSec, this task is accomplished using the Diffie-Hellman (DH) algorithm. DH is based on exponential computations. During the process, both sides exchange digits, allowing both peers to derive the same key, but nobody who sees these numbers can do the same. DH in IPSec can work with keys of different lengths: 768-bit (DH Group 1), 1024-bit (DH Group 2), and 1536-bit (DH Group 5). Group 5 keys are stronger, but require more processing power.

# Pros of IPSec

The IPSec protocol, as defined by the IETF, is "a framework of open standards for ensuring private, secure communications over Internet Protocol networks, through the use of cryptographic security services." This means that IPSec is a set of standards used for encrypting data so it can pass securely through a public medium, such as the Internet. Unlike other methods of secure communications, IPSec is not bound to any particular authentication method or algorithm, which is why it is considered an "open standard." In addition, unlike older security standards that were implemented at the application layer of the OSI model, IPSec is implemented at the network layer.

**NOTE**

Remember that IPSec is implemented at the network layer, not the application layer.

The advantage to IPSec being implemented at the network layer (versus the application layer) is that it is not application-dependent, meaning users do not have to configure each application to IPSec standards.

IPSec can be used to secure any protocol that makes use of IP. It also enjoys the support of the medium over which IP runs. Other encryption schemes to secure data, like PGP, expect a user to remember his or her passphrase, ensure the passphrase is safe, and the user must follow procedures to validate the correspondent's keys. IPSec is independent of the overhead in terms of expectation from a user to secure data. It is transparent to a user. IPSec authentication mechanism also provides prevention against many attacks on a high-level protocol. For example, a man-in-the-middle attack is not possible for an application using IPSec.

## Cons of IPSec

The IPSec protocol is an open protocol. The different design choices among different vendors have often resulted in IPSec-compliant products that differ from each other, which will cause these products to not operate with each other. IPSec-based VPN is tightly coupled with the operating system, so there is a longer packet processing time. IPSec has been designed to provide authentication between computers. It does not provide the concept of user ID, or support authentication of users, which is required for many other security mechanisms. If we want to design some sort of access control to our e-mail server or database server, a non-IPSec mechanism will be desired. IPSec provides encryption at the IP layer between two computers, which again is different from encrypting messages between users or between applications. For example, to secure e-mail, PGP is still preferred.

To ensure the integrity of data being transmitted using IPSec, there has to be a mechanism in place to authenticate end users and manage secret keys. This mechanism is called Internet Key Exchange (IKE). IKE is used to authenticate the two ends of a secure tunnel by providing a secure exchange of a shared key before IPSec transmissions begin.

For IKE to work, both parties must use a password known as a *pre-shared* key. During IKE negotiations, both parties swap a *hashed* version of a pre-shared key. When they receive the hashed data, they attempt to recreate it. If they successfully recreate the hash, both parties can begin secure communications.

IPSec also has the capability to use digital signatures. A digital signature is a certificate signed by a trusted third party (CA) that offers authentication and *nonrepudiation*, meaning the sender cannot deny that the message came from him. Without a digital signature, one party can easily deny he was responsible for messages sent.

Although *public key cryptology* ("User A" generates a random number and encrypts it with "User B's" *public key*, and User B decrypts it with his *private key*) can be used in IPSec, it does not offer nonrepudiation. The most important factor to consider when choosing an authentication method is that *both parties must agree on the method chosen*. IPSec uses an SA to describe how parties will use AH and encapsulating security payload to communicate. The security association can be established through manual intervention or by using the Internet Security Association and Key Management Protocol (ISAKMP). The Diffie-Hellman key exchange protocol is used for secure exchange of pre-shared keys.

Certain fields like source and destination gateway address, packet size, and so forth in IPSec can be used for traffic analysis. IPSec is prone to traffic analysis. IPSec cannot provide all the functionality of other security protocol working at upper layers. For example, IPSec cannot be used to digitally sign a document. IPSec and the applications that make use of IPSec are still prone to DoS attacks. Another serious drawback of IPSec VPN is the inability to work behind NAT devices. The authentication header in the IPSec mode hashes the source addresses during the authentication process. If NAT changes the source address, the VPN on the other end will see a different hash when it receives the packet. It will drop the packet, thinking it has been tampered with. Errors due to mismatched hashes because of a changed address can be avoided by running IPSec in tunnel mode using only Encapsulating Security Payload (ESP). IPSec cannot be used with non–IP protocols like AppleTalk, IPX, NetBIOS, and DECnet.

# SSL VPNs

Many years ago, accessing corporate resources and being productive while away from the office was a dream. With the advent of the IPSec VPN, accessing resources remotely is becoming a reality. However, using IPSec, company had several hundred or even a thousand employees who all needed remote access. There was software to install and update the policies to create. Generally speaking, when you deploy IPSec client software you must also purchase licenses. This can become extremely costly if you have a fairly large user base. The ability to access a company's resources while on the go is now at an all-time high.

This is where SSL VPN comes into play. SSL VPN allows you to secure your internal resources behind a single entry point device; the remote users only require a Web browser capable of SSL encryption. The user connects to the SSL-VPN gateway and begins his or her secure session. At this point, the user can access many different types of resources. This provides secure ubiquitous client access and because you don't have to deploy a client, you can easily deploy access to thousands of users in a matter of hours (Figure 5.14).

**Figure 5.14** SSL-Based VPN

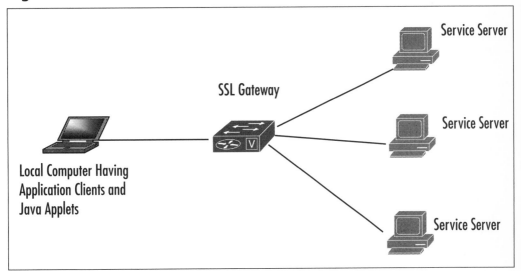

## Technical Description

A secure tunnel between computers provides secure communication channel between two computers. SSL uses asymmetric cryptography to share secrets between the local computers and then uses symmetric keys to encrypt the communication between the SSL gateways. To rehash, an encrypted tunnel between two computers over an insecure network such as the Internet is known as a virtual private network. SSL-VPN thus creates a secure tunnel by making sure both the users are authenticated before allowing access, and encrypting all data transmitted to and from the users by using SSL.

Earlier, we discussed the IPSec-based VPN. The difference between the IPSec-based VPN and the SSL-based VPN is that IPSec operates at the IP layer or at network layers, and SSL–VPN establishes connection using SSL, which works at the transport and session layers. They can also encapsulate information at the presentation and application layers. Thus, you can see that SSL-based VPN is the most versatile.

SSL between client and server as shown in Figure 5.14 can in turn be divided into two phases: handshake and data exchange. The handshake phase between the local machine and the server requires three phases.

# First Phase

During the first phase, client and server exchange hello, which in turn enables the client and server to exchange information about the encryption ciphers and the compression algorithms.

- **Client's hello** Comprised of protocol version supported, Session ID, list of supported data and key encryption ciphers, supported compression methods, and a nonce.

- **Server's hello message** Protocol version to be used, Session ID, one cipher for data and one for key exchange, one compression method and a nonce.

Based on the cryptography and compression algorithms, the client and server decide to cancel or proceed with the session. The next handshake phase involves authentication and key exchange between both the parties.

# Second Phase

The second phase involves the authentication, between client and server, and is done by exchanging digital certificates.

**Server's authentication** Server certificate or Server's public key, certificate request, "hello done" notification.

**Client's authentication** Clients certificate or client's public key, certificate verification.

A digital certificate is issued and signed by the private key of the CA and comprises the following:

- Owners public key
- Owner's name
- Expiration date of the public key

- Name of the issuer (the CA that issued the digital certificate)

- Serial number of the digital certificate

- Digital signature of the issuer

The CA can be some trusted third party such as VeriSign. The client must possess the public keys of the trusted party to verify that it has the public keys of the correct server. Digital certificates then help in handing over the public keys in a secure manner. The client will then use the public keys of the server to encrypt a pre-master secret and send it to the server. This pre-master secret is then used to generate a master secret, which aids in the generation of symmetric keys for data exchange. The symmetric keys between client and the server are then used to encrypt data.

## Third Phase

In the third phase, client and server wrap up the communication. Closing communication is performed by sending a 1-byte value that conveys finished notification.

Server Finish is comprised of change cipher spec, which is a 1-byte value, "finished notification." Client Finish in turn is comprised of change cipher spec and "finished" specifications. Once the client and server have finished authentication, the next stage involves the data exchange stage of SSL, which involves various stages.

First, data is fragmented into 18kB and then compressed. After compression, SSL appends a message authentication code MAC to the compressed data:

```
MAC{data} = hash { secret_key + hash{ secret_key  + data + time_stamp}}
```

The message authentication code is added to the packet and is then forwarded to the next layer, which involves encryption of the message. After encryption is complete, the SSL header is added to the packet and sent to the SSL layer. The packet is ready to be sent to the other side.

## SSL Tunnels in Linux

One of the most commonly used open source SSL VPNs is Open VPN, which uses TAP and TUN virtual drivers. For Linux version 2.4.x or later, these driver are already bundled with the kernel. Open VPN tunnels traffic over the UDP port 5000. Open VPN can either use TUN driver to allow the IP traffic or TAP driver to pass the Ethernet traffic. Open VPN requires configuration to be set in the configuration files. Open VPN has two secure modes. The first is based on SSL/TLs security using public keys like RSA, and the second is based on using symmetric keys or pre-shared secrets. RSA certificates and the keys for the first mode can be generated by using the **openssl** command. Details about these certificates or the private keys are stored in our *.cnf files to establish VPN connection.

The .crt extension will denote the certificate file, and .key will be used to denote private keys. The SSL–VPN connection will be established between two entities, one of which will be a client, which can be your laptop, and the other will be a server running at your office or lab. Both these computers will have .conf files, which define the parameters required to establish SSL–VPN connection.

For the server side, let's call the file tls-srvr.conf, details of which are shown in Figure 5.15.

## Figure 5.15 Configuration of the *.conf File on Server Side

```
# may be used to delimit comment. (Line 1)
dev tun
# 12.23.34.56 is the IP address of Server   (Line 2)
# 12.23.34.57 is the IP address of the Client  (Line 3)
 ifconfig 12.34.56 12.23.34.57
#scripts will establish routes when a VPN is alive (Line 4)
up ./srvr.up
# the script will be for server (Line 5)
tls-server
# Diffe –Hellman parameters (Line 6)
dh dh1234.pem
# Certificate Authority File (Line 7)
ca  my-ca.crt
 # Our certificate / Public Key (Line 8)
cert srvr.crt
# Private Key  key of Server (Line 9)
key srvr.key
# Open VPN uses port 5000 by default
# Each VPN must use a different Port (Line 10)
Port 5000
#UID and GID should be initialized to "nobody"  (Line 11)
user nobody
group nobody
#Verbosity Level  (Line 12)
#0 --quite except for fatal error
#1 – mostly quite , but can display non-fatal network error
#3 – Medium output, good for normal operations
#9 – Verbose, good for trouble shooting
verb 3
```

The configuration of srvr.up, which is mentioned after line 4, is shown in Figure 5.16.

The *.cnf file (let's call it clt.cnf) on the client side will look similar to Figure 5.12. However, there will be modifications in some of the parameters in the file. After line 3, the parameters of ifconf will change to ifconfig 12.1.0.2 12.1.0.1  # from client side to server side. 12.23.34.57 is the IP address of the client, and # 12.23.34.56 is the IP address of the server.

After line 4, modification will be

```
up ./cnt.up
```

After line 5, modification will be

```
tls-client
```

## Figure 5.16 Configuration of the srvr.up File

```
# !/bin/bash
route add –net  12.0.1.0 netmask 255.255.255.0 gw $5
```

Again, the certificate on the client side will point to the certificate of the client. If local.crt is storing the certificate of client and the private key of client is key local.key, then

```
cert home.crt
key local.key
```

will have to be added after line 8 and line 9.
The remaining part of the configuration file for the client side will remain the same.
    The configuration of the clt.up to start a VPN server is shown in Figure 5.17.

## Figure 5.17 Configuration of the clt.up File

```
#!/bin/bash
route add –net 12.23.34.0 netmask 255.255.255.0 gw $5
```

Once these files are configured, to start a VPN at the server side execute the command
*$ open vpn –config tls-srvr.cnf*

and similarly to start at the client side, use

*$ openvpn –config tls–clt.cnf*

# Pros

SSL VPN is one way to transfer the information since a web browser can be used to establish an SSL VPN connection. Since SSL VPN is clientless, it will result in cost savings and can be configured to allow access from corporate laptops, home desktops, or any computer in an Internet café. SSL VPNs also provide support for authentication methods and protocols, some of which include:

- Active Directory (AD)
- Lightweight Directory Access Protocol (LDAP)
- Windows NT LAN Manager (NTLM)
- Remote Authentication Dial-In User Service (RADIUS)
- RSA Security's RSA ACE/Server and RSA SecurID

Many SSL VPNs also provide support for single sign-on (SSO) capability. More sophisticated SSL VPN gateways provide additional network access through downloadable ActiveX components, Java applets, and installable Win32 applications. These add-ons help remote users access a wide range of applications, including:

- Citrix MetaFrame
- Microsoft Outlook
- NFS
- Remote Desktop
- Secure Shell (SSH)
- Telnet

However, note that not all SSL VPN products support all applications.

SSL VPN can also block traffic at the application level, blocking worms and viruses at the gateway. SSL VPN is again not bound to any IP address; hence, unlike IPSec VPN, connections can be maintained as the client moves. SSL VPN differs from IPSec VPN in that it provides fine-tuned access control. By using SSL VPN, each resource can be defined in a very granular manner, even as far as a URL. This feature of SSL VPN enables remote workers to access internal Web sites, applications, and file servers. This differs from IPSec VPN, since the entire corporate network can be defined in a single statement. SSL-based VPN uses Secure HTTP, TCP port 443. Many corporate network firewall policies allow outbound access for port 443 from any computer in the corporate network. In addition, since HTTPS traffic is encrypted, there will be limited restrictive firewall rules for SSL VPN.

# Cons

As you know, SSL-based VPN offers a greater choice of client platforms and is easy to use. However, an organization that wants to be sure their communication channel is encrypted and well secured will never assume that any computer in an Internet café is trusted. This in turn requires a trust association with an un-trusted client connection. To address the concern of an untrusted client, whenever a client from an untrusted platform connects to the VPN, a small java applet is downloaded to the client that searches for malicious files, processes, or ports. Based on the analysis of the computer, the applet can also restrict the types of client that can connect. This may sound feasible theoretically; practically, it requires the mapping of policies of one anti-virus and anti-spyware tool into an endpoint security tool used by VPN. In addition, these applets are prone to evasion and can be bypassed. However, note it carefully; you also need to have administrative access to perform many of the operations like deleting temporary files, deleting cookies, clearing cache, and so forth. If you have administrative rights in an Internet café, be assured that the system will be infected with keystroke loggers, sophisticated malicious remote access tools like Back Orifice using ICMP as a communication channel and RC4 to encrypt the payload.

By using SSL VPN, a user can download sensitive files or confidential, proprietary corporate data. This sensitive data has to be deleted from the local computer when an SSL VPN is terminated. To ensure the safety of confidential data, a sandbox is proposed and used. A sandbox is used to store any data downloaded from a corporate network via SSL VPN. After the SSL VPN session is terminated, the data in the sandbox is securely deleted. After a session is terminated, all logon credentials require deletion as well. You know that SSL VPN can be established even from a cyber café. It might happen that a user can leave the system unconnected. To prevent such issues, periodic authentication is required in some systems. As SSL VPN works on the boundary of Layers 4 and 5, each application has to support its use. In IPSec VPN, a large number of static IP address can be assigned to the remote client using RADIUS. This in turn provides the flexibility to filter and control the traffic based on source IP address. In the case of SSL VPN, the traffic is normally proxies from a single address, and all client sessions originate from this single IP. Thus, a network administrator is unable to allocate privileges using a source IP address. SSL-based VPN allows more firewall configurations as compared to IPSec VPN to control access to internal resources. Another cause of concern with SSL-based VPN is packet drop performance. IPSec will drop the malformed packet at the IP layer, whereas SSL will take it up the layer in the OSI model before dropping it. Hence, a packet will have to be processed more before it is dropped. This behavior of SSL-based VPN can be misused, used to execute DoS attacks, and if exploited, can result in a high capacity usage scenario.

# Layer 2 Solutions

A Layer 2 solution from Microsoft and Cisco makes use of both the Point-to-Point Protocol and Cisco Layer 2 protocols. Since the Layer 2 VPN solution provides a significant amount of revenue for the independent local exchange carriers (ILECs) and PTT (Post, Telephone, and Telegraph) service providers, the need for Layer 2 VPN has been increasing. However, the connections for a Layer 2 solution are costly, and the customers want more effective cost solutions. To aid customers, ILECS and PTT are using more effective solutions such as Multiprotocol Label Switching (MPLS), which offers Layer 2 VPN services. L2TP, as the name suggests, operates at the data link layer of the OSI networking model. L2TP is discussed in more detail in the following section. In the Layer 2 VPN solutions, there is no separate private IP network over which traffic is sent. Layer 2 VPNs take existing Layer 2 traffic and send it through point-to-point tunnels on an MPLS network backbone. Layer 2 MPLS VPNs are also called as Transparent LAN Services (TLS ) or VPLS Virtual Private LAN Services.

Some vendors who provide MPLS VPN include Avici Systems (www.avivi.com), Cisco Systems (www.cisco.com), CoSine Communications (www.cosineco.com), Juniper Networks (www.juniper.com), Lucent Technology (www.lucent.com), Nortel Networks (www.nortelnetworks.com), and Riverstone Networks (www.riverstonenetworks.com).

## L2TP

L2TP is a combination of PPTP and Layer 2 Forwarding (L2F), put forth by Cisco Systems. L2TP can encapsulate PPP frames just as PPTP can, but in contrast can then be sent over IP, ATM, or frame relay. It is rather more complicated than PPTP, and more secure.

The IPSec Encapsulating Security Payload (ESP) protocol is used to encrypt L2TP traffic. As you can see in Figure 5.18, one advantage of IPSec is that it encrypts more than just the PPP data packet.

As to security, L2TP is extremely strong. In addition to requiring user authentication through PPP, L2TP requires machine authentication via certificates. Although

certificates are covered in Chapter 3, you need to understand the following requirements for an L2TP implementation of a LAN-to-LAN VPN. First, a user certificate
needs to be installed on the calling router, and a computer certificate needs to be
installed on the answering router.

**Figure 5.18** An L2TP Packet

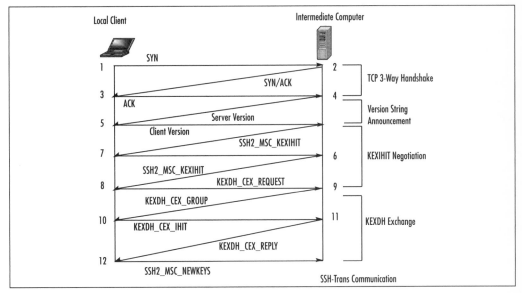

---

**TIP**

If the answering router is a member server in a domain, a computer certificate is required for L2TP. However, if the router is a domain controller
(DC), a DC certificate is needed.

---

# PPTP versus L2TP

When choosing which layering protocol to use for a secure VPN, you should under-
stand some of the differences between them. One of the largest differences between
PPTP and L2TP is the method of encryption each uses. PPTP uses MPPE, and
L2TP uses IPSec ESP.

When PPTP negotiations happen between a client and the VPN server, the
authentication phase is not encrypted, even when using the strongest form of MPPE
(128-bit RSA RC4). IPSec encryption, however, is negotiated even before the L2TP

connection is established. This allows the securing of both data and passwords. Moreover, IPSec can be configured to use Triple DES (3–DES), which is based on three separately generated 56-bit keys, for true 168-bit encryption. It is the strongest encryption method natively supported by Windows Server 2003.

Another consideration when choosing between L2TP and PPTP is how to implement packet filtering. In RRAS, packet filters can be implemented through the external interface's property sheet, located in the General IP Routing section. To allow only PPTP traffic through, the VPN server requires the dropping of all traffic except TCP port 1723 and protocol ID number 47 on both the input and output filters. L2TP, however, is more complicated. It requires the dropping of all traffic except UDP ports 500, 4500, and 1701.

Even though the implementation of L2TP is more administrative work than PPTP, it is recommended for all high-security environments. However, keep in mind that both L2TP and PPTP can be used on the same VPN server. It is also recommended that you use packet filtering and firewalls on all LAN-to-LAN and remote access VPNs.

# Technical Description for MPLS

Figure 5.19 shows the architecture for Layer 2 in a Layer 2 VPN. For the rest of the discussion about a Layer 2 solution, CE will represent the customer edge router, and PE will correspond to the provider edge router. PE performs the functionality of egress/ingress routing. The devices that perform the functionality of transit routing are called as provider routers, or P. Provider routers are less complex than PE.

**Figure 5.19** The Connection between Different Provider Edge Routers when There Are Three Customers' Sites

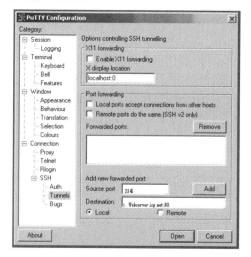

As shown in Figure 5.19, in a Layer 2 solution, traffic is forwarded to the provider edge PE router in a Layer 2 format. Interior Gateway Protocol (IGP) or static routes are enabled on the provider edge routers. The traffic is carried in MPLS format over the provider's network and is converted back to the Layer 2 traffic at the sending computer. MPLS works by pre-pending packets with an MPLS header, containing one or more "labels"—called a label stack. Figure 5.20 shows the structure of the MPLS stack. The label stacks as shown in Figure 5.20 contain four fields. The first field is a 20-bit label value. The next field is of size 3 bits; currently, this is reserved for any future use. Following the EXP field is 1-bit stack flag. If the stack flag is set (s=1), it signifies the current label is the last. Following the stack flag, is an 8-bit TTL (time to live) field.

**Figure 5.20** MPLS Packet Structure

Instead of lookup in the IP Tables, MPLS packets are forwarded by label lookup. When the ingress router encounters an unlabeled packet, it inserts the MPLS header. The packet is then forwarded to the next hop. The MPLS router, based on the contents of the MPLS packet, can perform three operations: SWAP, PUSH, or POP. The routers can also have built-in lookup tables that in turn can aid in deciding which kind of operations to perform based on the topmost label of the incoming packet so they can process the packet very quickly. In a PUSH operation, a new label is pushed on to the top of the label. This in turn aids in hierarchical routing of packets. For a SWAP operation, the packet label is replaced with the other label. For POP operation, the packet label is removed. The process of removing the label from the MPLS header is called *decapsulation*. At the egress router, the popped label is the last label of the packet. When the last label is removed from the MPLS packet, the packet contains only the payload. Therefore, the egress router must contain the information about the routing of the packet without any label lookup. In a Layer 2 VPN, IPSec, and more specifically its ESP protocol, provides the encryption for L2TP tunnels. L2TP also requires digital certificates, which in turn also computer authentication.

## Pros

A Layer 2 solution service provider provides only a Layer 2 solution to the customers. Hence, in a Layer 2 solution, routing of the packets, which is done at Layer 3, is the responsibility of the customer or the local host. This in turn results in privacy of routing, and customers are free to choose their own Layer 3 protocol. Also notice that overhead in maintaining information on the service provider router is also reduced in terms that they will not have to do anything to keep a customer's route separate from other customers or from the Internet. As shown in Figure 5.12, each PE in Layer 2 will transfer small information about every CE, that it is connected to every PE. Each PE will have to keep information from each CE in each VPN and keep a single "route" to every site in every VPN. In a Layer 2 VPN, if customers believe the Layer 2 service is insecure, they can use IPSec on top of a Layer 2 solution.

## Cons

The important problem with Layer 2 VPNs is that they will tie up the service provider VPN to Layer 2 circuits; for example, x.25, frame relay, and ATM (Asynchronous Transfer Mode). If there are n local hosts, and each is connected to each other (i.e., meshed network), the complexity of configuring is O (n*n), and is exponential in nature. Therefore, as the number of local hosts increases, the complexity of configuration increases exponentially. For n CEs, n*(n−1) /2 DLCI PVC must be provisioned across the service provider network, and at each CE, (n−1) DLCIs must be configured to reach each of other CEs. In addition, when a new CE is added, n new DLCI PVCs must be provisioned. Existing CEs must also be updated with a new DLCI to reach the new CE. (See the upcoming "Notes from the Underground" sidebar for more information on PVC, DLCI, and CDs.)

The Layer 2 solution is costly for the provider, and hence the topologies in a Layer 2 solution can be dictated by the cost rather than traffic patterns. Multiple Layer 2 solutions can result in an increase of administrative costs. In a Layer 2 VPN, if a CE is under the control of a customer, he may decide to use IPSec to secure his communication channel. However, the overhead involved in providing this extra security can result in slightly slower performance than PPTP. The client has to perform two authentications for dial-in users with the VPN carrier L2TP model; one when it encounters VPN carrier POP, and on contact with Enterprise gateway security.

## Notes from the Underground…

### What Are PVC (Permanent Virtual Circuits) , DLCI (Data Link Connection Identifier), and CE (Customer Edge Router)?

PVC provides frame relay service. It is a data link connection that is predefined on the both ends of the connection. The actual path taken through the network may alter; however, the beginning and end point of the circuits remain the same.

PVCs are identified by the DLCI, which is a 10-bit channel number attached to a data frame that aids in routing the data. Frame relays are multiplexed statistically, which results in transmission of one frame at a time. The DLCI, helps in logical connection of data to the connection; when a data goes to the network, the network knows where to send it.

A CE router interfaces the customer network with the provider network. Using it, a customer can limit the number of MAC addresses to the provider network.

# SSH Tunnels

Let's take the case of an organization in which all computers on the network have public IP addresses. This means that you can access any computer from anywhere in the world. This definitely is convenient for the mobile workforce or the employees because they can directly connect to the computers in their offices, research labs, and so forth (see Figure 5.21).

Public IP addresses can also cause problems. Since the computers on public IP addresses are universally accessible, they could be attacked by anyone on the global Internet. These computers could be attacked by viruses or worms, and thereby become infected and capable of spreading the infection to others.

**Figure 5.21** Connections between Local Machines and between Computers on a Private IP Using SSH Tunnel

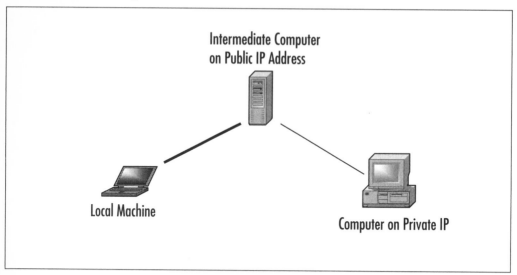

By using SSH tunnels, as you can see in Figure 5.21, you can access the computers that have public IP addresses. You can then forward the traffic to a computer with a private IP address such as an office or research lab computer. This method in turn provides the security of a private IP address, while retaining the convenience of a public IP address. An SSH tunnel provides the same functionality as a VPN, but with a simpler configuration.

# Technical Description

An SSH tunnel is a connection that takes traffic from an arbitrary port on one machine and sends it through an intermediate machine to a remote machine. Since it uses SSH to create the tunnel, between your computer and the computer on a public IP address, all your data is encrypted.

There are three basic steps to creating a tunnel to a privately addressed machine, and it requires three computers: your local computer, an intermediate computer with a public IP address, and the privately addressed destination computer to which you want to establish a connection.

Before you start an SSH connection from your local computer to the intermediate computer with a public IP address, you have to install SSH clients on your local computer. Some of the common SSH clients are Putty for Windows, MacSSH, MacSFTP, and Nifty Telnet for Mac OS. There are two main, incompatible versions of the SSH protocol: SSH1 (1.5) and SSH2. SSH1 uses CRC32 (cyclic redundancy check) to check the integrity of a message. CRC32s are prone to collision and are normally used to detect accidental errors in transmissions (IP, TCP, and UDP, for example, use a checksum in their headers). SSH2 (which is the latest version of SSH), on the other hand, uses MACs to check the integrity of messages. Integrity of messages in SSH2, is strengthened by using a cryptographic hash such as MD5 or SHA1. Since SSH1 and SSH use two different schemes to ensure the integrity of the message, make sure you use the recent version of SSH2, or the SSH1 between the client on a local host and on the server are the same.

Care has to be taken when you establish the connection to a computer having a public IP address for the first time—make sure you are connecting to the right computer. The SSH2 client will prompt with a warning that it has never seen that computer before. It will then store the public key of the computer having a public IP address in a cache so that on follow-up connections it can compare the received public key with the cached version and verify it hasn't changed.

Figure 5.22 shows the packets exchanged while establishing an SSH connection. Notice that packets 1, 2, and 3 are being used to establish the TCP 3-way handshake. As previously discussed, an SSH connection is successfully established only when both the client and the server have the same version number; if not, either peer can force termination of connection. Packets 4 and 5 as per Figure 5.22 while establishing SSH connection are being used for version string announcement. The server sends its version number first, and then the client sends it. A special code "1.99:" demonstrates that the server supports both SSH1 and SSH2. After the version number is verified, the next phase involves key exchange, bulk data encryption, message integrity, and compression. The primary objective of the SSH2_MSG_KEX-INIT exchange (packets 6, 7) the primary objective is to negotiate the algorithms for key exchange, bulk data encryption, message integrity, and compression. The peers will also let each other know the accepted host key types. As mentioned earlier, if diffie-hellman-group-exchange-sha1 is selected as the key exchange method, in SSH2_MSG_KEXDH_GEX_REQUEST (packet 8) the client notifies the server of its minimum, preferred, and maximum prime size for the group.

SSH2_MSG_KEXDH_GEX_GROUP (packet 9) is the server's response to the request and contains an appropriate size for the group's prime packet, and two multiprocessing integers containing the prime to be used (p) and the corresponding generator (g). After receiving this message, both client and server know the Diffie Hellman group to use. There are only two remaining packets in the key exchange (packets 10 and 11) before enough parameters are negotiated to start encrypting data. The client receives p and g, generates a random number x, such that $1 < x < (p-1)/2$, and then calculates $e = g^x \bmod p$. The value of e is sent in

SSH2_MSG_KEXDH_GEX_INIT (packet 10). After the server receives the client's SSH2_MSG_KEXDH_GEX_INIT message, the server generates its own random number y, calculates f = g^y mod p, and sends "f" to the client in SSH2_MSG_KEXDH_GEX_REPLY (packet 11). The server also calculates k = e^y mod p, which is the value of the shared secret. The client, after receiving the reply SSH2 _MSG_KEXDH_GEX_REPLY, does the same, using formula k = f^x mod p. If everything goes right, the client and server should compute identical values for k. This is very important, because k is one of the elements used to create the exchange hash signature, which is the primary factor in server authentication. SSH2_MSG_NEWKEYS (packet 12) contains the notice that keying materials and algorithms should go into effect from this point on.

**Figure 5.22** SSH Packet Exchange Diagram between Client and Intermediate Machine

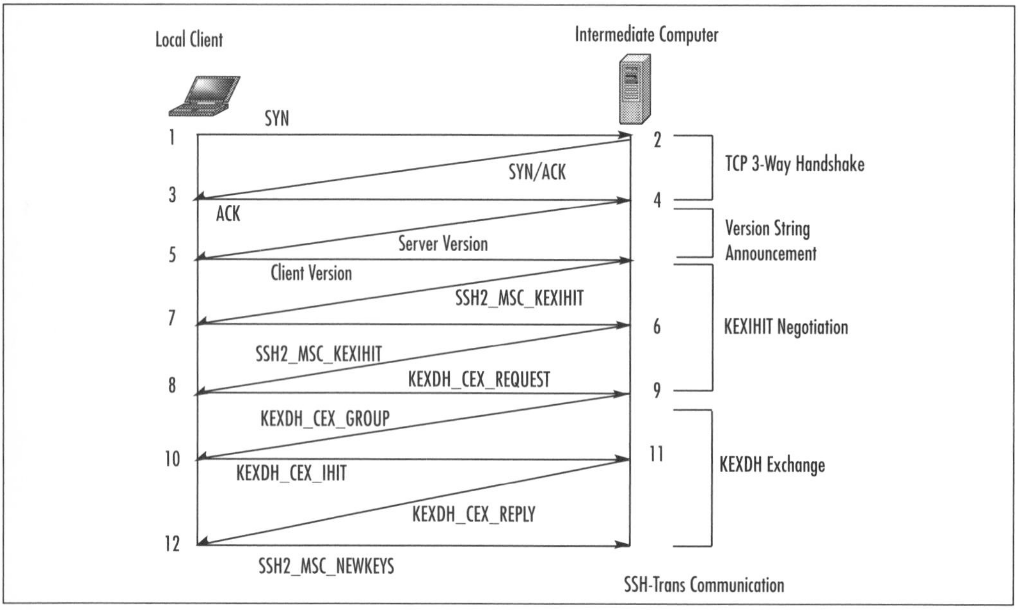

Once you have successfully established an SSH connection with the intermediate computer, the next step is to configure the connection to listen for traffic, to some port on your local machine. This port on the local machine is called forwarded. In the second step, the forwarded port is bound to the local host. When a process connects to the local host on forwarded port on the client machine, the /usr/bin/ssh client program accepts the connection. The SSH client informs the SSH server, over the encrypted channel, to create a connection to the remote computer (or the computer having a private IP address as shown in Figure 5.22). The client takes any data to the forwarded port, and sends it to the SSH server on a public IP, inside the encrypted SSH session. The SSH server after receiving the data decrypts it and then sends it in the clear to the computer on a remote IP address. The SSH server also takes any data received from the remote computer having a private IP and sends it inside the SSH session back to the client, who decrypts and sends them in the clear to the process connected to the client's on the forwarded port.

On your local machine, use the application you want to connect to the remote computer, and tell it to use the forwarded port on your local computer. When you connect to the local port, it will look like you have established connection to the destination computer on a private IP.

## SSH Tunnel in Linux

This section will help you understand how to create an SSH tunnel in Linux. SSH tunneling requires wrapping a TCP connection inside an SSH session. You will have to first configure your computer to send traffic to the tunnel instead of to the Internet. To establish an SSH tunnel, you will have to pick up a port on your computer that is called as a forwarded port. For this section, we will be using port 2345 as a forwarded port. Before doing so, ensure that no other application is listening on port 2345. This can be done by using netcat. Type the command **nc localhost 2345** at the command prompt. If the result of the command is **connection refused**, no other application is listening on port 2345 and it can be used for port forwarding.

Next, you have to set up a tunnel with SSH, and finally you should connect to the tunnel using the application you want to access the remote machine. SSH provides an option -L port:host:hostport. This option specifies that the given port on the local (client) host is to be forwarded to the given host and host port on the remote side. Host will have a private IP and will be streaming data at the host port. By allocating a socket to listen to the port on the local host, whenever a connection is made, the connection is forwarded over the secure channel to the host port from the local machine.

```
dummy$ ssh -L 2345:mailserver.isp.net:110 intermediateserver.usp.net
$ dummy@intermediateserverpassword: *********
dummy@intermediateserver $ hostname
intermediateserver
```

When the command

```
$ ssh -L 2345:mailserver.isp.net:110 intermediateserver.usp.net
```

is executed, the SSH client logs in to the intermediate server. After entering the password for dummy, authentication is complete.

The SSH client also binds to the port 2345 on loopback interface. When any process tries to access connection to 127.0.0.1 on port 2345 on the client machine, the /usr/bin/ssh client program accepts the connection.

Open a different window on your local host and establish a connection to the local computer using netcat.

```
dummy@desktop$ nc localhost 2345
 +OK POP3 mail server (mailserver.isp.net) ready.
 USER <Type POP3 user name>
 +OK
 PASS   <Type password>
```

Now we know that port 2345 is bounded by our SSH process, and the TCP connection to local port 2345 is tunneled through SSH to the other remote mail server. The local host takes data sent to port 2345, and forwards it to the intermediate server inside the encrypted SSH session. The intermediate server then decrypts the data and sends it in the clear to the destination computer, on port 110 of the Mail server.

The intermediate server also takes data received from the Mail server's port 110, and sends it inside the SSH tunnel back to the client , who decrypts and sends it in the clear to the process connected to the client's bound port, port 2345.

# SSH Tunnel in Windows

To establish SSH tunnel in Windows, you will have to ensure an SSH client in installed on your computer. We will be using Putty as our ssh client.(Putty is a free ssh client, and can be downloaded from www.chiark.greenend.org.uk/~sgtatham/). In the previous section, we used an SSH tunnel to secure access to our mail. For Windows, we will be discussing in depth how to establish a secure SSH tunnel from your local computer to access Web pages from a remote Web server on a private IP address.

After **Putty** is successfully installed on your computer, in the Category pane of the application window, click Session, and as shown in Figure 5.23, type **localhost** in the Host Name box. Ensure SSH is selected as your protocol. In the field Source port , enter the port number where you wish to forward the connection. Here we will be using 2345 as the forwarded port. After adding the port, click **Add**.

**Figure 5.23** Entries to Create SSH Tunnels

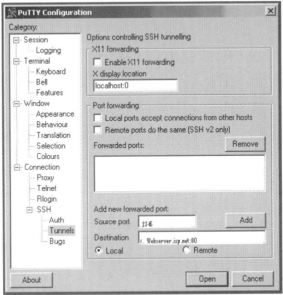

After adding the configuration, next in the Category pane, click **Session** and, as shown in Figure 5.24, enter the host name of the computer with a public IP address through which you want to establish your tunnel. Here we will be using intereme-diate.isp.net. Make sure this computer is running sshd. Select SSH as your protocol, which will automatically set the port number to 22. Figure 5.24 shows the image of the configuration. Once you click **Open**, it will prompt for username and password. Enter your username and password and log in to the intermediateserver.isp.net on a public IP address.

To receive Web pages from an SSH tunnel ( or from computer on a private IP address (WebServer.isp.net) running a web server), open your Web browser, and in the location bar enter **http://localhost:<PORTNUMBER>/,** where <PORT-NUMBER> is the number of the port on your local machine that you forwarded to the remote machine when you established your connection. In this case, we are using 2345. When you enter, the browser communicates with the remote computer on a private IP address, via an SSH tunnel. It fetches the Web pages served by web-server.isp.net and appears in the browser of your local computer.

**Figure 5.24** Establishing an SSH Connection to an Intermediate Computer on a Public IP Address

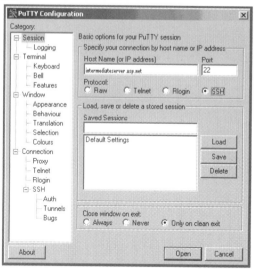

## Notes from the Underground…

### Can I View Web Pages Using an SSH Tunnel in Linux?

Yes, you can. To view Web pages from the Web server running on a remote computer, use the command **ssh -L 2345:webserver.isp.net:80 intermediateserver.isp.net**. After successful login to the intermediate server, specify **http://webserver.isp.net: 2345** in your browser.

## Pros

SSH operates at the application layer, whereas IPSec operates at the network layer. An SSH tunnel provides advantages in that any application with a fixed port number can be tunneled for a session. Hence, an SSH tunnel is an excellent way to tunnel insecure protocols through a secure communication channel. Various services like POP3 (port 110), FTP (port 21), SMTP (port 25 ),HTTP (port 80), Telnet (port 23), NNTP (port 119), VNC (port 5900), and NTP (port 123) can be tunneled by using SSH. An SSH tunnel reduces the unnecessary network overhead of encrypting all the applications as compared with IP VPNS. Tunneling of static TCP ports can also be automated. Moreover, another important advantage of SSH tunneling is that SSH was developed outside the United States, so it does not fall within U.S. government restrictions. Secure Shell, which provides support of encryption in an SSH tunnel, also provides support to many software/algorithms to generate one-time passwords, some of which include SecurID, S/Key, Kerberos, and TIS. SSH provides support for a wide variety of encryption algorithms such as RSA public key, Triple DES, IDEA, and Blowfish. You can also use port forwarding to secure some games; for example, *Age of Empires II* (port 23978) *Baldur's Gate* (port 15000), and *Dark Reign 2* (port 26214).

# Cons

Even though an SSH tunnel is lightweight, and can be used to secure insecure protocols like IMAP, SMTP, POP3, HTTP, and FTP, SSH only tunnels applications that use TCP for communication. SSH cannot be used to tunnel applications that do not have known ports, like applications using UDP, port ranges, or dynamic ports. Hence, applications like NFS cannot be protected by using port forwarding. An SSH daemon also does not provide any access control or any restriction against what port or ports can or cannot be forwarded as per the user.

In some computers, SSH is compiled with TCPWRAP options. TCPWRAP controls who can access a particular service on a computer. If a wrapper disallows a user from accessing a service, the SSH tunnel connection will be aborted. In SSH, a user can specify the encryption algorithms he can use for encrypting the channel. Many encrypting protocols can be used in SSH; for example, IDEA, DES, 3DES, and Blowfish. Even though IDEA is considered one of the most secure algorithms available in SSH, it is slowest while transmitting the data. Other algorithms like Blowfish are considered fastest; however, they come at the cost of security. Hence, in SSH tunnel, you will have to compromise on latency of transmitting data.

# Others

Besides the aforementioned SSL VPN, and SSH tunnels, there are other solutions to establish a VPN tunnel to a secure communication channel. One of them is CIPE, which stands for Crypto IP encapsulation. CIPE works by tunneling IP packets in UDP packets, and in a similar manner as IPSec. It too provides encryption and tunneling at the IP layer. This is different from SSL or SSH tunnels, which provide tunneling at the TCP layer. Even though CIPE gives much better performance in respect to IPSEC, IPSEC is more standardized and has more interoperability. CIPE makes use of Blowfish and 128-bit IDEA to secure the communication channel.

Point-to-Point Tunneling (PPTP) is the Microsoft proposed version of VPN, and is comprised of two channels. The first channel is called as the control channel over which link management information is passed, and the second channel is called as data channel over which private data network traffic is passed. The control channel connects to port 1723 on the server, and the data channel uses a generic encapsulation protocol. Although PPTP support is built into Windows, RRAS (Routing and Remote Access Server) needs to be installed and configured, which is a major upgrade on the Windows VPN server.

Microsoft implementation of the PPTP is considered unsecure, and the authentication protocol is prone to dictionary attack. By using a standard sniffer, the following information can be obtained from a Microsoft PPTP server:

- Client machine IP address

- Server machine IP address

- Number of available PPTP virtual tunnels at the server

- Client machine RAS number

- Client machine NetBIOS name

- Client vendor identification

- Server vendor identification

- Internal Virtual Tunnel IP address handed to the client

- Internal DNB servers handed to the client

- Client username

- Enough information to retrieve user's password hash

- Information to retrieve the initialization value used inside MPPE

- Current value of the encrypted packet for the client before RC4 re-initialization

- Current value of the encrypted packet for the server before RC4 re-initialization

To prevent information leakage, you can encrypt the control channel, or remove the channel, and everything the channel does can be done via PPP negotiations or the unused portions of the GRE header. There is no authentication of the control channel. Implementation of the encryption scheme uses output-feedback-mode stream cipher, whereas a cipher block-chaining-mode block cipher would have been more appropriate. Encryption key is a function of the user password instead of using a key-exchange algorithm like Diffie-Hellman. During the cryptanalysis of the PPTP protocol done by Bruce Schneier, they were able to open connections through a firewall by abusing PPTP negotiations. They were able to crash the Windows NT server by sending the malicious crafted packets from outside the firewall without any authentication. Some of the malicious crafted packets included sending invalid values in the PPTP control packet header, or iterating through all the valid and nonvalid values that could be held in the Packet Type field inside the PptpPacket header. Microsoft's Point-to-Point Encryption protocol provides a way to encrypt PPTP packets. It assumes the existence of a secret key shared by both ends of the connection and uses RC4 with either 40 bits or a 128-bit key. In the cryptanalysis attack against these encryption schemes, they claim to completely negate the usefulness of the encryption protocol. For further details, readers are encouraged to read Bruce Schneier's paper, "Cryptanalysis of Microsoft's Point-to-Point Tunneling Protocol (PPTP)," available at www.schneier.com/paper-pptp.pdf.

The PPP negotiation occurs before and after the encryption can be applied. A PPP CCP packet is being used for the resynchronization of the keys. Since there is no authentication of packets, spoofing the configuration packet containing the DNS server can be exploited to force all name resolution to happen through a malicious name server. Windows 95 can be classified as an obsolete version of Windows; however, the Win 95 client fails to properly sanitize the buffer and the information leaks in the protocol messages. As per the PPTP documentation, characters after the host name and the vendor string should be 0x00 (in the PPTP_START_SESSION_REQUEST) packet. Unfortunately, Windows 95 fails to do it. For Windows NT, all these bytes are set to null.

PPP-SSH VPN is also one of the common methods to establish VPN connection. In the next section, we discuss CIPE and PPP-SSH.

# Technical Description

The CIPE protocol involves two parts. The first part is encryption and checksumming of data packets and dynamic key exchange. In CIPE, an IP datagram is padded with the zero to seven random octet so length is congruent to three modulo eight. The packet is then padded with a value of P, which again is one octet. CRC 32 bit checksum is then calculated. The packet is then encrypted with the 64-bit block cipher in CBC mode. IDEA is generally used to perform this. It also makes use of Blowfish with 132-bit keys. The value of P, which is appended to the packet, is calculated as follows: Bits 4, 5, and 6 indicate the length of the packet between the original packet and P; bits 2 and 1 indicate the type of packet. Value 00 denotes the packet is a data packet, 01 denotes the packet is a key exchange packet, and 10 is reserved. Bits 0, 3, and 7 are reserved and must be zero. CIPE is available for download at http://sourceforge.net/projects/cipe-linux, and CIPE for Windows version is available at http://cipe-win32.sourceforge.net/. Details about the installation procedure for CIPE for a Linux computer can be found at www.redhat.com/docs/manuals/linux/RH-9-Manuals/security-guide/sl-vpn-cipe-install.html.

PPP is generally configured and designed to support single dial-up users Figure 5.25). A PPP connection is established when a user runs the PPP program. By using SSH, you can log on to a remote computer and run a program on the server. SSH ensures that the data stream between the client and the server is encrypted. If the locally and reciprocally running program on a LAN is PPP, and is triggered by SSH, the communication channel becomes encrypted and we can call the data transmission channel to be PPP-SSH VPN. In this scheme, SSH is being used to create a tunnel connection, and pppd is used to run TCP/IP traffic. Further details about the installation procedure for PPP-SSH can be found at www.tldp.org/HOWTO/ppp-ssh/index.html.

**Figure 5.25** Packet Encapsulation in a PPP Connection

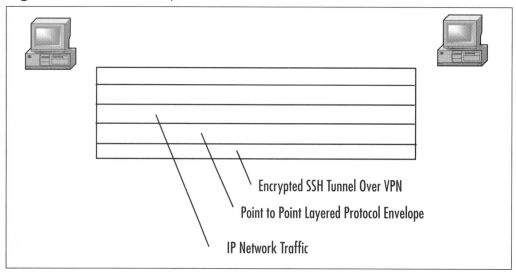

In PPP-SSH when a network load becomes very high, one TCP connection may get all the bandwidth, resulting in timeouts and dropping of other connections. Overheads and latency on PPP-SSH are also very high. If the ping time on 57.6 modem connections is in 135–175 ms range, the PPP-SSH ping time is around

310—340 ms range. Keep alives are the small packets used to find out if the connections between the computers are alive. In the case of PPP-SSH if the network load is too high, there will be latency in the arrival of packets. This in turn will delay the keep alive packets, and hence you cannot reliably tell if the network connections are down. When your SSH TCP connection is broken, the VPN connection is also disconnected, and all tunneled TCP connections are broken. PPP-SSH is running IP over TCP stream. This may result in weird delays, dropouts, and oscillations, and definitely the concept of IP over TCP is against the concept of the OSI model.

# Pros

Besides IPv4, CIPE also provides support for IPv6. CIPE uses Blowfish, which again is not prone to U.S. export restrictions. CIPE is a software-based VPN, and any computer able to run Linux can be used as a CIPE gateway. Organizations can save money by not purchasing dedicated hardware-based VPNs. CIPE has been designed to work with iptables, ipchains, and other rule-based firewalls. CIPE configuration is done through text files, which makes configuration easy. While graphical tools look good, they are often a burden over a network.

PPP-SSH comes with most of the Linux distributions, and many of the Linux kernels are preconfigured, thus saving time when installing, configuring, or recompiling the kernel. By ensuring distinct IP addresses for each tunnel to a single computer, you can establish multiple tunnels to a computer. PPP-SSH can establish VPN connections over dynamic IP addresses. You can have a VPN connection over a dialup connection. If the rules of your firewall are configured to allow SSH, PPP-SSH will work in that configuration as well. Routing in the case of SSH-PPP is a simple task; pppd automatically establishes the routing. If you require complex routing, you will have to update the Perl script with the custom routing command; PPP-SSH VPN thus can be termed as the poor man's VPN.

# Cons

Connections making use of CIPE will be slow on dialup modems. It is generally recommended to turn off the compression in the modem. A DoS attack is possible in CIPE. Vulnerability against the key generation process exists in CIPE, and happens when the sender is overrun with bogus packets. Hence, the sender will be using the static keys for a long period of time. To prevent this situation, stop sending the data completely after a long burst of static key sends.

# Summary

VPNs have quickly come to supplant traditional WAN technologies such as frame relay, leased lines, and dialup networks. They reduce the total cost of ownership of the WAN by eliminating recurring costs associated with those technologies and using the underlying and nascent IP technology a company has deployed. IPSec is the one of the most commonly used VPNs. Other methodologies to secure communication include SSL VPN, SSH Tunnel, and Layer 2 solutions.

SSL VPN, being the clientless VPN, is the most versatile VPN, whereas SSH Tunnel helps to secure nonsecure protocols. Each of these techniques to secure communication has its advantages and disadvantages; the best scheme to secure a channel depends on a user or an organization.

# Solutions Fast Track

## Solution IPSec

☑ The four topologies for VPNs are mesh (both fully and partially), star topology, hub-and-spoke, and remote access.

☑ The difference between a star topology and a hub-and-spoke topology is that in a star topology, the branch or stub networks are not able to communicate with one another. They can only communicate with the central corporate network.

☑ IPSec is not capable of traversing NAT devices without some modification. The problem comes when the NAT device changes information in the IP header of the IPSec packet. The changes will result in an incorrect IPSec checksum that is calculated over parts of the IP header. There are workarounds for this problem, however.

☑ When the number of VPNs connecting to the router, firewall, or VPN appliance becomes sufficiently large, it might be necessary to install a VPN accelerator module (VAM) into the device to offload many of the cryptographic functions used in the VPN.

☑ There are three main choices for encryption schemes in IPSec: DES, 3DES, and AES. AES deployment is not as widely used at present, so it might not be possible to use that encryption algorithm. DES has been proven insecure against an attack with sufficient resources. 3DES is the only current algorithm that is widely available and provably secure.

☑ Message integrity is provided using the MD5, SHA-1, or HMAC hash algorithms.

☑ Before an IPSec VPN tunnel can be established, the session parameters must be negotiated using Internet Key Exchange.

☑ IPSec security policies define the traffic permitted to enter the VPN tunnel.

# Solution SSL VPN

☑ SSL VPN is a clientless VPN. A VPN connection can be established from an Internet café.

☑ SSL VPN provides very fine-tuned access control over the resources.

☑ In SSL VPN, care has be taken to ensure that the downloaded sensitive data or information has been deleted from the clients.

# Solution SSH Tunnels

☑ SSH tunnels can be used to secure insecure protocols like POP3 and HTTP traffic.

☑ SSH tunnels can secure only applications using fixed ports.

☑ In SSH tunnels, security of insecure channel comes with the cost of latency. If you are using encryption algorithms that provide more security, latency on the network will be high.

# Solution Layer 2 Solution

☑ In Layer 2 solutions, the customer takes care of Layer 3 functionalities such as routing.

☑ Configuring of provider edge routers in a Layer 2 solution increases as new nodes are added.

☑ MPLS packets are forwarded by label lookup.

# Others

- ☑ CIPE provides tunneling in UDP packets. Like IPSec, it also works at the IP layer.

- ☑ PPP-SSH comes with many standard Linux distributions, and can be considered a poor man?s VPN. PPP-SSH is a TCP connection over TCP; even though it is secure, connection is unreliable.

# Frequently Asked Questions

The following Frequently Asked Questions, answered by the authors of this book, are designed to both measure your understanding of the concepts presented in this chapter and to assist you with real-life implementation of these concepts. To have your questions about this chapter answered by the author, browse to **www.syngress.com/solutions** and click on the **"Ask the Author"** form.

**Q:** What is the significance of terminating a VPN tunnel on a firewall's internal interface?

**A:** Terminating a VPN tunnel on a firewall's internal interface allows all VPN traffic to access the internal directory in one hop. This might not be desirable, and if IP filters cannot be applied to VPN tunnel traffic, other methods, such as having the VPN tunnel terminate within an isolated VLAN, must be employed to restrict the traffic.

**Q:** How does IKE work?

**A:** The Internet Key Exchange (IKE) protocol is designed to provide mutual authentication of systems and the establishment of a shared secret key to create in IPSec SA. IKE operates in two phases. Phase 1 provides mutual authentication of the systems and the establishment of session keys and is known as the ISAKMP SA. Phase 2 provides for setting up the IPSec SA.

**Q:** In SSH VPN, is the communication channel between a computer on a public IP and a computer on a private IP encrypted?

**A:** No. SSH VPN is being used to protect the computers on a private address from being accessed by the Internet. The communication channel between the client and the computer on a public IP is secured using SSH.

**Q:** Is it possible for many clients on a computer to use IPSec simultaneously?

**A:** Yes; however, there might be minor problems. IPSec defines a parameter for identifying the traffic by the Security parameter Index. (SPI). Unfortunately, SPI for inbound traffic is different from outbound traffic. Thus, there is no association between inbound and outbound traffic; hence, the connection for many clients on a computer to use IPSec is not reliable.

**Q:** Does IPSec uses the same encryption algorithm as SSL? Why or Why not?

**A:** No. IPSec works at THE IP layer which is a loss environment. SSL uses stream ciphers like RC4, which depend on the endpoint synchronization and are suitable for      reliable connections like HTTP over TCP. In an environment where there are chances of packets getting lost, a block cipher like 3DES, CAST-128 is used.

**Q:** Does SSL and IPSec VPNs work at the same layer in the OSI model?

**A:** No. SSL works at the application layer, and IPSec works at the network layer.

**Q:** Can I use VPN to secure my wireless network?

**A:** Yes. Create a separate LAN that will connect all the access points and one more Ethernet interface on the VPN server. You also have to ensure that DHCP service is provided to the wireless LAN. Use dhrelay to provide DHCP service. Ensure that the DHCP server is updated with the new Subnet details and there exists a route to the VPN wireless LAN interface. This can be done by using the **Route add** command. Update the VPN server by adding the DNSname service to ensure clients can access the VPN server by name.

# Chapter 6

# Deciding on a VPN

## Solutions in this chapter:

- **Hardware VPN Solutions**
- **Software VPN Solutions**

☑ **Summary**

☑ **Solutions Fast Track**

☑ **Frequently Asked Questions**

# Introduction

In this chapter, we examine the solutions for constructing VPNs. Many of the same principles in the previous chapter govern the choice of a VPN solution; however, we'll still examine them in detail in this chapter.

VPNs have recently been experiencing greater popularity and wider deployment due to increases in telecommuting, wireless technologies, and mobile workers—each of which poses particular problems associated with the secure access of data from remote locations. Telecommuters want to be able to work from home and have much the same experience as if they were sitting in the corporate offices. Wireless technologies, while improving laptop to wireless access point (WAP) encryption, have yet to see wide deployment of the encryption technologies. In addition, locations such as hotels and coffee shops rarely offer encryption, and are ripe for hackers to sniff the wireless traffic between laptops and WAPs to later analyze it for useful information including usernames and passwords. Mobile workers who must travel to many locations and use whatever Internet access is available are especially vulnerable to sniffing attacks on their traffic, and often require access to corporate resources quickly and securely. A well-configured VPN solution offers the solution to most, if not all, of these problems. In addition, a VPN provides a secure channel between geographically dispersed offices without the cost of private leased lines.

So, what exactly is a VPN? As the name implies, it is a way of creating what appears to be a private network using the publicly available Internet. The devices on each end of the VPN have a mutually agreed upon way of encrypting and decrypting all the data between the two points. Thus, when the packets enter the public Internet stream, they are unreadable. Often, VPN devices will automatically change the encryption key or sequence to avoid the possibility that someone could capture enough packets and work out the encryption. VPNs are a mature and well-trusted technology and reliably perform secure communications. There should never be a question as to if a *well-configured* VPN will protect the data. The question should be, "Where can we use a VPN to protect communications that are currently in danger of being compromised?" Figure 6.1 shows an example of VPN tunnels connecting branch offices with the main office.

**Figure 6.1** VPN Tunnels between Main and Branch Offices

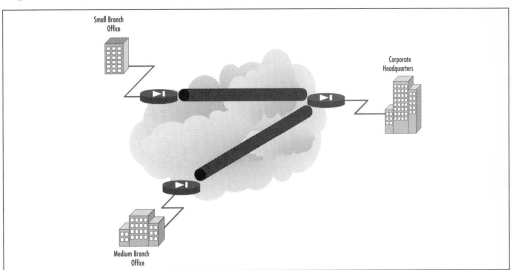

# VPN Types

VPNs come in several flavors and it is very important to understand the differences before examining the options on the market today. All the RFC (Request for Comments) numbers can be referenced at http://tools.ietf.org, where you will find detailed information on how each protocol works.

## IPSec

Generally considered one of the most secure ways for two devices to communicate, *IP Security* (IPSec) signs and encrypts traffic at the network level. The signing of packets, which insures that information sent has not been tampered with in transit, is handled by the *Authentication Header* (AH) cryptographic protocol. The encryption of packets to prevent snooping of data is handled by the *Encapsulating Security Payload* (ESP) protocol. Both of these protocols provide mutual authentication between two devices using *Internet Key Exchange* (IKE). IPSec virtually eliminates a possible *man-in-the-middle* attack, in which someone places himself between the two devices and pretends to be device A to device B, and vice versa. In this way, that person can decrypt all the traffic and read it. Finally, by working at the network level, it is much faster than those protocols that work at higher levels of the network stack. Details can be found in RFCs 4301–4309 (Note, there are earlier RFCs dating back to 1995; however, these are the most recent).

# PPTP

The *Point-to-Point Tunneling Protocol* (PPTP) was created by Cisco and then widely deployed by Microsoft. By adding the *Generic Routing Encapsulation* (GRE) protocol to the standard *point-to-point protocol* (PPP) and authenticating with MSCHAP-v2 (Microsoft Challenge-Handshake Authentication Protocol), a stable, reasonably secure connection is created. The primary weakness with PPTP is the authentication protocol. MSCHAP-v2 can be easily compromised if a strong, long password is not used. PPTP has been used since Windows 95 OSR2 and is currently available on all major operating systems. You will find VPNs that support PPTP, but it is generally only used between desktops and the appliances, not between appliances themselves. PPTP cannot be used through a firewall, in most cases. Details can be found in RFC 2637.

# L2TP

The *Layer 2 Tunneling Protocol* (L2TP) developed out of the combined work of Microsoft and Cisco to overcome the weaknesses of PPTP and Cisco's older *Layer 2 Forwarding* (L2F) protocol. L2TP works at Layer 2, the data layer, which make it very fast, and can use X.509 certificates for mutual authentication. IPSec can be added for additional security. L2TP does work through firewalls (details can be found in RFC 2661). A new version of L2TP, L2TPv3, is a simplified version of the original, and includes most of the good features with less work to use them.

# SSL

Secure Sockets Layer (SSL) VPN is the most confusing, primarily because different vendors mean different things by the term *SSL VPN*. OpenVPN, which we discuss later, secures the entire network stack like L2TP or IPSec. It consists of a binary client installed on both the client and server and completely encrypts all communications via the SSLv3/TLSv1 (*Transport Layer Security)* protocol. TLS details may be referenced in RFC 4346. While SSL and TLS are generally TCP-based protocols, there is an implementation in OpenSSL for Datagram TLS (DTLS). This protocol is based on TLS and is capable of securing datagram transport (UDP). Since UDP is a connectionless protocol, it is less secure and therefore not recommended for the purposes of this discussion.

Other options may only function as a *web proxy*—that is, the ability to authenticate to a device and indirectly, but securely, connect to protected network services, which are generally secure Web sites or Web-based applications. This is not a true VPN and has a number of dangers, including that the device functioning as the proxy can be a man-in-the-middle point for unscrupulous administrators to view all traffic traversing it. Mutual authentication is generally lacking and packet integrity is absent.

We will try to differentiate between these two types of SSL VPN implementations and warn you of options that only support the latter.

# Appliance / Hardware Solution

## Basic Description

As with firewalls, a hardware VPN solution is often preferred due to the perceived higher security a dedicated appliance can provide. This is not necessarily true. However, it will obtain higher performance with less work if a hardware solution is purchased.

Another distinct advantage of using the same brand, if not model, of VPN hardware in two locations, such as two offices in two different cities, is the ease with which a permanent VPN *tunnel* can be created and maintained. This is ideal for the scenario mentioned previously of various offices that need to act as if they are on a single network. While the same can be done with software solutions, or with different brands of VPN appliances, it often takes more work and, at times, finesse.

Finally, as mentioned with hardware firewalls, compliance with laws such as The Federal Information Processing Standards (FIPS www.itl.nist.gov/fipspubs), The Health Insurance Portability and Accountability Act (HIPAA www.hhs.gov/ocr/hipaa), and in Canada, The Security of Information Act (SOIA www.tbs-sct.gc.ca/pubs_pol/gospubs/tbm_12a/sia-lpi1_e.asp#effe) may require certified hardware solutions rather than software solutions.

## Own Hardware

Generally, there are stand-alone VPN appliances whose sole function is to provide VPN services, and other appliances, mostly firewalls, which incorporate VPN services into their package of service offerings. Each has advantages and disadvantages.

Stand-alone appliances usually have much higher data transfer rates than the same class of multifunction appliances. They also usually have multiple authentication protocols available, including RADIUS, LDAP, Active Directory, and built-in databases. Multifunction devices may or may not support all these protocols, or may have only limited support. The inclusion of integrated client software to be installed on laptops (or any other computer) for easy and secure connection to the appliance is often an advantage, as is larger numbers of permitted connections, if there is a limit at all. Perhaps the biggest downside of stand-alone appliances is the cost. You will be purchasing a single function appliance—is this a cost-effective use of your budget? It will depend on the number of users connecting and the throughput required.

Multifunction devices are more cost effective, especially for smaller companies. Purchasing a single firewall/VPN solution will protect your internal network while permitting secure remote connections. Generally, the minor loss in throughput and/or functionality is well worth the cost savings for smaller companies. However, for larger companies, such a compromise may lead to unacceptable performance reductions.

# Specialized Operating System

As with firewalls, VPN appliances can run their own specialized and optimized operating system (OS), or may run a hardened version of a commercial OS such as Linux, Solaris, or Windows. In all cases, the OS is hardened and optimized for VPN applications. Primarily, the OS is optimized for encryption/decryption, since this is the primary operation of the OS.

# Examples of Appliance Hardware Solutions

There are many commercial hardware-based VPN solutions. We will examine some of the larger manufacturers; however, do not discount a manufacturer just because it is not listed here. The network hardware market is dynamic and new vendors are coming on the scene frequently. However, do not jump on an unproven appliance to protect your data just because it is new or inexpensive. Study both the appliance specifications and reviews available on such sites as www.eweek.com and www.zdnet.com.

## Juniper SSL VPN

Juniper Networks Secure Access is one of the dominant manufacturers in the SSL VPN market segment. Juniper Networks SSL VPNs are based on the Instant Virtual Extranet (IVE) platform, which uses SSL (Secure Sockets Layer), the security protocol found in Web browsers. These appliances support both the OpenSSL and Web proxy methods of SSL VPN, the latter being available on the lower end appliances via an optional upgrade.

## Juniper SSL VPN Appliance Line

Table 6.1 presents the detailed features about the Juniper products that offer SSL VPN. Further details about any of these appliances are available at www.juniper.net/products/ssl/.

**Table 6.1** SSL Product Line Offered by Juniper

| Product | Designed for | Enterprise Class Features |
| --- | --- | --- |
| Juniper Networks Secure Access 700 | Small to mid-sized companies | Secure access for remote/mobile employees, with no client software required<br>Optional upgrade enables access from any PC anywhere<br>Plug-n-play deployment<br>Robust security features |
| Juniper Networks Secure Access 2000 | Small to mid-sized enterprises | Secure LAN, intranet, and extranet access for employees, business partners, and customers<br>Three access methods allow administrators to provision access by purpose<br>Dynamic access privilege management<br>Advanced software enables sophisticated functionality, including simplified administration with Central Manager<br>Common Criteria Certified |
| Juniper Networks Secure Access 4000 | Mid-sized to large enterprises | Scalable platform allows medium to large enterprises to offer secure extranet, intranet, and LAN access from one platform<br>Enterprise performance/high availability<br>License-based SSL acceleration and compression for all traffic types<br>Dynamic access privilege management, with three access methods<br>Common Criteria Certified, FIPS appliances available |

*Continued*

**Table 6.1 continued** SSL Product Line Offered by Juniper

| Product | Designed for | Enterprise Class Features |
|---|---|---|
| | | Advanced software enables sophisticated functionality, including simplified administration with Central Manager |
| Juniper Networks Secure Access 6000 | Large and multinational enterprises | High-performance platform for the largest, most complex and secure extranet, intranet, and LAN access deployments |
| | | Built-in SSL acceleration and compression for all traffic types |
| | | Redundant, and/or hot swappable hard disks, power supplies, and fans |
| | | Dynamic access privilege management, with three access methods |
| | | Common Criteria Certified, FIPS appliances available |
| | | Advanced software enables sophisticated functionality, including simplified administration with Central Manager |
| Juniper Networks Secure Access 6000 SP | Service provider managed services | SSL VPN platform with comprehensive virtualization enabling SPs to deliver network-based SSL VPN services to multiple enterprises of any size from a single appliance/cluster |
| | | No client to install and no firewall/NAT traversal issues result in reduced support overhead and high ROI |
| | | Differentiated revenue opportunities with services such as extranet access, disaster recovery, intranet LAN security and mobile device access. |

In addition to the SSL–VPN appliances, Juniper integrates VPN capabilities into its NetScreen firewall product, which allows for access control and authentication and network segmentation. NetScreen firewalls use a "security zone–based" model in which the network is separated into areas, or zones, that are distinct and separate from one another (see Chapter 4—this is an important and unique feature of NetScreen appliances).

By combining the firewall and VPN technologies, Juniper offers comprehensive security in a single package. In addition, Juniper's VPN technologies are based on IPSec, which is ideal for the connection of networks. Central and branch offices can make use of NetScreen appliances and, with a single device, connect the offices and offer client-to-network VPN services. *NetScreen Remote* is the client used to connect workstations to the NetScreen appliance. Unfortunately, the client is only available for Windows machines.

Configuration of the VPN features is accomplished by a Web-based interface. Figures 6.2 and 6.3 show the standard and advanced configuration pages.

**Figure 6.2** Standard VPN Configuration

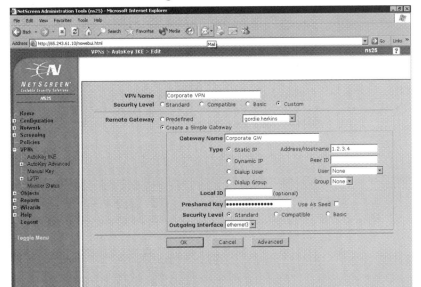

If you are interested in knowing more about NetScreen firewall and VPN, see www.juniper.net/products/integrated/ and refer to Syngress title *Configuring NetScreen Firewalls* (ISBN: 1-932266-39-9).

**Figure 6.3** Advanced VPN Configuration

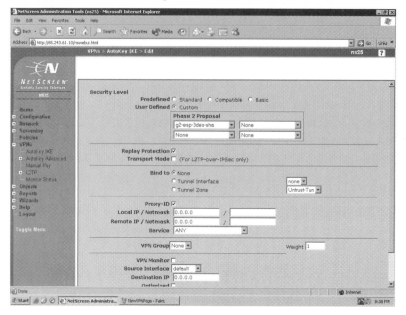

# F5

F5's SSL VPN appliance, FirePass, has the sole use of connecting remote clients to the corporate network. These appliances are not designed to create a VPN tunnel between two different networks. FirePass can be configured to accept connections as a Web proxy and/or from a proprietary binary client for Windows.

Some of the internal network protection features of FirePass include:

- Automatic detection of security compliant systems, preventing infection

- Automatic integration with the largest number of virus scanning and personal firewall solutions in the industry (over 100 different AV &and Personal Firewall versions)

- Automatic protection from infected file uploads or e-mail attachments

- Automatic re-routing and quarantine of infected or noncompliant systems to a self remediation network—reducing help desk calls

- A secure workspace, preventing eavesdropping and theft of sensitive data

- Secure Login with a randomized key entry system, preventing keystroke logger snooping

FirePass is especially suited for specific client/server application access via Web browsers. Administrators can restrict server access to specific applications and thereby protect other network resources.

- Enables a native client-side application to communicate back to a specific corporate application server via a secure connection between the browser and the FirePass Controller. Thus, user pre-installation and/or configure any software.

- On the network side, requires no additional enabling software on the application servers being accessed.

- Uses the standard HTTPS protocol, with SSL as the transport, so it works through all HTTP proxies including public access points, private LANs, and over networks and ISPs that do not support traditional IPSec VPNs.

- Supported applications include Outlook to Exchange Clusters; Passive FTP, Citrix Nfuse, and network drive mapping. Administrators can also support custom applications, including CRM and other applications that use static TCP ports.

- Supports auto-login to AppTunnels, Citrix, and WTS applications, and auto-launch of client-side applications.

- Unique support for compression of client/server application traffic over WAN to offer better performance.

- Users of Windows 2000/XP can be automatically switched to a protected workspace for their remote access session. In a protected workspace mode, the user cannot write files to locations outside the protected workspace, and the temporary folders and their contents are deleted at the end of the session.

Figure 6.4 shows the various modules used by FirePass and some examples of application access.

**Figure 6.4** FirePass Modules

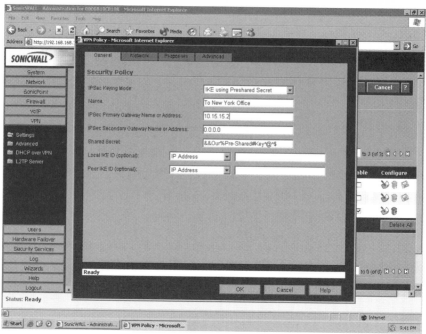

Table 6.2 lists the different FirePass appliances and their salient features. Further details about the products are available at www.f5.com/products/FirePass/.

**Table 6.2** SSL Product Line Offered by F 5 VPN

| | |
|---|---|
| FirePass 1000 Series | 1U rack-mount server.<br>Designed for small to medium enterprise locations.<br>Supports up to 100 concurrent users.<br>Offers a comprehensive solution for secure Web-based remote access to corporate applications and desktops. |
| FirePass 4100 Seriesn | 2U rack-mount server.<br>Designed for large enterprise locations.<br>Supports up to 2000 concurrent users.<br>Supports clustering for load balancing and high availability.<br>Offers a comprehensive solution for secure Web-based remote access to corporate applications and desktops. |

**Continued**

**Table 6.2 continued** SSL Product Line Offered by F 5 VPN

| | |
|---|---|
| FIPS SSL Accelerator Hardware Option | FIPS compliant to meet the strong security needs of government, finance, healthcare, and other security conscious organizations.<br>Offers support for FIPS 140 Level-2 enabled tamper proof storage of SSL keys and FIPS certified cipher support for encrypting and decrypting SSL traffic in hardware.<br>FIPS SSL Accelerator is available as a factory install option to the base 4100 platform. |
| SSL Accelerator Hardware Option | Offers hardware SSL Acceleration option to offload the SSL key exchange.<br>Encryption and decryption of SSL traffic. |

# SonicWALL

SonicWALL provides two stand-alone solutions?SSL-VPN 2000 and SSL- VPN 200—and VPN solutions integrated into their entire firewall series. SonicWALL SSL-VPN 2000 is for organizations having 1000 or fewer employees, whereas SonicWALL SSL VPN 200 is focused on organizations with 50 or fewer employees. Both appliances are primarily Web proxies and are not designed to connect networks. More details on the SonicWALL are available at www.sonicwall.com/products/sslapp.html. Readers interested in SonicWALL VPN are encouraged to refer to Syngress title *Configuring SonicWALL Firewalls* (ISBN: 1597490601).

Some interesting features of the SonicWALL appliances are:

- No restrictions on the number of concurrent tunnels. Thus, there are no additional costs associated with an increase in the number of remote users.

- The *NetExtender Client*, a binary client for Windows, permits the extension of services beyond just Web-based applications to legacy binary applications. Another separately sold client, *Enforced Client Anti-Virus and Anti-Spyware*, will enforce administrator policies for anti-virus and anti-spyware versions. This helps protect the internal network.

- Tokenless two-factor authentication is achieved by combining a unique one-time password, with the user's network username and password, providing enhanced protection against key loggers.

## Notes from the Underground…

### One-Time Password Vulnerabilities

Recently, Citibank experienced problems with one-time passwords, man-in-the-middle attacks, and phishing schemes. The phisher convinces a victim to visit their false site and thus obtains the victim's valid Citibank credentials. These are then passed to the actual Citibank site along with the one-time password. Now the phisher has all the information needed to steal the victim's identity, money, or other information. The only positive news is that this scheme will only work for a short time, and will unlikely be repeatable. The downside is that a single compromise can be devastating for the victim. For a full treatment of this topic, see Russ Cooper's July 19, 2006 article in Security Watch (http://mcpmag.com/security).

This same sort of compromise can happen to your network. Be very careful when implementing such authentication!

Table 6.3 compares the two SonicWALL appliances.

**Table 6.3** SonicWALL SSL-VPN Appliances

|  | SSL-VPN 200 | SSL-VPN 2000 |
| --- | --- | --- |
| **Deployment Environment** | | |
| Type and Size of Deployment Environment | Small organizations up to 50 employees | Mid-size organizations up to 1000 employees |
| Recommended Maximum Number of Concurrent Users | 5 heavy* /10 typ. usage | 50 heavy* /100 typ. usage |
| Concurrent User License | Unrestricted | Unrestricted |

*Heavy usage is defined as involving multiple concurrent HTTP, HTTPS, and FTP proxy sessions and/or requiring continuous downloading of files.

**Continued**

**Table 6.3 continued** SonicWALL SSL-VPN Appliances

| | SSL-VPN 200 | SSL-VPN 2000 |
| --- | --- | --- |
| **Application Support** | | |
| Proxy | HTTP, HTTPS, FTP, SHH, Telnet, RDP, VNC, Windows File Sharing (Windows SMB/CIFS) | HTTP, HTTPS, FTP, SHH, Telnet, RDP, VNC, Windows File Sharing (Windows SMB/CIFS), Citrix (ICA) |
| NetExtender | Most TCP/IP-based applications: ICMP, VoIP, IMAP, POP, SMTP, etc. | Any TCP/IP-based application: ICMP, Citrix, VoIP, IMAP, POP, SMTP, etc. |
| **Security Features** | | |
| Encryption | DES, 3DES, AES—128, 192, 256-bit, ARC4—128-bit, MD5, SHA-1 | DES, 3DES, AES—128, 192, 256-bit, ARC4—128-bit, MD5, SHA-1 |
| Authentication | Internal User Database, RADIUS, LDAP, Microsoft Active Directory, Windows NT Domain | Internal User Database, RADIUS, LDAP, Microsoft Active Directory, Windows NT Domain / Out-of-the-box one-time passwords (tokenless two factor authentication) |
| **Key Features** | | |
| Seamless Integration with Virtually Any Firewall | ☑ | ☑ |
| Clientless Connectivity | ☑ | ☑ |
| Unrestricted Concurrent Users | ☑ | ☑ |
| Enhanced Layered Security in a SonicWALL Environment | ☑ | ☑ |
| Granular Policy Configuration | ☑ | ☑ |
| NetExtender Technology | ☑ | ☑ |
| Multiple NetExtender IP Ranges and Routes | | ☑ |
| Virtual Host/Domain Name | | ☑ |
| Optional Client Certificate | | ☑ |
| Citrix (ICA) Support | | ☑ |

Continued

**Table 6.3 continued** SonicWALL SSL-VPN Appliances

| | SSL-VPN 200 | SSL-VPN 2000 |
|---|---|---|
| **Key Features** | | |
| File Shares Access Policies | | ☑ |
| Standalone NetExtender Client | | ☑ |
| One-Time Password Protection | | ☑ |
| Create System Backup | | ☑ |
| Graphical Usage Monitoring | | ☑ |
| RDP5—Non-Windows Platforms | | ☑ |
| Context-Sensitive Help | | ☑ |

Like many other VPN appliances, SonicWALL uses a Web-based interface for ease of management. Figure 6.5 shows the VPN summary page.

**Figure 6.5** SonicWALL VPN Summary Page

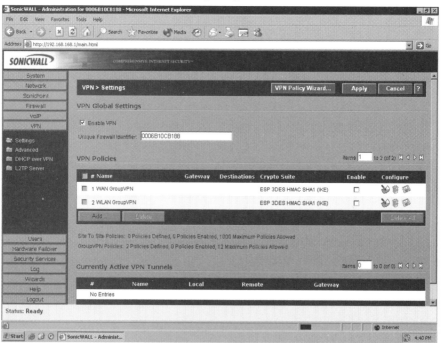

# Aventail

Aventail also provides three appliances for Smart SSL-VPN. The EX series of SSL-VPNs provides both Web proxy and client-based connectivity for Windows, Windows Mobile, Macintosh, and Linux workstations. As with other devices, client isolation and policy enforcement are supported. In addition, Aventail offers an interesting feature: should a client be stolen or otherwise lost, "Device Watermarks" based on client certificates permits access revocation. Figure 6.6 shows Aventail's primary features.

**Figure 6.6** Aventail Features

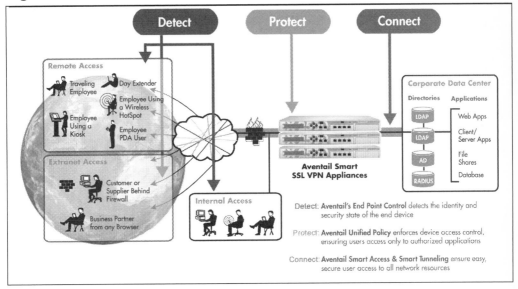

Table 6.4 lists the Aventail device specifications. Further details about Aventail SSL VPN appliance are found at  www.aventail.com/products/appliances/default.asp.

**Table 6.4** Aventail Device Specifications

| Model | EX-2500 | EX-1600 | EX-750 |
|---|---|---|---|
| Company size | You are an enterprise with hundreds or thousands of remote access users. You need high availability to ensure anytime access to critical applications. | You are a growing mid-sized company, an enterprise department, or you have a remote facility. You support 25 to 250 concurrent remote access users who need anytime access. | You are a small to mid-sized company, an enterprise department, or you have a remote facility. You support up to 25 concurrent remote access users. |
| Availability features and user base size | Clustering and high availability (HA) support: Up to eight nodes of externally sourced HA. Two nodes for internal HA with integrated load balancing. Supports up to 2000 concurrent users. | Can be paired for high availability (HA) and load sharing. Supports up to 250 concurrent users. | A cost-effective unit intended for stand-alone use. An ideal solution if your user base will not grow beyond 25 concurrent users. |

# Cisco

Cisco has integrated VPN technology into most of its networking products. These products include routers, PIX firewalls, and the VPN 3000 series concentrator. Most if not all of Cisco's IOS images for its routers have a version that includes VPN and firewall services as a feature set. Each of these devices provides approximately the same level of VPN services, as described in the sections that follow.

## Cisco IOS VPN

IOS VPN services allow the network administrator to terminate network-to-network VPN tunnels at an external or internal interface of the router. This allows considerable flexibility in the design of the VPN. Some of the more important site-to-site VPN features available in Cisco IOS include:

- **Diverse networking environment support**   IPSec is a Unicast, IP-only protocol, but Cisco's IOS (Integrated Operating System) VPN software features accommodate multicast and multiproctocol traffic. In addition, routing protocols are supported across the VPN. Scaled mesh VPN topologies are supported through Cisco's Dynamic Multipoint VPN (DMVPN) feature. DMVPN allows network administrators and users to better scale large and small IPSec-based VPNs by combining GRE tunnels, IPSec encryption, and Next-Hop Resolution Protocol (NHRP). This allows for an easier deployment of meshed VPN topologies by automating the provisioning of connections between spoke sites and dynamically setting up connections based on network traffic.

- **Timely, reliable delivery of latency-sensitive traffic**   Cisco's IOS VPN feature set enables traffic to be prioritized up to the application layer. This facilitates differentiated QoS (Quality of Service) policies by application type rather than just TCP port number. This system results in increased transmission reliability and better response time of business-critical applications traversing the VPNs.

- **V3PN solution**   By combining advanced QoS, telephony, networking, and VPN features with purpose-built hardware platforms, Cisco's VPN offerings are able to deliver a VPN infrastructure capable of transporting converged data, voice, and video traffic across a secure IPSec network. This is known as Voice- and Video-Enabled IPSec VPN, or V3PN.

- **VPN scalability and feature set**   Cisco's IOS VPN supports a wide variety of features that are essential to VPNs. These features include data encryption, tunneling, broad certificate authority support for public key infrastructure (PKI), stateful VPN failover, certificate auto-enrollment, stateful firewall, intrusion detection, and service-level validation.

- **VPN management framework**   Managing multiple VPN devices over multiple sites requires robust VPN configuration management and monitoring capabilities, and device inventory and software version management features. Cisco's CiscoWorks VPN/Security Management Solution (VMS) combines Web-based tools for configuring, monitoring, and troubleshooting enterprise VPNs and other devices such as firewalls and network- and host-based IDS.

## Notes from the Underground…

### Cisco IOS IKE Vulnerability

On April 8, 2004, Cisco released an advisory that there was a problem with their implementation of the Internet Key Exchange protocol (IKE). A malformed IKE packet sent to any system running IOS, which included most of the Cisco brand routers and switches, would cause the device to reboot. While not a problem that would compromise security, consider the disruption to network communications throughout an organization should a malicious person begin rebooting all the organization's switches and routers on a random basis. All communications would become susceptible to corruption, as they were terminated midstream. Applications connected to databases via the network could corrupt the database. Secure communications would be terminated and take time to reestablish.

Cisco rapidly addressed this vulnerability; however, it took until March 30, 2005 for the full extent of the vulnerability to be known and addressed. It turned out that it was not a small subset of devices running only the VPN Service Module, but all devices running the crypto feature set as shown here:

```
Router#show version

Cisco Internetwork Operating System Software

IOS (tm) c6sup2_rp Software (c6sup2_rp-PK9S-M), Version
12.2(18)SXD3, RELEASE SOFTWARE (fc1)

Technical Support: http://www.cisco.com/techsupport

Copyright (c) 1986-2004 by Cisco Systems, Inc.

Compiled Thu 09-Dec-04 19:35 by pwade

Image text-base: 0x4002100C, data-base: 0x422E8000
```

## PIX Firewall VPN

The PIX firewall line of products also provides VPN capabilities that are designed to allow businesses to securely extend their networks across low-cost Internet connections to mobile users, business partners, and remote offices. The PIX firewall VPN provides several key features:

- **Standards-based IPSec VPN** The PIX solution provides for a standards-based site-to-site VPN using the Internet Key Exchange (IKE) and IPSec protocols.

- **Multiplatform, multiclient support** The PIX firewall VPN supports a wide range of remote access VPN clients, including Cisco's own software VPN client on various platforms (Microsoft Windows, Linux, Solaris, and Mac OS X) and Cisco hardware-based VPN clients (PIX 501, 506E, VPN 3002 client, and the Cisco 800 and 1700 series routers). In addition to supporting IPSec-based VPNs, the PIX also supports PPTP and L2TP clients that are found in Linux, Mac, and Microsoft operating systems.

- **Encryption** The PIX uses one of three cryptographic algorithms for data confidentiality and integrity protection. These algorithms are the 56-bit Data Encryption Standard (DES), the 168-bit Triple DES (3DES), and the Advanced Encryption Standard (AES) algorithm. The AES implementation in the PIX supports up to 256-bit encryption.

## 3000 Series VPN Concentrator

The third major product in Cisco's VPN lineup is the 3000 series concentrator, which provides dedicated VPN services for remote access and LAN-to-LAN connectivity. The 3000 series provides for a wide range of models, from the 3005 for small enterprise networks to the 3080, designed for large enterprise networks. The 3000 series concentrator includes a software client that allows for easy configuration of IPSec tunnels by remote users. Additionally, a hardware version of the client, the 3002 concentrator, provides remote IPSec connectivity for telecommuters.

## Cisco Easy VPN

A recent software enhancement that simplifies VPN deployment in Cisco devices is Cisco Easy VPN. This feature centralizes VPN management and provides for the single deployment of consistent VPN policies and key management methods, thereby simplifying remote-site VPN management. The software consists of two components: the Easy VPN Remote and the Easy VPN Server.

The Cisco Easy VPN Remote feature allows Cisco IOS routers, Cisco PIX firewalls, and Cisco VPN 3002 hardware clients or software clients to act as remote VPN clients. These devices can receive security policies from a Cisco Easy VPN Server, thus minimizing VPN configuration requirements at the remote location. This cost-effective solution is ideal for remote offices with little IT support or large customer premises equipment (CPE) deployments in which it is impractical to individually configure multiple remote devices.

The Cisco Easy VPN Server allows Cisco IOS routers, Cisco PIX firewalls, and Cisco VPN 3000 concentrators to act as VPN headed devices in site-to-site or remote access VPNs, where the remote office devices are using the Cisco Easy VPN Remote feature. Using this feature, security policies defined at the head end are pushed to the remote VPN device, ensuring that those connections have up-to-date policies in place before the connection is established. In addition, a Cisco Easy VPN Server-enabled device can terminate VPN tunnels initiated by mobile remote workers running Cisco VPN client software on PCs. This flexibility makes it possible for mobile and remote workers, such as salespeople on the road or telecommuters, to access their headquarters' intranet on which critical data and applications exist. Figure 6.7 shows an architecture where the user will connect to the PIX firewall to establish an IPSec tunnel using a Cisco VPN client on a Windows workstation.

**Figure 6.7** Remote Access VPN via IPSec

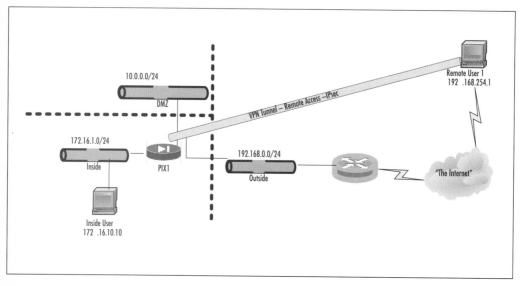

# Nortel

Nortel offers VPN gateways and VPN routers. The gateways are designed as secure remote access portals supporting Web proxy and traditional IPSec connectivity. The routers provide OpenSSL and IPSec connectivity between sites.

Nortel VPN solutions are the VPN Gateway 3050 and 3070 (Table 6.5). Both appliances support Voice/Data/Multimedia applications (Session Initiated Protocol (used in Voice-over-IP technologies), Video, Instant Messaging, etc.). *Security Host*

*Checking* is integrated into the appliances to prevent clients from infecting the internal network.

**Table 6.5** Nortel Gateway VPN Models

| Hardware Specifications | VPN Gateway 3050 | VPN Gateway 3070 |
|---|---|---|
| Maximum concurrent VPN sessions | 2000 (SSL and/or IPSec) | 5000 (SSL and/or IPSec) |
| Deployment positioning | Medium to large enterprise | Large enterprise and VPN service providers |
| CPU | (1) Intel P4 2.4GHz | (2) Intel Xeon 2.8GHz |
| Memory | 1GB DDR 266MHz | 2GB DDR 266MHz |
| On-board LANs | (2) 10/100/1000-TX | (2) 10/100/1000-TX |
| Expansion (Fixed) | (1) dual 10/100/1000-TX | (1) dual 10/100/1000-FX (fiber) |
| Drives | (1) 40GB IDE | (1) CD-ROM |

The Router series supports IPSec, L2TP, PPTP, and L2F tunneling protocols and DES, 3DES, or Advanced Encryption Standard (AES) encryption protocols. Authentication is handled by RADIUS, LDAP, SecureID, X.509 digital certificates, token cards, or smart cards. Fine control over access is handled by a packet filter protocol where each user, group, or branch office connection—internal or external—can have a unique filtering profile with different access rights. As of this writing, Nortel has renamed its "Contivity Secure IP Services Gateway" series to the "VPN Router" series. Table 6.6 shows the current models and naming scheme.

**Table 6.6** Nortel VPN Router Series

| Current Model Name | Previous Model Name | Office Size |
|---|---|---|
| VPN Router 200 Series | Contivity 200 Series VPN Switches | Telecommuters and small offices/home offices (SOHO) |
| VPN Router 600 | Contivity 600 Secure IP Services Gateway | Branch offices |
| VPN Router 1010 | Contivity 1010 Secure IP Services Gateway | Branch offices |
| VPN Router 1050 | Contivity 1050 Secure IP Services Gateway | Branch offices |

*Continued*

**Table 6.6 continued** Nortel VPN Router Series

| Current Model Name | Previous Model Name | Office Size |
|---|---|---|
| VPN Router 1100 | Contivity 1100 Secure IP Services Gateway | Branch offices |
| VPN Router 2700 | Contivity 2700 Secure IP Services Gateway | Large organizations |
| VPN Router 5000 | Contivity 5000 Secure IP Services Gateway | Large organizations that require built-in redundancy |

# Software Solutions

Software-based VPN solutions can offer a significant cost savings over hardware-based solutions, and they can perform as well; however, they require familiarity with host hardware, operating system, and VPN application itself. While this adds to the level of difficulty, it does not preclude the secure and effective deployment of such solutions. Some software VPN packages require modifications to routing tables and network addressing schemes on either the VPN system or the network as a whole. If such changes are necessary, be certain of your skills and network knowledge before taking on this task.

Patching and hardening become slightly more complicated when you opt for a software solution. Most hardware solutions issue single patches that update both the OS and the VPN component. Hardware solutions come with pre-hardened, optimized, OSs that have been modified to compliment the hardware. When you choose a software solution, you must take on the task of hardening and you will be patching the OS and VPN components separately, as well as patching any additional software that may be running on the OS.

The consideration that should rank the highest in your choice between hardware and software is security certifications. Just as with firewalls, if you fall under laws such as FIPS (Federal Information Processing Standard) or HIPAA (Health Insurance Portability and Accountability Act), you may be required to have a certain standard of VPN solution. A software solution may or may not comply with these laws, and an open source solution will most likely not. (Note that just because an open source solution does not comply with laws does not mean it is ineffective or more vulnerable to information disclosure.)

# Basic Description

The seven-layer Open Systems Interconnection (OSI) Reference Model of networking was developed by an International Organization for Standardization (ISO) subcommittee. Its seven layers act as a logical framework of protocols for computer-to-computer communications.

- **Layer 7:** Application layer
- **Layer 6** : Presentation layer
- **Layer 5**: Session layer
- **Layer 4**: Transport layer
- **Layer 3**: Network layer
- **Layer 2**: Data link layer
- **Layer 1**: Physical layer

Depending on how the VPN software integrates with the host OS, authentication, integrity checking, and encryption/decryption of data can occur anywhere from Layer 7 down to Layer 4. The lower in the stack the software is able to operate, the faster the VPN performance. Some solutions sit completely on top of the OS and operate at the application layer, meaning they operate much as a word processor would, with no integration with the OS. They communicate with the OS by standard calls. The OS must then process the information and process it. Other software integrates with the OS, sometimes inserting itself into the network stack, between either the session layer and transport layer or transport layer and network layer. Many of the binary clients for hardware solutions install this way. Depending on where in the stack the software installs, it could be a great disadvantage to throughput, but it could be a great advantage to cost savings. In most cases, there will be a throughput advantage to using a hardware solution; however, unless you require extremely high throughput, this should not be a major consideration when choosing between a hardware and software solution.

## Hardware Platform

Software-based VPN provides some flexibility as compared to the hardware-based VPN where there is no flexibility. You have your choice of hardware vendor and form factor (rack mountable vs. desktop box). You can select the processor speed and amount of memory. Perhaps most advantageous, you can select how expandable you want your hardware to be; in other words, how many more slots you will have for network cards. You can also select network cards that offload the encryption/decryption to a special chipset on the card rather than forcing it all on the central processor. These *offload cards* can greatly improve performance of otherwise mediocre hardware.

# You Need to Harden the OS

A VPN solution is used to protect the confidentiality of information. One of the biggest problems with the software-based solution is that many other applications are also executing on the computer. If the OS or any other application is vulnerable, the entire system, including the confidentiality of the information being protected becomes vulnerable. Hence, a software-based VPN solution has the basic requirement of operating system hardening and requires separate patching and maintenance of the OS and VPN software.

Any application running on a computer that must talk to another computer does so by opening a *port*. The biggest danger comes from applications and services that *listen* on ports for incoming traffic. By sending malicious crafted packets to listening ports, an attacker can first determine the software and/or operating system listening and then use the information to launch a series of attacks/exploits against them. The technique of determining the operating system is called *operating system fingerprinting*.

Let's look at the example of an Apache Web server. You can telnet to the Web server on port 80, and request header using the command

```
GET/http/1.0.
```

The server will respond with a line similar to:

```
Server: Apache/1.3.19 (Unix) (Red-Hat/Linux) mod_ssl/2.8.1 OpenSSL/0.9.6
DAV/1.0.2 PHP/4.0.6 mod_perl/1.24_01.
```

The response indicates that the computer is running Apache Web Server version 1.3.19, OpenSSL version 0.9.6, DAV (Web-based Distributed Authoring and Versioning) version 1.0.2, PHP (PHP Hypertext Preprocessor—an open-source, reflective scripting language) version 4.0.6, and mod-perl (Practical Extraction and Report Language—a programming language) version 1.24_01 on Red-Hat/Linux. This provides an attacker a great deal of information concerning possible exploits to run against this system. If any of these versions contain exploits that can be run remotely, your system will most likely be *owned* by the attacker. Many of the exploits against applications and the operating systems are published online on sites such as Canvas, Metasploit, Karalon, and Secunia.

The aim of operating system hardening is to ensure that the exposure of the OS to current and future threats is minimal. Operating system hardening comprises an end-to-end custom security configuration of the server, including all patches and updates. This can reduce the risk of attacks by 90 percent.

## Hardening List

Let's look at hardening examples for a Solaris and a Windows system.

**Disk Segmentation**  Disk segmentation separates various kinds of data to different disks or disk partitions for security. The data in a server can be broken up into four parts: system files, swap files, user data, and applications. System files are the OS. Swap files are used by the OS to write volatile memory to disk when physical memory fills up. Keeping this on a separate disk system greatly increases performance because the disk input/output can be dedicated to memory. It also increases security because if a hacker could access this data, it is possible he could insert malicious code into a location the OS would run. User data is self-explanatory. Applications pose a particular problem. While it is wise to install applications on a separate partition, it is not always practical. Many applications, particularly applications that integrate with the OS such as VPN software, write to files into the OS system files. A little experimentation on a test system will tell you if it is worthwhile to install the VPN software on a separate partition. In most cases, the answer will probably be no.

The practice of disk segmentation adds security gains and increases the efficiency of the system by dedicating disks to specific tasks. Note that if you are forced to use partitions rather than disks, you will not see the efficiency gains. Segregating important data in the disk prevents directory traversal attacks. As a practical example of disk segmentation configuration's inherent security value, consider Nimda. Most Nimda attacks rely on breaking out of the Web site root directory, traversing the file system, and running the Windows command interpreter by issuing GET requests like this:

```
GET /scripts/..%5c../winnt/system32/cmd.exe
```

Because we have separated the operating system from the Web site through disk partitions, this specific attack becomes impossible, even when no security hot fixes are applied.

**Access Control on the Files**  Most OSs on the market today support file level permissions. The permissions control that files a particular user can read, modify, and/or delete. By regulating the file permissions, it is possible to protect OS files, data, and application files against manipulation by most user accounts.

Windows has, in the past, offered the option of installing FAT32 (File Allocation Table—32-bit version) or NTFS (New Technology File System) file systems. FAT32 does not support file permissions, while NTFS does (along with a number of other features). It is always recommended to install using NTFS and, as of Windows Server 2003, FAT32 is no longer an option. By installing NTFS when you install Windows, strong file permissions are set on sensitive operating system files permitting change only by administrators. In addition, you can further strengthen permissions by using a *security template* in the *Security Configuration and Analysis* management console. In addition to the built-in security templates, more detailed and specialized templates are available from www.sans.org and http://nsa2.www.conxion.com/win2k/download.htm. For the latest detailed information on applying security templates, refer to the Microsoft Knowledge Base article 816585. *Never* apply a security template to a production system without testing! Even the best security templates can harm functionality due to particulars of your environment. Microsoft also provides the Baseline Security Analyzer that checks for many potential problems and is available at www.microsoft.com/technet/security/tools/mbsahome.mspx.

For Solaris, file access control lists are an extension of the permission set. They are implemented at the file system level and designed to enforce security policy on a much more granular level. The command-line tools chmod `setfacl` and `getfacl` are used to manipulate these permissions and the File Manager GUI under CDE (Common Desktop Environment). You also have to ensure that the setuid/setgid bits are set correctly for the inheritance of permissions. You can manually audit the file system using the **find** command with the `-perm` switch. For further information on hardening a Solaris system, refer to www.princeton.edu/~psg/unix/solaris/solarissecurity.html or www.yale.edu/its/security/securing/unix/workstation/index.htm. Sun Microsystems offers a free Security Toolkit available at www.sun.com/security/.

The Linux environment has the automated security tool Computer Oracle and Password System (COPS). COPS audits the local system for insecure file permissions, executables with elevated privileges, and weak passwords and is available from www.ciac.org/ciac/ToolsUnixSysMon.html. Although somewhat dated, it is well written and still extremely useful. RedHat Linux provides security resources at www.redhat.com/security/.

**Default Accounts** Some operating systems and applications have build-in accounts that can be used by default. These unused accounts can be prone to various brute force password-guessing attacks, or worse, have default, well-known passwords. While not entirely applicable to our study of VPNs, it is worth noting that Oracle databases are particularly notorious for the use of default usernames and passwords. At a minimum, the default passwords should be changed before exposing Oracle to the open network. As a best practice on all systems, any unused accounts should be either disabled or deleted. In particular, it is important to set a long random password on the built-in Guest account and disable it. The Administrator or Root account should always have a long complex password. If possible, these accounts should not be able to log in to the system remotely; they should only be accessible from the console. On Linux/Unix systems, the su command should be used for administration rather than logging in as Root.

> **NOTE**
>
> A natural companion to the operating system hardening section is Syngress Publishing's *Hack-Proofing Windows 2000*, which goes into more detail on a number of topics not covered in depth here due to space considerations. It covers many in detail, such as Microsoft's implementation of the IPSec protocol suite, and authentication infrastructures.
>
> Similarly, for the Solaris platform, Syngress Publishing's *Building DMZ's for Enterprise Network* provides details about hardening a Solaris/Linux/Unix system.

**Maintain System and Application Patches**   Operating systems and applications are written by humans, and all humans make mistakes. Therefore, it is necessary to correct those mistakes as they are discovered. Often, these mistakes lead to security vulnerabilities that can be exploited for malicious purposes. It is essential to apply patches as quickly as possible because it appears that no sooner does a patch come out than an exploit is developed by hackers to take advantage of the vulnerability patched.

It is also essential to realize that *no* operating system is immune to patching. There was a time when Microsoft products had the bad reputation of being easily hackable and the false belief that all other operating systems were far less vulnerable. The reality was that Microsoft was a very large target with wide distribution and other OSs were less widely distributed and did not look so appealing as hacking the giant corporation. This is no longer true. Every OS has vulnerabilities and every OS can be, and is, a target for hackers. Witness the recent long list of vulnerabilities that have been patched in the Mozilla Firefox Web browser—the very browser that was touted as the "safe" alternative to Microsoft's Internet Explorer. Recent vulnerabilities have been patched that could have resulted in the compromise of any OS running the browser.

## Configuring & Implementing…

### Windows Patch Management

Microsoft provides new security updates on the second Tuesday of each month. These security updates are for the Windows operating system, and for Microsoft applications like Microsoft Office, Exchange, Media Player, and Internet Explorer. www.microsoft.com/athome/security/update/bulletins/default.mspx provides links to the security bulletins. http://update.microsoft.com provides automatic analysis of your system and recommends the proper updates for your configuration.

### Solaris Patch Management

The main clearinghouse for Solaris patches is the SunSolve site, located at http://sunsolve.sun.com. From this site, you can gain access to the latest patch cluster via either HTTP or FTP download. In addition, automated tools are available to manage patches on Solaris systems, such as the Sun PatchManager utility. More information is available at http://sunsolve.sun.com/patchpro.

### Linux Patch Management

Because Linux comes in so many flavors, it is impossible to address every single source for patches. Here are a few places to start:

- Security patches for SuSE Linux are available at www.novell.com/linux/security/securitysupport.html.
- RedHat Linux patches are available at www.redhat.com/security/.
- OpenBSD security notifications are at www.openbsd.org/security.html.

# Examples

There are various commercial and open-source software-based VPN solutions. We will examine some open source options and then the commercial offerings.

# Openswan

Linux Openswan grew out of the FreeS/WAN IPSec implementation for Linux. FreeS/WAN was last released in 2004. Since that time, Openswan has continued to develop IPSec/VPN technologies for Linux. Openswan uses a three-part VPN scheme. The first part is Kernel IPSec (KLIPS) that implements Encapsulating

Security Payload (ESP), the module that provides encryption and authentication. Pluto, part 2, is an Internet Key exchange daemon, which implements IKE negotiating connections with other systems. The third part uses various scripts to provide an administrator interface.

The FreeS/WAN project also introduced the concept of opportunistic encryption, which has been continued in Openswan. Using a public/private key pair, the objective is to allow encryption for secure communication without any pre-arrangement specific to the pair of systems involved. DNS is used to distribute the public keys of each system involved. This is resistant to passive attacks. The use of DNS Security (DNSSEC) secures this system against active attackers as well, preventing DNS cache poisoning with false information. The VPN administrators must pre-configure the authentication information in the DNS, and must set up the VPN gateways with opportunistic encryption enabled. The gateways look for opportunities to encrypt, and create a tunnel whenever they can. Acceptance of unencrypted communication is again a decision of an administrator.

The technique of opportunistic encryption provides two inherent advantages:

- It reduces the administrative overhead for IPSec enormously. The requirement of configuration of the system on a per-tunnel basis is eliminated. Gateways can be configured automatically, and thereafter everything is automatic. Openswan allows specifically configured tunnels to co-exist with opportunistic encryption.

- Opportunistic encryption provides more secure Internet, allowing users to create an environment where message privacy is the default. All messages can be encrypted, with the help of the other end.

Further details about Openswan are available at www.openswan.org. There you will find all the documentation needed to install and configure the latest version. In addition, complete documentation is provided in the Openswan distribution file.

# OpenBSD

The Linux distribution of OpenBSD (www.openbsd.org) provides out-of-the-box, built-in IPSec functionality. Since the OpenBSD project is based in Canada and the Export Control List of Canada places no significant restriction on the export of cryptographic software, strong encryption protocols are built into the OS. The IPSec protocol stack has been included since 1997 and is certified by the Virtual Private Network Consortium (VPNC). One restriction to note: It is recommended by the OpenBSD developers to use network cards with on-board cryptographic processing. While this is recommended in any software-based implementation of VPN, it is particularly vital for OpenBSD for the highest performance standards. www.openbsd.org/crypto.html lists the supported cards and other important information concerning the IPSec implementation.

# CheckPoint

CheckPoint's solution for enforcing VPN security includes Firewall-1/VPN-1 Pro, VPN-1 Edge, and VPN-1 VSX. These server products are designed to run on Linux, Solaris, and Windows. The client software includes a Mac-compatible offering.

VPN-1 Pro is an enterprise-level solution designed to provide secure tunnels between sites. It includes *Application Intelligence* that can detect application-level attacks and prevent them from infecting your internal network. VPN-1 Pro also supports Voice over IP.

VPN-1 Edge is designed for branch offices as both a tunneling device to the main office and for secure access to the branch office network.

Integrity Secure Client and VPN-1 Secure Client provide client connectivity to the VPN gateway and enforce corporate policies. Such policies can include patch level and the installation of anti-virus software. It also provides host intrusion prevention and firewall functionality.

CheckPoint also provides SSL Network Extender, a Web-based plug-in that allows network-level access through your Web browser.

Firewall-1 also integrates with the VPN solutions to provide a cost-effective single point solution for both network protection and secure remote access.

# Microsoft

Microsoft has integrated VPN solutions into its Windows 2000, Windows XP Home Edition, Windows XP Professional, and Windows 2003 products. The implementation of VPNs in Windows is based on a combination of IPSec and L2TP, as described in RFC 3193. It is important to note that to fully implement L2TP in Windows, x.509 certificates must be issued to the client machines. The easiest way to issue certificates is to use Microsoft Certificate Server in a Windows Active Directory forest. The full integration of server/workstation, automatic certificate issuance, and Active Directory Group Policy makes the VPN invisible to the end user. Very little training is needed to get the user securely connected to the Microsoft VPN solution.

## Notes from the Underground...

### Microsoft VPN Complexity

While a Microsoft VPN can be set up securely, a great deal of knowledge is required to configure all the pieces correctly. You must first know the Microsoft Windows OS and how to lock it down. You must know the Microsoft PKI (Public Key Infrastructure) and securely deploy a certificate server. You must have Active Directory deployed securely and have Group Policy properly configured for certificate deployment and for the enforcement of other security policies. Finally, you must have your workstations properly installed and configured.

Microsoft VPN works best and most securely in a 100-percent Microsoft shop with uniform hardware and only Windows XP and Windows 2003 Server deployed. If it is deployed per Microsoft's recommendations, you can have a solid, easy-to-use VPN solution. If you try to "wing" it and don't do your research, you will be breached. Microsoft implementations are not as "plug and play" as many of the hardware solutions are.

In addition to the L2TP/IPSec VPN solution from Microsoft, there is also support for PPTP. This is a much less secure protocol and it is not recommended that you rely on this protocol to protect your data. We mention it here to make you aware it exists. Should you require secure dialup, PPTP might be considered; otherwise, you should only implement L2TP.

PPTP functions are divided between a PPTP Access Controller (PAC) running on a dial-access platform and a PPTP Network Server (PNS) that operates on a general-purpose operating system. It uses an enhanced GRE mechanism to provide a flow- and congestion-controlled encapsulated datagram service for carrying PPP packets. Some service providers do not allow GRE packets to traverse their networks, which could be an obstacle to deploying PPTP as a VPN solution.

## SSL Explorer

SSL Explorer is a Web-based SSL VPN server that has been designed to provide an SSL-VPN solution. It is available at www.sshtools.com/showSslExplorer.do under GPL. Available for Windows, UNIX, Mac, and Linux, it provides a Web-based interface to configure users, access policies, define authentication methods, access network resources, access, updates, upload and download files, and use remote

applications.  It supports multifactor authentication using LDAP, SSL client certificates, public-key, PIN, and one-time-password via SMS to a cell phone or PDA
There are two editions of it, Enterprise (paid) and Community (free). Community
edition comes with source and requires ANT (available at http://ant.apache.org) and
JDK, available at http://java.sun.com/j2se/1.5.0/download.jsp. Details about installation and configuration procedure can be found at http://sourceforge.net/project/
showfiles.php?group_id=116065&package_id=154305.

# Summary

A VPN is a secure way of sending data over public networks. It works by encapsulating your data in an encrypted form inside a TCP/IP packet.

Hardware solutions have hardware, operating system, and VPN software optimized to work together for maximum efficiency. In addition, the entire system is hardened against attacks. The following companies are a sampling of those offering VPN solutions.

Juniper offers the Secure Access line of VPN appliances, and VPN functionality within their NetScreen firewall line. Unique to the Juniper appliances is the concept of *zones*. Zones permit the administrator to gather interfaces, IP addresses, and/or VPN tunnels into groups and apply a single policy to that group. Thus, it is much easier to isolate a given group from other groups.

F5 offers the FirePass line of appliances. These appliances come with automatic detection of corporate policy compliance and attempt to provide a tunnel, and prevent infection of the internal network from a compromised machine using the VPN tunnel from the outside.

The Cisco line of appliances provides VPN capabilities within most of their router and switch product lines, in the PIX Firewall line, and as a separate VPN Concentrator line. All the Cisco products except the VPN Concentrator are more focused for site-to-site VPN connections, while the Concentrator is designed for workstation to corporate network connectivity.

Nortel appliances have recently undergone a renaming process and several products have been discontinued. The appliances on the market offer, like the F5 appliances, a built-in client compliance check to help prevent internal network infections.

Software solutions can offer an initial significant cost savings. However, great care must be taken to harden the host operating system and then carefully maintain and patch the OS and VPN application.

Openswan and OpenBSD are two offerings from the open source community of free IPSec-based VPNs. These are free to obtain; however, you must carefully harden the Linux or OpenBSD OS before implementing them, and you must maintain patches that are not automatically made available.

CheckPoint offers several levels of software VPNs designed for enterprise down to individual users. These are designed to run on Windows, Solaris, or Linux.

Windows offers a built-in VPN solution. The VPN supports L2TP and PPTP. PPTP is not recommended, but to securely implement L2TP, a number of steps must be completed correctly. In a 100-percent Microsoft enterprise, the effort is worth it for the integration. Otherwise, a hardware solution is a better option.

# Solutions Fast Track

## Solution Appliance Hardware Solution

☑ Hardware is dedicated to the function of providing a VPN.

☑ Operating system is optimized for the hardware and for providing VPN services.

☑ Legal compliance may require a certified hardware solution.

## Solution Appliance Software Solution

☑ Software-based solutions require familiarity with the host operating system and the application itself.

☑ Some software solutions require extensive setup time and/or network cards with on-board excelerator modules to be fully efficient.

☑ Some of the best practices in operating system hardening are disk segmentation, access control on files, and proper management of default accounts.

☑ The operating system must be patched separately from the VPN application.

# Frequently Asked Questions

The following Frequently Asked Questions, answered by the authors of this book, are designed to both measure your understanding of the concepts presented in this chapter and to assist you with real-life implementation of these concepts. To have your questions about this chapter answered by the author, browse to **www.syngress.com/solutions** and click on the **"Ask the Author"** form.

**Q:** Is Opportunistic Encryption part of IPSec VPN?

**A:** Opportunistic Encryption is the concept that any two Openswan gateways will be able to encrypt their traffic, even if the two gateway administrators have had no prior contact and neither system has any present information about the other. Concept of Opportunistic Encryption is not a part of the IPSec VPN standard, nor is it offered by any other company.

**Q:** How do I stop my OS from announcing information such as in the Apache Web Server example?

**A:** In some cases, there are *hacks* that can stop certain information from being published, or provide false information. For example, using the tool URLScan from Microsoft, you can change or remove the header announcing that the Web server is running IIS. While this may fool inexperienced hackers, it is far from foolproof. *Security through obscurity* is not security.

In other cases, you simply cannot stop this information advertisement. It will break how the computer functions. You cannot hide the type of operating system hosting a file system, for example. What would happen if a Mac attempted to connect to a Linux server and it did not know it was a Linux server? How would the Mac authenticate? How would it translate the files?

The best defense against exploitation of ports is not hiding them, but having a fully patched and hardened system with as few open ports as possible. Use of an application proxy will also mitigate possible attacks by filtering malicious code before it reaches the destination server.

**Q:** Under what circumstances is a software-based VPN preferred?

**A:** Software-based VPNs are best suited when cost is a primary issue, legal compliance is not an issue, and, most importantly, where there is a strong expertise to harden and maintain the underlying operating system.

**Q:** Under what circumstances is a hardware-based VPN preferred?

**A:** Hardware-based VPNs are best used where legal compliance and high performance are required. In addition, when there is a demand for high availability (24 x 7 uptime). Hardware VPNs should also be considered if a "plug and play" solution is favored over lower cost.

**Q:** Are automatic updates of either an underlying OS and VPN software solution, or the OS of a hardware solution recommended.

**A:** This is a difficult question to answer. Most updates will require restart of the VPN system. This will disconnect anyone with an active session and result in downtime as the system reboots. It is also *possible* that an update could be faulty and result in downtime as you either back out the update or restore the system from backup. Note this is *possible*, not *probable*. Most vendors thoroughly test updates and patches to insure they will not bring a system down. The danger in not automatically patching is, of course, the possibility that an exploit will appear, and if you don't have the patch on soon enough, your system will become compromised. How much time do you have to insure patches are applied as quickly as possible, manually? How willing are you to take the risk that automatic patching will not damage your system? Answer those questions, and you'll be on your way to making a decision.

# Part IV
# Implementing
# Firewalls and VPNs
# (Case Studies)

# Chapter 7

# IT Infrastructure Security Plan

## Solutions in this chapter:

- Infrastructure Security Assessment
- Project Parameters
- Project Team
- Project Organization
- Project Work Breakdown Structure
- Project Risks and Mitigation Strategies
- Project Constraints and Assumptions
- Project Schedule and Budget
- Infrastructure Security Project Outline

☑ Summary

☑ Solutions Fast Track

☑ Frequently Asked Questions

# Introduction

Infrastructure security is at the root of your entire corporate security plan. Other individual security area plans (ISAPs) may overlap with your infrastructure security plan to some extent. For example, a wireless network is part of your infrastructure, but it's also a large enough area to be addressed in a separate project plan. You'll need to ensure that your corporate IT security project and your ISAPs cover all the bases, but be aware that there are overlapping areas that should be clearly delineated if you're working on several projects in parallel. You don't want project teams wrestling over ownership of one part of your network or another. In this chapter, we'll look at the basic infrastructure components and how to secure them; then we'll create a project plan utilizing this information.

# Infrastructure Security Assessment

There are two distinct processes: audit and assessment. An *assessment* is intended to look for issues and vulnerabilities that can be mitigated, remediated, or eliminated prior to a security breach. An *audit* is normally conducted after an assessment with the goal of measuring compliance with policies and procedures. Typically, someone is held accountable for audit results. Some people don't like the term *auditing;* perhaps it's too reminiscent of ol' Uncle Sam scouring through your tax return from three years ago when you claimed that one vacation as a business trip because you talked to your boss on your cell phone while waiting at the shuttle to your beachfront hotel. Though the terms *assessment* and *audit* are often used interchangeably, in this chapter we focus on assessments.

As we've discussed throughout this book, there are three primary components of IT security: *people, process,* and *technology.* A balanced approach addresses all three areas, because focusing on one area to the exclusion of others creates security holes. People, including senior management, must buy into the importance of security, and they must understand and participate in their role in maintaining security. Process includes all the practices and procedures that occur and reoccur to keep the network secure. Technology obviously includes all hardware and software that comprises the network infrastructure. Part of the technology assessment required to assess and harden infrastructure security includes deploying the right technological solutions for your firm and not the "one size fits all" or the "it was all we could afford" solution. In IT, we often focus a disproportionate amount of time and energy on securing the technology and overlook the importance of both people and process to the overall security environment.

To secure your infrastructure, you need to understand its building blocks. These include:

- Network perimeter protection
- Internal network protection
- Intrusion monitoring and prevention
- Host and server configuration
- Protection against malicious code
- Incident response capabilities
- Security policies and procedures
- Employee awareness and training
- Physical security and monitoring

We'll discuss policies, procedures, and training in the chapter on operational security later in this book, so we won't discuss that material here.

We can look at the infrastructure security assessment in three segments, as shown in Figure 7.1.

**Figure 7.1** Infrastructure Assessment Overview

| Environment | People and Process | Technology |
|---|---|---|
| ⊙ Information criticality<br>⊙ Impact analysis<br>⊙ Systems definitions<br>⊙ Information flow<br>⊙ Scope | ⊙ User profiles<br>⊙ Policies, procedures<br>⊙ Organizational needs<br>⊙ Regulatory/compliance | ⊙ Server/host security<br>⊙ High assurance devices<br>⊙ Network security<br>⊙ Application security<br>⊙ Point of entry<br>⊙ Configuration management |

# Internal Environment

Security assessments should begin by looking at the overall environment in which security must be implemented, since security does not exist in a vacuum. Looking at the relative importance of your company's information is a good starting point, because you need to find the right balance between security and information criticality. As part of that analysis, you also need to look at the impact of a network infrastructure intrusion and what that would cost to defend and repair. You need to define the various systems you have in place and look at how information flows through your organization to understand the infrastructure you're trying to protect. Finally, you need to create an initial assessment of scope to define what *is* and *is not* included in your project. We'll look at scope later in the chapter, when we begin developing our project plan.

# Information Criticality

It's important to begin by looking at information criticality. We've discussed this topic throughout this book, and it will continue to be a common theme because there's really no point in securing something that no one wants. It's why a new Lexus RX-330 comes with a lo-jack system, but a 1993 Dodge Dart with serious body damage is not likely to need any protection (in fact, there might be an economic benefit to having such a vehicle stolen—no offense intended to any 1993 Dodge Dart owners). Information criticality is an assessment of what your network holds and how important that is in the overall scheme of things. Not all data is created equal, and if your company manufactures steel troughs for horse feed, there's a good chance your network data is not nearly as interesting to a potential attacker as the data in an online stock brokerage firm or a bank or credit card processing house network. Therefore, you need to look at the criticality of your information and decide how much you're willing to spend to secure that information. No one ever wants a security breach, but it would not make good business sense to spend $15 million to secure a network for a company that pulls in $5 million annually and doesn't store sensitive personal data such as credit card numbers or medical records. That said, just because your company makes $5 million annually doesn't mean that you *shouldn't* look seriously at the criticality of your data, to be sure you don't have excessive exposure. If you are storing credit card numbers or medical records, you'd better be sure your security solutions are up to standards, because your legal liability could significantly outstrip that $5 million annually in a big hurry.

# Impact Analysis

You'll notice as you read the chapters for the individual security area plans that some of this information overlaps. It's hard to perform an impact analysis on an infrastructure breach without also seeing how it would impact your wireless network components, your Web site, or your policies and procedures. However, in looking at the impact to your infrastructure, you'll need to understand how a breach could impact the very foundation of your organization. The impact analysis should include:

- **Cost of network infrastructure—failure (downtime)** Server down, database server down, routers down, etc.

- **Cost of network infrastructure—unavailable (slow or unresponsive)** Denial-of-service attacks, packet flooding, etc.

- **Cost of network infrastructure breach—data confidentiality, integrity, availability** Man-in-the-middle, spoofing, phishing, etc.

- **Cost to company reputation** Lost sales, lost customers, loss of long-term business relationships.

- **Cost to company** Cost of remediation, cost of litigation.

You should combine information criticality with the findings of your impact analysis to form a clear picture of what you're trying to protect and why. When you understand the impact, you can see where the important areas are in your organization, and you can use this information, in part, to prioritize your approach to securing the network.

# System Definitions

Infrastructure systems clearly include the "backbone" services, including DHCP servers, DNS servers, Directory Services servers, e-mail servers, database servers, firewalls, DMZs, routers/switches, operating systems, Web servers, and security applications (antivirus, antispyware, IDS/IPS, etc.). If it's helpful, you can also look at your systems from the OSI model perspective—from the physical layer all the way up through the application layer, whatever makes the most sense to you and your team.

Creating (or updating) network diagrams can also be included in the system definitions overview, since the way everything fits together is part of understanding the whole.

# Information Flow

One area that is sometimes overlooked in the assessment phase is the flow of information through the infrastructure. This area can be used in conjunction with your systems definitions to help map your network and to discover the key areas that need to be protected and how an attacker would get to those assets.

It sometimes helps to look at information flow from different perspectives. For example, how does information from a user computer flow? How does DNS or DHCP traffic flow through the network? How is external traffic coming into the network managed, and where and how does it enter? How is traffic leaving the network for the public network (Internet) managed? Creating a map of your network infrastructure and information flow will help you visualize your network and identify potential weak spots.

# Scope

You might want to limit the scope of your infrastructure security project for a variety of reasons. While you're looking at your internal environment, you might choose to limit the scope. "Scoping" is often done at this point when you're engaging an external security consultant. However, if you're doing this work internally, you may limit your scope here, or you may choose to do a full assessment and then limit the scope after you see what's what.

# People and Process

Clearly, people and processes impact network security in a big way. Most security breaches occur from the inside, not the outside, despite the media's sensationalized focus on external security breaches. The people in your organization can be your defenders or your downfall, depending on how they approach security. Savvy, well-informed users can augment the technical security measures by avoiding becoming victims of social engineering, by reporting suspicious activity, by avoiding responding to phishing e-mail, or by not leaving their computer logged in and unattended. All the security in the world can't prevent problems if users are not pulling their weight. There are many ways to inform and involve users, and unfortunately, many IT departments don't leverage these opportunities very successfully, because they often fall victim to a "user as pain in the hind quarters" mentality. Let's look at how users and organizational processes should be reviewed during an infrastructure assessment.

# User Profiles

What kinds of users do you have? Where and how do they work? If you begin by looking at your user population, you will see segments that have higher and lower risk profiles. The clerk in the mailroom might only have access to e-mail and the mailroom application, but does he or she also have Internet access and the ability to download and install programs? What about the marketing staff who travel worldwide? What kinds of information do they keep on their laptops (usernames, passwords, domain names, sensitive documents, contacts, and the like), and how does this impact your network security?

Users can be categorized in whatever ways work for you in your organization, but here's a list of potential risks by employee type, to get you thinking:

- **Executive** High-profile targets, often not extremely "tech savvy," potentially easy to get information about (from press releases, public filings, legal filings, and so on).

- **Director**  High-profile targets, may travel extensively with sensitive information, may need to connect to the network in a variety of insecure locations.

- **Finance**, **marketing**, **HR, legal**  Access to extremely sensitive data, may be high-profile targets due to their access to sensitive data, may travel extensively and be desirable targets of social engineering.

- **IT staff**  Access to network resources, ability to grant/deny access, potentially desirable targets of social engineering (especially via help desk), highly desirable targets (IT usernames and passwords with administrative privileges are the Holy Grail for hackers).

- **Users**  Access to sensitive company information, often targets of social engineering.

In addition to these categories, you may have user groups defined in your network security management system (which manages access control) that you want to use. Microsoft defines users as administrators, power users, and the like, and that might also work for you. Again, the point is to use a categorization method that's meaningful to the way your company and your existing network infrastructure are organized, so you can understand the risks users bring into the organization and the strategies for keeping the network secure in light of the way various users work.

# Policies and Procedures

We won't spend a lot of time discussing policies and procedures in this chapter; we'll focus on them in an upcoming chapter on operational security. As we've discussed, no single security topic exists in a vacuum or silo, and as you move through your project planning, you'll notice areas of intersection and overlap. There are few hard-and-fast rules about where these overlapping elements should be placed; the important factor is to be sure they *are* included *someplace*.

Infrastructure policies and procedures touch on the day-to-day operations of the IT staff, including the way security is monitored (auditing functions, log files, alerts) and how it is maintained (backups, updates, upgrades). Policies regarding user behavior are also crucial to ensuring that the network infrastructure remains safe. Finally, corporate policies regarding the use of data, computer and electronic equipment, and building access, to name just three, are areas that should be reviewed and revised to support and enhance security across the enterprise.

# Organizational Needs

The internal environment is shaped by the organization's business profile, including the type of business, the nature of sales and marketing functions, the types of customers, the kinds of employees, and the flow of work through the company. What does your company require from the network services you provide, and how can these needs be secured? If you believe your organization's network, data, and computer needs are being met, delineate what they are and check with a few users to see if you're on the mark or if you're really off-center by a wide margin. Make sure that you understand how the network fits into the organization, not the other way around, and then design your security solution around it.

# Regulatory/Compliance

Any infrastructure assessment and security plan must incorporate regulatory and compliance requirements. These vary greatly from state to state and country to country, and as you're probably well aware, keeping up with them can be more than a full-time job. Many companies are hiring compliance officers whose primary job is to manage corporate compliance. If your company has a compliance officer, you should certainly make sure he or she is a member of your IT project team, at least during the definition phase, when you're developing your functional and technical requirements, since these are often the method by which compliance occurs. We've included a short list here with a few Web site links, but it's not exhaustive; you should seek legal advice regarding regulatory and compliance requirements for your firm if you don't have a knowledgeable and experienced compliance officer in place.

## Business Intelligence…

## Common Compliance Standards

There are numerous compliance issues facing organizations today. Below are just a few of the compliance standards you should be aware of and should evaluate whether your firm is subject to these regulations or not.

**British Standard 7799** (BS7799), eventually evolved into ISO17799.

**Child Online Protection Act** (COPA), www.copacommission.org.

**Health Insurance Portability and Accountability Act** (HIPAA), www.cms.hhs.gov/hipaa/hipaa1/content/more.asp.

**Continued**

**Family Educational Rights and Privacy Act** (FERPA), www.ed.gov/policy/gen/guid/fpco/ferpa/index.html.

**Federal Information Security Mgmt Act** (FISMA), csrc.nist.gov/seccert/.

**Gramm-Leach Bliley Act** (GLBA), www.ftc.gov/privacy/glbact/.

**Homeland Security Presidential Directive 7** (HSPD-7), www.whitehouse.gov/news/release/2003/12/20031217-5.html.

**ISO 17799**, www.iso.org (International Organization for Standardization's INFOSEC recommendations).

**National Strategy to Secure Cyberspace**, www.whitehouse.gov/pcipb/.

**Sarbanes-Oxley Act** (SOX), www.aicpa.org/sarbanes/index.asp.

# Technology

The technology assessment involves the three elements: people, process, and technology. However, the technology portion of the assessment will probably take up 80% of your time due to the vast number of technological components involved in securing the infrastructure. Servers and hosts must be updated, patched, and secured. Applications must be updated, patched, and secured. The perimeter of your network must be secured, tested, and monitored. Remote access and wireless access must be secured, tested, and monitored. Data traveling across the network needs to be secured against a variety of attack types, which is done through various protocols at different network layers, depending on where the data originates, where it's headed, and what it contains. We'll spend the remainder of the chapter looking at the technology components of infrastructure security, holding off discussing the policies and procedures (which impact user behavior and the *people* aspect) until a later chapter.

# Establishing Baselines

The point of performing these assessments is not to prove that your network is secure or insecure but to find out exactly what level of security you actually have and to establish baselines. When you know the starting point, you can improve security incrementally and document it as you go. Baselines are created by establishing a known starting point, in this case your current settings.

It might be tempting to correct problems as you perform this assessment, but it's not the best way to proceed. As you know, making a configuration change at Point A can cause a ripple effect through your network and show up at Point C in a strange and unexpected way. As you develop your project plan, be clear with your project team that they need to document existing configurations, settings, versions, and so on, without making changes. If a team member finds a serious security hole, it should be brought to your attention immediately for action. The point is that if a serious problem is found, it should be quickly addressed but not in an ad hoc manner. It should be assessed and addressed in a calm, rational, thoughtful manner, and possibly incorporated into your project plan. Does that mean that you wait until your project planning is complete to address a serious security hole? Absolutely not. You should, however, use a well thought out strategy for addressing it outside the project planning cycle, then document the changes and incorporate them into your project plan. What you want to avoid is having every person looking at the network making small tweaks here and there to "tighten up security" as they go, because you'll end up with a mess at the end of your evaluation period. Serious problems should be brought to your immediate, and minor issues should be well documented.

# Addressing Risks to the Corporate Network

Once you have created a prioritized list of risks to your network as well as their associated costs, your next step will be to determine a course of action in handling each risk. When deciding how to address risks to your network, you typically have one of four options:

- **Avoidance** You can avoid a risk by changing the scope of the project so that the risk in question no longer applies, or change the features of the software to do the same. In most cases, this is not a viable option, since eliminating a network service such as e-mail to avoid risks from viruses would usually not be seen as an appropriate measure. (Network services exist for a reason; your job as a security professional is to make those services as secure as possible.) One example of how avoidance would be a useful risk management tactic is a case where a company has a single server that acts as both a Web server and a database server housing confidential personnel records, when there is no interaction whatsoever between the Web site and personnel information. In this scenario, purchasing a second server to house the employee database, removing the personnel database from the Web server entirely, and placing the employee database server on a private network segment with no contact to the Internet would be a way of avoiding Web-based attacks on personnel records, since this plan of action "removes" a feature of the Web server (the personnel files) entirely.

- **Transference** You can transfer a risk by moving the responsibility to a third party. The most well-known example of this solution is purchasing some type of insurance—let's say flood insurance—for the contents of your server room. Although the purchase of this insurance does not diminish the likelihood that a flood will occur in your server room, it does ensure that the monetary cost of the damage will be borne by the insurance company in return for your policy premiums. It's important to note that transference is not a 100-percent solution—in the flood example, your company will likely still incur some financial loss or decreased productivity in the time it takes you to restore your server room to working order. As with most risk management tactics, bringing the risk exposure down to zero is usually an unattainable goal.

- **Mitigation** This is what most IT professionals think of when implementing a risk management solution. Mitigation involves taking some positive action to reduce the likelihood that an attack will occur or to reduce the potential damage that would be caused by an attack, without removing the resource entirely, as is the case with avoidance. Patching servers, disabling unneeded services, and installing a firewall are some solutions that fall under the heading of risk mitigation.

- **Acceptance** After you have delineated all the risks to your infrastructure that can be avoided, transferred, or mitigated, you are still left with a certain amount of risk that you won't be able to reduce any further without seriously impacting your business (taking an e-mail server offline as a means to combat viruses, for example). Your final option is one of acceptance, where you decide that the residual risks to your network have reached an acceptable level, and you choose to monitor the network for any signs of new or increased risks that might require more action later.

There is no one right way to address all risks to your infrastructure; you'll most likely take a blended approach to security. There are some risks you absolutely need to avoid, other risks you can reasonably transfer or mitigate, and still others that you simply accept because the cost of avoiding them is just not worth it.

## Business Intelligence...

### Depth in Defense

*Depth in defense* is a key concept to understand before heading into an infrastructure security project. The concept is a fairly straightforward one: Security comes not from one source but from many layers of protection. Almost any attacker can find a way in through a single-defense system, but it's much more difficult (but not impossible) to find a way in through a maze of security measures. When security measures are used in combination, it's like having a deadbolt, a padlock, a keypad, a card reader, and a biometric scanner attached to the network. An attacker can get through one or two, maybe even three, but it's the fourth and fifth layers that finally stop the would-be intruder and cause him or her to look for another, easier target. In the world of IT security, nothing is 100-percent secure unless it's powered off and locked in an isolated box, at which point it becomes completely useless. Understanding the depth-in-defense approach will help you as you try to evaluate the measures you should take to secure your network infrastructure. You may choose to implement something less iron-clad (at a drastically lower cost) in one area, knowing that the "layering" effect will likely give you a strong enough level of defense against most known threats.

## External Environment

The external environment includes the changes in technology that might impact your business, the changes in the regulatory and legal environments that could impact your business, and the changing landscape of threats to your network. It's not a static picture; you'll need to implement policies and procedures that allow you and your IT staff to remain up to date with these changes so that you can continually monitor, assess, and address these changes in a proactive and positive manner.

We've talked about the legal implications of compliance and the importance of understanding those compliance issues when you're planning your IT security project. Because these issues are numerous, industry specific, and ever changing, we're not going to get into specific compliance data in this book. We recap some of the more common ones in this section, just in case you missed them earlier. We've also provided some Web links for you to learn more about these standards. There may be serious legal issues involved with compliance and noncompliance, so be sure to check with your firm's legal counsel to determine the regulations that apply to your firm. You might want to complete the internal assessment prior to contacting your attorney, so that you have a clear understanding of the kinds of information your network stores and the criticality of that information. For example, if your company recently started storing segments of people's medical records as part of a new business partnership with another firm, you will most likely have to comply with HIPAA standards (and possibly others). Recent changes to your company's business may have pulled you into areas in which regulation and compliance are mandatory, so be sure to do a full assessment here.

# Threats

Predicting network threats and analyzing the risks they present to your infrastructure are among the cornerstones of the network security design process. Understanding the types of threats that your network will face helps you in designing appropriate countermeasures and in obtaining the necessary money and resources to create a secure network framework. Members of an organization's management structure will likely be resistant to spending money on a threat that they don't understand; this process will also help them understand the very real consequences of network threats so they can make informed decisions about the types of measures to implement. In this section, we discuss some common network attacks that you will likely face when you're designing a secure network and how each of these attacks can adversely affect your network.

When classifying network threats, many developers and security analysts have taken to using a model called STRIDE, which is an acronym for the following terms:

- **Spoofing identity** These include attacks that involve illegally accessing and using account information that isn't yours, such as shoulder-surfing someone's password while he types it on his keyboard. This type of attack affects the confidentiality of data.

- **Tampering with data** These attacks involve a malicious modification of data, interfering with the integrity of an organization's data. The most common of these is a man-in-the-middle (MITM) attack, where a third party intercepts communications between two legitimate hosts and tampers with the information as it is sent back and forth. This is akin to sending an e-mail to Mary that says, "The meeting is at 3:00 P.M.", but a malicious attacker intercepts and changes the message to, "The meeting has been cancelled."

- **Repudiation** These threats occur when a user can perform a malicious action against a network resource and then deny that she did so, and the owners or administrators of the data have no way of proving otherwise. A repudiation threat can attack any portion of the confidentiality, integrity, and availability (CIA) triad.

- **Information disclosure** This occurs when information is made available to individuals who should not have access to it. Information disclosure can occur through improperly applied network permissions that allow a user to read a confidential file or give an intruder the ability to read data being transmitted between two networked computers. Information disclosure affects the confidentiality of your company's data and resources.

- **Denial of service** So-called DoS attacks do not attempt to alter a company's data; rather, they attack a network by denying access to valid users, by flooding a Web server with phony requests so that legitimate users cannot access it, for example. DoS attacks affect the availability of your organization's data and resources. A new variation is a distributed DoS (DDoS), also called a *zombie net* or *zombie attack*.

- **Elevation of privilege** This type of attack takes place when an unprivileged, nonadministrative user gains administrative or "root level" access to an entire system, usually through a flaw in the system software. When this occurs, an attacker has the ability to alter or even destroy any data that he finds, since he is acting with administrative privileges.

This type of threat affects all portions of the CIA triad, since the attacker can access, change, and remove any data that he or she sees fit. When you are analyzing a potential network threat, try to remember the STRIDE acronym as a means of classifying and reacting to the threat. You can use the STRIDE model throughout the life of your corporate network when you're designing and maintaining security policies and procedures.

# Recognizing External Threats

Now that we've discussed a model for classifying network threats, we can look at some of the common attacks in more detail. Entire books can be (and have been) written that solely discuss the kinds of threats that we look at in this section, so we'll be giving you a "birds-eye" view of the kinds of attacks that your network security design will need to guard against.

## Denial-of-Service Attacks

As we've already mentioned, the DoS attack (and its first cousin, the DDoS attack) works to disrupt services on a network so that legitimate users cannot access resources they need. Some examples include attempts to disrupt the connection between two specific machines, or more commonly, attempts to flood an entire network with traffic, thereby overloading the network and preventing legitimate traffic from being transmitted. There can also be instances in which an illegitimate use of resources can result in denial of service. For example, if an intruder uses a vulnerability in your FTP server to upload and store illegal software, this can consume all available disk space on the FTP server and prevent legitimate users from storing their files. A DoS attack can effectively disable a single computer or an entire network.

A common venue of attack for DoS is against an organization's network bandwidth and connectivity; the attacker's goal is to prevent other machines from communicating due to the traffic flood. An example of this type of attack is the *SYN flood attack.* In a SYN flood, the attacker begins to establish a connection to the victim machine but in such a way that the connection is never completed. Since even the most powerful server has only a certain amount of memory and number processor cycles to devote to its workload, legitimate connection attempts can be denied while the victim machine is trying to complete these fake "half-open" connections.

Another common DoS is the so-called *Ping of Death,* where an attacker sends so many *PING* requests to a target machine that it is overloaded and unable to process legitimate network requests. An intruder might also attempt to consume network resources in other ways, including generating a massive number of e-mail messages, intentionally generating system errors that need to be included in Event Viewer logs, or misusing FTP directories or network shares to overload available disk space. Basically, anything that allows data, whether on a network cable or hard drive, to be written at will (without any type of control mechanism) can create a DoS when the attack has exhausted a system's finite resources.

## Distributed Denial-of-Service Attacks

Distributed denial-of-service (DDoS) attacks are a relatively new development, made possible (and attractive to attackers) by the ever-expanding number of machines that are attached to the Internet. The first major wave of DDoS attacks on the Internet appeared in early 2000 and targeted such major e-commerce and news sites as Yahoo!, eBay, Amazon, Datek, and CNN. In each case, the Web sites belonging to these companies were unreachable for several hours at a time, causing a severe disruption to their online presence and effectiveness. Many more DDoS attacks have occurred since then, affecting networks and Web sites large and small.

Most publicity surrounding DDoS attacks has focused on Web servers as a target, but remember that any computer attached to the Internet can fall victim to the effects of a DDoS attack. This can include everything from file servers or e-mail servers to your users' desktop workstations.

The DDoS attack begins with a human attacker using a small number of computers, called *masters*. The master computers use network scanners to find as many weakly secured computers as it can, and they use system vulnerabilities (usually well-known ones) to install a small script or a service (referred to in the UNIX world as a *daemon*) onto the insecure computer. This machine becomes a *zombie* and can now be triggered by the master computer to attack any computer or network attached to the Internet. Once the organizer of the DDoS attack has a sufficient number of zombie machines under control, he or she will use the "zombi-fied" machines to send a stream of packets to a designated target computer or network, called the *victim*. For most of these attacks, these packets are directed at the victim machine. The distributed nature of the DDoS attack makes it extremely difficult to track down the person or persons who began it; the actual attacks are coming from zombie machines, and the owners of these machines are often not even aware that their machines have been compromised. Making matters even more difficult, most network packets used in DDoS attacks use forged source addresses, which means that they are essentially lying about where the attack is coming from.

## *Viruses, Worms, and Trojan Horses*

Viruses, Trojans, and worms are quite possibly the most disruptive of all security threats that we discuss in this section. These three types of threats, working alone or in combination, can alter or delete data files and executable programs on your network shares, flood e-mail servers and network connections with malicious traffic, and even create a "back door" into your systems that can allow a remote attacker to entirely take over control of a computer. You'll often hear these three terms used interchangeably, but each type of threat is slightly different. A *virus* is a piece of code that will alter an existing file and then use that alteration to recreate itself many times over. A *worm* simply makes copies of itself over and over again for the purpose of exhausting available system resources. A worm can target both hard drive space and processor cycles.

## Business Intelligence...

### Even Symantec Is Vulnerable

On May 24, 2006, a research company, eEye Digital Security, announced it had discovered a *high severity* security vulnerability in the Symantec antivirus program used by 200 million computers worldwide. The vulnerability was characterized as severe because it didn't require any user interaction to be exploited, making it highly susceptible to worm attacks. The irony is, of course, that this vulnerability was discovered not a week after the CEO of Symantec slammed Microsoft's "security monoculture" as a source of vulnerability. Since no one single product or defense will provide adequate security in today's threat environment, this finding underscores the need for depth in defense. And, as Symantec's CEO discovered, it also underscores the danger of tossing rocks at security "glass houses."

## Software Vulnerabilities

Some network attacks target vulnerabilities in the way that a software application or entire operating system has been programmed. For example, a *buffer overflow attack* occurs when a malicious user sends more data to a program than it knows how to handle. For example, we've all seen Web forms that ask you to fill in personal information: first name, last name, telephone number, and so forth. A careless developer might program the "First Name" field to only be able to handle 10 characters; that is, a name that is 10 letters long. If the Web application does not check for buffer overflows, an attacker can input a long string of gibberish into the First Name field in an attempt to cause a buffer overflow error. At this point, the attacker could even embed the name of an executable file into that long string of text and actually pass commands to the system as if he or she were sitting at the server console itself. A similar software vulnerability is a format string vulnerability that would allow an attacker to insert random data into a file or database, including malicious code that can be executed against the server as though the attacker were sitting right in front of the keyboard.

Another attack that is specifically common to Web and FTP servers is a *directory traversal vulnerability*. This type of vulnerability allows a user to gain access to a directory on a server that he hasn't been specifically given permissions to, by virtue of having permissions to a parent or child directory. Say that someone goes to the URL www.airplanes.com/biplanes/cessna/model1.html. He decides to manually change this URL (in other words, not following an <HREF> link on the site itself) to www.airplanes.com/biplanes/piper, to see if the directory structure holds any information there. If the Web site hasn't been properly patched and configured with the correct security settings, the user might find that he now has access to every single file in the piper/ directory. Even worse, he can once again execute a command from the Web browser by changing the URL to something like www.airplanes.com/biplanes/piper/del%20*.*. (*%20* is used in HTML to represent a space, so that command would read *del *.** on a regular command line.)

Another common attack also occurred in NetMeeting and Windows Media Player some time ago, where an attacker could insert special characters during a file transfer that would allow him to browse an unsuspecting user's hard drive directory structure.

Unfortunately, the breadth and depth of software vulnerabilities grows almost daily due to the wonderfully wide variety of applications available on the market. This variety provides new and useful functionality to users, but it obviously can create headaches for IT staff just trying to keep up.

## Nontechnical Attacks

A final category of attack that we'll discuss here are those that use less technical means to circumvent network security. *Social engineering attacks* rely on an unsuspecting user's lack of security consciousness. In some cases, the attacker will rely on someone's goodwill, using a tactic like, "I've really got to get this done and I don't have access to these files. Can you help me?" (This works because most of us, at heart, really want to be helpful to those around us.) Other social engineering attacks use a more threat-based approach, insisting that the attacker is the secretary for Mr. Big-Shot VP who needs his password reset right away and heaven help you if you keep him waiting. This method relies on the assumption that a show of authority will cause someone without adequate training to bypass security procedures, to keep the "big-shot important user/client" happy. Since social engineering attacks are nontechnical in nature, the measures required to defend against them are more administrative than anything else. It's critical to have well-understood security policies in place that apply to everyone, regardless of their position in your company. This will assist in preventing an attacker from circumventing security procedures because a help desk or other staff member is unaware of them. We discuss user education and awareness campaigns later in this book.

# Top 20 Threats

The SANS organization publishes and maintains a top-20 list of network threats. You might want to refer to this list as you're developing your infrastructure security plan; it will give you excellent insight into the latest threats and how to address them. For the most up-to-date list, visit www.sans.org/top20/#threatindex. The current Top Vulnerabilities in Windows Systems list contains the following categories:

- W1. Windows Services
- W2. Internet Explorer
- W3. Windows Libraries
- W4. Microsoft Office and Outlook Express
- W5. Windows Configuration Weaknesses

The Top Vulnerabilities in Cross-Platform Applications list:

- C1. Backup Software
- C2. Antivirus Software
- C3. PHP-based Applications
- C4. Database Software
- C5. File Sharing Applications
- C6. DNS Software
- C7. Media Players
- C8. Instant Messaging Applications
- C9. Mozilla and Firefox Browsers
- C10. Other Cross-platform Applications

The Top Vulnerabilities in UNIX Systems list:

- U1. UNIX Configuration Weaknesses
- U2. Mac OS X

The Top Vulnerabilities in Networking Products list:

- N1. Cisco IOS and non-IOS Products
- N2. Juniper, CheckPoint and Symantec Products
- N3. Cisco Devices Configuration Weaknesses

Later in this chapter, we'll look at the major threats and vulnerabilities so you can build these into your project plan, as appropriate, based on your own unique network configuration.

---

### Business Intelligence...

## Hackers Turn to Security Software

An article in the *Washington Post* in late 2005 highlighted a new and growing trend among hackers: the new focus on security software used by millions of end users. In the "old days," hackers focused on attacking operating systems and exploiting known vulnerabilities. Although that still occurs, the new threat front is in the very software you rely on to secure your computer from the bad guys. As hackers look for and exploit these vulnerabilities, they expose users to a whole new realm of risk. Operating systems such as Windows and Linux are now regularly updated and patched, but security software programs typically were only updating virus signature files, not the program itself. Now security software program makers are finding their products under attack and are having to respond as operating system companies once did.

For more information and to read the whole article, head to this URL: www.washingtonpost.com/wp-dyn/content/article/2005/11/21/AR2005112101424.html.

---

# Network Security Checklist

This section is a lengthy one and is intended to provide you with a thorough review of the types of things you should review, assess, and think about when you prepare your infrastructure security project plan. Even though we've created a detailed list, there's always a chance there are additional elements your plan will need. Certainly, there's also a strong likelihood that there are things in these checklists that you don't have and don't need. That's okay. The point is to try to help you think through all the details you possibly can about your network infrastructure, to ensure that you are thorough and don't leave any stone unturned. At the end of this process, you may decide not to address some aspects of infrastructure security, or you might choose to work on some of these items in a Phase 2 or Phase 3 project plan. This should give you a great start in thinking all this through.

We've divided the infrastructure project into four main areas, though you may choose to parse it out differently. We'll look at devices and media and ways to secure network devices (excluding servers and user computers) and the network media. Media could mean secure network area storage devices (NAS), backup media, or other storage devices. The "Topologies" section includes how you segment the network for security, including creating DMZs and implementing firewalls, and how you secure network traffic. Intrusion detection and prevention systems are pretty popular these days (for good reason), so we'll look at best practices for implementing IDS/IPS that you can utilize in your project plan. Finally, we'll look at system hardening, including hardening infrastructure servers (DNS, DHCP, and so on), application and database servers, and other computers on the network. Keep in mind that this is not a "how to" as much as it is a list of things to consider and include in your project plan. There are volumes filled with information on these topics; it would be far outside the scope of this book to talk about how you do these things. Our intent is to provide a framework and a solid starting point for your infrastructure security project-planning process. If you're not sure what some of these things are or if you're uncertain as to how to address these issues, you'll need to do further research on these topics.

## Devices and Media

Network devices typically include routers, switches, firewalls, and other communication devices. We cover these items extensively at the end of this section (we placed it there because it's a long, wide-ranging list). The short story is that routers, switches, and other communication devices should be:

1. **Physically secured**  Place devices in a locked cabinet, locked room, and locked building, where possible. Where that's not possible, devices should be closely monitored or access should be controlled or limited.

2. **Physically inspected**  Remove extra cables, disable external ports, and disconnect unused connections.

3. **Hardened**  Remove unused software, disable unused ports, stop or uninstall unused protocols and services, disable unused functionality, remove unused user accounts, change default settings, use strong passwords, and remove or limit all but one administrative account.

4. **Monitored**  Audit, log, and monitor all access to devices, both physical and logical; monitor all successful logons; monitor all failed logons; review log files frequently; and store configuration data in a safe, secure location.

5.  **Encrypted**  Encrypt sensitive data files; encrypt and secure all removable media; create a secure system for handling removable media, including backup files; create a log file to track media handling; secure removable media in locked, access-controlled location; and store archives in a secure, off-site location.

# Topologies

Network infrastructure security:

1.  Create secure boundaries using firewalls, DMZs, and proxy servers.
2.  Create secure remote access.
3.  Create secure wireless access.
4.  Implement a segmented network.
5.  Implement network traffic security protocols for sensitive network traffic.
6.  Deploy network security technologies.

    1.  Use Encrypting File System (EFS) or similar file encryption.
    2.  Require and use strong user authentication, passwords and account policies.
    3.  Employ the concept of "least privileges" when assigning user rights.

Security infrastructure components include routers, proxy servers, firewalls, and DMZs. Firewalls are pretty straightforward and can be implemented as hardware or software solutions. Let's take a side street and take a quick look at DMZs.

*Demilitarized zones,* or *DMZs,* are isolated network segments that typically sit between the Internet and your network, whether in front of or behind your firewall (or between two firewalls). There are many different ways to set up a DMZ; again, it's outside the scope of this book to discuss the design, implementation, and configuration of a DMZ. However, it might be helpful to discuss a few highlights of DMZ design that might help as you look at implementing or tightening a DMZ for your network.

## Designing DMZs

DMZ design, like security design, is always a work in progress. As in security planning and analysis, we find DMZ design carries great flexibility and change potential to keep the protection levels we put in place in an effective state. The ongoing work is required so that the system's security is always as high as we can make it within the constraints of time and budget, while still allowing appropriate users and visitors to access the information and services we provide. You will find that the time and funds spent in the design process and preparation for the implementation are very good investments if the process is focused and effective; this will lead to a high level of success and a good level of protection for your network.

In this section of the chapter, we explore the fundamentals of the design process. We incorporate the information we discussed in relation to security and traffic flow to make decisions about how our initial design should look. Additionally, we'll build on that information and review some other areas of concern that could affect the way you design your DMZ structure.

Design of the DMZ is critically important to the overall protection of your internal network—and the success of your firewall and DMZ deployment. The DMZ design can incorporate sections that isolate incoming VPN traffic, Web traffic, partner connections, employee connections, and public access to information provided by your organization. Design of the DMZ structure throughout the organization can protect internal resources from internal attack. As we discussed in the security section, it has been well documented that much of the risk of data loss, corruption, and breach actually exists inside the network perimeter. Our tendency is to protect assets from external harm but to disregard the dangers that come from our own internal equipment, policies, and employees.

These attacks or disruptions do not arise solely from disgruntled employees. Many of the most damaging conditions occur because of inadvertent mistakes made by well-intentioned employees. Each of these entry points is a potential source of loss for your organization and ultimately can provide an attack point to defeat your other defenses. Additionally, the design of your DMZ will allow you to implement a multilayered approach to securing your resources that does not leave a single point of failure in your plan. This minimizes the problems and loss of protection that can occur because of misconfiguration of rule sets or ACL lists, as well as reducing the problems that can occur due to hardware configuration errors.

## Remote Access

Remote access is granted in a number of different ways, so the way it should be secured varies widely. The basics are that the remote access servers should be physically secured (as should all infrastructure servers) in an access-controlled location. The number of accounts that are authorized to log onto the server for administrative purposes should be limited and audited. The communication link between the RAS and the remote users should be secured, as should the data on that link, if needed. The network traffic security methods include signing, encryption, and tunneling.

The level of these methods is determined by the system with the least capabilities. Older operating systems cannot utilize the latest encryption technologies, for example, so you might include policies that require that remotely connecting users use the latest version of Windows XP Professional, to enable the entire end-to-end communication link to use the strongest available encryption. You can also require strong authentication across remote links. Different operating systems implement this differently; in Windows Server 2003, for example, it's implemented through policies set in Administrative Tools | Routing and Remote Access.

## Wireless Access

We've devoted a whole chapter to wireless security, so we will only discuss the top-level items here:

- Change access point default settings.
- Disable SSID broadcasting; create a closed system (does not respond to clients with "Any" SSID assigned).
- Transmission power control (limiting the amount of power used for transmission to control the signal range).
- Enable MAC address filtering.
- Enable WEP or WPA.
- Filter protocols.
- Define IP allocations for the WLAN.
- Use VPNs.
- Secure users' computers.

All these choices have pros and cons, distinct advantages and disadvantages; you'll need to decide the right approach for your organization. As with all things in IT security, it's important that you understand the result of the solutions you're using, understand the configuration and maintenance of these elements, and be sure you test them well in a lab or isolated setting before implementing them across the enterprise.

# Intrusion Detection Systems/ Intrusion Prevention Systems (IDS/IPS)

First, let's define IDS and IPS, because they're not one and the same. *Intrusion detection systems* (IDS) are passive in nature; they let you know an intrusion is taking place or has occurred. They do nothing to stop an intrusion. On the other hand, an *intrusion prevention system* (IPS) is an active system that works to stop an intrusion or to prevent one when "it thinks" one is occurring. How does "it" think? It does so based on how you configure it, so we end up back at that persistent *people* problem we've mentioned once or twice. An IPS has one major drawback, and that is the high likelihood of false positives. Depending on how you configure the IPS, the results of a response to a false positive might be far more devastating than an actual intrusion, so you're walking a fine line with IPS. That said, some excellent hardware and software solutions are available on the market today, many of which are a great improvement over IDS/IPS systems of the past. It is far outside the scope of this book to discuss the pros and cons, the highlights and lowlights of these systems, so we're not going there. However, we will mention a few different ways you can implement and secure your IDS/IPS systems and leave it up to you to develop a specific plan for implementing these systems, since they are so varied.

A word of caution: IDS/IPS is not a standalone defense. You should implement it with the understanding that it contributes to your depth of defense, but alone it will not keep your network safe. It's a great tool to have in your security toolkit, but it's not the magic bullet everyone wishes they had.

IPSs introduce fundamental performance and stability issues within the network or system they are designed to protect. The act of implementing automatic controls in response to detecting attacks does not come without a price. For example, an inline network IPS will not forward packets before inspecting Application-layer data. This inspection takes time and can result in a slowdown in the responsiveness and throughput of the local network. A host IPS that has been charged with the inspection and validation of an application's system calls can impact a kernel's ability to quickly service system calls, which may only be 1 to 15 percent but is probably noticeable.

## Network Active Response System

A *network active response system* has the ability to interact with network traffic indirectly through the modification of firewall policies and router Access Control Lists (ACLs). They also have the ability to take down switch ports (for locally generated attacks) and to spoof error code packets such as Transmission Control Protocol (TCP), RST, or Internet Control Message Protocol (ICMP) unreachable packets. Such an active response system is commonly implemented directly within a network IDS, where it can easily take advantage of its detection capabilities. This is useful for tearing down individual sessions or for trying to convince an attacking host that the target is unreachable due to ICMP errors. However, there is not usually much time between these measures and the goal of the attack. It's unclear whether the counter-measure will be successful.

There are four classes of countermeasure that a network IPS can utilize to thwart a network-based attack. Each class applies to one layer of the protocol stack, beginning at the Data Link layer:

- **Data Link layer countermeasures** Administratively shut down a switch port interface associated with a system from which attacks are being launched. This approach is feasible only for attacks that are generated from a local system. Having the ability to timeout the downed switch port is important, since the port probably should not be shut down indefinitely.

- **Network layer countermeasures** Interact with the external firewall or router to add a general rule to block all communication from individual IP addresses or entire networks. An inline IPS can accomplish the same thing without having to appeal to an external device, since packets from specific IP addresses can simply be blocked after an attack has been detected. Similarly to Data Link layer responses, timeouts are important at the Network layer, since the firewall rule set or router ACL modifications should be removed after a configurable amount of time.

- **Transport layer countermeasures** Generate TCP RST packets to tear down malicious TCP sessions, or issues any of several available ICMP error-code packets in response to malicious UDP traffic. (Note that ICMP is strictly a Network layer protocol and is the standard method of communi-cating various errors to clients that utilize UDP). Timeouts are not appli-cable here, because countermeasures are leveraged against an attacker on a per-session or per-packet basis.

- **Application layer countermeasures** Alter malicious Application layer data so as to render it harmless before it reaches the target system. This countermeasure requires that the IPS be in line in the communication path. Any previously calculated Transport layer checksum must be recalcu-lated. Similarly to the Network layer, timeouts are not applicable here, since the effects of replacing Application layer data are transitory and do not linger once an altered packet is forwarded through the IPS.

Later in this chapter, we'll walk through a number of "generic" countermeasures and hardening tasks related to these layers when we look at various ways routers, switches, and other network devices can be hardened in conjunction with whatever IDS/IPS system you implement.

## Host Active Response System

A *host active response system* is usually implemented in software and is deployed directly on a host system. Once a suspicious event has been detected on a host (through any number of means, such as log file analysis, detection of specific files or registry keys associated with known exploits, or a suspicious server running on a high port), a host active response system is charged with taking an action. As with network active response, the expectation for a host active response system is that countermeasures will not necessarily prevent an attack from initially being successful. The emphasis is on trying to mitigate the effects and damage caused by an attack after detection. After an attack is detected, automated responses can include alteration of file system permissions, changes in access that a system grants to users, automated removal of worms or viruses (anti-virus), and additions of new rules to a local firewall subsystem.

Before we move into system hardening, let's take a look at how IDS/IPS systems are implemented in the network infrastructure. Figure 7.2 shows the IDS system as part of the infrastructure. The IDS server, in this case, would be connected to a span port so that it would monitor all traffic on the local network. The IDS system is capable of spoofing a TCP RST or ICMP error code packet to thwart the attack but would not be effective against single-packet attacks.

**Figure 7.2** IDS System Placement in Infrastructure

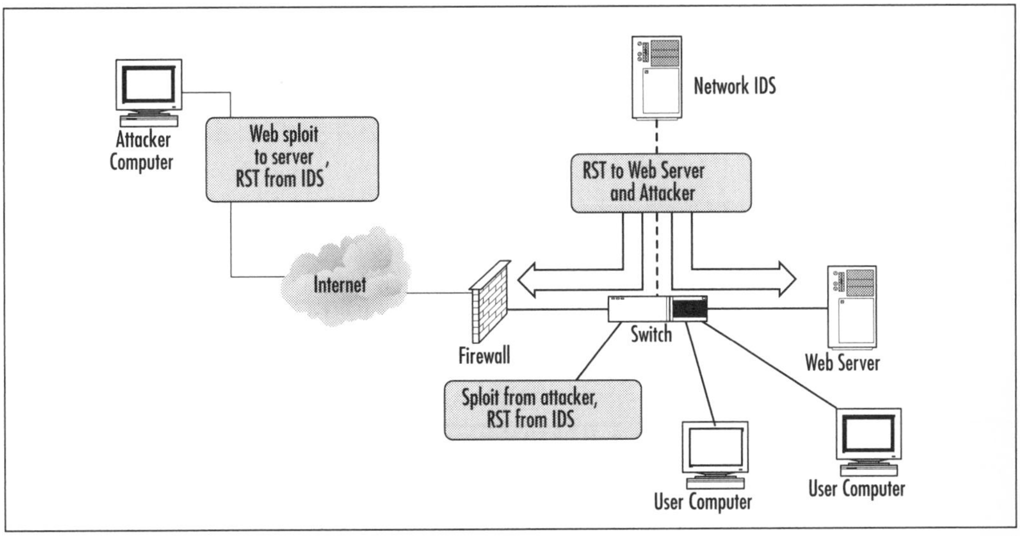

An inline system performs a bit differently, as shown in Figure 7.3. In this case, the inline system captures the *sploit* and modifies it to protect the local network. A typical deployment of the IPS occurs just inside the firewall. In this position, it captures all incoming traffic before it goes to the local network, providing ubiquitous protection, even for single-packet attacks. Because all traffic flows through an inline IPS, downsides such as false positives and slower response times must be factored in.

**Figure 7.3** IPS System Inline Placement in Infrastructure

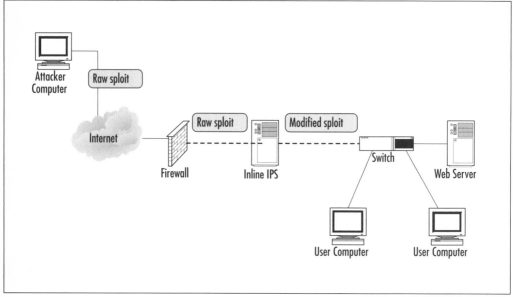

## Next Generation Security Devices

As you look at your current implementation of IDS or IPS (or if you're considering an implementation), you should also keep an eye on recent developments in the world of security devices. *Network processors* can be deployed in various architectures including parallel, where each processor handles $1/N$ of the total load or pipeline, where, as a packet moves through the pipeline, each processor typically handles a single specific repetitive task. The network processor was originally targeted to the routing market, but it is easy to see how it can be applied to the increased demands of packet inspection in network security. For example, one processor could handle the pattern matching for known worm signatures, another could analyze for protocol standards compliance, and yet another could look for protocol or usage anomalies. The network processor would have direct access to fast memory that stores policies and signatures, whereas slower, larger memory would store state information and heuristics information. New attacks could be mitigated by adding new code to the network processor. A separate processor can handle management functions such as logging and policy management. Network processors also offer the ability to scale, much like CPUs on computer systems.

## Business Intelligence…

### Intrusion Prevention and Detection Resource

At the risk of sounding a bit self-serving, if you have any desire to understand more about IDS/IPS, you really should check out another Syngress book. There may be other excellent IDS/IPS resources out there, but *Intrusion Detection and Active Response: Deploying Network and Host IPS*, by Michael Rash, Angela Orebaugh, Graham Clark, Becky Pinkard, and Jake Babbin, with a foreword by Stephen Northcutt (Syngress Publishing, Inc., 2005), is a great resource. If you're like most IT professionals, you're inundated with technical information on a daily (okay, hourly) basis and it's hard to stay up to date on every topic in the computer world. This book provides excellent background information and helps you understand the wild world of IDS/IPS so you can make informed decisions about how, when, and where to implement it in your organization. If you're looking for an excellent resource on this topic, do yourself a favor and check out this one-stop-shopping trip for an excellent IDS/IPS education.

## System Hardening

Server security:

1. Always control physical and network access to critical servers, especially domain controllers, DNS servers, DHCP servers, and other infrastructure servers. Keep infrastructure servers in an access–controlled location.

2. Always perform tasks on the servers with the least possible privileges. Do not perform tasks with Administrator privileges, if possible. Use the *Run As* command (or equivalent) when needed.

3. Restrict user and machine access to groups that have loose security settings. Provide users and computers with the least possible permissions while still meeting their needs to access and use network resources.

4. Secure the data on the computers using strong ACLs and, if needed, the *syskey* utility. The *syskey* utility provides protection against password-cracking software that targets the Security Access Management (SAM)

database or directory services. It uses strong encryption that is much more difficult (if not close to impossible) and time consuming to crack.

5.  Require the use of strong passwords via password policy settings.

6.  Restrict the downloading and installation of programs that do not come from known, trusted sources.

7.  Maintain up-to-date virus protection on all systems.

8.  Keep all software patches up to date. Patches often address newly discovered security holes. Applying patches in a timely manner on all affected machines can prevent problems that are easily avoided.

9.  Deploy server, application and client-side security technologies:

    ■  Secure server traffic traveling on the network.

    ■  Secure application and user data traveling on the network.

    ■  Secure network access points and network access.

    ■  Secure client devices including desktops, laptops, and PDAs.

    ■  Implement automatically updating virus and spyware protection systems.

# Other Infrastructure Issues

1.  Deploy network monitoring and auditing.

2.  Develop a disaster recovery plan that includes creating backups, documenting recovery options and using repair and recovery tools.

3.  Develop standard operating procedures that include strong monitoring, auditing, and documentation.

## Business Intelligence...

### Rootkits

There's been a lot of news in the recent past about the problems presented by rootkit attacks. As you're well aware, those little pieces of malware reside so deep in the system that you can't possibly remove them without completely starting

**Continued**

from scratch. After a system is compromised, all the affected software must be reinstalled from known "clean" sources. Since it can be difficult to determine precisely which pieces of software have been affected, the best way to guarantee security is to reinstall the entire operating system (OS) and all applications. OS kernels can also be compromised (see www.rootkit.com), and when they are, nothing on the system (even the most basic file system, memory, and network status information) can be trusted. An after-the-fact forensic analysis of the file system may turn up useful information if the disk is mounted underneath an uncompromised OS, but this is a time-consuming operation.

# Other Network Components: Routers, Switches, RAS, NMS, IDS

There are numerous components that should be checked during an infrastructure security project. The list in this section was compiled, in part, from a network checklist developed by the Defense Information Systems Agency (DISA) for the Department of Defense (DoD). Although not all items listed will apply to your network and it's possible that not all items that apply to your network appear on this list, this is an extensive list that you can use as the starting point for your own checklist. Some of the items in this list contain brief explanations included to help you understand their importance. Our assumption is that you're familiar with the ins and outs of network security, but there are a few places where a quick clarification will help, and we've included them as well. These are written in language that reflects problems you would find that should be remedied (for instance, highlighting the problem you're looking for, not necessarily the solution you should implement). The list is organized by device type, beginning with routers and other network devices and moving on to firewalls, VLANs, RAS servers, and so on.

## Network

- **Network infrastructure is not properly documented** You should begin with a clear understanding of how your network infrastructure is currently configured. This should be well documented and kept up to date.

- **Network connections exist without approval** All network connections should exist only with explicit approval or knowledge of the IT department. This is typically a problem with modems, wireless access points, and USB-type network devices.

- **Unmanaged backdoor connections, backdoor network connections bypass perimeter** Every network in the world has a variety of backdoor connections that network administrators use (or that software developers build in). When unmanaged, these connections create security problems for your network infrastructure. These are especially problematic when these backdoors bypass perimeter security systems. If you can use them, so can the bad guys.

- **Circuit location is not secure** The location of network circuitry, including the backbone and other highly critical components, should be secured physically.

- **Network devices are not stored in secure communications room** This is part of physical security; to the extent possible, network devices should be stored in a secure communications room. This should certainly be true for mission-critical devices. Physical security of the company's premises, coupled with physical security of key network devices, is part of a depth-in-defense strategy.

- **Minimum operating system release level** All network devices—from desktop computers to servers to firewalls to routers—should have the latest updates and patches for the operating system they are running. As seen from the top-20 threat list, many are threats to portions of the operating system, so all device operating systems should be kept up to date. Where possible, you may also choose to upgrade the operating system itself to a newer, more secure version, where appropriate. This OS release-level maintenance should also apply to routers and other devices that have operating systems, firmware, or other embedded software functionality.

- **DNS servers must be defined for client resolver** If a router or similar network device is specified as a client resolver (resolves DNS to IP address), the router should have a DNS server defined. If the DNS server is specified, it makes it more difficult for an attacker to substitute his or her IP address for that of the destination host. If this type of man-in-the-middle attack is successful, the unsuspecting host user could transmit sensitive information, including logon, authentication, and password data, to the attacker.

# External Communications (also see "Remote Access")

- **Modems are not disconnected** The problem with unsecured modems is that they can be attacked by wardialers who simply look for modems connected to corporate networks. These can create significant security holes and are often overlooked in our quest to lock down the wired network.

- **An ISP connection exists without written approval** In most companies, this might be a difficult trick to achieve, but it certainly warrants examination to ensure that the ISP connection(s) is managed by the IT department and not some errant user who managed to get the local ISP provider to run a cable into the office on a Saturday morning.

- **Communications devices are not password protected** This seems like a giant "Duh!" but you'd probably be surprised how often communication devices such as modems, routers, switches, and other "smart" devices are left unprotected by even a simple password or that use the default password that came with the device out of the box.

- **No warning banner** Failure to display the required login banner prior to logon attempts will limit the site's ability to prosecute unauthorized access. It also presents the potential for criminal and civil liability for systems administrators and information systems managers. Not displaying the proper banner will also hamper the site's ability to monitor device usage. Displaying a banner warning users of the consequences of unauthorized access helps warn off the bad guys and draws a line in the legal sand that you might need later.

## TCP/IP (Some TCP/IP Information Also Found in the "Routers" Section)

- **LAN addresses are not protected from the public** In later versions of the Windows operating system, even home users were able to easily implement Network Address Translation (NAT) to protect internal IP addresses from Internet users. Most businesses these days have implemented some method of protecting internal IP addresses so that hackers can't use this information to decipher the network structure and plan an attack.

- **The DHCP server is not configured to log hostnames** To identify and combat IP address spoofing, it is highly recommended that the DHCP server log MAC addresses or hostnames on the DHCP server.

- **TCP and UDP small server services are not disabled** TCP and UDP services are often available on network devices, including routers and servers. Disabling these services if they're not used helps reduce the attack footprint. TCP and UDP protocols include services that routers can support; however, they are not required for operation. Attackers have used these services to cause network DoS attacks.

- **TCP keepalives for Telnet session must be enabled** Enabling TCP keepalives on incoming connections can help guard against both malicious attacks and orphaned sessions caused by remote system crashes. Enabling the TCP keepalives causes the router to generate periodic keepalive messages, letting it detect and drop broken Telnet connections.

- **Identification support is enabled** Identification support allows you to query a TCP port for identification. This feature enables an unsecured protocol to report the identity of a client initiating a TCP connection and a host responding to the connection. With identification support, you can connect a TCP port on a host, issue a simple text string to request information, and receive a simple text-string reply. This is another mechanism to learn the router vendor, model number, and software version being run. Identification support should be disabled on routers and other network devices that provide this functionality.

## Business Intelligence...

### Whitelisting

*Whitelisting* is the ability to easily specify IP addresses or networks that should never be the subject of an automated response in an IDS/IPS system. For example, IP addresses associated with systems that are critical to a network (for example, the Domain Name Server, or DNS, or upstream router) should not be automatically blocked by an active response system, nor should sessions be altered by an inline IPS. Some active response systems include the ability to whitelist IP addresses and networks and to specify which protocols should be ignored. For example, if a DNS server sends an attack across the network to a Web server, it may be permissible for an active response system to capture the individual TCP session on port 80 but ignore everything else.

- **IP-directed broadcasts are not disabled** An *IP-directed broadcast* is a datagram sent to the broadcast address of a subnet that is not directly attached to the sending machine. The directed broadcast is routed through the network as a Unicast packet until it arrives at the target subnet, where it is converted into a link layer broadcast. Due to the nature of the IP addressing architecture, only the last router in the chain, which is connected directly to the target subnet, can conclusively identify a directed broadcast. IP-directed broadcasts are used in the extremely common and popular *smurf*, or DoS, attacks. In a smurf attack, the attacker sends ICMP echo requests from a falsified source address to a directed broadcast address, causing all the hosts on the target subnet to send replies to the falsified source. By sending a continuous stream of such requests, the attacker can create a much larger stream of replies, which can completely inundate the host whose address is being falsified. This service should be disabled on all interfaces when it's not needed to prevent smurf and DoS attacks.

- **Ingress filtering inbound spoofing addresses** Inbound spoofing occurs when someone outside the network uses an internal IP address to gain access to systems or devices on the internal network. If the intruder is successful, they can intercept data, passwords, and the like and use that information to perform destructive acts on network devices or network data.

- **Egress outbound spoofing filter** You should restrict the router from accepting any outbound IP packet that contains an illegitimate address in the source address field via egress ACLs or by enabling Unicast Reverse Path Forwarding. ACLs are the first line of defense in a layered security approach. They permit authorized packets and deny unauthorized packets based on port or service type. They enhance the network's posture by not allowing packets to even reach a potential target within the security domain. Auditing packets attempting to penetrate the network but that are stopped by an ACL will allow network administrators to broaden their protective ring and more tightly define the scope of operation.

## *Administration*

- **Devices exist that have standard default passwords** This is another major "Duh!" item; again, it's surprising how easy it is to get into a large number of devices just by using the default password that the device shipped with. Want to know the default password? Go up on the manufacturer's Web site, look for the user guide for the specific device, and the default password is almost guaranteed to be listed in the first five pages of the manual.

- **Group accounts or user accounts without passwords**  Without passwords on user accounts for network devices, one level of complexity is removed from gaining access to the routers. If a default user ID has not been changed or is guessed by an attacker, the network could be easily compromised, since the only remaining step would be to crack the password. Sharing group accounts on any network device should also be prohibited. If these group accounts are not changed when someone leaves the group, that person could possibly gain control of the device. Having group accounts does not allow for proper auditing of who is accessing or changing the network. Only allow individual user account access and require each user to have a unique user ID and a strong password.

- **Assign lowest privilege level to user accounts**  Across the enterprise, you should always assign the least privilege possible for all users. This prevents users from getting into places they shouldn't, and it also prevents hackers from upgrading their privileges if they manage to get in on a user account that has too many privileges. Even IT staff should have user accounts with least privileges for most day-to-day network tasks, and they should only log on with administrative privileges when needed. Network outages and security holes can be created by users with too many permissions or even by a well-meaning but inexperienced net admin.

- **Strong password policies are not enforced**  Strong passwords is an inadequate defense on its own, but it slows down a would-be intruder and can also alert a net admin to a potential problem if failed password attempts are monitored and accounts are locked down after too many failed attempts. Requiring users to use strong passwords, to change them periodically, and to prevent them from repeating old passwords too frequently are all parts of strong password policy. In addition, you can audit failed attempts, notify a net admin of too many failed attempts, and lock out an account with too many failed accounts as part of your strong password policy implementation.

- **Passwords are not recorded and stored properly**  User passwords should not be recorded and stored, but certain administrative ones absolutely should be. You can probably think of several scenarios where someone who doesn't normally require administrative access requires it. For example, suppose as part of your disaster recovery plan, you have an executive VP who is responsible for coordinating recovery efforts. He or she should have access to these passwords only for these emergency situations, because on a day-to-day basis, you operate on the principle of "least access" and the EVP really has nothing more than the equivalent rights of a power user. Having these passwords on a network server in plain sight or in a paper file someplace obvious is not a good idea. Making sure these emergency passwords are recorded and stored properly ensures security for the network on a day-to-day basis but provides an important fail-safe option in emergencies as well.

- **Passwords are viewable when displaying the router or other device** Many attacks on computer systems are launched from within the network by unsatisfied or disgruntled employees. It's vital that all router passwords be encrypted so they cannot be intercepted by viewing the console. If the router network is compromised, large parts of the network could be incapacitated with just a few simple commands.

- **Passwords are transmitted in clear text** There are many types of situations in which passwords are transmitted in clear text. This creates an opportunity for an attacker to seize passwords. Review how and where passwords are transmitted and secure the communication lines if the passwords themselves are transmitted in clear text.

- **Emergency accounts should be limited to one** Emergency accounts on devices such as routers or switches should be limited to one. Authentication for administrative access to the router should obviously be required at all times. A single account can be created on the router's local database for use in an emergency, such as when the authentication server is down or connectivity between the router and the authentication server is not operable. Verify that there is one and only one emergency account to prevent unnecessary opportunities for attack.

- **Unnecessary or unauthorized router or device accounts exist** This point is related to the previous item. You should eliminate any unused, unnecessary, or unauthorized device accounts except for one authorized emergency account.

- **Disable unused ports and services** On every server, every firewall, and every device, disable unused ports and services. Microsoft took a giant leap forward in the more recent versions of the Windows operating system when the company changed the default configuration from "open" to "closed." This meant that the net admin had to consciously enable and open services and ports after installation. Earlier versions came open and unlocked out of the box, and the net admin had to sift through the system to lock it down. For all devices, disable unused ports and services, uninstall unused applications, and remove unused hardware.

- **Auditing and logging files are not set to record *denied* events, not set to record system activity** Auditing and logging are key components of any security architecture. It is essential that security personnel know what is being done, being attempted, and by whom in order to compile an accurate risk assessment. Auditing the actions, particularly *denied* events, on routers provides a means to identify potential attacks or threats. Maintaining an audit trail of system activity logs (*syslog*) can help you identify configuration errors, understand past intrusions, troubleshoot service disruptions, and react to probes and scans of the network.

- **Configurations are stored in unsecured locations** To ensure network and data availability, the configuration data of key network infrastructure components should be maintained in a secure, offsite location. This is part of good disaster recovery planning practices and adds to security if these configurations are stored in secured locations offsite rather than in an unlocked file cabinet in the mailroom. Access to these configuration files should be restricted and logged to prevent unauthorized access.

## Network Management

- **Out-of-band network management not implemented or required** It's outside the scope of this chapter (and book) to get into a deep discussion of in-band and out-of-band network management, but we will toss out a couple of quick explanations before discussing the infrastructure security implications of both. In-band network management uses the same network infrastructure as the devices and data being managed. Most networking equipment basically sends out IP traffic for network management on the same medium as the traffic it's managing (routers, switches, and so forth). Out-of-band network management uses a separate connection, often a serial RS-232 port, instead of the network port used for in-band management. There are security pros and cons to both, so the key is to secure whichever method(s) you implement.

    Without secure out-of-band management implemented with authenticated access controls, strong two-factor authentication, encryption of the management session, and audit logs, unauthorized users may gain access to network managed devices such as routers or communications servers (CS). If the router network is compromised, large parts of the network could be incapacitated with only a few commands. If a CS is compromised, unauthorized users could gain access to the network and its attached systems. The CS could be disabled, therefore disallowing authorized subscribers from supporting mission critical functions.

From an architectural point of view, providing out-of-band management of network systems is the best first step in any management strategy. No network production traffic resides on an out-of-band network.

- **Use of in-band management is not limited, restricted, or encrypted**  It is imperative that communications used for administrative access to network components are limited to emergency situations or where out-of-band management would hinder daily operational requirements. In-band management introduces the risk of an attacker gaining access to the network internally or even externally. In-band management should be restricted to a limited number of authorized IP addresses to improve security. The in-band access should also be encrypted for added security. Without encrypted in-band management connections, unauthorized users may gain access to network managed devices such as routers, firewalls, or remote access servers. If any of these devices are compromised, the entire network could also be compromised. Administrative access requires the use of encryption on all communication channels between the remote user and the system being accessed. It is imperative to protect communications used for administrative access because an attacker who manages to hijack the link would gain immediate access to the network.

- **Log all in-band management access attempts**  Since in-band traffic travels on the same pathways as normal network traffic, be sure that all inbound management access attempts are logged. This will give you an indication as to whether an intruder is attempting to gain control of key network devices. These attempts should not go unnoticed and should be verified against legitimate management activity of that device. For example, if the access attempts happen after business hours, it's possible (or likely) that the attempts are unauthorized.

- **Two-factor authentication is not used for in-band or out-of-band network management**  Without strong two-factor authorization, unauthorized users may gain access to network managed devices such as routers, firewalls, and remote access servers. If any of these devices are compromised, the entire network could also be compromised.

- **Filter ICMP on external interface** The Internet Control Message Protocol (ICMP) supports IP traffic by relaying information about paths, routes, and network conditions. ICMP unreachable notifications, mask replies, and redirects should be disabled on all externally-interfaced routers to prevent hackers using these messages to perform network mapping and infrastructure discovery.

- **SNMP access is not restricted by IP address** Detailed information about the network is sent across the network via SNMP. If this information is discovered by attackers, it could be used to trace the network, show the network topology, and possibly gain access to network devices. Access to SNMP should be for specific IP addresses only.

- **SNMP is blocked at all external interfaces** Clearly, using SNMP to map a network and discover the network infrastructure is a great hacker tool that should be secured to the greatest extent possible. This includes blocking SNMP on all external interfaces.

- **SNMP write access to the router is enabled** This allows an intruder to set various configuration settings to allow him or her greater access to the router and hence to the network. SNMP write access should be disabled.

- **Block identified inbound ICMP messages** Using inbound ICMP Echo, Information, Net Mask, and Timestamp requests, an attacker can create a map of the subnets and hosts behind the router. An attacker can perform a DoS attack by flooding the router or internal hosts with Echo packets. With inbound ICMP Redirect packets, the attacker can change a host's routing tables.

- **Block identified outbound ICMP traffic** An attacker from the internal network (behind the router) may be able to launch DoS attacks with outbound ICMP packets. It is important to block all unnecessary ICMP traffic message types.

- **Block all inbound *traceroutes*** If you're ever had to troubleshoot a network or Internet connection, you're familiar with the *traceroute* command. This is a helpful tool in troubleshooting, but it also provides great information to a would-be attacker to create a map of the subnets and hosts behind the router. These should not be allowed into the network through the router or other externally facing devices.

- **Secure NMS traffic using IPSec** To securely protect the network, Network Management Systems (NMS) and access to them must be controlled to guard against outside or unauthorized intrusion, which could result in system or network compromise. Allowing any device to send traps or information may create a false positive and having site personnel perform unneeded or potentially hazardous actions on the network in response to these false traps. These sessions must be controlled and secured by IPSec.

- **An insecure version of SNMP is being used** SNMP Versions 1 and 2 are not considered secure and are not recommended. Instead, use SNMP Version 3, which provides the User-based Security Model (USM), which gives strong authentication and privacy. Without Version 3, it's possible an attacker could gain unauthorized access to detailed network management information that can be used to map and subsequently attack the network.

- **SNMP standard operating procedures are not documented** Standard operating procedures will ensure consistency and will help prevent errors or omissions that could create a security hole.

- **NMS security alarms not defined by violation type or severity** Ensure that security alarms are set up within the managed network's framework. At a minimum, these will include the following:

  - **Integrity violation** Indicates that network contents or objects have been illegally modified, deleted, or added.

  - **Operational violation** Indicates that a desired object or service could not be used.

  - **Physical violation** Indicates that a physical part of the network (such as a cable) has been damaged or modified without authorization.

  - **Security mechanism violation** Indicates that the network's security system has been ccmpromised or breached.

  - **Time domain violation** Indicates that an event has happened outside its allowed or typical time slot.

  Also ensure that alarms are categorized by severity using the following guidelines:

- Critical and major alarms are given when a condition that affects service has arisen. For a critical alarm, steps must be taken immediately to restore the service that has been lost completely.

- A major alarm indicates that steps must be taken as soon as possible because the affected service has degraded drastically and is in danger of being lost completely.

- A minor alarm indicates a problem that does not yet affect service but may do so if the problem is not corrected.

- A warning alarm is used to signal a potential problem that may affect service.

- An indeterminate alarm is one that requires human intervention to decide its severity.

Without the proper categories of security alarm being defined on the NMS, responding to critical outages or attacks on the network may not be coordinated correctly with the right personnel, hardware, software, or vendor maintenance. Delays will inevitably occur that will cause network outages to last longer than necessary or expose the network to larger, more extensive attacks or outages.

- **The NMS is not located in a secure environment** Any network management server (or any other highly critical network component) should be kept in a physically secure location with restricted access. Since many attacks come from inside an organization, by people who are authorized to be on the premises, it's important to physically secure all critical network components to the greatest degree possible. Using keypad or card-swipe access control can also help identify specific administrative access, to allow you to further control and monitor access.

  Access to NMS and other network critical components should be restricted via access controls as well ,and all activity, including all successful and failed attempts to log on, should be logged. The log file, as with all log files, should be reviewed regularly, stored for 30 days, and archived for a year, unless regulatory or compliance requirements differ.

- **NMS accounts are not properly maintained** Only those accounts necessary for the operation of the system and for access logging should be maintained. This is true for all servers and network devices. Good "housekeeping" is an essential element to network security, and removing or disabling unused accounts as well as removing and investigating unauthorized accounts is critical.

# Routers and Routing

- **No documented procedures and maintenance for MD5 keys**
  Routing protocols should use MD5 to authenticate neighbors prior to exchanging route table updates, to ensure that route tables are not corrupted or compromised.

- **MD5 Key Lifetime expiration is set to never expire** MD5 is a public key encryption algorithm that uses the exchange of encryption keys across a network link. If these keys are not managed properly, they could be intercepted by unauthorized users and used to break the encryption algorithm. This check is in place to ensure that keys do not expire, creating a DoS due to adjacencies being dropped and routes being aged out. The recommendation is to use two rotating six-month keys, with a third key set as infinite lifetime. The lifetime key should be changed seven days after the rotating keys have expired.

- **Console port is not configured to time out** Console ports on routers or other network devices should be set to time out after some specified period of inactivity. In most cases, a 5- or 10-minute timeout is appropriate. A router is a highly desirable asset to an intruder, so setting a low threshold on timeout will help increase security.

- **Modems are connected to the console or aux port** There may be valid reasons to have a modem connected to the console or auxiliary port of a router or other network device, but you should first ensure that this connection is absolutely necessary. If not, remove it. If it is needed, be sure to secure it by requiring a username and password (and other security measures) and avoid default configurations.

- **The router or network device's auxiliary port is not disabled** If the router or other network device has an auxiliary port, be sure it is disabled it if it's not in use. These are the kinds of welcome backdoors hackers look for.

- **Login is not limited to three attempts** Login attempts for any network device that exceed three tries are likely the work of a hacker. Limiting login attempts to three is a reasonable limit, and most net admins will stop after three attempts if they cannot recall the appropriate login. This won't stop a hacker who is willing to try three times, wait some specified interval, and try again, but it will prevent automated attacks from going through quickly (or at all).

- **Secure Shell timeout is not 60 seconds or less** Many routes and network management devices use the Secure Shell (SSH) protocol to secure communications to the device. Reducing the broken Telnet session expiration time to 60 seconds or less strengthens the router or network device from being attacked using an expired session.

- **Key services are not disabled on all routers** The DHCP, finger service, HTTP, FTP, and BSD *r*-commands and *bootp* services should be disabled on routers and network devices for added security. All unused protocols and services should be disabled to prevent unauthorized use of these services.

- **Configuration autoloading must be disabled** The routers can find their startup configuration in their own NVRAM or load it over the network via TFTP or Remote Copy (*rcp*). Obviously, loading in across the network is a security risk. If an attacker intercepted the startup configuration, it could be used to gain access to the router and take control of network traffic.

- **IP source routing is not disabled on all routers** IP source routing is a process whereby individual packets can specify routing. This is a method that attackers can exploit, so this ability should be disabled on routers and network devices with this capability.

- **Proxy ARP is not disabled** When proxy ARP is enabled on some routers, it allows that router to extend the network (at Layer 2) across multiple interfaces (LAN segments). Because proxy ARP allows hosts from different LAN segments to look like they are on the same segment, proxy ARP is safe only when it's used between trusted LAN segments. Attackers can leverage the trusting nature of proxy ARP by spoofing a trusted host and then intercepting packets. You should always disable proxy ARP on router interfaces that do not require it, unless the router is being used as a LAN bridge.

- **Gratuitous ARP is not disabled** A gratuitous ARP is an ARP broadcast in which the source and destination MAC addresses are the same. It is used to inform the network about a host's IP address. A spoofed gratuitous ARP message can cause network mapping information to be stored incorrectly, causing network malfunction and resulting in various types of service denials, leading to an *availability* issue.

- **Routers are not set to intercept TCP *SYN* attacks** The TCP *SYN* attack involves transmitting a volume of connections that cannot be completed at the destination. This attack causes the connection queues to fill up, thereby denying service to legitimate TCP users. Routers and similar network devices should be configured to intercept TCP *SYN* attacks to prevent DoS attacks from an outside network.

- **Router is not configured to block known DDoS ports** Several high-profile DDoS attacks have been launched across the Internet. Although routers cannot prevent DDoS attacks in general, it is usually sound security practice to discourage the activities of specific DDoS agents (a.k.a. *zombies*) by adding access list rules that block their particular ports.

- **TFTP used without specific need or approval, access is not restricted** Trivial File Transfer Protocol (TFTP) is a simple form of FTP that uses the User Datagram Protocol (UDP) and provides no security features at all (not even a password). It is often used by routers, X-terminals, and servers to boot diskless workstations, but by its very nature it is an insecure protocol. It should not be implemented without a very specific need to do so, and access to the TFTP server should be restricted and monitored.

- **The FTP username and password are not configured** The FTP server should require the use of usernames and passwords to prevent anonymous use of the FTP functionality on the network.

## Firewall

- **Firewall not implemented and configured properly** You should ensure that one or more firewalls are installed and properly configured. The default configuration should be the most restrictive configuration, *deny-by-default,* so that only specifically allowed traffic is allowed into the network.

- **A screened subnet (DMZ) is not implemented** Without the dual-homed screened subnet (a DMZ), architecture traffic that would be normally destined for the DMZ would have to be redirected to the site's internal network. Computers on the inside of the firewall should send outbound requests through the firewall and into the DMZ. The DMZ, in turn, routes or redirects these outbound requests. Typically, a firewall will not accept inbound requests from the DMZ computers, which adds another layer of protection to the network clients.

- **Using an application-level firewall** All networks should use an application-level gateway or firewall to proxy all traffic to external networks. Devices such as SSL gateways, e-mail gateways that will proxy services to protect the network, are also acceptable. A Layer 4 or stateful inspection firewall, in collaboration with application-level proxy devices, can be used to secure all connections.

- **Firewall does not require authentication, does not lock out after three attempts** Firewalls are the enforcement mechanisms of the security on the network, and they are ideal targets for attackers. Firewall placement in the network and the level of access granted to the users accessing the device also increase the risk profile associated with remote management. Therefore, all personnel who access the firewall both locally and remotely should be granted the minimum privilege level needed to perform their duties. The standard three-attempt lockout should be enforced, with the exception that when a firewall administrator is locked out, the senior net admin (or network security officer, if one exists) should be responsible for unlocking the account.

- **Firewall remote access is not restricted** Only the firewall administrator should be able to access the firewall remotely. Remove unused accounts and remove access for all staff other than the administrator.

- **Firewall is not configured to protect the network** Ensure that the firewall is actually configured to protect the network. Configuration of the firewall will vary from site to site, but in general, it should at least be configured to prevent TCP *SYN* flooding and the Ping of Death attacks.

- **Firewall has unnecessary services enabled** As with all network devices, disable, uninstall, and deconfigure any unused or unnecessary services. The fewer services that are enabled, the smaller the attack footprint.

- **Firewall version is not a supported or current** As with all network devices, it's critical to keep the firewall software (and hardware, if appropriate) up to date with current versions, patches, and updates. It's extremely common for attackers to exploit known security issues days, weeks, or even months after a patch is available. This type of hacking is pretty lazy stuff and is a bit of an embarrassment if it occurs, because it's 100-percent preventable. Keep your firewall up to date.

- **The firewall logs are not being reviewed daily** There's really no point in creating log files if you're not going to review them. Reviewing and analyzing log files is part art, part science, but the only way you'll ever know what's going on is to actually review those files on a regular basis. If you don't know that a hacker was chopping away at your network security last night, you'll probably be surprised when he or she manages to hack in tomorrow night.

■ **Firewall log retention does not meet policy** The firewall logs can be used for forensic analysis in support of incidents (after the fact) as well as to aid in normal traffic analysis. It can take numerous days to recover from a firewall outage when a proper backup scheme is not used. Firewall logs should be stored in secure locations; they should be stored for 30 days and archived for one year.

■ **The firewall configuration is not backed up weekly** It's quite a chore to properly configure a corporate firewall, as you probably well know. Therefore, it's wise to back up the configuration data for the firewall on a weekly basis or whenever the firewall configuration changes. This provides excellent forensic support and helps in disaster recovery efforts.

■ **The firewall is not configured to alarm the admin** If someone is knocking at the door but no one's home, an intruder may well decide to just barge right in. That's the net result of having a firewall that is not con-figured to alarm the administrator to unusual traffic.

■ **The firewall is not configured properly** The firewall should be config-ured to protect the network. The following are suggested settings:

  ■ Log unsuccessful authentication attempts.

  ■ Stamp audit trail data with the date and time it was recorded.

  ■ Record the source IP, destination IP, protocol used, and the action taken.

  ■ Log administrator logons, changes to the administrator group, and account lockouts.

  ■ Protect audit logs from deletion and modification.

## Intrusion Detection/ Intrusion Prevention

■ **The company does not have an incident response policy** An IDS is pretty worthless if you don't also have an incident response policy in place. Develop an incident response policy so there are clear lines of responsibility and reporting. Also clearly delineate how, where, and to whom to report suspicious activity.

- **Unauthorized traffic is not logged**  Audit logs are necessary to provide a trail of evidence in case the network is compromised. With this information, the network administrator can devise ways to block the attack and possibly identify and prosecute the attacker. Information supplied by an IDS can be used for forensic analysis in support of an incident as well as to aid in normal traffic analysis.

- **No established weekly backup procedures**  IDS data needs to be backed up to ensure that it is preserved in the event of a hardware failure of the IDS or in the event the IDS is breached.

- **IDS antivirus updates procedures not in the standard operating procedure**  IDS systems require antivirus updates. Be sure that these updates are in the standard operating procedures for IT staff. Sometimes it's the little things we overlook that bite us the hardest; this one's a no-brainer but easy to overlook.

- **Switches and cross-connects are not secure**  Since the intrusion detection and prevention system includes all hardware required to connect horizontal wiring to the backbone wiring, it's important that all switches and associated cross-connect hardware are kept in a secured location, a locked room or an enclosed cabinet that is locked. This will also prevent an attacker from gaining privilege mode access to the switch. Several switch products require only a reboot of the switch to reset or recover the password.

## Remote Access

- **The management VLAN is not secured**  In a VLAN-based network, switches use VLAN1 as the default VLAN for in-band management and to communicate with other networking devices using Spanning-Tree Protocol (STP), Cisco Discovery Protocol (CDP), Dynamic Trunking Protocol (DTP), VLAN Trunking Protocol (VTP), and Port Aggregation Protocol (PAgP)—all untagged traffic. As a consequence, VLAN1 may unwisely span the entire network if it's not appropriately pruned. If its scope is large enough, the risk of compromise can increase significantly.

- **Remote Access Servers do not require encryption for end-user access** You should ensure that only users who require remote access are granted it and that all remote access traffic is encrypted to the fullest extent possible.

- **RAS does not use two-factor authentication** Without strong two-factor authorization, unauthorized users may gain access to network services, devices, and data. Clearly, if an intruder gains control of network infrastructure devices, he or she could inflict damage to either the data or the network, causing loss of confidentiality, integrity, or availability.

- **Remote Access Server connectivity isn't logged** Logging is your friend; keeping a log file of RAS connectivity is critical to keep track of who is attempting to log in, who did log in and when, and how long they were logged in. Reviewing log files daily will help you notice patterns and problems earlier in the cycle than reviewing log files infrequently (or never).

- **RAS session exceeds 30-minute inactivity** An RAS session that is inactive should be terminated to prevent session hijacking. Terminate idle connections after no more than 30 minutes of inactivity.

- **RAS log retentions do not meet requirements** Depending on organizational, legal, or regulatory requirements, you should keep log files for 30 days and archive them for one year.

- **The logs are not viewed on a weekly basis** Reviewing log files daily will help you notice patterns and problems earlier in the cycle than reviewing log files infrequently (or never).

- **Modems are not physically protected** Limiting the access to infrastructure modems and keeping accurate records of the deployed modems will limit the chance that unauthorized modems will be placed into the infrastructure. If an unauthorized person has physical access to a site's modems, the switch or software settings can be changed to affect the security of a system.

- **An accurate list of all modems isn't maintained** Keeping accurate records of the deployed modems will limit the chance that unauthorized modems will be placed into the infrastructure. It will also help you keep track of modems that are no longer used so they can be physically removed or disabled.

- **Modems are not restricted to single-line operation**  Modems should be connected to phone lines that have very basic capabilities. If a phone line has advanced features such as call forwarding, it's possible an intruder could take control of a modem, computer, or network. Keep it simple for better security.

- **Proper call logs are not being maintained**  Logs of all in-bound and out-bound calls for modems and phone lines should be logged and reviewed on a regular basis. Hijacked modems could conceivably allow an attacker to steal phone time and incur long-distance charges on your company's dime. Make sure you know what's going on with modems and phone lines to avoid big phone bills or network intrusion.

- **Callback procedures are not configured correctly**  One way to increase security is to implement a callback feature on the modem so that a caller's call disconnects and the modem calls back a preprogrammed number. Ensure that if callback procedures are used, on establishment of the callback connection the communications device requires the user to authenticate to the system.

- **RAS/NAS server is not located in a screened subnet**  Allowing a remote connection to the private network unchecked by the firewall enables a mobile user to violate the security policy and put the network infrastructure in a vulnerable position. The risk would be magnified if a remote access session were hijacked.

- **The RAS/NAS is not configured to use PPP**  To securely protect the network, Network Access Servers (NAS) and access to them must be controlled to guard against outside or unauthorized intrusion, which could result in system or network compromise. If the NAS is accessed remotely, the risk of compromising a password or user ID increases. The authentication of the remote nodes must be controlled by encryption such as CHAP with MD5 or MS-CHAP with MD4.

- **VPN gateway is located behind the firewall**  Allowing a remote connection to the private network unchecked by the firewall enables a mobile user to violate the security policy and put the network infrastructure in a vulnerable position. The risk would be magnified if the VPN connection were hijacked.

- **The VPN connection is not using IPSec's ESP tunnel** Ensure that remote access via VPN uses IPSec ESP in tunnel mode. For legacy support, L2TP may be used if IPSec provides encryption or another technology that provides security such as AES, 3DES, SSH, or SSL.

- **VPN is not configured as a tunnel type VPN** Be sure that VPNs are established as tunnel type VPNs, which terminate outside the firewall (in other words, between the router and the firewall, or connected to an outside interface of the router). If VPNs terminate inside the firewall, you basically have taken the firewall out of the security mix and reduced your line of defense by one. Improperly deployed VPNs take away a firewall's ability to audit useful information.

We've walked through a lot of very specific security information in this section, some of which might be relevant to your organization, some of which might not be. What is highly likely, though, is that if you even scanned this section, you thought of a few things you might otherwise have overlooked, or it sparked you to make a note to check one thing or another. The key is to be thorough, and to that end, this list should have helped you make sure you covered some of the nitty-gritty details of network infrastructure security.

# Project Parameters

It's time now to plan your infrastructure security project. We've covered a lot of detail, and now we'll try to focus it down into a project plan that you can use to secure your infrastructure. Let's start with our problem and mission (outcome) statements. Remember, this is a good time to gather your core IT project team together to help you begin defining the basic project parameters. You probably could do some (or all) of this preliminary work on your own, but there's a lot to be said for getting the core team fired up and engaged with the project from the very start. You're less likely to have gaps in the project plan if you start relying on the "two heads are better" theory right from the start. Here are two sample problem statements you can use to begin developing your own:

> Our network infrastructure is vulnerable to attack because our security technologies have not kept pace with changes in the external environment. We currently do not have a meaningful approach to security, and all measures in place have been ad hoc or reactive. We are not confident of our level of security across the enterprise.

> We recently experienced a security breach that caused a network outage for three days. We were fortunate that no sensitive data appears to have been stolen or compromised. We took remedial measures, but we are not confident that our data or our network is secure.

Next, let's look at the mission or outcome statement for these problem statements. What's the desired outcome in both of these cases? The short answer is a secure network. We can probably use a single outcome statement for both problems, and it might look something like this:

> We want to create and implement a comprehensive infrastructure security plan so that we are confident we have developed and can maintain as secure a network environment as is reasonably possible.

Your possible solutions run the gamut, but we're going to assume that you've made the decision to secure your network infrastructure by developing a security plan focused on network infrastructure. That being the case, let's look at the requirements for this project.

# Requirements

If you haven't done so, gather your core project team to work with you on the requirements. Requirements are those areas the project must address; in some respects, this is the real foundation of your project. Whatever is defined in the requirements should be implemented in the project, and whatever's in the project should be defined by the requirements. Success factors, those things required to make the project successful, can be defined within your requirements here or as part of your assumptions (discussed later in this chapter).

## Functional Requirements

The functional requirements for your infrastructure security project will vary from the list we're providing, but your list should have the same overall elements. Where we would expect to see more divergence is in the technical requirements, which we'll discuss in a moment. Functional requirements might include:

- Physically secure premises
- Secure network infrastructure servers
- Secure network components (firewalls, routers, switches)

- Secure local communication (authentication, access control, encryption)

- Secure remote communication (authentication, access control, encryption)

- Secure user devices (operating system, antivirus, antispyware, application, file system)

- Create secure operating procedures

- Create documentation

# Technical Requirements

Clearly, the technical requirements for your infrastructure security project will vary greatly from whatever list we provide, because the technical requirements are based on the specific network topology, server types, server operating systems, communication methods, authentication methods, and more. The lengthy list of items presented earlier in this chapter should provide you with plenty of ideas and material for creating your technical requirements for the project. Instead of going into detail here, we present the categories that you should include; the details under those categories are up to you, based on your unique requirements.

Remember, technical requirements should describe the "how" of your functional requirements. So, as you work through this section, keep in mind that you should be describing, very specifically, how you will implement the functional requirements via technology. Your technical requirements should be detailed in describing how these things will be accomplished, but be careful to stick to describing the *requirement*. Let's take "Physically secure the premises" as an example. You don't need to describe how the premises will actually be secured ("Phil will get a screwdriver and install a dead-bolt …"); you need to describe the *technical details* of how it will be secured. So, let's say you're the only tenant in a building. You might describe your technical requirement in this manner:

- Upgrade all external entry doors to card-swipe system. Card-swipe system should be compatible with the existing employee card system, XYZ. (You might include the technical specs of this system here as well.)

- Install security monitoring system (with cameras) focused on parking lot and all external doorways (3). System should be able to record continuously for 24 hours, cameras should be able to record in slow motion and high resolution, the system should be able to "respond" to potential incidents, and the system should record events and have at least three methods of administrator alert.

These are just some of the ways you can capture technical requirements. Clearly, if you're talking about a server, you would include processor speed, memory specifications, disk drive specifications, operating system, and so on. However, other kinds of less technical elements, such as how to secure the premises, might look like the example provided. If your card-swipe system, for example, must conform to certain standards, those standards should be included as well.

# Legal/Compliance Requirements

Create a list of the functional, technical, and administrative requirements for your infrastructure security project based on the legal, regulatory, and compliance requirements. Taking time to translate these requirements into project requirements at this juncture will help ensure that you build compliance requirements into your project. In standard project management, it's always easier to build something in at the front end than to add it at the back end (it reduces errors, omissions, time, and cost), so now's the time to add these requirements to the greatest extent possible. Also, be sure to add milestones and documentation requirements to your project plan based on compliance needs.

# Policy Requirements

Policy requirements may fall under functional requirements, but there's no rule that you can't include policy requirements as a distinct category of requirements if doing so helps you cover all the bases. We'll look at policies in more detail in a later chapter, but for now, let's walk through a few ideas for policies related to securing the infrastructure:

- User policies
- Network access policies
- Remote access policies
- Wireless policies
- Network administration/network management policies
- Server policies
- Firewall, IDS/IPS, DMZ policies
- Regulatory/compliance policies
- Corporate policies
- Legal policies

# Scope

At this point, you should have an idea of the scope of your project. You could choose to address your complete infrastructure security needs during this project, or you might choose to parse it out into smaller subprojects and time them in stages or phases to meet organizational needs. Making changes to the infrastructure comes with risk, and you'll need to be careful to take this fact into consideration as you plan your project. This starts with determining the proper scope for your project. For example, you might have recently implemented an IDS that you're satisfied with, so you could choose to include IDS in your project only to the extent that it ties in with other infrastructure security measures. However, you might feel that your biggest exposure is on network servers such as DHCP, DNS, and directory servers, so your primary focus will be to harden these servers and related network traffic. Your assessment should tell you where you need to focus and what must be included in the plan and perhaps what can safely be omitted from your plan. Then clearly define what is and what is not part of your project so that you leave nothing open to interpretation.

# Schedule

Since we haven't created a detailed work breakdown structure (WBS) yet, we can't develop a detailed schedule, but we can begin to develop a higher-level schedule. First, you should take a look at your organization and see if there are any events or timelines that might come into play. You certainly don't want to be in the middle of a network outage (due to an upgrade) when an important client is visiting, when your marketing department has a big presentation coming up, or when your manufacturing group is working overtime to get a large order out. Taking organizational needs into consideration is critical to project success and helps grease the political gears as well.

In addition to organizational needs, you might know about other timelines or constraints that should be considered in the schedule. Are other security initiatives being planned or under way? If so, is there a logical order to the plans themselves? It might make sense to complete early phases of an infrastructure security project before implementing a new wireless network security plan, for example. Also, look at other IT projects to determine how they might impact the infrastructure security plan or how the infrastructure security activities might disrupt or alter other projects that are in the planning or implementation stages.

Finally, look at your talented IT staff and determine if there are any scheduling issues that would impact your project, such as your best wireless or IP person heading out for vacation or your encryption specialist planning to be out for a month on paternity leave. Whatever the case, if you already know about these scheduling issues, you might as well begin addressing them here.

You might have a rough idea of how long this project will take, given what you've looked at thus far, and you may be able to see where it will fit in your overall IT schedule. You'll have to balance the demands for your IT resources with the need to secure the infrastructure, so this is a good point to try to get a handle on some of those schedule constraints.

# Budget

Your budget will be large or small depending on how well secured your infrastructure currently is and how large your company is. For example, if you already know that you're going to have to upgrade some of those old servers still running Windows NT (gasp), then your budget is going to have to include a whole host of things like the server box itself, the operating system, license upgrades, and updated applications. As with scheduling, you won't have an exact amount in mind yet, but you might have some large segments defined or at least identified. Begin making a list of the components you believe you've identified in terms of purchases so you can verify (or modify) this list after you've created your WBS. Also keep in mind that with an infrastructure security project, a large percentage of your budget might be expended on labor costs (if you track internal labor costs in your project) because much of the work entails checking configurations and modifying settings.

# Quality

You could define quality as the level of protection you're willing to accept, though it might be difficult to quantify. As we've stated, quality is a mindset, and you should instill this mindset in your IT project team. As you define your project plan, you'll have the opportunity to create specific quality metrics related to your infrastructure and incorporate them into your task details. Remember that security comes from depth of defense, so you want each layer you build to be as strong as it can be, within the defined constraints (time, cost, criticality, and so on) and understanding that no system is 100-percent secure.

Once you've defined the project parameters, it's essential that you develop your priorities. If you haven't checked in with your project sponsor, this would be a good time to discuss the priorities. What's the least flexible element here? Are you expected to meet a particular deadline, or were you handed a set budget? Understanding which of these parameters must be met will tell you how to make decisions during the project work phase. If you have a deadline, you'll focus your efforts on making sure that the schedule stays on track, which might mean spending a bit more on overtime than was in the original budget. As you know, in projects something always changes and something *has* to give. Understanding where that flexibility should come from will help you meet organizational requirements. Understand which parameter is least flexible and which is most flexible. Discuss this with your project sponsor, and make sure you're clear and in agreement. That way, when project work is under way, you won't have to keep going back to your sponsor to make basic decisions, and you'll know you're making decisions that support these priorities.

# Key Skills Needed

For your network infrastructure security project, you're going to need a very wide variety of skills. Here we list some of the obvious ones; you can add to (or modify) this list as you define your project:

- **Network services** Securing the infrastructure requires a solid look at security settings on infrastructure servers such as DHCP, DNS, and directory services servers. These key servers require a deep understanding of the services they provide as well as an understanding of best practices in each of these areas.

- **Network perimeter services** Securing the perimeter involves installing, configuring, and managing components such as firewalls, routers, proxy servers, and DMZs. These typically require a strong background and ability to work with various protocols, including SNMP, ICMP, TCP, IP, FTP, HTTPS, SSH, SSL and more.

- **Intrusion detection/intrusion prevention** Installing and configuring IDS/IPS systems require a strong skill set in networking, understanding how information and IP traffic flows through the network infrastructure, and understanding the kinds of threats that are commonly launched (TCP, ICMP, etc.).

- **Remote access** Securing remote access requires an understanding of communication devices and protocols as well as of various authentication and encryption standards and methods. RAS, VLAN, VPN, and tunneling are just a few of the concepts needed in this area.

- **Wireless access** Securing a wireless LAN is discussed in a later chapter, but the skills here are the ability to understand and use various wireless network tools (the same ones the hackers use) and an understanding of how wireless networks are vulnerable and can be protected using a variety of tools.

- **Servers and hosts** These entail understanding operating systems, patches, upgrades, and vulnerabilities as well as how to secure files, folders, data, and user accounts.

- **Network administration** A strong understanding of network administration tools and techniques, including the ability to audit, review, and manage user and group accounts, access control lists, services and protocols, and other administrative tasks, is critical.

- **Documentation** You need people who are excellent at documenting the systems, the proposed changes, the implemented changes, and the final infrastructure configuration data. Documentation may be required for legal or compliance requirements as well.

- **Communication** You should have one or more people on your team who are good at communicating and creating connections within the organization. Since infrastructure changes can have a big impact on business operations, you will need to effectively and proactively communicate with various stakeholders and users during the course of the project.

- **Training** You might need to train users or IT staff on new methods, technologies, or other changes that occur as a result of implementing the infrastructure project plan.

# Key Personnel Needed

Now that you've developed your list of needed skills, you can develop your wish list for project team members. You might want to create your "A" list and a backup list, but for political purposes, you might want to call it your Primary and Secondary teams, to avoid ruffling any feathers. Be sure to highlight the skills needed for which there are no internal matches. This will indicate places you need to seek staff training or external expertise. Also look at your personnel needed and get a sense for how much you're relying on a two or three people. It's often the case that we want the three people who are best to work on everything, but that will slow your project down tremendously. Develop your personnel list, then determine where your gaps are and how you'll address those gaps.

# Project Processes and Procedures

As with any project, you should identify the processes and procedures you'll use during the duration of the project. We are assuming you have a whole stash of those at your disposal, so we won't run through the basics here. However, there are five areas to keep in mind when you're working on an infrastructure security project; you might want to check that these are in your processes and procedures. If not, add them as needed:

- **Testing procedures** Define how, when, and where you'll test security solutions before implementing them on the live network. Clearly, some things can be done on live systems; others should be tested before going live. Define what should be tested offline and how those testing scenarios should proceed.

- **Rollback procedures** For any major changes you're making, be sure you've identified and tested reliable rollback plans so you can roll back to a known good state in case things go wrong.

- **Escalation procedures** These are standard in any project, but when you're dealing with the infrastructure, you might need to beef this area up a bit to make sure you have the right people on standby or on call when critical portions of the project are being implemented.

- **Critical issue reporting** As with other security projects, you might want to review your critical issue-reporting procedures to see whether you need to create a "team red response" that will enable you and your project team to quickly address any vulnerabilities or issues that are deemed critical, severe, or extreme. Develop the process for defining these kinds of issues, and develop an agreed-on scale or measurement system so your team can quickly deal with imminent or urgent issues that may arise.

- **Documentation** Depending on the nature of your project as well as your regulatory or compliance requirements, you might need to revisit your typical project documentation processes and procedures so that you can create the kinds of documentation your project requires, without sorting back through the project to develop the documentation after the fact.

# Project Team

We always recommend gathering at least your core team together to help define the project, but at this point, you have defined the skills and personnel you need, so you should be ready to create your project team. As with almost all IT projects, you should involve subject matter experts from outside the IT department so that you get a well-rounded view of life within the organization, not just within the IT department. Also keep in mind that with infrastructure issues, many areas are technically beyond the grasp of many employees within the organization (well, most everyone outside the IT department). Be patient, be prepared to explain things in nontechnical ways, and don't discuss technical details when it isn't absolutely necessary. You want to involve users and stakeholders in appropriate ways, but there will be a more limited role for them in this type of project than in most of the other kinds of IT security projects you might undertake.

An infrastructure security project spans the entire enterprise and is as deep as it is wide. To be successfully completed, the project requires an extensive set of first-rate skills. Be sure that your project team has all the skills delineated in your skills assessment. If it does not, your project is at risk because gaps in skills or skills that are not up to standards will create problems in quality or scheduling down the line. Be sure you have all the requisite skills; if you don't, be sure to create a plan to address those gaps. Whether you need additional external staff or just some training for internal staff, be sure to add this to your budget and possibly your schedule.

Develop your team, create a team roster, and get the team ready to create the detailed project plan, especially the work breakdown structure.

# Project Organization

You might want to organize your project by the topic areas we've defined so that you have subteams dedicated to: devices and media, topologies, IDS/IPS, and system hardening. You could choose to parse it out differently, or you might have the whole team, if it is small, work through each stage of the project plan together. It's up to you, and it's certainly somewhat dependent on the size of your company, the size of the project, and the size of your IT staff. Be sure that everyone is clear about what their roles are within the team and within the project. Organizing your team will provide the necessary structure for the team to be productive. Since we're assuming you've managed a lot of projects (or have read up on your project management skills recently), we won't delve into the details of organizing this project except to make one note: The work in the various segments of this project overlaps a lot, and if your project and team are not well organized, you're going to have people working at cross-purposes and creating a big mess. Keep the project and your team organized to avoid this scenario.

# Project Work Breakdown Structure

Your approach to creating your work breakdown structure (WBS) might be different from the method we provide; that's fine as long as you cover the basics. Our recommended approach is to start with your mission statement and your selected solution and create three to five high-level objectives. From there, you can parse each of those objectives down into smaller components until you have tasks that actually make sense and are understandable. Tasks should be broken down until they represent an understandable and manageable unit of work. The 80/8 rule is a good one to keep in mind; it states that no task should exceed 80 hours or be less than 8 hours. If a task is longer than 80 hours, it needs to be broken down into smaller components. If you define tasks of less than 8 hours, you'll end up with a scheduling nightmare on your hands.

We'll start with the four major areas we discussed at the opening of this chapter:

1.  Devices and media

2.  Topologies

3.  Intrusion detection/intrusion prevention

4.  System hardening

These are not properly written as tasks or even as objectives; they're topic labels. So, let's fix that and create the top-level objectives based on these four areas of concern:

1.  Audit and secure devices and media

2.  Audit and secure network topology

3.  Implement or harden intrusion prevention/detection systems

4.  Harden systems

Now we have a better starting point for our WBS. From here, we can break these down into smaller tasks. We're not going to dig down as deep as you'll need to, because once you get beyond a certain level of detail, the plan is very much dependent on the nature and structure of your organization and how you and your team decide to approach the project. So, don't fight with the structure presented here; use it as a guide to create one that works for you. Also note that where servers or other devices may be called out, the numbers or types of devices may not track with standard networking practices. They are presented as examples of a WBS tree, not necessarily examples of best practices in networking. In reality, you will have more or fewer DNS servers, but we only mention one. You will have a long list of tasks under Task 3.4, "Assess and harden routers, switches, and other network communication devices." We didn't dig down at all levels of the WBS but provided samples of how or where you might develop additional tasks and subtasks. And, while this list is long, it's not as long as your infrastructure security project plan's WBS will end up being. However, this should give you a running start:

1. Audit and secure devices and media.

2. Audit and secure network topology.

    2.1 Create secure boundaries using firewalls, DMZs, and proxy servers.

    2.2 Create secure remote access.

        2.2.1 Secure all Remote Access Servers.

            2.2.1.1 Physically secure Remote Access Servers.

            2.2.1.2 Secure Remote Access Servers.

                2.2.1.2.1 Remove excess administrative accounts.

                2.2.1.2.2 Disable all unused services, ports, and protocols.

                2.2.1.2.3 Remove all unused applications.

                2.2.1.2.4 Disable all unused modems.

        2.2.2 Secure remote communications.

            2.2.2.1 Evaluate the feasibility and desirability of implementing VLAN.

            2.2.2.1 Evaluate the feasibility and desirability of implementing VPN.

    2.3 Create secure wireless access.

        2.3.1 Change all wireless access points' default settings.

        2.3.2 Disable SSID broadcasting, create a closed system.

        2.3.3 Enable MAC address filtering.

        2.3.4 Evaluate and implement encryption (WEP or WPA).

        2.3.5 Filter wireless protocols.

        2.3.5 Define IP allocations for the WLAN.

2.3.6 Evaluate VPNs for possible implementation.

2.3.7 Secure users' wireless devices.

2.3.8 Develop wireless policies for users.

2.3.9 Develop wireless policies for IT operations.

2.4 Implement a segmented network.

2.5 Implement network traffic security protocols for sensitive network traffic.

2.6 Deploy network security technologies.

2.6.1 Use Encrypting File System (EFS) or similar file encryption.

2.6.2 Require and use strong user authentication, passwords, and account policies.

2.6.3 Employ the concept of "least privileges" when assigning user rights.

3.  Implement or harden intrusion prevention/detection systems.

3.1 Assess security of current IDS/IPS system or evaluate need for implementing IDS/IPS system.

3.1.1 Evaluate intrusion detection system feasibility and desirability.

3.1.2 Inline intrusion prevention system feasibility and desirability.

3.1.3 Network active response system feasibility and desirability.

3.1.4 Host active response system feasibility and desirability.

3.1.5 Network processors feasibility and desirability.

3.2 Assess and harden DMZ or evaluate need for implementing DMZ.

3.3 Assess and harden firewall or evaluate need for implementing additional firewalls.

3.4 Assess and harden routers, switches, and other network communication devices.

4.  Harden systems.

4.1 Evaluate physical security and access control to critical servers.

4.1.1 Evaluate and secure access to domain controllers.

4.1.1.1 Evaluate and secure domain controller 1.

4.1.1.2 Evaluate and secure domain controller 2.

4.1.1.3 Evaluate and secure domain controller 3.

4.1.2 Evaluate and secure access to DHCP server.

4.1.3 Evaluate and secure access to DNS server.

4.2 Review and revise administrative accounts on infrastructure servers.

4.2.1 Remove unused or superfluous administrative accounts.

4.2.2 Remove unused or unnecessary non–administrative accounts.

4.2.3 Remove unused rights and privileges.

4.3 Implement strong authentication and password policies on all infrastructure devices.

4.4 Review, record and update (as needed) operating system and application version levels.

4.4.1 Review and record operating system versions on all infrastructure servers.

4.4.1.1 Review and record operating system version on domain controller 1.

4.4.1.2 Review and record operating system version on domain controller 2.

4.4.1.3 Review and record operating system version on domain controller 3.

4.4.1.4 Review and record operating system version on DHCP server.

4.4.1.5 Review and record operating system version on DNS server.

4.4.2 Update operating systems on all infrastructure servers.

4.4.2.1 Update operating system on domain controller 1.

4.4.2.2 Update operating system on domain controller 2.

4.4.2.3 Update operating system on domain controller 3.

4.4.2.4 Update operating system on DHCP server.

4.4.2.5 Update operating system on DNS server.

4.5 Review current status of virus protection software installed on servers.

4.6 Assess and implement server, application, and client-side security technologies.

4.6.1 Secure server traffic traveling on the network.

4.6.2 Secure application and user data traveling on the network.

4.6.3 Secure network access points and network access.

4.6.4 Secure client devices including desktops, laptops, and PDAs.

4.6.4.1 Upgrade all insecure "legacy" operating systems.

4.6.4.2 Update all operating systems with latest revisions, patches, and updates.

4.6.4.3 Update all applications with latest revisions, patches, and updates.

4.6.4.4 Update all virus protection programs.

4.6.4.4.1 Ensure latest virus definition file is loaded.

4.6.4.4.2 Ensure virus program is configured to automatically download the latest definition file from secure server or Internet site (WSUS in Windows or vendor Web site).

4.6.4.5 Enable file encryption for mobile devices.

4.6.4.6 Implement strong passwords.

4.6.4.7 Update user policies to prevent downloading or installing of unsigned programs.

5. Document all infrastructure changes.

5.1 Document changes to all infrastructure configuration settings.

5.2 Document changes to network topology, layout, or structure.

5.3 Document changes to standard operating procedures.

5.4 Document changes to user policies and procedures.

6. Perform compliance audit.

Once you've completed the WBS, you need to go through with your subject matter experts and develop the task details. Details can include task owners, resources, known constraints, or requirements for the task, task duration, task cost or budget, tools or equipment needed for the task, completion criteria, deadline or due date, and any other data relevant to the task and its successful completion. Remember that the functional, technical, and legal requirements should be fully incorporated into the project task detail or they will get lost. This is a great opportunity to review your requirements and go through your task details to ensure that everything is included, before project work starts.

This is also a point at which you should do a scope check and make sure that the WBS describes your intended scope. It's fairly common for the scope described by the WBS to be larger than the stated scope. In fact, this is often the first source of "scope creep." Look at your scope statement and at your WBS and reconcile any discrepancies. For example, you might have stated in your scope statement that something was not part of the project scope but that element shows up in the WBS. Decide if that element should be in or out, then adjust either your scope statement or your WBS accordingly. If there are substantive changes to your scope, check in with your project sponsor to gain agreement as to the modified or updated scope and WBS.

# Project Risks and Mitigation Strategies

This section of your project plan defines the risks to your project and the strategies you'll use to avoid or mitigate your risk. There are always risks with every project, and it's important to take time to identify those risks while you're calm, cool, and collected. There are some projects for which the risks outweigh the benefits and you decide, as a team or an organization, to not go down that path. Securing the infrastructure is not likely to fall into that category, but it's always important to keep this in mind—that sometimes doing nothing is a better choice.

However, you've decided to strengthen security on your network infrastructure and there are attendant risks. Let's look at one risk you might have, and you can then use this structure to develop additional risk and mitigation strategies. We'll use the following ranking system: 1 = Extremely high, 5 = Extremely low.

**Risk: Improper configuration could completely disable network.**

1. Criticality: 1
2. Likelihood of occurrence: 3
3. Relative risk ranking: 2

4. Mitigation strategy 1: Test all configurations in lab prior to rollout.

5. Risk of mitigation 1: Not all lab tests will completely mirror actual conditions.

6. Mitigation strategy 2: Develop fail-safe rollback plans for all critical configuration changes.

7. Risk of mitigation 2: Rollback will take time and set back project completion timelines.

8. Trigger 1: One week prior to scheduled configuration change.

9. Trigger 2: Forty-five minutes after network outage occurs.

10. Notes: All configuration changes will be tested in the lab first, but the there is still a chance that the configuration change could cause the network to crash. If this occurs, rollback plans will be implemented after 45 minutes of network downtime have elapsed.

As you can see from this single example, you can develop sound contingency plans for risks you decide are worth planning for. Some risks are too small to bother planning for; other risks are significant but unlikely to occur, and planning for them would also not be a good use of time.

Once you've listed every risk you can think of, you can develop a ranked list based on both criticality and likelihood of occurrence. From there, you can develop mitigation strategies for just the most critical and most likely-to-occur risks. You may choose to develop more than one mitigation strategy. In our example, our first choice was to test in the lab, but we also conceded that testing in the lab may not mirror real-world results and the risk of our mitigation strategy had to be addressed as well. In this case, we developed a secondary or backup mitigation strategy as a fail-safe option. Both mitigation strategies require a defined trigger—how will you know when to implement your risk mitigation plan? In this case, you might choose to build lab testing into your project plan for all configuration change tasks and avoid this first mitigation strategy. However, you would still need the second mitigation strategy and trigger in the event that you ran into a configuration problem that you couldn't immediately find. In this case, after a 45-minute outage you'd go to Plan B, your predetermined rollback plan. It's nice to have Plan B ready to go when you're running around like you hair is on fire because you have 47 different people asking you when the network will be back up, what the problem is, and why they can't log onto the network.

# Project Constraints and Assumptions

Constraints for an infrastructure security project might come in all shapes and sizes. You may well face budgetary constraints that limit the scope of your project. You might face scope problems because the infrastructure needs a lot of upgrading but your company isn't willing to implement all the changes needed, for a variety of financial, political, and organizational reasons. You might face resistance within the organization because some changes impact users' computing behaviors, and this can cause problems. In addition, you may face specific constraints or limits within portions of your project. For a variety of reasons, you might not be able to make changes to application servers or database servers due to other projects under way or other organizational issues. The infrastructure security is core to your network's security, so constraints to the project should be clearly identified and discussed. If the constraints are too great or impede your project too much, you should have a talk with your project sponsor. Although every project has to deal with a variety of constraints, you must decide whether the constraints are reasonable or if they place an undue burden on your project. You are responsible for project success and, ultimately, for the security of the infrastructure, so it's up to you to clear away these obstacles or get your project sponsor involved with removing them so the project can be successful.

Equally important is delineating the assumptions you're working under as you move into the project. For example, if you assume certain resources will be available or if you assume that other projects will be completed first, you should state that clearly. Your assumptions should be clearly delineated so that you and your team can *challenge*, *clarify*, or *confirm* those assumptions before proceeding with the project. The most dangerous assumptions are the ones we don't know we're making.

For example, if you've been in the midst of deploying a particular encryption method, your project would work on the assumption that the encryption scheme was already in place or was being deployed. This fact is critical to note in your project because, if something outside your control changes the encryption scheme on which your infrastructure project is based, you'll have to rework your project plan. This could (and probably would) impact both your schedule and your budget. It's hard enough to bring a project in on time and on budget without having the project environment shift around on you. Listing the assumptions you're making going into the project will help you as you develop your plan as well because others on the team or in the organization can challenge your assumptions, if they know what they are. To go back to the encryption example, if you list this as an assumption and someone on your project team lets you know that the encryption project was put on hold for one reason or another, it's good to know that ahead of time rather than planning based on that incorrect assumption.

Some project managers like to list project success factors in their list of assumptions because they are assuming these factors will be in place or will occur. You can also discuss and define success factors at the front of your project-planning process, if that's a more logical flow for you. Some teams don't know what it will take to be successful until they've neared the end of their definition and planning work; others like to define these elements right up front. Whatever works for you is fine. Just be sure to define these so you'll know what it will take for your project to succeed.

You and your project team will have to look at the project environment and list the constraints and the assumptions you're making in order for your project to get off to a good start and to have a better-than-average chance for success. These elements are unique to each project and each company, so we can't give you a list of things to place in this section, but now that we've discussed them in general terms, you and your team should be able to dig in and find the constraints and assumptions for your own, unique infrastructure security project.

# Project Schedule and Budget

You can see from the lengthy project plan we've created that your schedule and budget are going to be challenging to develop. Once you've created your WBS, you can look through your task details and begin developing your schedule. The schedule is best developed in a project management software program since you will have a lot of moving parts to handle. If you have subteams working in parallel on different aspects of the project plan, be sure you address this in your schedule. First, you'll have to be sure you're not double-booking someone and throwing your schedule off. Second, you want to keep an eye on how different segments of the project will impact other segments so you don't end up working at cross-purposes, or worse, damaging something another team just implemented. If one team is upgrading the firewalls and another team is working on IPS, it's entirely possible one team's work will greatly impact the other team's work and cause confusion, problems, errors, or omissions.

Be sure to check your critical path tasks after you've loaded your schedule into the software program, since these tasks will determine the longest, least-flexible path through your project. Although we haven't discussed the more technical aspects of scheduling (we assume you know them), recall that you can indicate lead and lag times as well as float to create a more realistic schedule. If everything in your project plan ends up on the critical path, or if none of your tasks end up on the critical path, there's a good chance you have a fundamental problem with how your schedule is set up.

As for budget, you should have a pretty clear idea of what this project will cost at this point, with one notable exception. If you are using your infrastructure security project plan to evaluate the need for an IDS, IPS, DMZ, or other network equipment, you might not yet have sufficient data with which to get bids for these systems. In that case, you need some sort of placeholder to indicate that a system will be purchased but the system has yet to be clearly defined and therefore cannot be spec'd out or priced. If you know the order of magnitude, it might be good to add a dollar-amount placeholder. For example, suppose you know that one type of system you're looking for costs about $18,000, plus or minus $2,000. You might want to put $20,000 into your budget as a placeholder so that when your project budget is approved, you have that cost built in. It's usually difficult to get your budget increased after it's been approved, unless you specifically get your budget approved with the understanding that it does *not* include the cost of new hardware or software solutions that may be recommended as a result of the project assessment.

If you've made it this far, you've made it to the end of the chapter and the end of your planning cycle for your infrastructure security project plan. It's a lot to cover because the infrastructure is wide and deep, but if you take time to step through your planning in a measured, thoughtful manner, you'll end up with better results than if you just rush headlong into the project work. That's a guarantee. Your project might not be perfect, it could come in late or over budget, but whatever result you turn in will be far better than if you used no consistent approach or framework at all.

# IT Infrastructure Security Project Outline

- Audit and secure devices and media
- Audit and secure network topology
  - Create secure boundaries using firewalls, DMZs and proxy servers.
  - Create secure remote access.
  - Create secure wireless access.
  - Implement a segmented network.
  - Implement network traffic security protocols for sensitive network traffic.
  - Deploy network security technologies.

- Implement or harden intrusion prevention/detection systems

  - Assess security of current IDS/IPS system *or* evaluate need for implementing IDS/IPS system.

  - Assess and harden DMZ *or* evaluate need for implementing DMZ.

  - Assess and harden firewall *or* evaluate need for implementing additional firewalls.

  - Assess and harden routers, switches, and other network communication devices.

- Harden systems

  - Evaluate physical security and access control to critical servers.

  - Review and revise administrative accounts on infrastructure servers.

  - Implement strong authentication and password policies on all infrastructure devices.

  - Review, record, and update (as needed) operating system and application version levels.

  - Review current status of virus protection software installed on servers.

  - Assess and implement server, application, and client-side security technologies.

- Document all infrastructure changes.

  - Document changes to all infrastructure configuration settings.

  - Document changes to network topology, layout or structure.

  - Document changes to standard operating procedures.

  - Document changes to user policies and procedures.

- Perform compliance audit.

# Summary

We've covered a lot of ground in this chapter because your network infrastructure is literally and figuratively the backbone of your network. Infrastructure security touches every aspect of your network, and a thorough assessment will take time and careful effort to complete so that your network is as secure as it can reasonably be, given the organizational constraints and considerations you'll have to deal with. It's often helpful to break the network infrastructure down into it systems or areas to help ensure that you cover all the areas, including devices and media, topology, intrusion detection and prevention, system hardening, and all the network components such as routers, switches, and modems. Once you've identified all the areas, you need to take a top-to-bottom look at how security is currently implemented and what threats exist. By looking at issues such as information criticality and performing an impact analysis, you can decide what should be included in your project and what can reasonably be left out or delayed for a later phase if needed. Understanding the threat environment and your network's vulnerabilities is also important during your planning phase.

Requirements need to be thoroughly developed because they form the foundation of your project's scope. Functional requirements should be developed first, followed by technical, legal, and policy requirements. Be sure to build these into your task details when you create your WBS so that all required elements will be present and accounted for in your project plan.

In an infrastructure security project, you'll need a wide variety of skills that span the depth and breadth of networking knowledge. Be sure you define the skills you'll need so that you can assess your team and your organization to identify skills gaps. These will have to be addressed before your project can proceed, and this often requires hiring outside contractors or providing training for internal staff members. Either way, this can impact both your budget and your schedule, so be sure you do a gap analysis between needed and available skills prior to proceeding with your project.

The WBS defines the scope of your project, so once you've identified all the work through delineating the tasks, be sure to do a scope check. If the defined scope is smaller than the scope outlined in your WBS, you need to reconcile the differences. Also be sure to discuss any scope changes with your project sponsor so that you start off with the same expectations about project results.

Scheduling an infrastructure security project can be challenging due to all the moving parts involved. You'll run into scheduling conflicts, resource usage conflicts, timing issues, and more. These should be resolved to the greatest degree possible before starting the project, because things will only get more complicated and difficult to resolve once project work is under way. One important scheduling note is that with all areas of your network being poked and prodded, you'll need to make sure subproject teams are not working at cross-purposes and undoing work just done or inadvertently injecting false indicators into the process through their own task work.

When it's all said and done, you should be able to define, implement, manage, and close a very successful infrastructure security project, if you follow a consistent methodology and make teamwork and quality topmost priorities. This is the foundation of all other security projects; it touches on everything in your organization, so success here will create the framework for a very secure network that will help you sleep at night, knowing you've done everything possible to keep your organization's assets secure.

# Solutions Fast Track

## Infrastructure Security Auditing

☑ Auditing or assessing the infrastructure security is a large task that encompasses every aspect of your network.

☑ Infrastructure projects cross several boundaries, and you should be sure that any overlap is addressed so you are not working at cross-purposes.

☑ The infrastructure project can be parsed out in numerous ways. One way is to look at it in terms of these systems: network perimeter, internal network, intrusion monitoring and prevention, host and server configuration, malicious code protection, incident response capabilities, security policies and procedures, employee awareness and training, and physical security and monitoring.

☑ The internal and external environments should be assessed thoroughly prior to planning your project.

☑ Internal factors include understanding information criticality, the potential impact of a breach, the information flow, policies and procedures, user needs, and regulatory/compliance issues.

☑ Externally, you need to consider the types of threats your network is vulnerable to, including spoofing, repudiation, data tampering, denial of service, and elevation of privileges.

☑ The SAN Institute publishes a list of the top 20 vulnerabilities that can serve as a great starting point for assessing your network's vulnerabilities.

☑ The assessment should look at devices and media, topologies, intrusion detection/intrusion prevention systems, and system hardening.

☑ Devices and media include all the network infrastructure devices that must be secured, including routers, switches, and modems.

## Project Parameters

☑ Defining the functional and technical specifications for your infrastructure project will define the scope of work you need to accomplish.

☑ There could be specific legal or regulatory compliance issues to be addressed within the scope of your infrastructure security plan; you should include these issues in the early stages of project planning.

☑ Defining scope, initial budget, initial schedule, and quality guidelines based on the functional, technical, legal, and policy requirements gives you a solid starting point.

☑ Developing the relative priority of your parameters and gaining project sponsor agreement is important in helping you know how to make decisions for your project, moving forward. The least flexible parameter will be your constraint; the most flexible parameter will be what "gives" when things change in the course of project work.

☑ Technical skills needed for the project include network services, network perimeter, intrusion detection/prevention, remote access, wireless access, server and host administration, familiarity with protocols, ports, and services as well as skills in documentation, communication, and training.

## Project Team

☑ Your core project team should help in defining the project.

☑ Your infrastructure project team should include people with the needed skills, which, in an infrastructure security project, are extensive.

☑ Your project is at risk if you don't have the skills you need on your team. Be sure to address skills gaps before you start project work and add any associated costs into your project budget.

# Project Organization

- ☑ The project should be organized around areas of the network and areas of expertise.

- ☑ Typical organizational methods should form the foundation of your project organization.

- ☑ Infrastructure projects require extra coordination to ensure that subteams are not working at cross-purposes.

# Project Work Breakdown Structure

- ☑ The work breakdown structure, or WBS, for an infrastructure project should begin with the high-level objectives for your project, which might include securing devices and media, securing the perimeter, securing infrastructure components, or whatever way you choose to segment the work in this project.

- ☑ Task details should reflect the functional, technical, and regulatory requirements for your project. Check task details against requirements to be sure everything is included at the outset.

- ☑ The scope statement and the scope described by the WBS might not be in sync. Compare them and make any modifications needed to either your scope statement or your WBS before proceeding.

- ☑ If there are significant changes to your scope statement, check in with your project sponsor before proceeding to ensure that you're both on the same page with regard to scope.

# Project Risks and Mitigation Strategies

- ☑ The risks inherent in an infrastructure project are many because this type of project touches every aspect of your network.

- ☑ Identify all potential risks and rank them according to criticality and likelihood of occurrence, then look over the list and make any reasonable adjustments.

- ☑ Determine how far down your risk list you will plan, then develop mitigation strategies and triggers for each defined risk.

☑ If you determine that there are one or more significant risks, you should sit down and talk them over with your project sponsor. In some cases, the risks outweigh any potential benefit and the project should be canceled, redefined, or postponed until those risks can be more clearly evaluated and addressed.

# Project Constraints and Assumptions

☑ Constraints are present in every project, but in an infrastructure security project, you could have constraints on several fronts.

☑ If the constraints are too great, they can hinder or prevent project success. Discuss major constraints with your project sponsor to determine the best course of action. Otherwise, develop ways to address these constraints or plan around them.

☑ Clearly delineating assumptions is an important part of your infrastructure security plan because you have to work from a known good point.

☑ If your assumptions are stated, they can be challenged, clarified, or confirmed.

☑ Assumptions may also include success factors, since you might be assuming certain factors must be in place for the project to succeed. Success factors are also sometimes developed in the requirements phase of the project-planning process, depending on how you go about identifying them.

# Project Schedule and Budget

☑ After you've developed your project's WBS, you should have sufficient data to create a fairly realistic and feasible project schedule and budget.

☑ Keep in mind that the project schedule has a lot of moving parts, and you're likely to run into issues around conflicting resource demands or subteams working at cross-purposes.

☑ Be sure your budget provides for adequate training or hiring of needed resources.

☑ Large purchases such as IDS/IPS or other major components might not be decided at the outset of the project. Create ballpark estimates or insert placeholders in your budget so it is clear whether or not large-ticket items are included or specifically excluded from your project budget.

# Infrastructure Security Project Outline

- ☑ Audit and secure network topology.
- ☑ Audit and secure network topology.
- ☑ Implement or harden intrusion prevention/detection systems.
- ☑ Harden systems.
- ☑ Document all infrastructure changes.
- ☑ Perform compliance audit.

# Chapter 8

# Case Study: SOHO (Five Computers, Printer, Servers, etc.)

## Solutions in this chapter:

- Introducing the SOHO Firewall Case Study
- Designing the SOHO Firewall
- Implementing the SOHO Firewall

☑ Summary

☑ Solutions Fast Track

☑ Frequently Asked Questions

# Introduction

The Internet continues to grow as small businesses and home users realize the opportunities available to them with a wider audience for goods. Using personalized Web sites and e-mail addresses, and having a permanent Internet connection create a closer customer experience with remote users. This closeness comes at a price as systems are made accessible 24x7. With accessibility, unwelcome guests and customers have invitations to use the network. The exploitation of vulnerabilities on a system include misusing protocols, or applications, by connecting to an IP address on an open TCP or UDP port of a system on the network. Security for the home isn't as well developed as in a corporate environment. Users often do not have the time to become experts, while maintaining their business or working remotely.

## Using *netstat* to Determine Open Ports on a System

The *netstat* command does many useful things other than determining open ports on a system, including displaying memory and network buffer usage, system route table information, and interface statistics. To understand more about those options, read the documentation online about *netstat*. The following focuses on using *netstat* to determine the open ports and whether they should be open.

When a remote system or user wishes to access a service on your computer (e.g., Web server), the underlying OS on the remote system creates a connection to a port on your computer system on behalf of the remote user.

A process listening on a port will accept incoming connections to that port. A large part of securing your system from network attack is an audit of these services. Once you know what is running, you can turn off services that have opened ports that you don't need, and make sure to secure the services you do need. It will also establish a baseline as to what should be running. When the system starts acting sluggishly, or responding in an abnormal fashion, you can quickly check to make sure there are no rogue processes running on unrecognized ports.

The *−a* flag tells *netstat* "show the state of all sockets." One understanding of a socket is as a listening port. The *-n* flags tells *netstat* to not attempt to resolve names via DNS. This is generally a good practice because you remove a dependency on working DNS, and *netstat* will return information more quickly. If you need to look up an IP-to-name mapping, you can always do that later with the *host*, *nslookup*, or *dig* commands.

Here is an example of *netstat* output using the *−a* and *−n* flags.

## Sample *netstat*—Output on a UNIX Server

```
Active Internet connections (including servers)
Proto Recv-Q Send-Q  Local Address        Foreign Address        State
tcp      0      0  6.7.8.9.60072   221.132.43.179.113    SYN_SENT
tcp      0      0  6.7.8.9.25      221.132.43.179.48301  ESTABLISHED
tcp      0    120  6.7.8.9.22      24.7.34.163.1811      ESTABLISHED
tcp      0      0  6.7.8.9.60124   67.46.65.70.113       FIN_WAIT_2
tcp      0      0  127.0.0.1.4000  127.0.0.1.60977       ESTABLISHED
tcp      0      0  127.0.0.1.60977 127.0.0.1.4000        ESTABLISHED
tcp      0      0  *.4000                *.*             LISTEN
tcp      0      0  6.7.8.9.22      24.7.34.163.50206     ESTABLISHED
tcp      0      0  6.7.8.9.62220   216.120.255.44.22     ESTABLISHED
tcp      0      0  6.7.8.9.22      24.7.34.163.65408     ESTABLISHED
tcp      0      0  6.7.8.9.22      67.131.247.194.4026   ESTABLISHED
tcp      0      0  6.7.8.9.64015   217.206.161.163.22    ESTABLISHED
tcp      0      0  6.7.8.9.22      82.36.206.162.48247   ESTABLISHED
tcp      0      0  *.80                  *.*             LISTEN
tcp      0      0  *.993                 *.*             LISTEN
tcp      0      0  *.25                  *.*             LISTEN
tcp      0      0  *.22                  *.*             LISTEN
tcp      0      0  *.21                  *.*             LISTEN
tcp      0      0  127.0.0.1.53          *.*             LISTEN
tcp      0      0  6.7.8.9.53      *.*             LISTEN
udp      0      0  127.0.0.1.123         *.*
udp      0      0  6.7.8.9.123     *.*
udp      0      0  *.123                 *.*
udp      0      0  *.65510               *.*
udp      0      0  127.0.0.1.53          *.*
udp      0      0  6.7.8.9.53      *.*
Active Internet6 connections (including servers)
Proto Recv-Q Send-Q  Local Address        Foreign Address        (state)
tcp6     0      0  *.25                  *.*             LISTEN
tcp6     0      0  *.22                  *.*             LISTEN
udp6     0      0  fe80::1%lo0.123       *.*
udp6     0      0  :: 1.123              *.*
udp6     0      0  fe80::2e0:81ff:f.123  *.*
udp6     0      0  *.123                 *.*
udp6     0      0  *.65509               *.*
```

```
Active UNIX domain sockets
Address   Type   Recv-Q Send-Q     Inode     Conn     Refs  Nextref Addr
c204c440 dgram      0      0        0 c1fd80c0          0 c2026540 ->
/var/run/lo
g
c20fd040 stream     0      0        0 c1fcd3c0          0        0
c1fcd3c0 stream     0      0        0 c20fd040          0        0
c1fd3300 stream     0      0        0 c1fd8680          0        0
c1fd8680 stream     0      0        0 c1fd3300          0        0
c2129e40 stream     0      0        0 c20db500          0        0
c20db500 stream     0      0        0 c2129e40          0        0
c204cb40 stream     0      0        0 c20fdb00          0        0
c20fdb00 stream     0      0        0 c204cb40          0        0
c20fdc00 stream     0      0        0 c2129800          0        0
c2129800 stream     0      0        0 c20fdc00          0        0
c2026540 dgram      0      0        0 c1fd80c0          0 c1f9c740 ->
/var/run/lo
g
c1f9c740 dgram      0      0        0 c1fd80c0          0        0 ->
/var/run/lo
g
c1fd80c0 dgram      0      0 cc32615c          0 c204c440          0
/var/run/log
c1fd8300 dgram      0      0 cc3260b4          0        0          0
/var/chroot/na
med/var/run/log
```

Examine the parts that have TCP and UDP ports in the first section of the output. Unless you're actively running IPv6, you can safely ignore the tcp6, and udp6 output. Additionally, UNIX domain sockets are local within the machine and not network related.

## Sample *netstat*—TCP Output on a UNIX Server

```
tcp        0        0 6.7.8.9.60072  221.132.43.179.113     SYN_SENT
tcp        0        0 6.7.8.9.25     221.132.43.179.48301   ESTABLISHED
tcp        0      120 6.7.8.9.22     24.7.34.163.1811       ESTABLISHED
tcp        0        0 6.7.8.9.60124  67.46.65.70.113        FIN_WAIT_2
tcp        0        0 127.0.0.1.4000        127.0.0.1.60977
ESTABLISHED
tcp        0        0 127.0.0.1.60977       127.0.0.1.4000
ESTABLISHED
```

```
tcp    0    0   *.4000                      *.*                  LISTEN
tcp    0    0   6.7.8.9.22       24.7.34.163.50206    ESTABLISHED
tcp    0    0   6.7.8.9.62220    216.120.255.44.22    ESTABLISHED
tcp    0    0   6.7.8.9.22       24.7.34.163.65408    ESTABLISHED
tcp    0    0   6.7.8.9.22       67.131.247.194.4026  ESTABLISHED
tcp    0    0   6.7.8.9.64015    217.206.161.163.22   ESTABLISHED
tcp    0    0   6.7.8.9.22       82.36.206.162.48247  ESTABLISHED
tcp    0    0   *.80                        *.*                  LISTEN
tcp    0    0   *.993                       *.*                  LISTEN
tcp    0    0   *.25                        *.*                  LISTEN
tcp    0    0   *.22                        *.*                  LISTEN
tcp    0    0   *.21                        *.*                  LISTEN
tcp    0    0   127.0.0.1.53                *.*                  LISTEN
tcp    0    0   6.7.8.9.53                  *.*                  LISTEN
```

Notice the last field contains different words like *ESTABLISHED* and *LISTEN*. This denotes the state of the socket. The sockets that show active services waiting for connections are lines that contain LISTEN. The * fields describes a port open to any IP address, so *.80 in the local address field tells us that this machine has port listening on every IP interface in this machine. Generally, a system will only have one IP address, but occasionally can have multiple interfaces.

So, a short way of getting the listening TCP ports on a UNIX system would be netstat -an | grep LISTEN, extracting only the LISTEN lines.

```
slick: {8} netstat -an | grep LISTEN
tcp     0    0   *.4000              *.*                LISTEN
tcp     0    0   *.80               *.*                LISTEN
tcp     0    0   *.993              *.*                LISTEN
tcp     0    0   *.25               *.*                LISTEN
tcp     0    0   *.22               *.*                LISTEN
tcp     0    0   *.21               *.*                LISTEN
tcp     0    0   127.0.0.1.53       *.*                LISTEN
tcp     0    0   6.7.8.9.53    *.*             LISTEN
tcp6    0    0   *.25               *.*                LISTEN
tcp6    0    0   *.22               *.*                LISTEN
```

Okay, we have a list of TCP, so let's move on to the UDP section. UDP doesn't have any state field, because unlike TCP, UDP is a stateless protocol model. Each packet is discrete and disconnected in any way to the previous packet arriving on that port. There is no provision in the protocol for retransmission of dropped packets. Applications like NTP and DNA rely on UDP.

```
slick: {9} netstat -an | grep udp
udp      0      0   127.0.0.1.123           *.*
udp      0      0   10.1.2.3.123      *.*
udp      0      0   *.123                   *.*
udp      0      0   *.65510                 *.*
udp      0      0   127.0.0.1.53            *.*
udp      0      0   10.1.2.3.53       *.*
udp6     0      0   fe80::1%lo0.123         *.*
udp6     0      0   ::1.123                 *.*
udp6     0      0   fe80::2e0:81ff:f.123    *.*
udp6     0      0   *.123                   *.*
udp6     0      0   *.65509                 *.*
```

Ignore the udp6 (IPV6) lines. The third field is the same as the TCP output from before. This is the listening address and port. The IP address of this machine is 6.7.8.9, and there is a localhost interface, 127.0.0.1, for local TCP and UDP communication. 127.0.0.1 is the localhost and not visible to the Internet.

Anything that is not recognizable and requires further information should be audited.

## Sample Ports Requiring Auditing

```
tcp      0      0   *.4000                  *.*                    LISTEN
tcp      0      0   *.80                    *.*                    LISTEN
tcp      0      0   *.993                   *.*                    LISTEN
tcp      0      0   *.25                    *.*                    LISTEN
tcp      0      0   *.22                    *.*                    LISTEN
tcp      0      0   *.21                    *.*                    LISTEN
tcp      0      0   127.0.0.1.53            *.*                    LISTEN
tcp      0      0   6.7.8.9.53        *.*             LISTEN
udp      0      0   10.1.2.3.123      *.*
udp      0      0   *.123                   *.*
udp      0      0   *.65510                 *.*
udp      0      0   10.1.2.3.53       *.*
```

Now we need to figure out what processes on the local system correspond to those services. Looking in the/etc/services file, we can determine what UNIX services usually reside on these ports. This does not mean that a service hasn't hijacked a well-known port specifically to hide its footprint, but it gives us a better idea of what could be running.

## Sample /etc/services Output

```
ftp             21/tcp          # File Transfer Protocol
ssh             22/tcp          # Secure Shell
ssh             22/udp
telnet          23/tcp
# 24 - private
smtp            25/tcp          mail
# 26 - unassigned
time            37/tcp          timserver
time            37/udp          timserver
```

Looking at the audited ports, we can determine what service is potentially being served and whether this service should be open to the outside world to function correctly. Recording the information for later use will help us determine problems in the future (see Table 8.1).

**Table 8.1** Partial Audited Ports

| Connection Type | IP + PORT | Possible Service |
|---|---|---|
| tcp | *.4000 | |
| tcp | *.80 | Web server |
| tcp | *.993 | IMAPS server |
| tcp | *.25 | SMTP server |
| tcp | *.22 | Secure shell |
| tcp | *.21 | FTP server |
| tcp | 6.7.8.9.53 | DNS server |

There is no way to know that this service is actually what is being used on the port without querying the system. We use another useful tool, *lsof*, to inspect each open port.

# Determining More Information with *lsof*

Query the kernel data structures to return what process is associated with each particular port. The command that allows us to do this deep digging is *lsof*. This is a tool for listing open files on a UNIX system. In the UNIX world, pretty much everything is a file, and so *lsof* will also list open ports, and tell you which process is holding that port open.

*lsof* also has many flags, but we will keep it to a few simple examples. We examine a UDP connection on port 53. From the following output, we can see that it is named, which serves DNS as expected.

```
slick: {38} lsof -n -i UDP:53
COMMAND  PID  USER    FD    TYPE     DEVICE SIZE/OFF NODE NAME
named    1177 named   20u   IPv4 0xc1f5f000     0t0  UDP 6.7.8.9:domain
named    1177 named   22u   IPv4 0xc1f5f0d8     0t0  UDP 127.0.0.1:domain
```

Checking UDP port 65510, we see that it is also named. This is most likely the rndc control channel.

```
slick: {39} lsof -n -i UDP:65510
COMMAND  PID  USER    FD    TYPE     DEVICE SIZE/OFF NODE NAME
named    1177 named   24u   IPv4 0xc1f5f1b0     0t0  UDP *:65510
```

Examining TCP port 4000 with *lsof*, we see that this is a user process. We should talk to user Paul and discover what the service running on port 4000 is.

```
slick: {40} lsof -n -i TCP:4000
COMMAND    PID USER   FD    TYPE     DEVICE SIZE/OFF NODE NAME
telnet   16192 paul    3u   IPv4 0xc2065b44     0t0  TCP 127.0.0.1:60977-
>127.0.0.1:4000 (ESTABLISHED)
razors   22997 paul    4u   IPv4 0xc1ff2ca8     0t0  TCP *:4000 (LISTEN)
razors   22997 paul   16u   IPv4 0xc206516c     0t0  TCP 127.0.0.1:4000-
>127.0.0.1:60977 (ESTABLISHED)
```

Using *netstat −an*, create a list of listening ports. With *lsof*, check each of these ports to figure out what processes are actually listening, and confirm that the services match the processes as expected. Figure out if those processes are needed, and either turn them off, or set up an ACL on your firewall to allow that service through.

# Using *netstat* on Windows XP

With Windows XP, there are additional flags −*b*, -*v*, and −*o* that will show additional information. −*b* displays the executable involved in creating the connection. In the following example, you can see that Apache is running on the local system and it has port 80 open. −*v* when used with −*b* will display the sequence of components that created the connection. −*o* will display the process that has the port open (see Table 8.2).

```
C:\Documents and Settings\jdavis>netstat -anvb


Active Connections
```

```
Proto   Local Address        Foreign Address        State        PID
TCP     0.0.0.0:80           0.0.0.0:0              LISTENING    1268
C:\WINDOWS\system32\imon.dll
C:\Program Files\Apache Software Foundation\Apache2.2\bin\libapr-1.dll
C:\Program Files\Apache Software Foundation\Apache2.2\bin\libhttpd.dll
C:\Program Files\Apache Software Foundation\Apache2.2\bin\httpd.exe
C:\WINDOWS\system32\kernel32.dll
[httpd.exe]


TCP     0.0.0.0:135          0.0.0.0:0              LISTENING    252
C:\WINDOWS\system32\imon.dll
C:\WINDOWS\system32\RPCRT4.dll
c:\windows\system32\rpcss.dll
C:\WINDOWS\system32\svchost.exe
C:\WINDOWS\system32\ADVAPI32.dll
[svchost.exe]
```

**Table 8.2** Common Ports Associated with Popular Services

| | | | | |
|---|---|---|---|---|
| 20 FTP data | 68 DHCP | 123 NTP | 161 SNMP | 993 SIMAP |
| 21 FTP | 79 Finger | 137 NetBIOS | 194 IRC | 995 SPOD |
| 22 SSH | 80 http | 138 NetBIOS | 220 IMAP3 | 1433 MS SQL Svr |
| 23 SMTP | 110 POP3 | 139 NetBIOS | 389 LDAP | 2049 NFS |
| 43 whois | 115 SFTP | 143 IMAP | 443 SSL | 5010 Yahoo! Messenger |
| 53 DNS | 119 NNTP | | 445 SMB | 5190 AOL Messenger |

Closing all ports on a system makes the system useless on a network. Anytime a browser is used, or e-mail, is read, traffic is tunneling across open ports. Protect ports by using a firewall.

**NOTE**

As an individual worrying about the needs of a SOHO's firewall infrastructure, also make sure you "AUDiT" your systems by following these basic security steps to better ensure the company's security:

Apply the latest patches to any systems. This could be as simple as turning on Windows Auto Updater, or downloading the latest security patches for your favorite Linux distribution.

Update any firmware on appliances you are running. This includes the firewall, the printer, the wireless router, and any other networked appliance if applicable.

Determine which data is critical data. Set up an automated process for backing up that data. Make sure to have copies of those backups in multiple locations.

Turn off unneeded services on your servers, and appliances.

---

Due to the small size of a SOHO, there is often a misconception that there is no need for a firewall, that the company is insignificant to any would-be crackers or script kiddies. Everyone connected to the Internet should be aware of the potential dangers inherent in the medium. Just as you don't leave your front door open for any would-be thieves, the "front door" and any other open access points into the SOHO should be protected. Every open port on an Internet-visible host is an open access point into your system.

By visiting random Web sites or opening dangerous e-mail, a user exposes himself to potential virus infections. Every time a user interacts with other systems on the Internet, his IP address is logged. Using this IP address, malicious users can hack in to the network using known vulnerabilities with standard applications. The malicious user will be looking for credit card numbers, bank accounts, or passwords to subscription Web sites, among other activities. For future abuse of the network, the malicious user could install a Trojan horse that would allow him to revisit the system later.

## NOTE

A firewall doesn't solve all the potential security risks. It is a perimeter security measure that will stop a percentage of attacks. It will help prevent systems from being zombiefied, and then attack other systems and networks.

Additionally, if a malicious user manages to crack a valid user's password, he can access the internal network with that user's credentials. Then it is just a matter of taking advantage of the vulnerabilities on the systems to get elevated privileges.

There are a number of Internet-ready devices on the market to address the needs of a SOHO firewall. Depending on the number of servers, and environment of the SOHO, it is also possible to install and manage a firewall built on top of NetBSD, Linux, or other familiar OSs. Some appliances come with VPN features for remote access to network and resources. By using one of the Internet-ready devices, you lower the bar to entry in getting your firewall set up and blocking the traffic needed.

This chapter and the case study explore the SOHO firewall. They examine the advantages, problems, and possible solutions, and then extend to design and implementation of a simple firewall solution that includes a VPN.

# Employing a Firewall in a SOHO Environment

Any system is vulnerable to infiltration, infection, and compromise in a network. Systems can be turned into zombie systems and then remotely controlled by the attacker, and used to attack other systems and networks. E-mail, future project plans, and competitive information could expose the company to an unknown degree of liability. This would brand a company to its customers, and potential customers as less than reliable. Do not be the low-hanging fruit that is easily snatched by an attacker. Safeguard yourself, company, brand name, and customers by seriously analyzing your security needs. As one aspect of a comprehensive security solution, the firewall protects the home and small office from external attack by only allowing authorized users and applications to gain access, while allowing network pass through for authentic data.

## Host-Based Firewall Solutions

Use a host-based firewall as one element in your defense in-depth strategy, but do not rely on that application alone to protect your data and systems. Zone Fire Alarm, Windows XP Internet Connection Firewall, and other host-based firewalls protect individual systems. Having a firewall that sits outside the system that runs the applications you are using means the firewall is protecting all your assets in a unified fashion, minimizing problems of application interference. If a host-based firewall solution crashes, it can take the system down with it. If an appliance crashes, only the appliance is affected. Finally, a host-based firewall uses the resources of your system to protect you. An appliance does not take away CPU, and memory resources, to protect access to resources.

Make sure to update all systems on a regular basis for patches, or updates to applications. Install antivirus software, antispyware software, and a software firewall to the host. This will harden the host considerably. Protect the system behind a firewall appliance. This creates two layers of protection for each system.

# Introducing the SOHO Firewall Case Study

The following case study illustrates the design of a simple SOHO firewall intended for the average user without much hands-on systems or security experience. The user is interested in securing his networked business assets, while allowing his family general use of the broadband network access. He wants to protect all systems from attack on the outside, and prevent dangerous outgoing traffic. He also wants to encourage external traffic to a personalized company Web site, and to interact with his customers with a personalized e-mail address. This section describes the user's current situation, the problem, the proposed solution, and the implementation of the solution.

## Assessing Needs

Tom Little is a sole trader in the home office space. He has set aside a room in his home as an office for tax deductions. He has two desktops in his office that are the core of his business infrastructure. One contains billing invoices, customer account information, and account management software that his wife uses in her role as secretary for the business. The other system includes all of his e-mail correspondence with vendors and customers, and his project plans for the various accounts he is currently working. Tom has a printer connected to his main work system that is shared. Tom has a networked 160GB Ethernet hard drive on which he stores backups of his files. He also uses his laptop connected to the network.

Tom's two children have their own PCs. Tom grants them Internet time while watching over them, allowing them to explore and broaden their knowledge in a supervised environment.

Tom currently has broadband access to his home. All his systems are connected via cat 5 cable from the DSL router provided by his ISP.

Tom wants to create a more segregated network. He also wants to move the kids' systems out of his office. He plans to implement a wireless solution to allow him to access his business resources remotely with his laptop. He also wants a personalized Web site and e-mail address so he can e-mail his clients from a @company.com address rather than the @yahoo.com address he has been using. Tom does a little investigation of the products available and realizes many of the solutions are well within his budget (see Figure 8.1).

**Figure 8.1** Tom's Current Network Topology

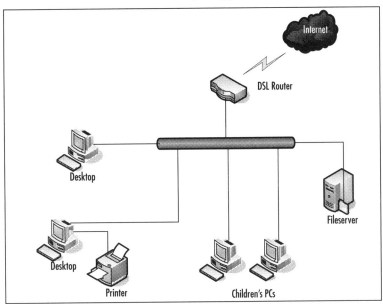

# Defining the Scope of the Case Study

Tom's challenge is that he needs to protect his company's assets without interfering with the running of his business, or his family's access to the Internet. All equipment he uses must be readily available, and inexpensive.

# Designing the SOHO Firewall

This section explains how Tom determines his needs, and plans, designs, and implements a firewall with VPN. Tom learns more about the available features, differences in firewall technology, and costs of different vendor solutions. Tom proceeds by:

- Determining the requirements.

- Analyzing the existing environment.

- Creating a preliminary design.

- Developing a detailed design.

- Implementing the firewall with VPN, and modifying the network.

Tom begins his investigation by:

- Determining the functional requirements of his family and business.
- Talking to local user groups for recommendations.
- Drawing a physical map of his home.

# Determining the Functional Requirements

The users of the network are Tom, his wife, and their children. Tom and his wife both use the Internet for recreational purposes, and for the home business. His children use the Internet for school projects, and gaming. Tom works with his family to define expectations of the home network.

## Determining the Needs of the Family

Although Tom's wife sees the benefits of separating the children's PCs from the home office, she is worried that she won't be able to get the access she needs to the Internet. She also doesn't see how she will be able to supervise the kids' browsing habits.

The kids aren't sure how they will be able to print their school papers, and are concerned that a firewall will adversely affect the bandwidth that is available for their gaming. They are excited about having the computers in their own space.

Tom plans to buy his wife a laptop to facilitate her working remotely and watching over the kids, and a printer for the kids to print their schoolwork. Tom is considering either running a Web server, and e-mail server locally, or paying for hosted services. This limits his budget for modifying his network to include a firewall to $200.

## Talking to Local User Groups

Tom has heard of the local user group BayLISA, a group of system and network administrators ranging in skill levels. The group meets once per month to discuss issues related to their professions. It can also be a social atmosphere. Tom decides to e-mail the group with a detailed list of his problem. He registers with the BayLISA group by sending an e-mail to the mailing list manager majordomo@baylisa.org with the body "subscribe baylisa." He follows the verification mechanism. After watching traffic for a few days, he submits his request.

Tom receives a number of responses from his query and notes all of the information. He categorizes product recommendations and experience separate from the general comments about his problems. Many users recommend he use a hosted site, as he does not have the expertise to manage a Web or e-mail server. He could accidentally expose all his private files with the Web server, and expose his business network to more vulnerabilities by having incorrectly configured servers, or nonpatched servers.

He is reassured that the process of setting up a wireless network is painless, so he can move his children's computers out of the office. Additionally, although he could set up a firewall on a Linux- or Unix-based system, he doesn't have the finances to spend on the hardware, or the expertise to support the OS, applications, and firewall tuning that would be required. He is better off purchasing a firewall appliance he just has to remember to update regularly.

# Creating a Site Survey of the Home

Based on his preliminary investigations and guidance from the user group, Tom comes up with the following design considerations:

- He needs to purchase a firewall with VPN capabilities.

- He needs to purchase a wireless access point to connect the laptops and children's systems.

- He needs to purchase two wireless cards for the children's desktop computers.

- He needs to invest in a hosted service plan that will allow him to have a personalized Web site, and e-mail address.

The next step is to analyze the existing environment. This includes:

- Identifying current technology options and constraints.

- Investigating the costs.

- Weighing the costs and benefits of each solution.

Tom determines that there is an equal amount of business, school, and entertainment content being used for the broadband access. He determines the second printer for the kids is a good choice, as it will limit the access the children need to the office network. He also determines that he does not want the Web server, and e-mail server, affecting the family's bandwidth, so he has decided to remotely host these services.

Tom's existing network is very simple. The broadband service is delivered to the house from a DSL modem. From the modem, the service is wired to the PCs via a cat 5 Ethernet cable. The printer is a peripheral of his main business PC via the PC's serial port. It is shared out to the local network. The networked disk is connected via a cat 5 Ethernet cable that sits

# Identifying Current Technology Options and Constraints

After talking to the local user groups, exploring the options available on the store shelves, and doing searches on the Internet using the words *SOHO firewall best practices*, Tom realizes he has several options in configuring his firewall.

Tom creates a list of the options available so he can better examine the choices he has to make. He fills out a list of important features, technical specs, and the pricing associated for each model. His list looks similar to Table 8.3 with a column for each solution.

**Table 8.3** Vendor Feature List

| Vendor | | Netgear |
|---|---|---|
| Product | Website | Prosafe FVS 114 |
| Features | | |
| | Firewall Type | Stateful Packet Inspection |
| | VPN Type | IPSec (ESP, AH), MD5, SHA-1, DES, 3DES, IKE, PKI, AES |
| | Intrusion Prevention | Y |
| | Intrusion Detection | Y |
| | Antivirus Protection | N |
| | Content Filtering | Some |
| | Update Mechanism | Via Web Browser |
| | Licensing | NA |
| | Management | Via Web Browser |
| Technical | | |
| | Processor | 200 MHz 32-bit RISC |
| | OS | |
| | Memory | 2MB Flash, 16MB SDRAM |
| | Ports | 4 |
| | Wireless | N |
| | Console/Modem | N |
| | Certifications | VPNC Compliant |
| Price | | $79.99 |

He then populates the list with the various vendor offerings he finds at the local Fry's Electronics, Best Buy, and online listings. He would prefer to purchase the hardware locally, because if it doesn't work, he wants the ease of returning it quickly. He quickly determines that the Linksys Wireless G Broadband Router at $59.99, and the Netgear Prosafe VPN Firewall model FVS 114 at $79.99 fit perfectly into his budget, and have all the functionality he needs.

# Implementing the SOHO Firewall

This section describes at a high level how Tom builds his firewall protected VPN accessible network. He approaches the implementation by:

- Assembling the network components.
- Installing the components.
- Testing the configuration from the various access points.

## Assembling the Components

Tom visits his local hardware store, Fry's Electronics, and picks up a Linksys Wireless G Broadband Router, a Netgear Prosafe VPN Firewall model FVS 114, and two ASUS 802.11b/g Wireless LAN cards. He already has the cat 5 cables that will connect his business systems to the firewall.

## Installing the Components

Tom is reasonably experienced with hardware installation, having previous upgraded the children's desktops. He feels comfortable having assembled the components, and tools, so he shouldn't have any problems putting the network together.

### Remote Virtual DMZ

After looking at the various options available for hosting his Web and e-mail servers, Tom chooses to go with the Yahoo! Small Businesses Services site. He has been using his @yahoo.com address for years and has not had any problems with it. He knows that Yahoo! has a reliable and redundant network due to the nature of its business. He is also impressed with their use of regular snapshots, and backups of Web sites. He feels secure in the knowledge that his Web site will not just disappear at a moment's notice. Tom searches for a descriptive domain name widgets.com at http://smallbusiness.yahoo.com/webhosting. He tries tomswidgets.com, and it is available. He clicks on **compare all plans**. Looking at the disk space and other features, he realizes that for now, he just needs the starter plan. He pays a $25 setup fee, and $11.95 for 5GB of space, 200 possible business e-mail addresses, and other features. He knows that it will take approximately 24 hours before his domain is live, but he is immediately able to begin editing the site. His wife logs in to the site, and replicates a brochure she made for the company using the site builder tools.

He is investing in a solution that means he doesn't have to rely on understanding all the technical decisions on how to build a reliable, fault-tolerant mail and Web server solution, and manage the spam and anti-virus protection for his inbound and outbound e-mail. For now, the space will just hold his Widget catalog, and contact information but his wife has many creative ideas on how to improve the site.

This solution has created a remote virtual DMZ that separates his Web server and mail server from his home systems. It maximizes his time in not having to manage servers that would also consume the bandwidth into his home.

## Installing the Wireless Cards

Tom puts on an antistatic wristband before he opens the children's PCs. He unplugs the power, and all of the cables, and sets the systems on a flat working surface. He opens each PC in turn, attaching the wristband to the metal frame of the computer. He unscrews the screw holding the metal guard in place in front of the open PCI slot. He inserts one of the cards carefully, pushing until he feels the card firmly click into place. He repeats the procedure on the second computer. Tom closes each system, noting the MAC address for each card. He powers the systems back on after plugging them in. The Add New Hardware wizard appears, and Tom follows the instructions for installing the software for the cards. He confirms that the MAC addresses are what he expects by opening a command window with **Start | Run | command**. He types **ipconfig /all** and sees

```
Ethernet adapter Wireless Network Connection:


        Media State . . . . . . . . . . . : Media disconnected
        Description . . . . . . . . . . . : ASUS 802.11b/g Wireless LAN Card
        Physical Address. . . . . . . . . : 00-11-E6-AB-24-9C
```

He repeats this process on the second computer. While he is noting down MAC addresses, he checks the two laptops to confirm their addresses.

## Configuring the Wireless Router

Tom plugs in the wireless router into the DSL modem. He follows the instructions for connecting to the wireless router that came with the packaging. He first sets the wireless network name to WiHoInc and disables the SSID broadcast. According to the user group postings, this makes it less likely that individuals trolling for wireless access will discover his wireless network.

> **NOTE**
>
> The default username and password for the wireless router is blank username, and admin for the password. Change this as soon after the basic configuration.

He enables WPA Pre-Shared key, chooses AES for encryption, and creates a reasonable length shared key "Widgets for the Win." This is a pass phrase that will be easy for him to remember, but not easy for others to take advantage of. He records it in his PDA device in an encrypted format where he keeps the rest of his passwords that access his important data.

He enables MAC filtering, which will allow him to permit only PCs listed to access the wireless network. He edits the MAC filter address and adds his children's PCs, and the two laptops.

He clicks on the Security tab, and enables the firewall protection. Although this is not Tom's main firewall, this will protect his laptop, and kids' systems from some attacks. He makes sure Block Anonymous Internet requests is enabled. He also filters multicast, and IDENT requests. He does not filter Internet NAT redirection.

He logs in to each of the children's PCs, and the laptops, and configures them to connect to the WiHoInc network. After confirming that the connections work, he disassembles and reassembles the children's PCs in their rooms. He could configure the wireless firewall to only allow network traffic at certain times of day to prevent his children from browsing the network while he or his wife is not around, but he feels they will follow the rules for using the Internet. Additionally, he has logging turned on so he knows exactly where the systems are browsing. He also has the capability of enabling blocking of specific sites, or keywords. The firewall on the wireless appliance is limited, so in the future he may pick up another firewall appliance to put between the network router and the wireless appliance.

## Configuring the Firewall with VPN Router

Tom connects a cat 5 Ethernet cable from the wireless router to his firewall. He turns on the firewall. He then connects his computer and printer network ports to the firewall Ethernet ports. He checks that the lights for each of the ports are showing up as connected.

**NOTE**

The firewall separates the internal network from the other networks, keeping the interior of the network the most secure. If the wireless network is compromised, the servers on the internal network are not accessible.

He browses to 192.168.0.1 (the default IP address for this particular appliance). He accepts all the defaults allowing the wireless router to give the firewall a DHCP address, and let the firewall give his internal systems their own IP addresses.

**NOTE**

The default username and password for the firewall is admin, and password. Change this soon after the basic configuration.

Tom checks the Basic Settings. He can safely accept this basic configuration from the initial setup.

He then checks logging, and checks the All Websites and news groups visited, All incoming TCP/UDP/ICMP traffic, All Outgoing TCP/UDP/ICMP traffic, Other IP traffic, and Connections to the Web based interface of this Router, as he wants to get as much information as possible about what is happening in his internal network. Later, after he feels comfortable with what is normal behavior on his systems, he might turn off some of the logging so it is not as comprehensive. Tom doesn't worry about the syslog server configuration, as he does not have a logging infrastructure. For now, Tom isn't going to e-mail the logs to himself; instead, he chooses to look at them and clear them manually.

The logging is now comprehensive. The highlighted portion of the log in Figure 8.2 shows Tom's access to the Administrator Interface.

On the Rules tab, Tom sees that he can configure specific rules to allow and disallow services, and actions from happening. Tom plans to watch his log for a few days and determine what if anything he needs to tune.

Tom invested in a solution that would give him VPN functionality. This allows him to connect his laptop remotely to the internal system so he can print, or access records from his porch or anywhere in his house. Now that he has the basic firewall configured, he can configure the VPN access. He clicks on the VPN wizard, and gives the connection a name. He reuses his pre-shared key, and chooses remote VPN client.

**Figure 8.2** Administrator Access Logged

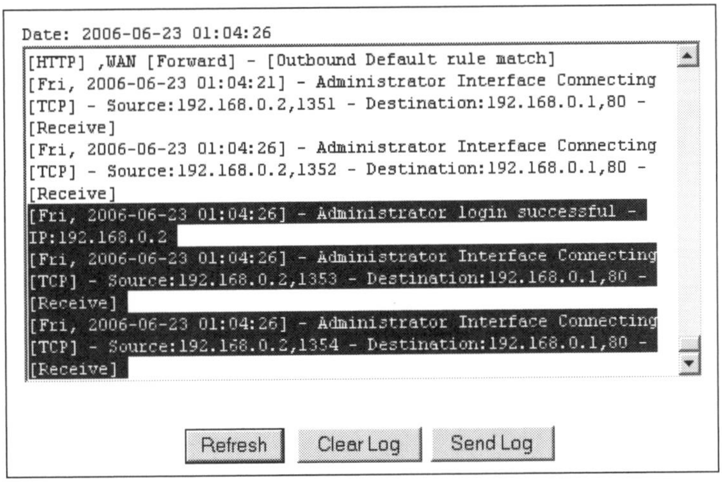

```
Date: 2006-06-23 01:04:26
[HTTP] ,WAN [Forward] - [Outbound Default rule match]
[Fri, 2006-06-23 01:04:21] - Administrator Interface Connecting
[TCP] - Source:192.168.0.2,1351 - Destination:192.168.0.1,80 -
[Receive]
[Fri, 2006-06-23 01:04:26] - Administrator Interface Connecting
[TCP] - Source:192.168.0.2,1352 - Destination:192.168.0.1,80 -
[Receive]
[Fri, 2006-06-23 01:04:26] - Administrator login successful -
IP:192.168.0.2
[Fri, 2006-06-23 01:04:26] - Administrator Interface Connecting
[TCP] - Source:192.168.0.2,1353 - Destination:192.168.0.1,80 -
[Receive]
[Fri, 2006-06-23 01:04:26] - Administrator Interface Connecting
[TCP] - Source:192.168.0.2,1354 - Destination:192.168.0.1,80 -
[Receive]
```

```
Refresh    Clear Log    Send Log
```

He downloads the Netgear VPN client software so he can use IPSec to connect to the VPN. Optionally, he could connect direct to another VPN firewall via his firewall if he were to bring on board a remote partner using this same VPN wizard setting on the VPN firewall.

# Testing the Configuration from Various Access Points

Tom first checks that his children can access the Internet. The speeds appear to be fine connecting to www.yahoo.com. He next tries to access his office printer, or his office server. Both appear to be inaccessible to his children.

Next, Tom checks that he has access to the Internet on his laptop. He knows he can browse the Web from his children's PCs, so he is not expecting any problems. He is not disappointed—the wireless works as expected. He turns on the VPN tunnel by clicking on the application software icon. He now has access to the printer, and servers, that are sitting in his office. He confirms this by accessing the printer and file shares available from his server.

Finally, Tom checks that his office servers have the access required to function within the scope of his business needs. He accesses the widget production site to download costs of materials. The connection works. He can also print from both systems, and access his backup file server. He is satisfied that his network is working the way he expects it to.

# Summary

A firewall acts as a border guard, filtering packets by application proxy, packet filtering, or state inspection. Tom's final network topology is comprehensive. He has an internal DMZ that creates an untrusted network that is still protected within his network, an external virtual DMZ via the hosted service, and an internal protected network behind the firewall (Figure 8.3).

**Figure 8.3** Tom's Network with Firewall

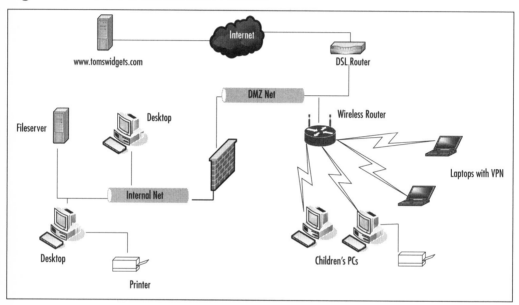

Choose the right firewall for your needs. If you don't have GB connection, 1000Mbps is not useful. 10/100 is sufficient. DHCP, decent management GUI for managing the firewall, wireless access point, virtual private network, along with the type of filters, and the mechanism of firewalling are all aspects you need to analyze to determine what will be the most cost effective with feature tradeoffs. Don't implement services you won't use.

# Solutions Fast Track

## Introducing the SOHO Firewall Case Study

☑ Security is an important function that SOHO users must address as they connect to the intranet.

☑ Protection of networked assets can be seen as securing your house on a virtual level.

☑ End services you do not need so you do not have open ports on your system that could be used to infiltrate your network. Use *netstat* to determine what services are running on which ports.

## Designing the SOHO Firewall

☑ Gaming, education, and business interactions are all components of the functional requirements.

☑ In the preliminary design, the user opts for a remote service hosting his Web and e-mail, a firewall, and wireless router.

## Implementing the SOHO Firewall

☑ In the detailed design, the user assembles the components, installs the hardware, configures the software, and tests access points.

☑ Configuration includes examining the default settings, enabling logging, and the VPN. Further modifications to the firewall can be enabled after examining typical usage from the logs.

☑ Depending on the functional requirements, there are a number of solutions that range in price from $50 to $600 for small businesses, and home office users.

☑ Change default passwords for all appliances.

# Frequently Asked Questions

The following Frequently Asked Questions, answered by the authors of this book, are designed to both measure your understanding of the concepts presented in this chapter and to assist you with real-life implementation of these concepts. To have your questions about this chapter answered by the author, browse to **www.syngress.com/solutions** and click on the **"Ask the Author"** form.

**Q:** How do I maintain an out-of-the-box solution firewall?

**A:** Check the Web site for the manufacturer of the Web site. Sign up for any mailing lists, and make sure to install any firmware patches that are recommended.

**Q:** One of my applications isn't working right. How do I make it work?

**A:** First, take the firewall out of the picture. Does it work now? If so, start working basic principles. Turn on the highest level logging on the firewall. Does it show in the logging that the connection is being refused? If so, configure a rule in the rule set to match that setting. You can figure out what settings are needed using *netstat* on the system that is running the application to see what ports it is looking for. If you aren't seeing a connection refused in the logs, check to see if you see any problems reported with this particular application and your chosen appliance. Finally, if all else fails, and you can't find the information on your own, contact the manufacturer for support. By going through these steps first, you can show that you have made a diligent effort to solve your own problem, and the support staff will be more attentive hearing the steps you have taken.

**Q:** If it doesn't work, whom do I talk to?

**A:** Contact support for the manufacturer. Check the documentation that came with the appliance, and the vendor's Web site. It is recommended to check the vendor's Web site prior to purchasing a solution to gauge the support level available. Check your favorite mailing lists, baylisa@baylisa.org, and sage-members@sage.org. Local Linux user group mailing lists like svlug@svlug.org can generally be helpful, or security mailing lists.

**Q:** What is the cost of the out-of-the-box solution?

**A:** This case study showed a solution that cost $130 for the wireless and firewall appliances, and then a Web services fee of $12 per month to host the Web site. Depending on the solutions you choose, you may spend less or more based on the functionality, and vendor.

# Chapter 9

# Medium Business (<2000 People)

## Solutions in this chapter:

- **Mapping Your Systems**

- **Improving Accountability with Identity Management**

- **Lowering Risks with Application Layer Filtering**

☑ Summary

☑ Solutions Fast Track

☑ Frequently Asked Questions

# Introduction

Added security concerns greet all growing organizations. Small organizations often have to rely on user pragmatism to get by. The increased numbers of users, workstations, servers, and network appliances can turn the enforcement of most security policies into a headache for the most experienced security professionals. A simple solution is to stick to the trusted "principle of least privilege," which dictates that only the lowest possible permissions be granted.

There are plenty of security appliances, software applications, and services that allow you to define and apply granular security policies. Unfortunately, those tools consume budgets quickly, thus leaving some areas of the infrastructure well protected and other areas sorely lacking security.

As a security professional, your job is to know the types of application traffic running on your systems, and to make every effort to minimize any identifiable risks. Dealing with different types of risks requires varying amounts of time and effort. You must be able to identify, prioritize, and handle risks. Where possible, you should apply suitable controls to help lower any potential damage to your organization, its data, and its employees. You must work closely with other managers and business owners to ensure that each different application is afforded the appropriate security budget, which will ultimately translate into your organization's enforcement and mitigation tools.

Firewall vulnerabilities are being exploited at the application layer; when new applications appear, new vulnerabilities appear. Allowing a new application past your firewalls without fully considering the consequences can lead to gaping holes in your defenses.

Security products used to be in niche areas. To address several security requirements, you had to have several separate products. These days, many security product manufacturer's combine various selections of these technologies into bigger, more feature-rich products (e.g., the recent trend by several firewall manufacturers to include anti-virus engines with their products.) Secure Computing, Fortinet, Cisco, and Checkpoint are among the list of manufacturer's that are now integrating anti-virus and other content-filtering technologies into their products. The idea of an all-in-one security appliance is appealing to cost-conscious organizations, because it allows them to apply basic levels of security to combat many types of threats without having to add multiple individual products (e.g., a firewall that allows embedded anti-virus scanning might offset the need for a specialist anti-virus or content-filtering server.) The down side to this approach is that these general-purpose devices rarely work well and do not provide the best solutions to defend against a specific type of threat. As organizations grow, they often replace equipment and deploy new applications to meet new business demands. Every organization is different and a security environment and policy that works for one organization may not work for another.

Many security professionals find that security projects do not always need a new implementation; they often inherit someone else's infrastructure. Occasionally, this infrastructure is well-secured and well-documented; however, this utopian vision is not always the case. Reconnaissance is usually required before you can successfully start implementing or improving security without inadvertently breaking mission-critical applications.

This chapter contains a case study of a medium-size business called the "Hot Cash Corporation," a financial products and services provider. It examines the issues faced by the Hot Cash Corporation as they expand their business and encounter limitations of their incumbent firewall environment. It also shows the areas where firewall and Demilitarized Zone (DMZ) design techniques can be applied throughout your organization to provide a holistic approach to network security.

# Mapping Your Systems

Mapping your systems and adding AAA to bolster security will certainly improve things but they are not the only measures that can be taken to improve security. This section briefly suggests some other security improvements that may be used.

## Ask Someone

You have just started to work for Hot Cash Corporation as their new information security manager. Your predecessor left in a hurry and did not leave much documentation. You ask your new colleagues for information about the company's offices and the network infrastructure and security tools they use.

You quickly learn that Hot Cash Corporation has offices located in Seattle, New York, and Dallas. The user population at headquarters is made up of:

- 25 management and office administrators,
- 5 Web developers,
- 15 IT, network, and security staff
- 10 call center supervisors
- 450 call center agents
- 10 business development, innovation, and partner program staff

The user populations at the New York and Dallas sites are:

- 10 managers and office administrators
- 5 call center supervisors
- 200 call center agents
- 5 business development, innovation, and partner program staff
- 3 local IT staff

In addition, Hot Cash Corporation has a contract with "Big Foot Sales" that effectively adds an additional 300 door-to-door sales specialists to the Hot Cash Corporation workforce. These contract employees do not have Hot Cash Corporation e-mail addresses; they access company Web sites and databases using a variety of handheld wireless Internet devices (not managed by Hot Cash Corporation).

---

**TIP**

If you are new to a site or organization, one of the quickest ways to gather information is to talk to the people who work there. Never over-estimate people's ability to keep good documentation; there are often details about applications or projects that never make it onto paper.

---

Talking to your technical colleagues, you find out that each office is connected via a fully meshed Frame Relay network. Each office operates its own local server for e-mail, file, and print applications. At the core of the organization's infrastructure are a number of database applications that are hosted on two database server clusters and hold customer, product, and financial information. The database server clusters replicate data between one another.

The company's only Internet connection is located at their headquarters in Seattle. This high-speed connection is used to provide company-wide e-mail and to update the company Web site, which is located on a DMZ network. The Web site is hosted on a server running the Linux Operating System (OS) (*www.linux.org*) with Apache Web server software (*www.apache.org*). The firewall has been configured to only allow encrypted connections using Secure Sockets Layer (SSL) to the Web server. The server is allowed to communicate with internal database servers, which allows the company to provide basic application access to their mobile sales force. These databases are hosted at the Seattle site.

The Hot Cash Corporation currently operates a Cisco PIX515E firewall appliance. The current firewall policy allows all internal users to access a limited number of "approved" Internet sites. The list of approved sites is maintained by manually editing an associated "trusted sites" object group on the firewall, which is used to limit access to external and potentially damaging content sources. Your colleagues inform you that one of the sites on the trusted list was hacked last month. They share your concern that without an application layer filter, the hacked Web site may have been accessed by users, which in turn may have resulted in a security breach of the Hot Cash Corporation.

## Are You Owned?

### You Can Never Be Too Careful

The Hot Cash Corporation does not have application-level inspection or content filtering for trusted Web sites. In this situation, an external trusted Web site may affect the company's security. Even if they used traditional white list- or black list-based Uniform Resource Locator (URL) filtering products, the company cannot assume that a trusted Web site will be safe. If an attacker determines one of the Web sites on the trusted Access Control List (ACL) and plants a Trojan horse on that external Web site, the firewall and its ACL may be powerless to stop it. Deploying a system to authenticate users before granting access to this external site does not guarantee that an unwanted Trojan horse file will be blocked.

It always makes sense to have a backup plan for your security mechanisms. If an authenticated firewall connection with a strict white-list ACL fails to block malicious content, you need to ask yourself if there is some other method of protection. Are anti-virus and anti-spyware applications for the internal hosts acceptable? Will an aggressive software update and maintenance policy help combat zero-day or zero-hour attacks?

You can see that there is almost always another angle from which your resources are vulnerable. Because attackers never stop looking for new vulnerabilities, you should never assume that your resources are fully secure.

The Hot Cash Corporation has configured a Microsoft Exchange 2003 server in their DMZ, and has dedicated Microsoft Exchange 2003 servers at each of the company's sites. The Microsoft Exchange server in the DMZ has been configured to accept and deliver Simple Mail Transfer Protocol (SMTP) e-mail through the Internet. It has also been set up to filter Unsolicited Commercial E-mail (UCE) using the server's native filtering features. Positioning a separate Exchange server on the DMZ reduces the risk of an Internet-based attacker gaining direct access to an internal resource, such as the Exchange server on the internal Local Area Network (LAN).

Hot Cash Corporation administrators are concerned about the number of previously reported vulnerabilities on the Microsoft Internet Information Server (IIS) Web server, so they have opted to use the free open source Apache Web server instead. This policy decision means that the company is not in a position to deploy Outlook Web Access, Microsoft's Web-based e-mail client.

Web-based e-mail is provided using SquirrelMail, a Web-based e-mail client that runs on Linux platforms with Apache Web servers. Users' mailboxes are located on internal e-mail servers. SquirrelMail is permitted to communicate with these e-mail servers using Internet Message Access Protocol (IMAP), the Internet standard protocol for e-mail.

Internal hosts run a variety of versions of the Microsoft Windows OS, and are configured with a centrally managed anti-virus product. Updates for the anti-virus product are pushed to protected hosts every eight hours at staggered intervals. OS patches are not handled consistently. In some cases, automatic updates are configured to be downloaded and applied on a daily basis. Some servers and some older hosts do not automatically download and install patches, because the company fears that untested patches may result in mission critical applications.

The LANs are maintained across multiple Cisco Catalyst 6500 switches, which typically contain three or more 48-port fast Ethernet modules, redundant power supplies, and redundant layer 3 management cards. The network has been segmented into logical divisions called Virtual LANs (VLANs), which are connected to one another using network devices such as firewalls and layer 3 modules. The network layer connections ensure that traffic between VLANs is routed through the gateway devices where traffic is filtered, authenticated, or throttled for Quality Of Service (QOS). There is no port authentication or other port security mechanisms configured on any of the internal switch ports.

Cisco 2611 routers are used to interconnect the offices, and a Cisco 1800 series router is used to connect to the Internet provider. The Wide Area Network (WAN) routers are configured in a full mesh topology; the ACLs have been used on the routers to block unnecessary inter-site traffic; and local administrator usernames and passwords have been configured on the routers. Information Technology (IT) staff admit that the router, switch, and firewall passwords have not been changed in two years.

Simple Network Management Protocol (SNMP) is used to poll network devices and servers for utilization information. Network devices use a standards-based protocol called syslog to transmit log information to a site-specific log server. Part of the company's security policy states that there be a regular inspection of logs for anomalies. Although this task has been handled manually to date, the administrator responsible finds it tiresome and admits that this task often gets neglected.

Once you have interviewed all of the necessary people, you should have a basic idea of your organization's geography, political divisions, and technical components. Figure 9.1 summarizes the information gathered to date.

**Figure 9.1** Overview of Network Topology

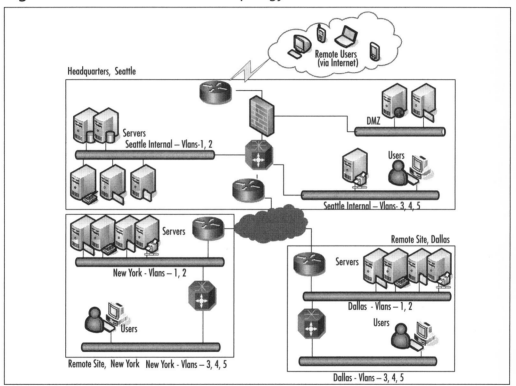

# Charting Cables

The most accurate picture of your network topology will come from an audit of your data cables and the devices they are plugged into. Ideally you should be able to account for every data cable, whether a telephone cable connected to a modem or a gigabit Ethernet cable connected to a server. By doing this, you can quickly identify anomalies such as unused legacy systems or unauthorized physical connections. Discovering and subsequently removing unused legacy systems can free up rack space, power outlets, and network connection points. The discovery and removal of unauthorized hosts is a sign that your security regime is working. You explain this auditing procedure to your colleagues and all agree that one IT staff member at each site will be responsible for cataloging all of the data cables in the patch panels and switches at that site. Your team has also agreed to log all of their work into the company's database server. The cable information will be stored in a separate table; however, hopefully this information can eventually be joined to the hardware inventory.

# IP Addressing and VLANs

Larger networks tend to use VLANs to compartmentalize sections of the network. VLANs are groups of switch ports that are virtually separated from the other ports on the same switch, which allows discrete groups of user hosts or servers to co-exist on the same switch equipment without affecting each other's network traffic. VLANs separate the network at the data link layer of the Open Systems Interconnection (OSI) network model. Routers, firewalls, and other network layer gateways can be used to join VLANs at the network layer. Connecting VLANs at the network layer causes inter-VLAN traffic to be routed. Routed traffic must pass through a gateway to get from a host in one VLAN to a host in another. Because routed networks require different network address ranges on each side of a gateway, it is common to see Internet Protocol (IP) subnets allocated to reflect VLAN topologies.

Hot Cash Corporation has allocated subnets and VLANs based on geography, resource type, and user population. In their Seattle office, they have allocated VLANs 1 and 2 to servers. The subnets allocated use */24*, network masks, which means there are approximately 500 IP addresses available for the servers in Seattle (not including those in the DMZ VLAN). Several subnets and VLANs have been allocated for users, each containing a discrete VLAN. Each user group also has its own subnet and VLANs. User groups with more than 120 users have been splintered into smaller groups based on where they are located in the office building. There are approximately 100 call center agents per floor. To simplify administration, a central DHCP server on each site is used to automatically assign IP addresses. Since there are different subnets assigned to each VLAN, the Dynamic Host Configuration Protocol (DHCP) server has been configured to assign the appropriate addresses to each VLAN.

# Software Tools

Once you have a good idea of where the main components of the organization are, you need to get more accurate details. Building a picture of how your systems interoperate will enable you to properly scrutinize change requests from a security perspective.

# OS Tools

There are other ways to gather host information. The troubleshooting utilities that are included with most OSs can be used to gather information. Although these utilities may vary slightly between platforms, there are several that are commonly available on default installations of popular OSs. Table 9.1 includes some examples.

**Table 9.1** Utilities for Gathering Detailed Host Information

| Utility Name | OS | Function |
| --- | --- | --- |
| arp | Windows & UNIX/Linux | Resolves interface hardware addresses from IP addresses |
| ping | Windows & UNIX/Linux | Tests connectivity to an IP address |
| traceroute | UNIX/Linux | Determines network path between two hosts |
| tracert | Windows | Similar to traceroute on UNIX/Linux |
| telnet | Windows & UNIX/Linux | Provides a remote command line interface (CLI) to a server |
| nslookup | Windows & UNIX/Linux | Translates IP addresses to host-names and back |
| snoop | Solaris (UNIX) | Command-line packet capture and analysis |

## *Address Resolution Protocol (ARP)*

Most modern LAN switches have features that allow you to enumerate all Media Access Control (MAC) addresses that are currently visible to the switch. Many switches also provide the ability to search for a MAC address and display the port and VLAN on the switch where the MAC address is visible. This allows you to correlate the information gathered in your cable database or hardware inventory.

If MAC addresses are listed on your switch but do not appear in your inventory, find the switch port in question and trace the cable until you find the unknown host. There may be some exceptions where valid virtual MAC addresses are not listed in the hardware inventories (e.g., Virtual Router Redundancy Protocol [VRRP] is commonly used as a high availability mechanism, and uses a virtual MAC address). A Cisco Catalyst 6500 switch running Cisco Internetworking Operation System (IOS) accepts the **show mac-address-table** command (see Figure 9.2).

**Figure 9.2** Displaying the MAC Address Table on a Cisco Catalyst 6500 Switch

```
Switch#show mac-address-table
          Mac Address Table
-------------------------------------------
Vlan    Mac Address       Type        Ports
----    -----------       --------    -----
 All    000e.83e9.47c0    STATIC      CPU
 All    0100.0ccc.cccc    STATIC      CPU
 All    0100.0ccc.cccd    STATIC      CPU
 All    0100.0cdd.dddd    STATIC      CPU
  1     0000.0c07.ac01    DYNAMIC     Fa0/1
  1     000a.5e1f.f443    DYNAMIC     Fa0/17
Total Mac Addresses for this criterion: 6
```

You can use the **ARP** command on routers or servers to display the ARP table, which consists of recently seen MAC addresses within the same broadcast domain or VLAN. On Cisco routers, the command to display the ARP table is **show arp** (see Figure 9.3), and on Microsoft Windows servers, the command is **arp –a** (see Figure 9.4).

**Figure 9.3** Displaying the ARP Table on a Cisco Router

```
router2#show arp
Protocol  Address         Age (min)  Hardware Addr   Type   Interface
Internet  192.168.103.41          0  00e0.299e.8c93  ARPA   Ethernet0
Internet  192.168.103.33          -  0000.0c07.ac01  ARPA   Ethernet0
Internet  192.168.103.200         -  0000.0c07.ac01  ARPA   Ethernet0
Internet  192.168.103.199         0  000e.83e9.47c0  ARPA   Ethernet0
```

**Figure 9.4** Displaying the ARP Table on a Windows Server

```
C:\>arp –a

Interface: 192.168.1.66 --- 0x10003
  Internet Address      Physical Address      Type
  192.168.1.3           00-01-02-f1-4c-2f     dynamic
  192.168.1.254         00-0f-cc-49-6d-c0     dynamic
```

```
Interface: 192.168.103.111 --- 0x10004
  Internet Address      Physical Address       Type
  192.168.103.41        00-e0-29-9e-8c-93      dynamic
  192.168.103.199       00-0e-83-e9-47-c0      dynamic
```

## Ping

Ping is a simple utility that is included with almost all OSs. Much like sonar, ping sends out a signal called an "echo request" and listens for an "echo response." Many implementations of ping, including the one shipped with Microsoft Windows, record the time taken to hear the "echo response," which is often used as a basic test for network latency.

Using ping on its own as a method for host discovery is not very productive, due to the fact that many host systems are equipped with personal firewalls that filter ping traffic. If traffic is filtered, the request may not be processed by the intended target and, therefore, a response is not sent. Similarly, a host-based personal firewall may have been configured to block the ping responses.

If pinging a host or range of hosts does not yield any responses and you are pinging an IP address within the same IP subnet, don't forget to check your ARP table. Even hosts with a personal firewall installed are likely to yield ARP responses and populate the ARP table of the host you run the ping from.

## Traceroute

Traceroute is a path discovery tool that is used to determine the routed path between source and destination IP addresses. If you are unfamiliar with a network topology, traceroute can be used to discover layer 3 gateways such as routers or layer 3 switches.

Advanced options for the **traceroute** command include the ability to specify a path by way of source routing.

## Nslookup

The nslookup utility is used to convert IP addresses into hostnames or hostnames into IP addresses. The utility depends on Domain Name Services (DNS) having been configured correctly. In environments where DNS has been well maintained, you will find it easy to determine server or workstation names based on IP addresses.

## *Telnet*

Although telnet is typically thought of as a terminal-style application for use with CLIs and text-based servers, it can also be used to test the availability of services on remote hosts (e.g., if you telnet to a remote host using port 80 instead of the default telnet port 23, you will connect to the Web server Hypertext Transfer Protocol [HTTP] service on that host. In this case, you will need to understand the target's service protocol commands). Connecting to a HTTP port is unlikely to result in a login or password prompt that you would expect to see when using telnet. Instead you can enter a HTTP-style command such as:

```
GET http://192.168.1.66/ HTTP/1.0
```

If you are connected to a Web server service, you should receive a response that details the Web server type and version (contained in the HTTP header at the start of the server's response).

Most Transmission Control Protocol (TCP)-based services accept connections from telnet clients. Knowing which protocol to use with a particular target is based on the information learned from the "services" file, or from simple trial and error. (The "services" file on Windows is located in the */windows/system32/drivers/etc* or */winnt/system32/drivers/etc* folder.)

Many services such as Internet e-mail (Post Office Protocol version 3 [POP3] or SMTP) display a telltale banner when you connect to them.

## *Windows Specific Tools*

The **nbtstat** command allows you to associate machine and user names with an IP address. Use **nbtstat** with no command-line options to get syntax and options help.

**Netstat** is a tool that is included on many host systems, including most versions of Windows and UNIX. Netstat allows you to view information related to established connections or applications that are waiting for network connections on a given host. Basic netstat commands are **netstat –a** and **netstat –r**. The **–a** option displays all network connections and listening services on the host that is being used, and the **–r** option displays the routing table for the host that it's running from.

Microsoft Windows netstat has changed recently. Windows XP and Windows Server 2003 both include a version of netstat that allows **–b** and **–v** options. Typing **netstat –abv** will display all connections or listening applications on your host, along with the application files used to generate the connection or listening process.

Network Monitor is a protocol analyzer (installed from the Windows installation media) that captures network traffic and translates it into a readable format. There are two versions of Network Monitor available. The Windows version is free but limited to capturing packets where the local host is marked as the source or the destination. The more advanced version of Network Monitor is included in Microsoft Systems Management Server. The advanced version operates in promiscuous mode, allowing it to capture packets for other network hosts.

> **NOTE**
>
> Some organizations have strict change control policies. In those cases, you may be faced with restrictions when installing software on those systems that are considered "stable" or "in production." If you are unable to install third-party software, you may still be able to use the tools that are installed by default with these systems.

## UNIX Specific Tools

Many of the more versatile security, auditing, and mapping tools available for the Windows platform started life on UNIX platforms. Although most of the popular tools are now multi-platform, there are still some tools that can be found on UNIX systems by default, including the following:

- **snoop** A utility that comes with Sun Microsystems' Solaris OS. Snoop is a command-line utility that offers packet capture and analysis features much the same way Network Monitor does on Windows platforms, but without the graphical interface.

- **rarp** (Reverse Address Resolution Protocol) is used to manipulate a system's rarp table. Rarp provides an IP address from the MAC address resolution, and arp resolves MAC addresses from IP addresses. Arp is available on Windows and UNIX systems. Rarp is not shipped with any versions of Windows.

## Freeware Third-party Tools

Not surprisingly, there are a number of applications that make the task of identifying hosts easier. These applications range from freeware to commercial "enterprise" products. Table 9.2 includes some examples of freeware applications that can help you audit your networks with a view to establishing a baseline for "normal" connections and activity.

**Table 9.2** Utilities for Identifying Hosts

| Utility Name | OS | Function |
| --- | --- | --- |
| TCPView | Windows | Shows applications associated with network traffic |
| Nmap | Windows & UNIX/Linux | Network mapper |
| Kiwi CatTools | Windows | Network device administration and reporting |
| Ntop | Windows & UNIX/Linux | Traffic reporting based on flow statistics |
| Tcpdump | UNIX/Linux | Command-line packet capture and protocol analysis |
| WinDump | Windows | Windows implementation of tcpdump |
| Wireshark | Windows & UNIX/Linux | Protocol Analyzer (formerly known as Ethereal) |
| IPTraf | Linux | IP Traffic statistics |
| EtherApe | UNIX/Linux | IP Traffic statistics |
| Nessus | Windows & UNIX/Linux | Network vulnerability scanner |
| Netcat | Windows & UNIX/Linux | General-purpose network utility |

## TCPView

In the previous section, you saw how the **netstat** command lists all open or listening connections on your hosts. In older versions of Microsoft Windows you may find that the options used to display process ID or associated application files using the **netstat** command are unavailable. A freeware Graphical User Interface (GUI)-based utility called TCPView is available from *www.sysinternals.com*.

TCPView provides similar functions to the latest versions of Microsoft's netstat implementation (see Figure 9.)

## Nmap

According to the product's home page, Nmap (Network Mapper) is a free open-source utility for network exploration and security auditing. This application allows you to quickly determine the:

- Network ranges for live IP addresses

- Individual hosts for active service ports
- Host OS versions
- Network application versions
- Types of firewalls

The Hot Cash Corporation is primarily based on Microsoft Windows OSs. Visit the Nmap Web site (www.insecure.org/nmap/download.html) for downloads and documentation.

Nmap is a command-line tool. Even though there are freeware graphical front ends available, it is recommended that you learn to use the command-line options, which will allow you to stack Nmap scans into batch files or Windows scripting files. To start Nmap, run the **nmap** command and add a network range or host IP address at the end of the command line.

To scan for IP addresses on subnet range 192.168.1.0/24, use the **nmap –sP 192.168.1.0/24** command.

Sample output from this command shows that three IP addresses are listed (see Figures 9.5 and 9.6). In this example, 192.168.1.3 does not show a corresponding MAC address, because it is the host you are performing the scan from.

**Figure 9.5** Output From an Nmap Scan to Discover Hosts

```
C:\WINDOWS\system32\cmd.exe

C:\Program Files\Nmap>nmap -sP 192.168.1.0/24

Starting Nmap 4.10 ( http://www.insecure.org/nmap ) at 2006-06-20 21:21 GMT Dayl
ight Time
Host 192.168.1.3 appears to be up.
Host 192.168.1.66 appears to be up.
MAC Address: 00:0C:F6:1B:5E:F7 (Sitecom Europe BV)
Host 192.168.1.254 appears to be up.
MAC Address: 00:0F:CC:49:6D:C0 (Netopia)
Nmap finished: 256 IP addresses (3 hosts up) scanned in 17.312 seconds

C:\Program Files\Nmap>

C:\Program Files\Nmap>

C:\Program Files\Nmap>

C:\Program Files\Nmap>

C:\Program Files\Nmap>ipconfig  /all

Windows IP Configuration

        Host Name . . . . . . . . . . . . : groundzero
        Primary Dns Suffix  . . . . . . . :
        Node Type . . . . . . . . . . . . : Unknown
        IP Routing Enabled. . . . . . . . : No
        WINS Proxy Enabled. . . . . . . . : No

Ethernet adapter Local Area Connection:

        Connection-specific DNS Suffix  . :
        Description . . . . . . . . . . . : 3Com EtherLink XL 10/100 PCI For Com
plete PC Management NIC (3C905C-TX)
        Physical Address. . . . . . . . . : 00-01-02-F1-4C-2F
        Dhcp Enabled. . . . . . . . . . . : Yes
        Autoconfiguration Enabled . . . . : Yes
        IP Address. . . . . . . . . . . . : 192.168.1.3
        Subnet Mask . . . . . . . . . . . : 255.255.255.0
        Default Gateway . . . . . . . . . : 192.168.1.254
        DHCP Server . . . . . . . . . . . : 192.168.1.254
        DNS Servers . . . . . . . . . . . : 159.134.237.6
        Lease Obtained. . . . . . . . . . : 20 June 2006 21:17:44
        Lease Expires . . . . . . . . . . : 20 June 2006 22:17:44
```

**Figure 9.6** Output From an Nmap Host Scan

## *Kiwi CatTools*

Kiwi CatTools from Kiwi Enterprises (*www.kiwisyslog.com*) provide the Report.ARP feature, which builds a report of the ARP table entries and tracks any changes. This allows you to find out which MAC addresses are appearing on what switch ports and VLANs. CatTools can highlight changes in the ARP table output from one report to the next, making it a useful tool for detecting rogue devices.

CatTools can be used to schedule tasks to run automatically and repeatedly against your devices, which makes for light work compared to the alternative of manually logging on to your switches and listing arp tables. Start by defining your devices using the **Add** button on the **Devices** tab of CatTools. Each device has to be identified by its IP address, device type, and model. You also have to define the connection method (telnet or secure shell [SSH]) and include the passwords for the device, so that CatTools can successfully log in (see Figure 9.7).

Once you have defined the device, you can add a scheduled task to the **Activities** tab by clicking the **Add** button. When setting up a new activity, you have to tell CatTools the type of activity you require (e.g., reports for the "mac address table" and the "port info table"). Comparing these tables allows you to determine the ports that do not have MAC addresses, which helps identify unauthorized packet capture devices. To finish creating the activity, you must define the device or devices you want to perform the activity on and the number of times the activity should be carried out (see Figure 9.8)

CatTools supports many types of equipment, including Cisco, Extreme, and Foundry switches. Different settings and output are available for different makes and models of network equipment.

**Figure 9.7** Device Configuration in CatTools

**Figure 9.8** Sample ARP Report from CatTools

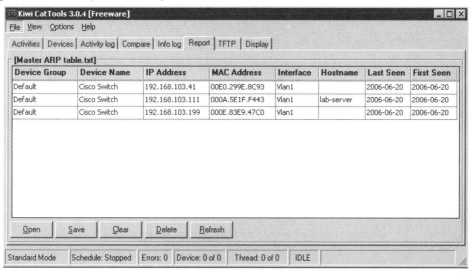

## *ntop*

ntop is freeware, open-source application. Originally written for the UNIX platform, the application is now available for Windows. Windows users have the option of downloading the source code and compiling ntop for themselves, or registering and making a small donation to the project in order to get the download link for the full version of the product. If you do not wish to register or compile the code yourself, ntop is available as a demo for windows from the ntop Web site (*www.ntop.org*).

ntop provides flow analysis and other network traffic analysis by collecting NetFlow and sFlow data from switches and routers, or by analyzing packets in the same way as a traditional packet sniffer application. NetFlow and sFlow are both technologies that report flow statistics from network equipment to a central collection point for analysis. The ability to collect NetFlow and sFlow from multiple routers or switches allows for massive visibility of the traffic on your networks.

Deploying ntop successfully requires some work, but it is well worth the effort. Apart from installing and configuring ntop, you also need to configure one or more of the following:

- Capture port traffic
- Configure NetFlow on routers
- Configure sFlow on switches

Capturing network traffic is synonymous with protocol analyzers and packet sniffers. The idea is that selected network traffic is made visible in real-time to the capturing device, which allows the capturing device to capture, log, decode, and analyze the network traffic. It also allows you to identify and track undesirable network activity. The mechanism required to pass the traffic to ntop is the same as the method used for packet sniffers. There is a difference in terms of what is done with the gathered data. Instead of capturing data like a packet sniffer, ntop simply records the traffic statistics. This statistical approach can be used to record the existence of certain types of network traffic without actually recording it (e.g., ntop can tell if a File Transfer Protocol [FTP] transfer took place between two hosts on your LAN, but it will not record the FTP session).

To steer the data towards the ntop host, you have to use a network tap, a Switch Port Analyzer (SPAN) port, or a Remote Switched Port Analyzer (RSPAN) port. SPAN and RSPAN are features on Cisco Catalyst 6500 switches that allow you to mirror traffic from one part of the network onto a port where ntop is connected. This does not affect the natural sources and destinations of packets that would flow through the port being mirrored. Network taps are devices that allow ntop to eavesdrop on conversations as they pass through the tap, which is typically inserted between a network switch and a router or firewall so that traffic can be monitored as it passes between subnets.

sFlow is a technology that samples packets and sends reports to a central collection point for analysis. Although the technology is somewhat different from NetFlow, the applications for its use are similar. Given that our case study uses Cisco LAN switches and routers, NetFlow is more appropriate.

There are two steps used to configure basic NetFlow export on your organization's Cisco Catalyst 6500 switches or routers. First, you must enable NetFlow on the interfaces you wish to gather statistics from using the **Router(config-if)# ip route-cache flow** command. Second, you have to tell the Cisco device where it should export the NetFlow information, using the **Router(config)# ip flow-export <ip-address> udp-port version 5** global configuration command .

Once you have configured the Cisco devices, you need to configure ntop so that it knows what kind of information to expect. ntop is configured using a Web interface. The default setting for ntop on Windows is to start the Web interface on port 3000. Once ntop is installed, you can browse to http://localhost:3000/ on the ntop machine. ntop allows you to add NetFlow devices to its configuration using the "plug-in" menu.

Once a device is added, you have to activate it and set a "local collector port." The default port used for NetFlow is 2055. If you do not explicitly configure this port setting, ntop will not be able to process your NetFlow data.

## Tcpdump

This freeware open source application is commonly found in Linux distributions and is also available on a range of other platforms. Tcpdump is also available for Windows where it is called WinDump. Tcpdump is commonly used on UNIX-based firewalls as a troubleshooting utility. Tcpdump allows you to filter and capture live network traffic in real time. If you are unsure of the service ports that an application uses, tcpdump can unveil the missing pieces.

When using tcpdump, it is wise to apply a filter to your capture so that the output is not overwhelmed by irrelevant packet information. Web sites for tcpdump and WinDump are www.tcpdump.org and www.winpcap.org/windump/, respectively.

## Wireshark

Formerly known as Ethereal, this GUI-based protocol analyzer allows for capture functionality similar to tcpdump. In addition, Wireshark presents the data collected in a more filterable way than tcpdump. The Wireshark Web site is at www.wireshark.org.

Wireshark can be used to view packet decodes in exceptional detail (see Figure 9.9 ), and can open previously saved capture sessions from Ethereal, tcpdump, WinDump, Network Monitor, or other common packet analyzers.

**Figure 9.9** Wireshark Identifies a Web Server as Microsoft IIS 6.0

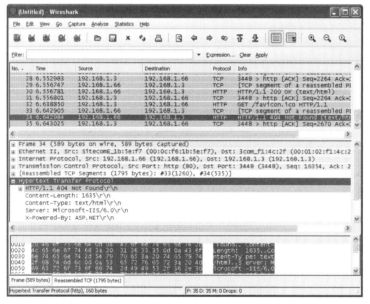

## IPTraf

IPTraf uses a text-mode interface and provides network statistics. This Linux-based network monitoring tool is available at http://iptraf.seul.org/.

## EtherApe

EtherApe allows administrators to view network traffic between different hosts on the network. To get the maximum benefit from EtherApe, deploy it using port mirroring features on your switches or use network taps. EtherApe only displays traffic that it "sees," much like the conditions required for Wireshark or tcpdump. This graphical UNIX-based network monitoring tool is available at http://etherape.sourceforge.net/.

## Netcat

This command-line tool, originally available only in UNIX environments, was ported to the Windows platform over a decade ago. Netcat can operate as a client or server for both TCP and User Datagram Protocol (UDP) protocols, which makes it an ideal tool for testing transport layer filtering configurations like the ones you might find in router ACLs or firewalls. Modifications and transported versions (ports) of the original netcat may be known as a variety of different names, including sock, socket, ncat and nc. The netcat TCP client is comparable to an advanced telnet client. It allows telnet-specific protocol traits to be removed to firewalls that are less likely to detect and possibly deny the unusual client connection. Netcat as a TCP server can be used to provide a remote command line on the destination server example (e.g., on Windows hosts that do not include a telnet server you can emulate a telnet server using the **nc -l -p 23 -t -e cmd.exe** command. This command tells netcat (**nc**) to listen (**-l**) on port 23 (**-p 23**) and to negotiate with telnet clients (**-t**) before executing (**-e**) the command prompt (**cmd.exe**) and joining it to the user's session.

A UDP client and server may be used to test for holes in your firewall rules (e.g., a common misconfiguration is to allow all sources to access UDP port 53 at all destinations). This port is normally used for DNS lookups, but if not properly secured can be used to tunnel data (e.g., if you run the command **nc -u -l -p 53** on a host on one side of the firewall, it will create a UDP server. Then, if you use netcat to communicate with that server (**nc -u 10.10.2.50 53**), you will be able to test connectivity using the DNS service port. Type some text at the client end and press **Return**. This text will be copied to the server side proving that the port is open. If the netcat client returns to a command prompt or the text is not echoed, the port is not active. In this case, there may be a firewall in the way or there may be a problem with the netcat server.

## Nessus

Nessus is undoubtedly the world's favorite free vulnerability scanner. Using Nessus on your network will help to reveal any vulnerabilities that may exist, by feeding fingerprinting techniques and known exploits to your hosts. Taken to extremes, this can cause vulnerable systems to malfunction or even crash. The positive side to this is that at least you learn about and remediate the vulnerability in a controlled manner, rather than have some unknown influence taking advantage of the vulnerability while you are not watching. Nessus is available for UNIX and Windows from www.nessus.org. For more information on Nessus, check the Syngress Web site for specialist titles.

# Mapping Results

There are countless other freeware and commercial utility applications available that can help you map your networks. At this stage, we have introduced several tools and techniques that allow you to gather intelligence and build a picture of how your network operates.

The security professionals at Hot Cash Corporation have gathered a full cable database and significant intelligence about the constitution of the network, using the tools and techniques just described. Drawing on this information, the next section describes the techniques that can be used to improve security.

# Improving Accountability with Identity Management

Management at Hot Cash Corporation has voiced their concern about the company's ability to comply with both internal and external security standards and requirements. Keeping their concerns in mind, let's examine the current firewall configuration (see Figure 9.10).

**Figure 9.10** Original Hot Cash Corporation Firewall Configuration

```
! PIX Version 6.3(5)

! set speed and duplex on interfaces
interface ethernet0 auto
interface ethernet1 auto
interface ethernet2 auto

! assign names and security levels to the interfaces
nameif ethernet0 outside security0
nameif ethernet1 inside security100
nameif ethernet2 outside security50

! assign access passwords
enable password ********** encrypted
passwd ********** encrypted

! set the system name
hostname hcc-PIX
```

```
domain-name hotcash.com

! default protocol 'fixup's (helps NAT compatability etc.)
fixup protocol dns maximum-length 512
fixup protocol ftp 21
fixup protocol h323 h225 1720
fixup protocol h323 ras 1718-1719
fixup protocol http 80
fixup protocol rsh 514
fixup protocol rtsp 554
fixup protocol sip 5060
fixup protocol sip udp 5060
fixup protocol skinny 2000
fixup protocol smtp 25
fixup protocol sqlnet 1521
fixup protocol tftp 69

! define names of objects used in access-lists
names
name 10.10.15.20 administratorPC
name 172.16.100.101 mailserver-dmz
name 172.16.100.100 webserver-dmz
name 87.65.43.100 webserver-public
name 87.65.43.101 mailserver-public
name 10.10.1.100 mailserver-inside
name 10.10.2.100 database1-inside
name 10.10.2.101 database2-inside
name 10.10.1.1 HQ-DC-01
name 9.8.7.0 ISP-dns
name 1.2.3.0 www.ft.com
name 2.3.4.0 www.antiviruscorp.com
name 3.4.5.0 www.financialtimes.com
name 4.5.6.0 www.hcc-remotepartner.com

! define groups of objects to be used in access-lists
object-group network database-servers
  description Database servers
  network-object host database1-inside
  network-object host database2-inside
```

```
object-group network approved-sites
  description Approved Internet websites
  network-object www.ft.com 255.255.255.0
  network-object www.antiviruscorp.com 255.255.255.0
  network-object www.financialtimes.com 255.255.255.0
  network-object www.hcc-remotepartner.com 255.255.255.0


! define rules for traffic coming from the Internet (see remarks)
access-list FromInternet permit tcp any host webserver-public eq https
access-list FromInternet remark --- allow only SSL access our web server
from Internet
access-list FromInternet permit tcp any host mailserver-public eq smtp
access-list FromInternet remark --- allow public to send us mail
access-list FromInternet permit icmp any interface outside echo-reply
access-list FromInternet permit icmp any interface outside unreachable
access-list FromInternet permit icmp any interface outside redirect
access-list FromInternet permit icmp any interface outside time-exceeded
access-list FromInternet permit icmp any interface outside information-reply
access-list FromInternet permit icmp any interface outside timestamp-reply
access-list FromInternet remark --- allow replies to traceroute and ping
access-list FromInternet remark --- implied deny all at end of list


! define rules for traffic originating in the DMZ (see remarks)
access-list FromDMZ permit udp host webserver-dmz ISP-dns 255.255.255.0 eq
domain
access-list FromDMZ permit udp host mailserver-dmz ISP-dns 255.255.255.0 eq
domain
access-list FromDMZ permit tcp host webserver-dmz ISP-dns 255.255.255.0 eq
domain
access-list FromDMZ permit tcp host mailserver-dmz ISP-dns 255.255.255.0 eq
domain
access-list FromDMZ remark ---  allow DMZ based servers to query ISP DNS
servers
access-list FromDMZ permit tcp host mailserver-dmz any eq smtp
access-list FromDMZ remark ---  allow our mail server to send mail to the
Internet
access-list FromDMZ permit tcp host webserver-dmz object-group database-
servers eq sqlnet
access-list FromDMZ remark ---  allow our web server to query the internal
databases
access-list FromDMZ permit tcp host webserver-dmz any eq 143
```

```
access-list FromDMZ remark ---  allow our web server to access internal mail
with IMAP
access-list FromDMZ remark ---  this is for external access to email without
using O.W.A.
access-list FromDMZ permit icmp any any
access-list FromDMZ remark --- permit ping and ping replies
access-list FromDMZ remark --- implied deny all at end of list


! define rules for traffic originating on the internal LAN  (see remarks)
access-list FromInside permit ip host administratorPC any
access-list FromInside remark --- allow admin PC unrestricted access to DMZ
& Internet
access-list FromInside permit tcp host HQ-DC-01 ISP-dns 255.255.255.0 eq
domain
access-list FromInside permit udp host HQ-DC-01 ISP-dns 255.255.255.0 eq
domain
access-list FromInside remark --- allow internal DNS servers to query ISP
DNS servers
access-list FromInside permit tcp any object-group approved-sites eq www
access-list FromInside permit tcp any object-group approved-sites eq https
access-list FromInside remark --- allow internal hosts access to 'approved'
sites
access-list FromInside permit icmp any any
access-list FromInside remark --- permit ping and ping replies
access-list FromInside remark --- implied deny all at end of list


! set interface IP addresses
ip address outside 87.65.43.21 255.255.255.0
ip address inside 172.16.1.254 255.255.255.0
ip address dmz 172.16.100.254 255.255.255.0


! default Intrusion detection/prevention settings
ip audit info action alarm
ip audit attack action alarm


! default failover (none - ignore this)
no failover
failover timeout 0:00:00
failover poll 15
no failover ip address outside
```

```
no failover ip address inside
no failover ip address dmz

! default arp timeout
arp timeout 14400

! activate access-list rules on respective interfaces
access-group FromInside in interface inside
access-group FromDMZ in interface dmz
access-group FromOutside in interface Outside

! set a default gateway to the Internet
route outside 0.0.0.0 0.0.0.0 87.65.43.20 1
! set a static route for WAN traffic
route inside 10.0.0.0 255.0.0.0 172.16.1.254 1

! default session table and address translation table timeouts
timeout xlate 3:00:00
timeout conn 1:00:00 half-closed 0:10:00 udp 0:02:00 rpc 0:10:00 h225
1:00:00
timeout h323 0:05:00 mgcp 0:05:00 sip 0:30:00 sip_media 0:02:00
timeout sip-disconnect 0:02:00 sip-invite 0:03:00

! default user authorization timeout (every 5 minutes)
timeout uauth 0:05:00 absolute

! default AAA settings (no AAA defined)
aaa-server TACACS+ protocol tacacs+
aaa-server TACACS+ max-failed-attempts 3
aaa-server TACACS+ deadtime 10
aaa-server RADIUS protocol radius
aaa-server RADIUS max-failed-attempts 3
aaa-server RADIUS deadtime 10
aaa-server LOCAL protocol local

! set snmp details
snmp-server location cabinet G24-3, HCC-HQ, Seattle
no snmp-server contact
snmp-server community hcc-RO-$tring
```

```
snmp-server host inside 10.10.2.50 trap
snmp-server host inside 10.10.2.51 poll
snmp-server enable traps


! default floodguard   (on)
floodguard enable


! define an access-list to allow ssh based administration ONLY from the
administratorPC
ssh administratorPC 255.255.255.255 inside


! define an idle timeout for ssh access (3 minutes)
! this low timeout will help ensure that the
! administrator does not accidentally stay logged in
ssh timeout 3


! define an idle timeout for the console (3 minutes)
console timeout 3
```

Note that although the firewall rules are relatively well-defined, there are a number of options that are still at their default settings (e.g., default connection table timeout settings on Private Internet Exchange [PIX] are geared towards application compatibility rather than security). Most implementations will benefit from lowering the timeouts associated with connections (**timeout conn**) and network address translations (**timeout xlate**). There may be other improvement in the following areas:

- Authentication, Authorization, Accounting (AAA)
- Time synchronization
- Content filtering
- Timeout settings
- Failover (high availability)
- Intrusion detection

# AAA Using Cisco ACS

A number of criticisms can be made of the current firewall configuration, the most notable being the lack of AAA. Specifically, there is no way of knowing which users accessed any of the approved sites, and what time they accessed those sites.

The intelligence gathering exercise revealed that call center users require access to an application that is hosted outside your organization. Management at Hot Cash Corporation wants to limit and track the users that access this application.

After a visit to the Cisco documentation site (www.cisco.com/univercd) and a few quick configuration tests, you discover that your firewall appliance is not optimally equipped to handle this task on its own. You determine that a dedicated AAA server is desirable, so you allocate some time and budget towards a pilot project.

You consider using either Lightweight Directory Access Protocol (LDAP) or Remote Authentication Dial-In User Server (RADIUS) protocols directly with Active Directory. RADIUS is compatible with Cisco PIX firewall, but the management interface for Internet Authentication Service (IAS), the RADIUS component of Windows server, does not provide all of the options required. Instead, you opt to try an evaluation of Cisco Access Control Server (ACS) software, which supports RADIUS and Terminal Access Controller Access Control System Plus (TACACS+) protocols. It allows you to define both user groups and Network Device Groups (NDG). It is possible, and in this case desirable, to allow specific groups of users to authenticate to specific resources such as the firewall. Even though you can still use Active Directory as a downstream authentication database, the ACSs ability to map user group policies to device groups will allow you to control users' traffic more efficiently, by enforcing per-user access restrictions at devices such as the PIX. This is not the same as restricting the source of a user's login attempt. Instead, destination restrictions are enforced. In addition, authenticated administrative users of devices such as the firewall, switches, or routers can use ACS to authorize specific commands and configuration options.

Start by installing Cisco ACS software default options on a server that meets the minimum hardware and OS requirements. A 90-day fully functional trial of Cisco ACS software is available from www.cisco.com.

## Network Access Restrictions

Cisco ACS uses the Network Access Restrictions (NAR) feature to control who can log on at a particular access point, such as the firewall. NAR is an optional configuration component; therefore, ACS may require you to enable the display of NAR settings in the ACS Web interface before you can access the appropriate settings. To enable NAR, login to the Web user interface, which can be accessed directly from the server at http://localhost:2002/.

Once connected to the ACS user interface, select the **Interface** button located to the left of the screen, and select the **Advanced Options** link. Now you can enable either "User-Level Network Access Restrictions" or "Group-Level Network Access Restrictions." Group-level NAR is preferable, because it becomes easier to manage as user numbers increase. Finally, click **Submit** to apply any changes (see Figure 9.11).

When NAR is enabled at either the user or group level, you will see NAR settings listed on the configuration screens for user or group properties, respectively.

**Figure 9.11** Configuring Group-level NAR with Cisco ACS

Defining NAR rules allows configuration under two similar headings in the ACS interface: Define IP-based access restrictions and Define CLI/DNIS-based access restrictions. You will use the IP-based option for PIX that the Caller-ID (CLI) and Dialed Number Identification Service (DNIS) refers to, both of which are used in dial-up situations to identify the telephone number the user is coming from and the telephone number they have dialed. For IP-based restrictions, the "Address" option refers to the user's source IP address. If you want to allow users in this group to authenticate to the firewall from all IP addresses, you can enter an asterisk (*) in the address field and in the port field.

This NAR configuration is a type of ACL, and as such, it allows a "permit of deny" action to be applied to all entries on the list. You can pick either permit or deny for the entire list. This limitation is likely to affect the way you define the group's NAR list.

# External Authentication Databases

Now you can start challenging users for their login credentials when they want to access external content. When configuring users or groups in ACS, they can be set to authenticate using a variety of methods. At its most basic, ACS offers a per-user password mechanism, where usernames and passwords are stored together in the ACS database. If you have invested considerable effort setting up users in another authentication database (e.g., Active Directory) or on a token server (e.g., RSA SecurID or Safeword from Secure Computing), you can allow ACS usernames to reference those databases. This allows user's to use the same login credentials that they use on other systems, while ACS transparently adds authorization attributes specific to where user's want to login. You want users to authenticate using their Active Directory username and password, and you want ACS to decide the type of access they are allowed. Before a user or group can reference an external authentication database, you have to inform ACS of those external databases (see Figure 9.12). From the ACS Web interface, click **External User Databases**.

**Figure 9.12** External User Databases Options

Clicking on **Database Configuration** allows you to select the type of external database you want to make available to ACS. Multiple external databases may be included in the ACS. Support external sources include:

- Network Admission Control (NAC)
- Windows Database
- Novell Novell Directory Services (NDS)
- Generic LDAP
- External Open Database Connectivity (ODBC) Database
- LEAP Proxy
- RADIUS Server
- RADIUS Token Server
- RSA SecurID Token Server

The "Windows Database" option usually works best for Active Directory, and is used for Hot Cash Corporation. In cases where the Windows environment is hardened, the "Generic LDAP" or "RADIUS Server" options may be suitable alternatives. After selecting **Windows Database**, click **Configure** and add the Active Directory domains you want to query into the **Domain List** of the **Configure Domain List** section. Click **Submit** to apply any changes.

Once you have an external database set up in the ACS, you can direct the user's authentication to look for Active Directory. Configure this referral under the user's properties as follows:

1. From the ACS Web interface, click **User Setup**.
2. Next, enter the username and click **Add/Edit**.
3. Change the **Password Authentication** drop down box to the required external database (configured in the previous step), and click **Submit**.

Now when this user logs in their password will be compared against Active Directory, but their authorization and other settings will be determined by ACS.

If you have a lot of users and don't want to input all of the usernames into ACS, use the **External User Databases** configuration button to set up an "Unknown User Policy." If you opt to use this feature, your ACS server will query its internal database for the username first. If ACS cannot find a username, the unknown user policy refers to the list of configured external databases to try to find the username. External databases are queried in an order of preference set by you. If a user is not found in an external database, ACS will query the next database and so on until there are no more places to search. If ACS finds a user in an external database using the "Unknown User Policy," it will automatically populate its own database with the username and password authentication required to access the appropriate database. Consequently, the next time this user logs in, the ACS will already have a copy of their username and will know where to refer authentication requests to. If ACS cannot find a username in any of databases, the user authentication fails.

# User and Group Authorization

Once you can account for who is using the network, you will want to create authorization rules that define what those users are allowed to do or access on the network.

Two examples of authorization that can be used to improve security at the Hot Cash Corporation are:

- Downloadable IP ACLs
- Command authorization

Downloadable ACLs define what destination IP addresses or services a user or group is permitted or denied access to. Users authenticate with the firewall using telnet or HTTP, and the firewall dynamically assigns ACLs based on the ACS configuration. Downloadable IP ACLs allow you to move the list of trusted destinations off the firewall and onto the ACS server. In addition, you can now associate different trusted destination lists with different users or groups, which allows you to control which users get access to which sites (e.g., the IT staff might be permitted access to support sites for software updates, while other users are denied access to these sites).

Command authorization is particularly useful if you have different administrators with different administrative privilege levels on the same equipment. Command authorization allows you to selectively assign commands to users or groups. One application of this feature allows first-level support specialists access to commands that allow them to view the status of devices, but not to change the configuration.

> **NOTE**
>
> Potentially damaging commands such as a **reboot**, or shutting down a network interface, should be left to users with extensive expertise.

The options to configure downloadable IP ACLs may not be visible in your version of ACS. To enable this option, click **Interface Configuration** in the ACS Web interface and select **Advanced Options**. Here, you can enable the check boxes to display **User-Level Downloadable ACLs** and **Group-Level Downloadable ACLs** (see Figure 9.13) User-level settings take precedence over group-level settings.

**Figure 9.13** Cisco ACS Interface Configuration Options

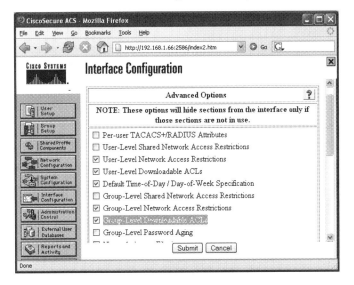

Downloadable IP ACLs are defined under the "Shared Profile Components" section of the ACS. Access this section by clicking **Shared Profile Components** in the ACS Web interface and follow the **Downloadable IP ACLs** link.

The downloadable ACLs allow you to configure multiple sets of rules per downloadable ACL. Each downloadable ACL is given a name, description, and rules. Each rule consists of ACL definitions that look similar to the native ACL entries found on the intended device (e.g., a downloadable ACL for a PIX firewall may contain a rule with the ACL entries) (See Figure 9.14.)

**Figure 9.14** Downloadable ACL for PIX

```
permit tcp any host 50.24.30.2.4
permit tcp any host 65.41.99.2.66
deny tcp any host 215.74.132.2.102
permit tcp any 215.74.132.2.0 255.255.255.0
```

```
permit icmp any any
deny ip any any
```

Downloadable ACLs for PIX firewalls download differently than downloadable ACLs for Internetwork Operating System (IOS) devices. IOS support for downloadable ACLs has traditionally been provided through the configuration of vendor specific RADIUS Attribute-Value (AV) pairs. Another difference between PIX and IOS ACLs is that IOS ACLs use wildcard masks values, whereas PIX uses regular network mask values. Recent versions of IOS support downloadable ACLs, but it is recommended that you use the PIX firewall as an enforcement point.

Users have to authenticate to the enforcement device before ACS downloads and applies the user's ACL to the firewall. Users authenticate by opening a telnet or HTTP session to a firewall virtual IP address (PIX must be configured appropriately to allow this). (Additional information regarding configuring PIX devices for downloadable ACLs, can be found later in this chapter.)

When a packet attempts to traverse a firewall, the ACL statements are evaluated from top to bottom until a match is made, at which time the packet is permitted or denied according to the list entry. If a list does not contain a suitable match for the packet, it is dropped.

## NOTE

Both the name of the downloadable ACL and the content rules within it are limited to 27 characters each. These descriptions must not contain any spaces or any of the following characters: , - [ ] / \ " < > —.

One advanced option of using downloadable ACLs is that you can associate specific ACL content entries with network access filters, which allows you to control which devices are enforcing particular access restrictions. This is of particular interest if you are using multiple firewalls or other ACL-capable devices such as routers. Downloadable ACLs are supported on the following Cisco equipment:

- VPN 3000 series concentrators
- PIX Firewalls
- Cisco devices running IOS version 12.3(8)T or higher

Firewall technologies are typically associated with the perimeter of the network. As in the network mapping exercise, the Hot Cash Corporation uses Catalyst 6500 series switches on its LANs. ACS also allows you to use downloadable ACLs with this equipment, which offers the prospect of enabling access control mechanisms within the LAN, thereby giving you the potential to control access to otherwise unprotected resources on the internal network.

The final piece of the downloadable ACL configuration is to apply the downloadable ACL to a user or group of users, which can be done by clicking **Group Setup** in the ACS Web interface and then editing a user group by selecting a group from the dropdown list and clicking **Edit Settings**. Under **Downloadable ACLs** you can enable **Assign IP ACL** and choose a downloadable ACL from the dropdown box. To complete the changes, click **Submit and Restart** at the bottom of the Web page.

More information from this network mapping exercise reveals that there is a standalone database server on the network. This Windows server uses a Web front end and is maintained by the Hot Cash Corporation business development users, who access this resource by dialing modems that are directly connected to the server. This server does not have the latest patches applied, because of compatibility problems with the database application. Management wants you to remove the dial-in setup and make this server available on the Internet. They require that access be restricted to partners. The application on the server does not provide an authentication system of its own; therefore, use the Web server's authentication engine to solve this problem. Allowing direct access to the server, even with server-based authentication, would expose the unpatched system directly to the Internet. You can solve this server to a new partner DMZ and authenticate inbound access to it using ACS.

## Configuring PIX for Downloadable ACLs

To activate a downloadable ACL to PIX, user's should browse to http://172.16.99.99. Once authenticated, user access is valid for the length of time configured by the **timeout uauth** command. In this example, user access is valid for 15 minutes (see Figure 9.15).

**Figure 9.15** PIX Configuration for Downloadable ACL

```
aaa-server myACS protocol RADIUS
aaa-server myACS (inside) host 192.168.103.33 myAc$KeY
access-list authClients permit tcp any any
aaa authentication match authClients inside myACS
virtual http 172.16.99.99
timeout uauth 0:15:0
auth-prompt prompt Authenticate Yourself for access!
```

```
auth-prompt accept Welcome. Access granted.
auth-prmopt reject Access has been denied.
```

## Notes From the Underground...

### Downloadable ACL Vulnerability

In December 2005, Cisco posted field notice FN61965 describing vulnerabilities in downloadable ACL technology. Cisco updated this notice in April 2006 and although fixes and workarounds are available, at the time of writing, this field notice is still active and should be monitored. It is important that the appropriate software versions are applied to avoid security breaches.

# Authorization

Once a user has been authenticated we are in apposition that we trust the user is who they say they are. Authentication provides the next logical step by determining exactly what tasks that user is allowed to do or not to do as the case may be.

## Command Authorization

Part of the information gathered during your network mapping included a list of active switch ports without associated MAC entries. You discover that these ports are configured with the SPAN feature. SPAN mirrors traffic from chosen parts of the network onto the SPAN port, so that packet capture applications can process the traffic without disconnecting or interrupting production systems (see Table 9.3).

You trace the cables back to the attached hosts and discover that they are unauthorized packet capture devices. Removing the devices is an easy task; however, when you quiz your IT staff about the unexpected situation, they all claim ignorance. Hot Cash Corporation often uses contractors to perform server maintenance. You are concerned that an unauthorized individual, such as an external contractor, has learned the passwords for the network equipment and taken the liberty of configuring the switch themselves. To limit the ability of certain user accounts, you decide that command authorization is a suitable restriction mechanism.

**Table 9.3** Active Switch Ports with No MAC Addresses

| Switch Name | Site | Switch Location | Num. of MAC Addresses Seen | Port Status | Port ID |
|---|---|---|---|---|---|
| SE6506-2A | Seattle | 2nd Floor Cabinet | 0 | Up/Up | FastEthernet 3/22 |
| DA6513-CA | Dallas | Comms Room | 0 | Up/Up | Gigabit Ethernet 4/2 |
| DA6513-CB | Dallas | Comms Room | 0 | Up/Up | Gigabit Ethernet 4/2 |

Command authorization lets you limit the scope of the commands available to users. This can be used to allow a user to display status, but block them from configuring the device. It is possible to define and enforce command authorization by using local authorization features or by using RADIUS with an AAA server. Using an AAA server (e.g., Cisco ACS) allows you to centrally configure settings for many users and devices. For the Hot Cash Corporation, this means you can restrict command abilities in the exec shell on your routers, switches, and firewall. In this section you learn how to configure command authorization on ACS for Cisco IOS devices. Remote site IT staff will have access to a subset of commands for the network equipment at their sites, but the main IT department will be allowed full configuration control. Remote IT staff will not be allowed access to any AAA configuration or SPAN configuration commands.

PIX and IOS (routers and switches) authorization is configured under the "Shared Profile Components" section of the ACS. Click **Shared Profile Components** at the left of the ACS Web interface to access these configuration options. Next, follow the **Shell Command Authorization Sets** link. There are no default authorization sets in ACS, so click the **Add** button to create one. When the Shell Command Authorization Sets appear, you are presented with the option to enter an authorization set Name and Description. Below that is the option to Permit or Deny any Unmatched Commands that you have not explicitly included in your authorization set. Enter **limited-ios** as the name for this example. In this example, you will permit all commands except the ones for SPAN and AAA configuration. The default setting is to Deny any unmatched commands. Change this option to **Permit**.

To define a command that is explicitly permitted or denied by authorization, type the command in the text box above the **Add Command** button and click **Add Command**.

The command you added appears in the list box on the left. Click on the command that you just entered so that it is highlighted (see Figure 9.16). Now click in the right-hand box directly above the **Remove Command** button and enter Permit and Deny statements for the command arguments. The "Permit Unmatched Args" checkbox controls the default behavior of each command. In Figure 9.16, this is set to deny all arguments for the session command.

**Figure 9.16** Command Authorization Set Configuration

When your command authorization set is configured and ready to use, you need to associate it with a user group. To do so, go to the "Group Setup" page, select a user group, and click **Edit Settings**. Look for the **Shell Command Authorization Set** heading under the **TACACS+ Settings**. There are different ways of joining the authorization set to the user group. The **Assign a Shell Command Authorization Set on a per Network Device Group Basis** option offers the most useful combination. If you select this option, choose a **Device Group** and matching **Command Set** and click **Add Association**. You may add multiple device groups to command-set associations for each user group.

## Privilege Levels

The ACS **Group Setup** option allows you to define **Enable Options**, which governs the privilege level assigned to users of the group when they type the **enable** command on the IOS device. Privilege levels and authorization are closely related. Privilege levels have default command authorizations. Higher privilege levels have more authorized commands available. Privilege level 15 is known as "enable mode" or "privileged exec mode," and authorizes all commands by default. It is possible to assign privilege levels and command authorization to a user at the same time. Privilege level and authorization restrictions interact differently on different types of devices.

You may use NDG to associate different Privilege levels with user groups. Privilege associations may be enforced at the user level for greater granularity; however, it is recommended that you use the group level configuration to keep things relatively simple. If you have unexpected results when using privileged mode access for any user, check that their user-level Enable Options are configured to refer to the group settings. To make a user-level account refer to group level settings for Command Authorization, navigate to the **User Setup** page and check **Use Group Level Setting** located under the **TACACS+ Enable Control:** tab of the **Advanced TACACS+ Settings**. Another useful advanced TACACS+ setting that appears on the **Advanced TACACS+ Settings**, is the option to use the same password as is assigned for executive level access, or to choose a separate password or authentication method. In complex examples, you can assign a one-time password token from a token server (e.g. RSA SecurID, Secure Computing Safeword, or Vasco Digipass) to a user. You can then add security by requiring a separate token from a different token server to access "privilege" mode (also known as "enable" mode). To keep things simple the users, select the setting **Use CiscoSecure PAP password**, which will require the user to use the same password for exec and privileged mode. The user will be asked for the password a second time when they attempt to enter privileged mode.

## IOS Command Authorization

Commands to enable AAA on the router are used as follows:

```
aaa new-model
```

This command will activate AAA capabilities on the router, and is required before you configure other AAA statements.

```
tacacs-server host 192.168.103.111 key myPassword
aaa group server tacacs+ myTacacsServers
 server 192.168.103.111
```

Each AAA server must be defined separately, using an IP address and a shared secret key. Multiple AAA servers of the same type may be combined into a named group (shown earlier in this chapter).

```
aaa authentication login default group myTacacsServers local none
aaa authorization config-commands
aaa authorization exec default group tacacs+ if-authenticated none
aaa authorization commands 15 default group myTacacsServers
```

Different command modes require different types of authorization configuration example (e.g., configuration mode commands such as "interface" or "enable secret" require **config-commands** option, but exec mode commands such as "show" or "debug" require the **exec** and **commands** options).

---

**W**ARNING

Enabling PIX command authorization can lock you out of your firewall if it is not configured correctly. Save the configuration before you make changes; do not save the configuration again until you are sure that the command authorization is working as expected. In the event that something goes wrong and you lock yourself out, you can recover quickly by power cycling the firewall to go back to the last saved configuration. If you are locked out and have saved the incorrect configuration, go to www.cisco.com/warp/customer/110/34.shtml for recovery instructions.

---

## PIX Command Authorization

Setting up command authorization on PIX is similar to setting up for IOS devices, but with a few quirky differences. At the time of this writing, the PIX implements authorization based on shell command sets, not PIXshell command sets.

---

**N**OTE

Cisco ACS has an option in the "Shared Profile Components" section called "PIX Command Authorization Sets." This is misleading, because it is not actually used for PIX command authorization.

---

At some point, Cisco may intend to implement PIXshell command authorization on future hardware projects. Until then, avoid the "PIX Command Authorization Sets" feature and use "Shell Command Authorization Sets" for PIX and for IOS devices. PIX supports command authorization and enables authorization. Command authorization on PIX differs from IOS authorization when it comes to entering privileged exec mode and entering privileged mode commands.

For an IOS-based device such as a router, ACS can directly assign a privilege level from 0 to 15. If a user is assigned privilege level 15 in their ACS profile, they are logged straight into privileged mode exec. If the user is assigned a privilege level less than 15, the user may still use the **enable** command to increase their privilege level. When that user types a command that needs to be authorized, the router forwards the user's login name to ACS along with the command that needs to be authorized. ACS will permit or deny the authorization request based on the user or the user's group settings.

ACS does not assign a privilege level for PIX. PIX assigns privilege level 1 to all users authenticated by ACS. The user can type **enable** to increase their privilege level to level 15 only. If the PIX has been set up to use enable authentication, the username is maintained and any subsequent authorization requests use the username.

Here's where things start to get a bit tricky. If a user logs into the PIX without a username, the name sent to ACS for authorization of commands is "enable_1." If the user uses the **enable** command and has to use the enable password from global configuration on the PIX (i.e., if it is not using enable authentication), the username sent to ACS for authorization becomes "enable_15." If you do not authenticate a user for privileged exec mode access, you should ensure that usernames "enable_1" and "enable_15"exist on ACS and that these usernames are allowed to authenticate on the devices. PIX CLI login authentication is governed by the commands:

```
aaa authentication ssh console <myTacacsServer>
aaa authentication serial console <myTacacsServer>
aaa authentication telnet console <myTacacsServer>
```

PIX privileged exec authentication is governed by the command:

```
aaa authentication enable console <myTacacsServer>
```

**NOTE**

Cisco PIX authentication is available using RADIUS or TACACS+. PIX command authorization is only available using TACACS+. PIX downloadable ACLs are only supported using RADIUS. ACS only allows each AAA client (i.e. PIX or router or switch) to define one type of AAA protocol per device. In other words, if PIX uses RADIUS it cannot use TACACS+ on the same ACS server and vice versa. This leaves an unfortunate gap in functionality. If you want to take full advantage of all PIX's authentication and authorization features, you need separate RADIUS and TACACS+ servers.

Given that the commands for PIX and IOS CLIs are significantly different, separate Command Authentication Sets for each type of network device would be appropriate. Hot Cash Corporation can classify its devices into one of five groups:

- PIX firewall
- DMZ switch
- Internal LAN switch
- Internal router
- External router

Command Authorization Sets can be applied to multiple devices of the same type by associating the sets with a NDG. You learned during the network mapping exercise that Hot Cash Corporation uses multiple Catalyst 6500 series switches on their LANs. Each of these switches can be added into a device group called *Internal_Switches.*

## Accounting

Now that you have the details on how to authenticate users and how to authorize specific actions for those users, monitor their progress and check for anomalous behavior by using accounting (otherwise known as "logging.") The more information you log about the activities on your systems, the easier it will be to backtrack and find anomalies. For Hot Cash Corporation, this means configuring each of the AAA devices to deliver selected accounting information back to either a RADIUS or TACACS+ server. In other words, you need to configure your devices to send information about AAA activities to ACS. ACS then presents reports covering each of the following sections:

- TACACS+ Accounting
- TACACS+ Administration
- RADIUS Accounting
- Passed Authentications
- Failed Attempts
- Logged-in Users

Pay particular attention to the "Failed Attempts" report, which details any failed authentications and any failed authorizations. The Failed Attempts report shows the date and time of each failure along with the username, the AAA device, and details of the type of failure that occurred. Examples of failure types are "Unknown NAS," "Authentication Failure," and "Authorization Failure."

The logging of Passed Authentication information is not recorded by default. You need to enable this option under the **System Configuration**, **Logging**, **CSV Passed Authentications** section of ACS.

The AAA devices must be set up to record AAA information to the ACS server.

Use the **aaa accounting** command to configure accounting on Cisco IOS devices and PIX firewalls. For example, on a router you can use these accounting commands:

```
aaa accounting send stop-record authentication failure
aaa accounting update periodic 2
aaa accounting auth-proxy default start-stop group tacacs+
aaa accounting exec default start-stop group tacacs+
aaa accounting commands 0 default start-stop group tacacs+
aaa accounting network default start-stop group tacacs+
aaa accounting connection default start-stop group tacacs+
aaa accounting system default start-stop group radius
aaa accounting resource default start-stop group radius
```

You can choose RADIUS, TACACS+, or a mixture of both protocols to deliver accounting information. AAA accounting configuration on a PIX is much simpler. You can use a single **aaa** command on PIX to specify logging:

```
aaa accounting match <acl_name> <if_name> <server_tag>
```

## Content Filtering

Management at Hot Cash Corporation is keen to allow users access to more resources on the Internet; however, they want to ensure that users are denied access to undesirable Web sites. You realize that the current manually maintained list system will not work. There are two types of referral technologies that integrate with Cisco devices. The Web Cache Communication Protocol (WCCP) operates on IOS devices and transparently passes browser requests to a proxy server. Although in theory this could be sent to a filtering proxy server, the WCCP implementation currently operates in a fail-open configuration, which means that if the WCCP request does not receive a reply from the WCCP server, the request will be directed to the real destination. This ensures that Web pages are delivered even if the proxy if offline. For this reason, the WCCP feature is not suitable for Hot Cash Corporation.

The alternative PIX configuration option uses the **url-server** command to define an external filtering server. Websense and N2H2 are supported filtering engines. The N2H2 technology is now encompassed within Secure Computing's range of products.

A common alternative to using the referral technologies on IOS or PIX devices is to use a dedicated filtering proxy server. Filtering proxy servers such as NetIQ's Web Marshal or Network Appliance's NetCache products allow administrators to add content lists such as Websense or N2H2 with effects similar to those achieved with PIX. One major advantage of using a dedicated proxy server is that it has the ability to cache content, thereby improving response performance for users' Web browsers. Many filtering proxy server implementations also allow the addition of anti-virus engines, which makes them a thorough filtering option.

Hot Cache Corporation chooses to use a filtering proxy server with RADIUS-based authentication, a third-party filtering list, and a third-party anti-virus software. To use this proxy server, you need to reconfigure your company's Web browsers. Once you have all of Hot Cash Corporation's Web browsers reconfigured, you can change the firewall rules so that only the proxy server's IP address is allowed to go to external Web sites. Since the new proxy server supports RADIUS, you can configure it to communicate with your Cisco ACS server. Now, because you are authenticating your users at the proxy server, you can remove any firewall-based authentication for outbound browsing sessions.

All of Hot Cash Corporation users' PC's contain Web browsers and a lot of their computers need to have proxy settings configured (see Table 9.4). Rather than doing this manually, it is recommended that you use a group policy or login script to change this setting.

**Table 9.4** IP Subnet Allocations

| Subnet | Location | Intended Use | Hosts Identified by Nmap |
|---|---|---|---|
| 10.10.1.0/24 | Seattle | Servers | 7 |
| 10.10.2.0/24 | Seattle | Database Servers | 5 |
| 10.10.3.0/24 | Seattle | User PC's | 101 |
| 10.10.4.0/24 | Seattle | User PC's | 101 |
| 10.10.5.0/24 | Seattle | User PC's | 101 |
| 10.10.6.0/24 | Seattle | User PC's | 88 |
| 10.10.7.0/24 | Seattle | User PC's | 74 |
| 10.10.15.0/24 | Seattle | IT Dept. | 18 |
| 10.10.101.0/24 | Seattle | Business Development | 11 |
| 10.10.102.0/24 | Seattle | Admin & Managers | 26 |
| 172.16.100.0/24 | Seattle | Internet DMZ | 3 |
| 172.16.1.0/24 | Seattle | Inside of firewall | 3 |
| 87.65.43.0/24 | Seattle | Outside of firewall (ISP) | 2 |
| 172.16.2.0/24 | Seattle | WAN DMZ | 2 |
| 192.168.1.0/24 | Seattle | Security Servers VLAN | *Created for ACS server |
| 172.16.101.0/24 | Seattle | Web Application DMZ | *Created for application server |
| 10.20.1.0/24 | New York | Servers | 5 |
| 10.20.3.0/24 | New York | User PC's | 101 |
| 10.20.4.0/24 | New York | User PC's | 109 |
| 10.20.15.0/24 | New York | IT Dept. | 6 |
| 10.20.101.0/24 | New York | Business Development | 5 |
| 10.20.102.0/24 | New York | Admin & Managers | 8 |
| 10.30.1.0/24 | Dallas | Servers | 5 |
| 10.30.3.0/24 | Dallas | User PC's | 101 |
| 10.30.4.0/24 | Dallas | User PC's | 117 |
| 10.30.15.0/24 | Dallas | IT Dept. | 6 |
| 10.30.101.0/24 | Dallas | Business Development | 5 |
| 10.30.102.0/24 | Dallas | Admin & Managers | 11 |

# Other Security Improvements

Mapping your systems and adding AAA to bolster security will certainly improve things but they are not the only measures that can be taken to improve security.

## Synchronized Time

When you produce logs, it makes a lot of sense to ensure that all log entries are time stamped with the correct date and time. Computer clocks are notoriously bad when it comes to keeping time. Some clocks can slip by significant amounts during the course of a year, making event correlation from different logs difficult. Maintaining the correct time on all log-capable devices provides the ability to accurately correlate event information from logs. Network Time Protocol (NTP) can be used to synchronize clocks on your equipment.

Use the **ntp** command on PIX or IOS devices to set up NTP. For example:

```
ntp server 0.europe.pool.ntp.org source outside prefer
ntp server 1.europe.pool.ntp.org source outside
ntp server 2.europe.pool.ntp.org source outside
```

If you choose to use hostnames (as shown above), don't forget to configure a DNS or host name resolution for your device. A DNS can be set using the IOS commands:

```
ip name-lookup
ip name-server <ip-address-of-server>
```

For the PIX, you can use the name command to manually set host name resolution:

```
names
name 10.0.0.1  0. pool.ntp.org
name 10.0.0.2  1.pool.ntp.org
name 10.0.0.3  2.pool.ntp.org
```

## High Availability

Maintaining uptime is essential for production environments and to allow day-to-day business to take place. Single points of failure should be removed to lessen the risk of service outages. Deployment of redundant hardware and network resources in the right places can help lower and even eliminate outages. Hot Cash Corporation presently has only a single firewall in place; therefore, you should add a backup firewall. PIX supports a high availability peer firewall. The configuration and operating state is automatically replicated from the primary to the secondary PIX firewall.

On the LAN, high availability is maintained by assigning at least two 6500's to each VLAN. Having multiple layer 3 switches attached to each VLAN allows you to use Hot Standby Routing Protocol (HSRP) or Gateway Load Balancing Protocol (GLBP). Both HSRP and GLBP are mechanisms that provide a highly available gateway address to the hosts on the VLAN.

On the WAN, high availability is achieved through the full mesh Frame Relay setup. Because all sites are connected to each other, you can afford to lose a single WAN connection and not lose connectivity to any sites. This works fine for three sites, but full mesh topologies can be difficult to manage and do not scale well.

A single point of failure now exists with the link to the Internet Service Provider (ISP).

## Timeout Settings

Firewalls base a lot of their capabilities on the ability to police sessions. One of the things that a firewall does is maintain a list of the sessions passing through it. Sometimes sessions do not close properly, which can happen for a variety of reasons, including loss of power, a software crash, spoofed packets, and so on. The firewall has a list of timeouts that tell it when it is safe to assume that a stale session is dead. When a session timeout is detected, resources are freed up on the firewall. By default, the PIX session timeout values are conservatively high. The settings on the Hot Cash Corporation firewall are still at their default values. Many of the values in the **timeout** command can be lowered to improve security and performance.

## Manual Blocking and Filtering

The **shun** command can be used to block a single unwanted source address. Unwanted addresses may be identified from Intrusion Detection Software (IDS) logs or from an external source such as www.dshield.org, a site that tracks cracker activity and maintains an up-to-the minute block list. The block list contains network ranges that have been identified as the sources of scanning activity by multiple victims on the Internet. The block list is available from https://secure.dshield.org/feeds/block.txt and, because it is a text file, it can easily be downloaded and parsed using command-line utilities **curl** (http://curl.haxx.se/) and **awk** (www.cygwin.com). You may need to use a script to create a suitable ACL, because the **shun** command does not work for network ranges (e.g., the following script is used to create a condensed version of the block list without any comments or unnecessary information. You can use a similar technique to create an ACL for the firewall or the router connecting Hot Cash Corporation to your Internet service provider.

```
curl -s http://feeds.dshield.org/block.txt | awk '($1!="#" && $1!="Start" &&
NF>=2) {print $1"/"$3}' > newlist.txt
```

## Anti-spoofing

PIX firewalls support a feature known to Checkpoint administrators as anti-spoofing. **ip verify reverse-path** is a configuration command that tells PIX to check the routing table for entries that match an inbound packets source address. Normally, routing is checked only for destination addresses. In this case, checking for the source address using the same interface and path allows the PIX to determine if there is a path back to where the packet says it came from. If there is a mismatch, the packet is considered to be a spoofed packet and is discarded. The IP verify reverse-path must be enabled on a per-interface basis.

## Network-based Application Recognition

The Network-based Application Recognition (NBAR) feature allows IOS devices to identify protocols that would otherwise be difficult to identify. Relying on the destination port numbers of well-known services is not always the best way to correctly identify an application. Many peer-to-peer and instant messaging applications have the ability to use TCP port 80 or port 443, which are usually associated with browser traffic. NBAR offers the potential to differentiate protocols even if they are not running on their native well-known ports. Once an application's traffic has been identified, it can be subject to filtering or QOS adjustments.

## Intrusion Detection/Intrusion Prevention

Most firewalls have at least a basic ability to detect malicious traffic. PIX version 6.3.5 that is built into IDS, will detect approximately 50 common signatures using the **ip audit** configuration commands. Over time, PIX will likely be replaced by Cisco's new ASA5500 series firewall appliances. These appliances are Cisco's new flagship firewall product, and run on the same version of software starting with version 7.0. ASA5500 appliances include an added module slot that is not available on PIX. This module slot is capable of holding a specialist Intrusion Prevention System (IPS) module. The Cisco IPS module detects 1000's of signatures. If you have a requirement for intrusion detection and prevention, consider using a specific Intrusion Detection System (IDS)/IPS product.

# VPN Connectivity

Hot Cash Corporation currently uses a dedicated dial-in server to provide remote access for users and application support companies. This remote access server uses its own database and does not offer the ability to interface with the company's AAA server. Hot Cash Corporation wants to replace the solution with a remote access VPN solution, to hopefully improve security and cut the expenses associated with long distance calls from remote users. This can be achieved by enabling remote access Secure Internet Protocol (IPSec) VPN features on their PIX firewall. The Cisco PIX offers the following IPSEC VPN features:

- No additional license required on firewall

- Multiplatform VPN client

- VPN client with basic integrated personal firewall

- Triple Data Encryption Standard (3DES) and AES256 encryption

- Network Address Translation Transparency (NAT-T) support

- Network Extension Mode (NEM) or Port Address Translation (PAT) mode for Easy VPN (EZVPN) support

- Group-based address and parameter assignment

- Authenticates from AAA server

NAT-T allows IPSec VPN connections to operate in NAT environments such as from behind home Digital Subscriber Line (DSL) routers or external firewalls. With increasing limitations being put on public IP address allocation, NAT-T is now an essential component of IPSec implementations.

The EZVPN client is a simplified configuration option for hardware-based VPN clients that require site-to-site VPN connectivity. An EZVPN client specifies basic parameters such as tunnel head end IP address, username, and password. This basic configuration connects the remote EZVPN client to the central resources with minimal effort. Normally, when a VPN client connects to the head end, it is assigned an IP address from a central pool. Because EZVPN supports site-to-site connections, but is in fact a client connection, the remote site will, by default, hide its addresses behind the assigned IP address using PAT. PAT only allows one-way communication from the remote site to the central site. Cisco refers to this software VPN client emulation as "client mode." This is fine for simple applications such as telnet access to a central server or browsing to a central intranet server, but PAT does not allow connections to be made in the opposite direction. An alternative connection method, Network Extension Mode (NEM), allows EZVPN clients to make the connection and forward traffic from the remote site without changing the remote site IP addresses. If the central site needs to be able to reach individual hosts on the remote site, you should use NEM or a dedicated site-to-site (non-EZVPN) configuration (see Figure 9.17.)

**Figure 9.17** Sample Pix VPN Configuration

```
! define phase 1 encryption
isakmp policy 50 encr 3des
isakmp policy 50 hash sha
isakmp policy 50 authentication pre-share
isakmp policy 70 encr 3des
isakmp policy 70 hash md5
isakmp policy 70 authentication pre-share

! define phase 2 encryption
crypto ipsec transform-set 3desMd5 esp-3des esp-md5-hmac
crypto ipsec transform-set 3desSha esp-3des esp-sha-hmac

!define authentication and other vpn client parameters
ip local pool myPool 10.1.1.1-10.1.1.254
vpngroup hotcash-IT address-pool myPool
vpngroup hotcash-IT default-domain hotcashcorp.com
vpngroup hotcash-IT idle-time 600
vpngroup hotcash-IT dns-server 10.10.1.144
vpngroup hotcash-IT password mySharedKey
crypto map Internet-VPNs client authentication myACS


! activate IPSEC policies
crypto dynamic-map VPN-clients 10 set transform-set 3desSha
crypto dynamic-map VPN-clients 20 set transform-set 3desMd5
crypto map Internet-VPNs 999 ipsec-isakmp dynamic VPN-clients
crypto map Internet-VPNs interface outside
isakmp enable outside

! deactivate NAT from center to remote sites
nat (inside) 0 access-list NoNat
```

In this example, the remote access clients are allowed to use IPSec Key Exchange (IKE) security associations of Triple Data Encryption Standard (3DES) encryption with Message Digest 5 (MD5) or Secure Hash Algorithm (SHA) as a hashing algorithm. Similarly, there is a dynamic crypto map policy that allows 3DES encryption with MD5 or SHA as a hashing algorithm for IPSec security associations. The dynamic crypto map name is VPN-clients, and is attached to the outside interface via a crypto map called Internet-VPNs. This crypto map has been assigned the AAA server myACS to authenticate incoming clients. Crypto maps and dynamic crypto maps are Cisco-specific terms that refer to the association of VPN-specific configuration details.

Aside from providing credentials for the AAA server, clients must also provide group credentials for authentication. Group credentials, as defined with the **vpn-group** command, allow multiple groups of users to be identified, and for separate attributes to be assigned to each group. Groups can be set up to authenticate using a pre-shared key (password) or by using certificates. Figure 9.17 shows a **vpngroup** called hotcash-IT which was defined with the mySharedKey pre-shared key . User and group authentication are separate processes. Using certificates to authenticate groups does not prevent using passwords for user authentication.

VPN connections have been enabled on the interface named outside using the **isakmp enable** command. And finally, **nat 0** has been used to create a NAT exception rule, which means that VPN traffic that matches permit statements on the NoNat ACL will not be NATed.

## Notes From the Underground…

### Using Only VPN Group Configuration to Identify Users

If an AAA server is not available to authenticate incoming users, VPN group authentication can be used on its own. In this situation, a unique group can be created for each individual user. Associating each group with a single user provides the ability to assign attributes (e.g., IP addresses) on a per-user basis. This may be useful if you do not yet have an AAA server. The down side is that this method does not scale well and does not provide optimal security. You should use this only as a temporary solution.

# Summary

Many small organization's implement firewalls at a very basic level. Often, it is only after they have experienced security-related problems that they realize the importance of documentation, audit, and accountability. There is an abundance of software available to allow you to audit your network and its systems. Some of this software is free and some of it is included with your OSs. Even without a budget for commercial auditing or network monitoring systems, you should perform self-audits, which allows organizations to gain awareness and better control over their IT resources.

VLANs may be used to split the network into manageable sections. Network devices such as firewalls, routers, and multi-layered switches can be used to enforce security between individual VLANs.

AAA can be used to authenticate and authorize inbound connections from the Internet and outbound connections form the LAN. Authentication and authorization of inbound connections serves to protect your internal- or DMZ-based servers against direct attack from the Internet. Authentication and authorization of outgoing connections serves to provide control over users' access to external and potentially dangerous resources. Accounting is used to create a per-user trail of activity on your network devices. In some industry sectors such as finance or healthcare, accounting may be required for legal compliance.

# Solutions Fast Track

## Mapping Your Systems

☑ Always ask people that are familiar with the systems before breaking out the software tools. Do this sooner rather than later so that information is not lost as people move to other departments or other companies. Documenting everything you find will make your job easier when you are called to troubleshoot a problem.

☑ A cable database can be a useful aid in identifying unauthorized hardware. Although it can be difficult to get up and running, it adds the ability to easily locate unauthorized network connections.

☑ Many OSs offer built in utilities that can be used to aid mapping of an unknown network; however, you will find that there are a lot of third-party software that is better suited to the task.

# Improving Accountability with Identity Management

☑ Using identity management with AAA can help track network activity at the user level. This is becoming increasingly important for regulatory compliance and improved operational security.

☑ Cisco PIX and Adaptive Security Appliance (ASA) firewall appliances are equipped with basic AAA abilities. Adding Cisco ACS software compliments the firewall solution and provides better scalability.

☑ Many firewalls now offer additional services such as anti-spyware and content filtering, in a bid to make their products the ultimate security solution. This has given rise to a new generation of firewall appliances.

# Lowering Risks with Application Layer Filtering

☑ Cisco devices support referral methods to pass URLs to external filtering servers.

☑ Dedicated proxy have the disadvantage of requiring browsers to be explicitly configured to use them, but they also offer added benefits such as caching, anti-virus, filtering, and authentication

☑n Identification and control of non-Web traffic can be achieved using Cisco NBAR or application-aware firewalls.

# Frequently Asked Questions

The following Frequently Asked Questions, answered by the authors of this book, are designed to both measure your understanding of the concepts presented in this chapter and to assist you with real-life implementation of these concepts. To have your questions about this chapter answered by the author, browse to **www.syngress.com/solutions** and click on the **"Ask the Author"** form. You will also gain access to thousands of other FAQs at ITFAQnet.com.

**Q:** Why do I need VLANs?

**A:** Without VLANs, the default operation of most switches will allow every host connected to that switch to communicate with every other host on that switch, which is not always desirable. For example, if the accounts department shares a switch with the sales department and no VLAN separation is used, it may be possible for the sales team to intercept confidential or restricted accounts department data.

**Q:** What happens if I connect VLANs together?

**A:** In simple terms, VLANs are discrete compartments on your network. Normally, these compartments are separated by network layer devices such as firewalls, routers, or layer 3 engines within your switches. Connecting VLANs together will bypass any intermediary network layer devices and is likely to cause security problems. Do not connect VLANs together unless you know what you are doing.

**Q:** I have a Mac. Can I use any of the software mentioned in this chapter?

**A:** Recent versions of Mac OS are UNIX-based. As such, most of the UNIX/Linux applications mentioned have been made available (ported) to this platform. In addition, Cisco has a version of their VPN client for the Mac platform.

**Q:** I use a firewall to filter users' traffic based on the IP address of their machine. Why do I need authentication and authorization?

**A:** In some cases machines are shared by multiple users. You may not want all users of a single machine to have access to the same Web sites.

**Q:** I already have anti-virus software on my internal hosts. Why do I need it on my proxy server, too?

**A**: Anti-virus software engines are not all the same. Sometimes one manufacturer's signature database may lag behind its competitors. Many organizations use a second anti-virus product on their proxy server or firewall to lower the associated risk.

**Q**: I have detailed documentation about my organization's systems, so why do I need to map my network? Isn't this overdoing it a little?

**A**: If you can personally vouch for every single system, cable, and piece of software that is installed on your network, then you have in effect already mapped your network. On the other hand, if you are not absolutely certain of what is installed and where, a regular audit of your network will help ensure that no anomalies exist.

**Q**: I need to protect an internal server from internal users. Can I use a downloadable ACL?

**A**: Yes, you can use the **auth-proxy** command on IOS devices to achieve this. The server will need to be on a different IP subnet from the users so that traffic is forced to flow at layer 3. Layer 3 traffic can be authenticated and filtered. Alternatively, you can use 802.1x to assign user restrictions during log on.

# Index

# Z

# Syngress: *The Definition of a Serious Security Library*

**Syn·gress** (sin‑gres): *noun, sing.* Freedom from risk or danger; safety. See *security*.

# Syngress: *The Definition of a Serious Security Library*

**Syn·gress** (sin-gres): *noun, sing.* Freedom from risk or danger; safety. See *security*.

## Syngress IT Security Project Management Handbook
Susan Snedaker

The definitive work for IT professionals responsible for the management of the design, configuration, deployment and maintenance of enterprise-wide security projects. Provides specialized coverage of key project areas including Penetration Testing, Intrusion Detection and Prevention Systems, and Access Control Systems.

ISBN: 1-59749-076-8

Price: $59.95 US    $77.95 CAN

## Combating Spyware in the Enterprise
Paul Piccard

Combating Spyware in the Enterprise is the first book published on defending enterprise networks from increasingly sophisticated and malicious spyware. System administrators and security professionals responsible for administering and securing networks ranging in size from SOHO networks up the largest enterprise networks will learn to use a combination of free and commercial anti-spyware software, firewalls, intrusion detection systems, intrusion prevention systems, and host integrity monitoring applications to prevent the installation of spyware, and to limit the damage caused by spyware that does in fact infiltrate their networks.

ISBN: 1-59749-064-4

Price: $49.95 US    $64.95 CAN

## Practical VoIP Security
Thomas Porter

After struggling for years, you finally think you've got your network secured from malicious hackers and obnoxious spammers. Just when you think it's safe to go back into the water, VoIP finally catches on. Now your newly converged network is vulnerable to DoS attacks, hacked gateways leading to unauthorized free calls, call eavesdropping, malicious call redirection, and spam over Internet Telephony (SPIT). This book details both VoIP attacks and defense techniques and tools.

ISBN: 1-59749-060-1

Price: $49.95 U.S.    $69.95 CAN

# Syngress: *The Definition of a Serious Security Library*

**Syn·gress** (sin–gres): *noun, sing.* Freedom from risk or danger; safety. See *security.*

## Cyber Spying: Tracking Your Family's (Sometimes) Secret Online Lives

Dr. Eric Cole, Michael Nordfelt, Sandra Ring, and Ted Fair

Have you ever wondered about that friend your spouse e-mails, or who they spend hours chatting online with? Are you curious about what your children are doing online, whom they meet, and what they talk about? Do you worry about them finding drugs and other illegal items online, and wonder what they look at? This book shows you how to monitor and analyze your family's online behavior.

ISBN: 1-93183-641-8

Price: $39.95 US   $57.95 CAN

## Stealing the Network: How to Own an Identity

Timothy Mullen, Ryan Russell, Riley (Caezar) Eller, Jeff Moss, Jay Beale, Johnny Long, Chris Hurley, Tom Parker, Brian Hatch

The first two books in this series "Stealing the Network: How to Own the Box" and "Stealing the Network: How to Own a Continent" have become classics in the Hacker and Infosec communities because of their chillingly realistic depictions of criminal hacking techniques. In this third installment, the all-star cast of authors tackle one of the fastest-growing crimes in the world: Identity Theft. Now, the criminal hackers readers have grown to both love and hate try to cover their tracks and vanish into thin air...

ISBN: 1-59749-006-7

Price: $39.95 US   $55.95 CAN

## Software Piracy Exposed

Paul Craig, Ron Honick

For every $2 worth of software purchased legally, $1 worth of software is pirated illegally. For the first time ever, the dark underground of how software is stolen and traded over the Internet is revealed. The technical detail provided will open the eyes of software users and manufacturers worldwide! This book is a tell-it-like-it-is exposé of how tens of billions of dollars worth of software is stolen every year.

ISBN: 1-93226-698-4

Price: $39.95 U.S.   $55.95 CAN

**SYNGRESS**®

# Syngress: *The Definition of a Serious Security Library*

**Syn·gress** (sin-gres): *noun, sing.* Freedom from risk or danger; safety. See *security*.

## Phishing Exposed

Lance James, Secure Science Corporation,
Joe Stewart (Foreword)

If you have ever received a phish, become a victim of a phish, or manage the security of a major e-commerce or financial site, then you need to read this book. The author of this book delivers the unconcealed techniques of phishers including their evolving patterns, and how to gain the upper hand against the ever-accelerating attacks they deploy. Filled with elaborate and unprecedented forensics, Phishing Exposed details techniques that system administrators, law enforcement, and fraud investigators can exercise and learn more about their attacker and their specific attack methods, enabling risk mitigation in many cases before the attack occurs.

ISBN: 1-59749-030-X

Price: $49.95 US   $69.95 CAN

## Penetration Tester's Open Source Toolkit

Johnny Long, Chris Hurley, SensePost,
Mark Wolfgang, Mike Petruzzi

This is the first fully integrated Penetration Testing book and bootable Linux CD containing the "Auditor Security Collection," which includes over 300 of the most effective and commonly used open source attack and penetration testing tools. This powerful tool kit and authoritative reference is written by the security industry's foremost penetration testers including HD Moore, Jay Beale, and SensePost. This unique package provides you with a completely portable and bootable Linux attack distribution and authoritative reference to the toolset included and the required methodology.

ISBN: 1-59749-021-0

Price: $59.95 US   $83.95 CAN

## Google Hacking for Penetration Testers

Johnny Long, Foreword by Ed Skoudis

Google has been a strong force in Internet culture since its 1998 upstart. Since then, the engine has evolved from a simple search instrument to an innovative authority of information. As the sophistication of Google grows, so do the hacking hazards that the engine entertains. Approaches to hacking are forever changing, and this book covers the risks and precautions that administrators need to be aware of during this explosive phase of Google Hacking.

ISBN: 1-93183-636-1

Price: $44.95 U.S.   $65.95 CAN

SYNGRESS®

# Syngress: *The Definition of a Serious Security Library*

**Syn·gress** (sin–gres): *noun, sing.* Freedom from risk or danger; safety. See *security*.

### Cisco PIX Firewalls:
### Configure, Manage, & Troubleshoot

Charles Riley, Umer Khan, Michael Sweeney

Cisco PIX Firewall is the world's most used network firewall, protecting internal networks from unwanted intrusions and attacks. Virtual Private Networks (VPNs) are the means by which authorized users are allowed through PIX Firewalls. Network engineers and security specialists must constantly balance the need for air-tight security (Firewalls) with the need for on-demand access (VPNs). In this book, Umer Khan, author of the #1 best selling PIX Firewall book, provides a concise, to-the-point blueprint for fully integrating these two essential pieces of any enterprise network.

ISBN: 1-59749-004-0

Price: $49.95 US   $69.95 CAN

---

### Configuring Netscreen Firewalls

Rob Cameron

Configuring NetScreen Firewalls is the first book to deliver an in-depth look at the NetScreen firewall product line. It covers all of the aspects of the NetScreen product line from the SOHO devices to the Enterprise NetScreen firewalls. Advanced troubleshooting techniques and the NetScreen Security Manager are also covered..

ISBN: 1--93226-639-9

Price: $49.95 US   $72.95 CAN

---

### Configuring Check Point
### NGX VPN-1/FireWall-1

Barry J. Stiefel, Simon Desmeules

Configuring Check Point NGX VPN-1/Firewall-1 is the perfect reference for anyone migrating from earlier versions of Check Point's flagship firewall/VPN product as well as those deploying VPN-1/Firewall-1 for the first time. NGX includes dramatic changes and new, enhanced features to secure the integrity of your network's data, communications, and applications from the plethora of blended threats that can breach your security through your network perimeter, Web access, and increasingly common internal threats.

ISBN: 1--59749-031-8

Price: $49.95 U.S.   $69.95 CAN

**SYNGRESS®**

# Syngress: *The Definition of a Serious Security Library*

**Syn·gress** (sin–gres): *noun, sing.* Freedom from risk or danger; safety. See *security*.

# Syngress: *The Definition of a Serious Security Library*

**Syn·gress** (sin-gres): *noun, sing.* Freedom from risk or danger; safety. See *security.*

### Snort 2.1 Intrusion Detection, Second Edition

Jay Beale, Brian Caswell, et. al.

"The authors of this *Snort 2.1 Intrusion Detection, Second Edition* have produced a book with a simple focus, to teach you how to use Snort, from the basics of getting started to advanced rule configuration, they cover all aspects of using Snort, including basic installation, preprocessor configuration, and optimization of your Snort system."

—*Stephen Northcutt*
*Director of Training & Certification, The SANS Institute*

ISBN: 1-931836-04-3

Price: $49.95 U.S.   $69.95 CAN

### Ethereal Packet Sniffing

Ethereal offers more protocol decoding and reassembly than any free sniffer out there and ranks well among the commercial tools. You've all used tools like tcpdump or windump to examine individual packets, but Ethereal makes it easier to make sense of a stream of ongoing network communications. Ethereal not only makes network troubleshooting work far easier, but also aids greatly in network forensics, the art of finding and examining an attack, by giving a better "big picture" view. *Ethereal Packet Sniffing* will show you how to make the most out of your use of Ethereal.

ISBN: 1-932266-82-8

Price: $49.95 U.S.   $77.95 CAN

### Nessus Network Auditing

Jay Beale, Haroon Meer, Roelof Temmingh, Charl Van Der Walt, Renaud Deraison

Crackers constantly probe machines looking for both old and new vulnerabilities. In order to avoid becoming a casualty of a casual cracker, savvy sys admins audit their own machines before they're probed by hostile outsiders (or even hostile insiders). Nessus is the premier Open Source vulnerability assessment tool, and was recently voted the "most popular" open source security tool of any kind. *Nessus Network Auditing* is the first book available on Nessus and it is written by the world's premier Nessus developers led by the creator of Nessus, Renaud Deraison.

ISBN: 1-931836-08-6

Price: $49.95 U.S.   $69.95 CAN

"Thieme's ability to be open minded, conspiratorial, ethical, and subversive all at the same time is very inspiring."–*Jeff Moss, CEO, Black Hat, Inc.*

**Richard Thieme's Islands in the Clickstream: Reflections on Life in a Virtual World**

Richard Thieme is one of the most visible commentators on technology and society, appearing regularly on CNN radio, TechTV, and various other national media outlets. He is also in great demand as a public speaker, delivering his "Human Dimension of Technology" talk to over 50,000 live audience members each year. *Islands in the Clickstream* is a single volume "best of Richard Thieme."

ISBN: 1-931836-22-1

Price: $29.95 US    $43.95 CAN

"Thieme's Islands in the Clickstream is deeply reflective, enlightening, and refreshing." —*Peter Neumann, Stanford Research Institute*

"Richard Thieme takes us to the edge of cliffs we know are there but rarely visit ... he wonderfully weaves life, mystery, and passion through digital and natural worlds with creativity and imagination. This is delightful and deeply thought provoking reading full of "aha!" insights." —*Clinton C. Brooks, Senior Advisor for Homeland Security and Asst. Deputy Director, NSA*

"WOW! You eloquently express thoughts and ideas that I feel. You have helped me, not so much tear down barriers to communication, as to leverage these barriers into another structure with elevators and escalators."
—*Chip Meadows, CISSP, CCSE, USAA e-Security Team*

"Richard Thieme navigates the complex world of people and computers with amazing ease and grace. His clarity of thinking is refreshing, and his insights are profound." —*Bruce Schneier, CEO, Counterpane*

"I believe that you are a practioner of wu wei, the effort to choose the elegant appropriate contribution to each and every issue that you address." —*Hal McConnell (fomer intelligence analyst, NSA)*

"Richard Thieme presents us with a rare gift. His words touch our heart while challenging our most cherished constructs. He is both a poet and pragmatist navigating a new world with clarity, curiosity and boundless amazement." —*Kelly Hansen, CEO, Neohapsis*

"Richard Thieme combines hi-tech, business savvy and social consciousness to create some of the most penetrating commentaries of our times. A column I am always eager to read." —*Peter Russell, author "From Science to God"*

"These reflections provide a veritable feast for the imagination, allowing us more fully to participate in Wonder. This book is an experience of loving Creation with our minds." —*Louie Crew, Member of Executive Council of The Episcopal Church*

"The particular connections Richard Thieme makes between mind, heart, technology, and truth, lend us timely and useful insight on what it means to live in a technological era. Richard fills a unique and important niche in hacker society!" —*Mick Bauer, Security Editor, Linux Journal*